SUN YAT-SEN

His Life and Its Meaning

A CRITICAL BIOGRAPHY

THE HUMAN SUN YAT-SEN

SUN YAT-SEN

His Life and Its Meaning

A CRITICAL BIOGRAPHY

by

LYON SHARMAN

ARCHON BOOKS
Hamden, Connecticut
1965

LIBRARY OF CONGRESS CATALOG CARD NUMBER: 65-19600
PRINTED IN THE UNITED STATES OF AMERICA

TO CHINA

Known by a memory, crisp but incomplete,
Home of my childhood, not of all the years,
Are you but a dear dream, colored by my youth,
Or are you half a dream and half a truth?
Dreams are what we feed on—dreams and fears;
Bare truth we cannot eat without some sweet
Of dreams. Spirit of what loveliest seems,
Teach me to bite the truth, yet taste my dreams.

THE LACQUERED IMAGE AND THE BIOGRAPHER

A PREFACE

THE Sun Yat-sen Cult was encroaching upon Peking along with the Kuomintang armies when, on a certain day, late in 1927, a sheaf of manuscript was laid upon my table. A Chinese friend was making the request that I revise its English. Replenished from week to week, the manuscript turned out to be a translation of some of Sun Yat-sen's more important writings. Because the rendering was made by a Chinese, no urbanity of phrasing stood between me and Sun Yat-sen's militant utterances. I could feel something of the Chinese idiom, and I got Sun Yat-sen's ideas unmediated and without selection. Since I am a passionate admirer of China, I was surprised and not a little regretful to find that I could not look with more admiration into Sun Yat-sen's mind. It was not reassuring to be told that his thinking represented the best that had been contributed to China's modern problem. I recall tapping the manuscript and remarking in my disappointment: This thinking is not great enough to save China. But my friend was not free to discuss Sun Yat-sen's inadequacy, if, indeed, he felt it; even then the Cult was inhibiting criticism.

If I had been indifferent toward China, Sun Yat-sen would not have mattered; I could have forgotten him. Instead, I came to realize that I must either draw off from China or come to a reckoning with Sun Yat-sen. To draw off from China seemed like closing a part of myself, as one would close a house on moving out. Rather than do that I had to make an effort to understand Sun Yat-sen. The present book is a product of that effort.

At first I did not find a real man; I found a hero already stiffened into an idol. The making of a lacquered god out of human flesh and blood has probably never been accomplished with such speed and thoroughness as in the case of Sun Yat-sen. It is only nine years now since he died; but upon what may a biographer reconstruct his life? There are hundreds of Chinese living who knew him and should be able to testify. But criticism of Sun Yat-sen and of his ideas has been forbidden in Nationalist China. When I began to write, the situation was so tense that it would have been compromising the future of a Chinese friend to associate him with an untrammeled biography of Sun Yat-sen. Only in recent months has it been possible to find even a few Chinese willing to whisper what they really think of their canonized leader. So, from the beginning of my work, it was clear that where free speech was impossible oral sources would have to be used warily; they would inevitably furnish accretions to the already too large store of heroizing material, and they might produce subtle deflections of the magnetic needle by which the biographer must steer. I asked myself the question: Must Sun Yat-sen then remain unreal and unknown to the West while the growing hero-legend in China yearly renders him more unreal? My answer was No! I refused to believe that a man who had lived so spectacularly in the world's eye could fail to be knowable. The story of his life, it seemed to me, must lie strewn through many contemporary sources of various kinds, which, just because they were contemporary, would have a value of their own that reminiscences, obfuscated both by sentiment and frailties of memory, could not have. Indeed, I could only hope to keep my feet on solid ground by giving full consideration to written sources—not only major ones, but also incidental records dropped here and there in periodicals and books of the years before Sun Yat-sen suffered hero-transformation. It would be a mistake, however, to suppose that my interpretation has been built upon literary sources alone. I have been fortunate in spending three recent years in China, where I was able to catch the vanishing figure of the real Sun Yat-sen. There much help came to me incidentally from oral sources, usually without its being suspected that I was to write a book; indeed, information began coming before I thought of writing about Sun Yat-sen. I am thinking of Chinese chiefly when I say this; occidental sources I have been able to approach frankly and directly.

As I worked, I came to see that the materials for certain major periods of Sun Yat-sen's life are not so accessible to his fellow-countrymen in China as to outsiders, for the simple reason that Sun Yat-sen lived much of his life away from his native land. He became President of China at forty-five; of those forty-five years he had spent about a dozen in education in foreign territories, and for sixteen other years he had been a revolutionary vagabond, living at various times in Europe, Japan and America. Even after his presidency he spent three more years in exile. The two longest periods which Sun Yat-sen ever spent on Chinese soil were his boyhood up to twelve years of age, and the last nine years of his life. It is a matter to be reckoned with that we foreigners have held and still hold the keys to some of the most important phases of Sun Yat-sen's career. And surely we can understand better than most Chinese the occidental influences that molded Sun Yat-sen as a youth, and played perpetually upon his thinking, planning and acting throughout life.

If the present book has any justification as another biography of Sun Yat-sen, it will be found in its central concern with history rather than with romantic episodes. There is no prying gossip about the veiled intimacies of Sun Yat-sen's life. From the beginning I have conceived of this biography as a narrative within a narrative. What happened to China is the large epic movement without which Sun Yat-sen's life has no meaning and little interest. What happened to Sun Yat-sen is a stream of episode within the larger movement. But it is a significant stream. The events of his life make the currents of the flowing river more readily observable. China, unfocussed in personalities, is apt to seem amorphous and chaotic. But, given a human being living in the chaotic conditions, and the result is adventure.

My method had better speak for itself. To parry certain types of argument I should perhaps confess that there are two tendencies represented in discussions of modern China which I have set my face against. The citing of Western analogues to Chinese conditions and events is one of them. Time was when I, also, did that sort of thing —until I came to see that I did it too often as a form of special pleading; surely China is a nation too august to call for such belittling tactics. Moreover, I have become convinced that for the present we shall make better progress in understanding China by looking more carefully at the facts and scrutinizing skeptically our facile historical parallels.

My other stubbornness is that I have purposely avoided accounting for Chinese situations by evolutionary generalizations. Thirty years ago a too ready assumption that thinkers in all fields understood the evolutionary process led to much unwarranted optimism. Now, what possibly are equally wrong inferences from biological evolution have made cowards and fatalists of many of us. I regret this so much that I fling out like one of Shakespeare's fools: God teach them evolution that talk it; and those that are human, let them know their humanity. If, in saying this, I am guilty of rationalizing a prejudice, the prejudice gives me an individual attack upon the life of Sun Yat-sen. Nor am I defrauding the honorable reader; for him there are already accessible excellent books setting forth the evolutionary interpretation of modern China. It may be, after all, simply because I was born in China that I cannot stand off and think of the chaos there as the inescapable program of an Evolutionary Fate. To me all that has happened in China has been wrought out of human endeavor and human resistance; it has been shot through and through with human passions and volitions; and it has been involved with human faults that attack national tissue like a disease. Gigantic as China's modern movements are, transcending our frail powers of analysis and understanding, the country's development, I still must believe, is in the hands of her citizens.

Because the number of personal names by which an individual may be known in China is a source of no little perplexity to Occidentals, I have avoided putting the reader through the mutations of Sun Yat-sen's names by calling him from first to last by the name best known in the Occident. That name I have not shortened, believing that it is conveniently short already. To call him Doctor Sun would not save even one syllable, and it would not only transgress our occidental usage in naming famous men deceased, but would depart from any truly Chinese usage. In the Chinese language Sun Yat-sen is not—as far as my knowledge goes—referred to by his medical title and surname. When used by Chinese, "Doctor Sun" is a distinctly hybridized courtesy-name, a substitute for the courtesy appellations now in use in China; one of these is simply the Kuomintang name for President, and another is, curiously enough, an alias under which Sun Yat-sen hid as an exile in Japan.

An observant reader will detect in the quoted passages considerable variation in spelling and other matters of usage. Unfortunately some indispensable sources were published in faulty English form. Others are in oriental English so picturesque that I would not—by editing—deprive the reader of their color. The amount of editing that would be required to standardize all the citations of this book would be unjustifiable; so I have adopted the only other logical policy—verbatim fidelity. If the resulting variegation of certain pages offends the typographically sensitive, I beg them to reflect that this international variety is typical of the many-patterned influences that played upon Sun Yat-sen.

There are Chinese in many parts of the world, possibly even in

Nanking, who will not be displeased to see a critical biography of Sun Yat-sen appear. Under present circumstances such a biography cannot be produced in China. It is doubtful whether any Chinese would, at the present juncture, risk his future by thoroughly criticizing Sun Yat-sen anywhere. The bravest dissenting voice has been that of Hu Shih, who has taken issue at points with Sun Yat-sen's thinking and has protested against the suppression of criticism in *The Crescent Moon,* published in that city of refuge for free speech, Shanghai. If the Kuomintang's prohibitions should be relaxed in time—that is, before the active participants in the events die off— the Chinese will be able to amplify and make more vivid a biography such as mine. But so long as it seems more important for China to worship Sun Yat-sen than to understand him, there can be little searching out of the truth and little objective evaluation except by foreigners. While the Chinese are being held off from criticism of Sun Yat-sen, the real man is being obliterated by a legend. This should create concern among historians. It seems now that if the human Sun Yat-sen is to be saved for posterity, it must be done by Western biographies.

As for my own interpretation and my critical judgments, I cannot expect that they will be always agreed with. What I ask is that they may be considered. If after consideration they are controverted I shall not be disturbed. Clarification comes sometimes only out of controversy.

Most thankfully would I make public acknowledgments to those who have helped me by answering inquiries or by reading and criticizing the manuscript; I refrain from naming them because, under the present inhibiting policies in regard to Sun Yat-sen, it might not in every case be a kindness to those who have been kind to me. Whatever blame there may be for the book must fall upon myself.

I am not thinking, as I lay down my pen, of those who will resist and deny what I have said; if their ideas or mine are thereby illuminated that will be all to the good. I am thinking rather of those who will suffer under what I have to say and make no outcry. Toward them my heart is tender. I can only honor them here in passing, whether they are known to me or unknown, whether they are working in the clear light on the fundamental problems or fumbling in their lack of confidence. If this book should give them courage to act more forcibly upon their own right intuitions I shall be made happier.

August 30, 1934

CONTENTS

SUN YAT-SEN

His Life and Its Meaning

A CRITICAL BIOGRAPHY

CHAPTER I

A Revolutionary in the Making

I. THE MAKING OF A CHINESE

A BOY of bronzed skin running barefoot among other village boys —such was Sun Yat-sen when he began to remember what was happening to him. His father was a farmer who made his home, as farmers usually do in China, in a village out on the countryside. Generations and generations before him those who worked the land had established the custom of building their dwellings near together for the joys and protections of community life. With a feeling worthy of outdoor workers these farmers had called their hamlet the Blue Thriving Village—Choyhung in local speech; the blue of its name was not the common blue of dyed clothes, but the blue of kingfishers' feathers. The village must often have looked as blue, for the sea mists were not far off on any side. Choyhung is situated about thirty miles north of Macao in the great delta of the West River, a region netted with waterways that are traveled by boats of many sizes and shapes and riggings. A characteristic hilliness won for the district about Choyhung the poetic name of Heungshan, the Fragrant Hills. That also was the name of the district's chief town, where the local magistrate had his *yamen*. This low-ranking but useful functionary represented the Emperor's will to the scores of villages like Choyhung that lay within his administrative area.

Like most of his fellow-farmers, Sun Yat-sen's father, Sun Tao-chuan, was poor; but the mud-plastered dwelling which housed his family is remembered as a room or two larger and somewhat better built than most of the village houses. Yet its floors were of

3

paving-tiles or hardened earth; its sleeping pallets were spread upon austere bed-boards; its lamps burned vegetable oil and were smoky and dim; the members of the family ate their bowls of plain food from plain tables. If they were not pinched for money, they could afford rice with their vegetables, and once in a long while a small seasoning of meat; if the money chest was low, they lived on the humbler sweet potato which could be grown on the stony hills.

When, as a famous man, Sun Yat-sen was talking with one whose freedom from snobbery he could take for granted, he said bluntly:

I am a coolie and the son of a coolie. I was born with the poor and I am still poor. My sympathies have always been with the struggling mass.[1]

Sun Yat-sen seems never to have been ashamed of his origin in the class that earned its livelihood, as the Chinese feelingly put it, by *koo lee,* bitter labor. It is significant of the lowliness of his origin that no record of the day of his birth can be found. Sun Yat-sen never knew on what day he was born and never bothered about it: that is the report recently made by the biographer to whom Sun Yat-sen supplied stories about his childhood. The last birthday celebration of his life was held Nov. 2, 1924, according to one who was present at it; but that seems to settle nothing. In default of exactitude, November 12th has been officially settled upon, and is now nationally celebrated as the birthday of this Chinese "father of his country."

Sun Yat-sen was born in 1866. His father was then of middle age. His mother was a bound-footed country woman of vigorous physique, who had borne her husband a son fifteen years before the birth of the child who became famous. There was also a girl in the family, and among the early memories of Sun Yat-sen's boyhood were the piteous cries of this sister when her tender bones were subjected to the cruel process of foot-binding.

The village of Choyhung would not have been complete without its shops for food-stuffs and for farming accessories; it had also its tea house for the refreshment of travelers, and its village temple for the worship of the protective gods of an agricultural people. Even simple households were mindful of the honor due to ancestors. At the New Year season the posterlike gate gods would be pasted afresh on the outer door-panels, and other "god papers," equally redolent of folklore, would ensure protection of the inner chambers or preside over the kitchen stove. Like other Chinese villages Choyhung was governed by a council of its leading citizens, men of ripe years, with whom sat also the aristocracy of the educated. If the village at any time was fortunate enough to have a resident who had acquired even the lowest degree in China's educational system, he was expected to share the responsibilities of local government no matter how young he might be; such was the respect for education in old China.

If Choyhung was not unlike other villages, it had an elementary school whenever some determined resident had children he wished to educate and was able to give a teacher the necessary guarantee of a living. To the school would be invited the children of such other parents as could contribute to the master's fees. In this school the village boys might at least set their feet upon the long, hard path of Chinese learning. For a period in Sun Yat-sen's boyhood such a school functioned in Choyhung. No one seems to know how long—whether for a year or two years or three—Sun Yat-sen was fortunate enough to have been included among its pupils. The robed and bespectacled teacher set the boys to learning the traditional textbooks. The triple rhythm of the *Three Character Classic* made it the easiest to remember; and the "project" of the old education was to memorize the classics. In order to get the phrases fixed in mind each individual was required to study his lesson by shouting it aloud, and that with no regard for uniformity in assignment, much less for unison in the chorus. A traveler through the village any time between early morning and dark could have located the school by the babel that issued from it. When summoned in his turn to the teacher's desk young Sun Yat-sen would make a respectful bow to the master, place his book, opened at the assignment, on the table in front of the teacher; then turning his own back on the book, he would recite the memorized passage with an accompanying swaying of his boyish body. If he made a mistake he was within reach of the master's ferule. During certain other hours of the day he was required to discipline his fingers in the intricate task of tracing characters with ink and brush on semi-transparent paper placed over beautiful models of penmanship; thus slowly the child would acquire visual familiarity with the strange symbols, by tens first, then a hundred and upward, later a thousand and upward; and that was the merest beginning of literacy in China.

It was a hard discipline, the old education—a direct drive to master the instruments of reading and writing without the thrill of discovering the uses to which they might be put. What the *Three Character Classic* or *The Great Learning* had to say was almost completely submerged in the effort to remember the archaic-sounding sentences and the difficult written symbols that stood for them. Of course the boy Sun Yat-sen was in a daze like the rest; that was to be expected. How should he know the meaning of what he was memorizing? When Sun Yat-sen became a man he hinted at boyish rebellions against the school discipline which seemed to get nowhere. But by that time he had a reputation as a rebel to live up to, and the temptation must have been strong to make his boyhood dramatically consistent with his career. He probably forgot how docile he had been as a lad; one may be at least a little skeptical as to the reasons for any indocility. He seems to have been a healthy and normal boy who enjoyed firecrackers and liked to fly a kite or spin a top.

II. THE MAKING OF AN ADVENTURER

Village boy though he was, Sun Yat-sen must have felt the lure of a greater world as soon as he felt anything. His father could scarcely have avoided making references to his bachelor youth, when he left the farm for the city and went all the thirty miles to gay Macao; there he learned the tailoring trade; but homesickness overcame the spirit of adventure, and he returned to his native village to till the land and to beget a famous son. Similarly from many of the villages of the Fragrant Hills men had ventured forth to the cities; some had gone even to distant Shanghai. Temptations to travel were not far off from Choyhung. Over the hills and beyond the rice fields lay a small harbor to which a sturdy boy might easily wander out of sheer curiosity. There Sun Yat-sen could see the lesser seacraft coming into port and could listen to the tales of the returning men.

Even in his own home circle there was a constant reminder of the vaguely engulfing world. Two frustrated aunts lived as members of the household into which Sun Yat-sen was born; they were the relicts of his father's missing brothers, whose story was both a lure and a warning. News of the discovery of gold in California had reached South China in the spring of 1848. California had suddenly become a place where every white man thought of himself as potentially too rich to hire out as a laborer; so it had occurred to some one that in China men could be found who would be content to do hard work for regular pay. Thus it came to pass that the white men, themselves lured by the yellow gold, set a lure for the yellow men in promises of wealth in wages—wages undreamed of by any Oriental. The steamship companies sent their agents to the farming villages of Kwangtung Province equipped with maps and graphic posters. By preaching the opportunities of California they drew vigorous young men from the agricultural districts to the ships that were waiting at Macao and at Hongkong to transport them over the ocean. By the end of 1851, so the amazing story runs, as many as twenty-five thousand Chinese were working in California, some at the processes of placer mining, but many more as cooks and manual laborers. This was the human tide that swept Sun Tao-chuan's able-bodied brothers far away from home. Dutifully their young wives remained in the Choyhung household into which they had married. For years they waited without news of their men. Only tardily did they learn that the husband of one had died at sea and the husband of the other in the California gold fields.

Some gold-rush emigrants fared better than they. In later life Sun Yat-sen told how, as a child, he had listened to one returned adventurer recounting his experiences to the stay-at-homes in the village tea house. What stuck in the mind of the lad was the hero's boast of having carried nuggets concealed in his clothing in two places, so that if a robber found one lot he might perchance be satisfied and fail to look for another lot more cunningly concealed.

While Sun Yat-sen was still a very young boy, his elder brother, Sun Mei, fifteen years his senior, emigrated to Honolulu. He was one of the pioneers in the development of the low land in the region of Pearl Harbor. Just what took him to Hawaii no one has troubled to explain. The Sun family were people of the south—of that province which above all others has been the mother of overseas adventurers, the Province of Kwangtung. Our Western generalization that the temperate and north temperate zones breed the more adventurous peoples seems to be denied by China, whose world-wanderers have gone out largely from her most tropical provinces. The migrating people *par excellence* have been the Cantonese and their fellow provincials. Sun Yat-sen began life in the part of Kwangtung most concerned in foreign trade. Macao is the oldest of the foreign commercial settlements now permanently established on the China coast. It was founded by Portuguese traders of the early sixteenth century. In Sun Yat-sen's youth Hongkong, quickly accessible across the water, was outstripping Macao, while Canton, with centuries of trading behind it, had already been a "treaty port" for upwards of twenty-five years.

Traders coming to Canton from the Pacific often carried in their cargo sandalwood from Hawaii; hence the Islands became known to China as the Sandalwood Hills. Now and then seagoing Chinese left the trading ships and settled in Hawaii. When news of their prosperity began to reach home, others followed. As sugar-raising developed in Hawaii, the Chinese were found particularly useful and were encouraged to come. The year before Sun Yat-sen was born, a Board of Immigration was formed and a commissioner was sent to China, who arranged for the transportation of five hundred Chinese laborers from Hongkong. A bonus of eight dollars was offered to each of these immigrants—a sum that must have been very tempting to the trivially paid Chinese coolie. Passage money and other forms of expense were advanced by the sugar planters, to whom the men were bound by a five-year contract. In subsequent years the bonuses rose to higher figures. In 1874 the Hawaiian Government signed an agreement with a firm of Chinese labor contractors for the importation of a hundred Chinese laborers at twenty-five dollars per man. When, as the result of a reciprocity treaty concluded with the United States in 1876, the raising of sugar-cane took a great leap forward, it was to the agricultural districts of Kwangtung Province that agents were sent to recruit more land-working laborers.

It could not have been far from this time when Sun Yat-sen's elder brother returned to Choyhung for a visit. He brought with him not only stories of prosperity, but evidence of it in money which he shared with his parents, lifting them noticeably in the scale of living. He inspired his young brother with the wanderlust: indeed, he tried to persuade his parents to let him take the child back with him, but they rightly considered him too young for such an adventure. So Sun Yat-sen remained a little while longer a Chinese farmer's boy, sometimes helping his father in the fields, sometimes picking up the hard morsels of Chinese learning in the village school. While at home, however, the elder brother set afoot a plan which soon enough carried the boy across the ocean.

From Sun Yat-sen himself comes the story of the shrewd scheme by which his brother, coöperating with a Kwangtung friend, arranged for the transportation to Hawaii of a shipload of immigrants and absorbed the government bonuses as a commission for the enterprise. So, not only by official encouragement but also by private initiative, Chinese immigration flowed into Hawaii. The wave was at its peak when in 1879 a British vessel of two thousand tons, the *Grannoch,* manned by British sailors, embarked from Macao for Honolulu well packed with human cargo. Any one who has seen Chinese immigrants on an ocean steamer can imagine the cramped decks and the crowded quarters below, overflowing with patient, good-natured people and their boxes of wood and of leather, their bamboo baskets, their rolls of bedding, and their blue kerchiefs neatly knotted over small belongings. Worming their way swiftly in and out among the packages and the people were active Chinese boys bound on absorbing adventures of their own; one of these was Sun Yat-sen, aged twelve. Emigrating with laboring colonists to a laborers' paradise, he was nevertheless being carried away from a laborer's life to opportunities of a wholly new kind. With this voyage, which took more than twenty days, the barefoot farmer boy passes out of the picture.

At Honolulu Sun Yat-sen was taken in hand by his brother, who at first set him to work in a small general store which he was carrying on in addition to his farming. This biographically important elder brother, Sun Mei—familiarly known in Hawaii as Ah Mi—seems not only to have taken seriously the Chinese ethics of the elder-brother relationship, but also to have had the generous impulses of a self-made man. He was eager to provide his young brother with opportunities which he himself had never enjoyed. He was living then in the village of Ewa, near Honolulu, and he was frequently in and out of the city. He had heard of an excellent school to which a Chinese boy might gain admittance. It was popularly known as the Bishop's School, because it was fostered by Bishop Willis of the Church of England, who had located the school on his own premises and personally took an interest in the boys. Properly known as Iolani, this school has more than once changed its site; it is still a very well-known Honolulu boys' school.

The Honolulu Diocesan Almanac for 1877 makes vivid the churchly atmosphere into which the boy from Choyhung was thrust in 1879. From its instructive pages, garnished at the bottom with quaint quotations from George Herbert, one may read a "History of the Introduction of the Anglican Church into Hawaii"; also about the laying of the foundation stone of the choir of a projected cathedral church to be dedicated to Saint Andrew. Not only are the Bishops of all the English dioceses fully listed in the Almanac, but also the Bishops of Ireland, Scotland, the United States, India, China and Japan, West Indies and South America, Africa, Madagascar, Australasia and the Hawaiian Islands. Such was the world pervasiveness of the ecclesiastical body into whose care the unconverted and under-educated Chinese villager, Ah Mi, was committing his receptive young brother. How firmly the Society for the Propagation of the Gospel had established itself in Hawaii is suggested by the register of the clergy of the Diocese of Honolulu with their churches and their missions. The educational institutions supported by the Church are also described, and first among them:

For Boys. "Bishop's College School" known as Iolani College, a Boarding and Day School for boys of Hawaiian birth. Principal—The Bishop of Honolulu. Master—Mr. Abel Clark. . . .

Every boarder should be provided with two pairs of sheets. . . .

The terms for boarders are $100 per annum. Books, &c., required by the scholars are supplied at cost prices from the school. . . . [2]

What a different world from Choyhung village! It was perhaps just as well that twelve-year-old Sun Yat-sen did not yet understand the English language and was thus spared too sudden a transition into all the complexities of a new religion as well as of a new culture. What he would be able to receive with his eyes would be strange enough to him. Surely it was progressive of Ah Mi to have sought out the Bishop and to have made the arrangements. Under a boyhood name (recorded as Tai Chu), Sun Yat-sen was received and enrolled as a boarding pupil after the summer vacation of 1879. There were also a few other Chinese among the pupils at Iolani. They wore their hair in the traditional queue of the old régime. It is the testimony of his Chinese schoolmates that Sun Yat-sen knew no English when he entered Iolani. Since at the Bishop's School the pupils were supposed to speak nothing but English, the boy was forced to learn the new language from his schoolmates as well as from his teachers. The masters at Iolani were all British except one; a Hawaiian named Solomon Meheule had the responsibility of helping the boys to make their first break into the English language. It was a thoroughly British discipline in which Sun Yat-sen received the first impress of an alien culture. The schooling was British in method and the textbooks were British. The atmosphere was saturated with monarchical ideas. Like the pro-cathedral Iolani enjoyed the patronage of the Hawaiian royal family.

It is true that American influences were very much abroad in Hawaii during this period. Missionaries of the Congregational Church of the United States had unwittingly put in a wedge when they braved the wild "Sandwich Islands" in 1820 for religious propaganda. By the '70's American enterprise was competing vigorously with British trade in the commercial development of Hawaii. The Reciprocity Treaty of 1876 tightened the economic bond with the United States, and conservative Hawaiians became apprehensive of a trend toward annexation. The Bishop-Principal of Iolani was one of the most outspoken resisters of what was termed "American aggression." When Sun Yat-sen became notorious as a rebel against the Chinese monarchy, Bishop Willis wrote in his *Diocesan Magazine* for Dec. 15, 1896, an article about him. To clear his school of the suspicion of having bred a republican he said:

As far as can be remembered, Tai Chu's school days gave no indications of his future career. He has left behind him no traditions of hatching plots against the magisterial authority, or of composing juvenile odes on the coming emancipation of China from the Manchu yoke. Nor will any one suppose that he was indoctrinated at Iolani with the love of a republican form of government, much less with the desire of revolutionizing the Celestial Kingdom after the model of the Hawaiian republic which was then unborn.[8]

At Iolani School the boarding pupils were so thoroughly regimented that few American ideas could have penetrated to Sun Yat-sen. But, of course, there were vacations, and a boy freed from restraint has both eyes and ears in his head. It is difficult to set limits to what Sun Yat-sen may have learned by asking questions in his newly acquired tongue.

The religious education of pupils was zealously looked after at the Bishop's School. Daily attendance at morning and evening prayer was a required routine, and on Sunday the boys were taken to services in the pro-cathedral. One of Sun Yat-sen's cherished memories of Iolani was of learning to sing; it is said that he attained the distinction of a choir boy's surplice. The Bishop concerned himself with the instruction of his pupils in Christian doctrine. He inculcated in them a critical attitude toward superstition and idolatry, and he associated in their tender minds the two ideas of progress and Christianity. Every reasonable persuasion was brought to bear on the boys to present themselves for baptism. When Sun Yat-sen saw his Chinese schoolmates being instructed for confirmation he also wanted to be a Christian. He went to talk with his brother about it. True to the teaching he had received, the adolescent lad preached to the grown man of the sin of idol worship and spoke disparagingly of his brother's household gods. From this Ah Mi judged with some wrath that his young brother had had enough of the foreigners' schooling. He would by no means consent to his baptism. It is reported that a letter was despatched to Choyhung setting forth the risks of too much foreign education. Moreover, the boy was ripening toward the traditional marriage age: he was in his seventeenth year by Chinese count, in his sixteenth year by our reckoning, when he finished his three years at Iolani. Since there is nothing the Chinese take more seriously than the guarding of the ancestral line from breakage and the ancestral altars from neglect, no boy could approach his maturity without having the duty of marriage pressed home upon him. The arrangements for so important an event were not left to the children; the parents made the betrothals.

Sun Yat-sen left Iolani in what must have seemed to him and to his brother a blaze of glory. The closing exercises for the year were held on July 27, 1882, and were attended by royalty. The Dowager Queen Emma was there, also the Princess Liliuokalani. The presentation of prizes was made by King Kalakaua personally, and among those who were called up to receive honors was Sun Yat-sen; he was given the second prize in English Grammar; proudly he carried it down—an English book about China. From Iolani he also carried away an English Bible and a habit of reading it. Until arrangements were complete for his return to China, he worked, as he had probably done in his other vacations, in his brother's store; in this business he had been allowed a partnership in place of wages.

There are distinguished residents in Honolulu today who, fol lowing Bishop Restarick, are under the impression that Sun Yat-sen spent as many as five or six years of his boyhood in Hawaii. What makes against this is our old and determined belief that no one can be in two places at the same time. The evidence that Sun Yat-sen was in China from 1883 to 1886 follows next in the story.

III. THE MAKING OF A PROGRESSIVE

When Sun Yat-sen, the youth, was put on the ship for China, in the latter months of 1882 or early in 1883, he carried something of Hawaii with him. He had received there the rudiments of a Western education together with a grounding in the English language; he had, moreover, been living in a wholly new world while he was of an age to take a great deal from it into the texture of his own being. For more than three impressionable years of adolescence he had been an overseas Chinese being plastically molded by both American and British ideas. Is it any wonder that he turned out to be a man extraordinarily ductile to foreign influences? Sun Yat-sen never wrote an article—as an Occidental might have done—on "What I Owe to Hawaii." He accepted his Hawaiian experience and said little about it. That as a boy he had been impressed by the foreign buildings, the banks, the newspapers, the sugar planta-tions and the coming and going of ships we may take for granted. That somehow, in spite of Iolani's British conservatism, American enthusiasm for the republican form of government had reached his boyish mind seems an inescapable conclusion. But what appears to have gripped his imagination more firmly than anything else, judging as we must by later events, was that process of change, of which Hawaii has been a notable illustration, namely, the lifting of a primitive people into a Westernized civilization. Before the coming of the white man the Hawaiians were a tabu-ridden people, inhibited by many superstitions. The white man's sense of humor, whether he was a missionary or a loafing sailor, made him a propagandist against many enslaving forms of the tabu. A continuous and determined assault upon idolatry and popular superstition had been going forward in Hawaii for sixty years before Sun Yat-sen landed on the Islands. Begun by some of the earliest navigators and settlers, helped by an unusually responsive royal family, the onslaught had been vigorously continued by missionaries from Puritan New England. Sun Yat-sen, though a mere boy, could see around him (in his schoolmates, for example) the results of liberation, and he could also see enough survivals of the old superstitions to give him a little knowledge of what had been encountered. It seems to have been in large measure due to his Hawaiian experience that he became obsessed with the idea that the breaking down of superstition was a condition of progress. This idea he carried back to China with him along with his Bible.

Sun Yat-sen had not even landed on his native soil before he began to feel irritation at the backwardness of China. After he reached Choyhung he discovered how much his years in Hawaii had altered his outlook. Everything in the village appeared as if in a new light. Some of the biographers, both Chinese and foreign, picture him on his return as a tactless and fanatic young radical going about his native village ruthlessly challenging customs and traditions. This is doubtless a dramatically exaggerated picture of a reformer-to-be. But that there is some truth in it is borne out by an episode which is as well validated as any incident in Sun Yat-sen's youth.

It was an escapade in the village temple—if an act so zealously intended to be reforming can be called an escapade. In it Sun Yat-sen appears to have had a collaborator. The son of another local family was also visiting in Heungshan at the time, Lu Hao-tung by name. Years earlier his father had gone to Shanghai and had there developed a business of his own in lightering ships. His son, brought up in Shanghai, had acquired a knowledge of the English language and some foreign schooling, and had become a Christian. He rose to a post in a telegraph office. When his father died in Shanghai, Lu Hao-tung gave up his position and took his father's body to the Fragrant Hills for burial. He had not left Heungshan when Sun Yat-sen returned from Honolulu at the age of sixteen.

These two youths who had seen a larger world found that they had much in common. In the first place there was Christianity, in which they were both believers. Sun Yat-sen fell into the habit of calling Lu Hao-tung his "doctrinal friend." Many customs and superstitions, which they were looking upon with new eyes, could be discussed freely between them. It was through Lu Hao-tung that Sun Yat-sen learned of some aspects of the Tai-ping Rebellion, which in his altered state of mind made a special appeal to him. It goes without saying that he must have heard from his babyhood of this rising, so ironically called "the Great Peace" Rebellion. Beginning in Canton, it had swept all South China and the Yangtze Valley with more than twelve years of war, leaving in its wake untold destruction and loss of life, and was finally quenched about two years before Sun Yat-sen was born. One of the most distinguished annalists of Sun Yat-sen's life asserts that while still a child in the Choyhung village school, Sun Yat-sen had heard stories of the Tai-ping leader and had felt the ambition stirring within him to become such a rebel leader himself. This may be truth or it may be legend; it is true, however, that Lu Hao-tung was able to tell Sun Yat-sen, the adolescent, certain facts about the rising which apparently had not come to his knowledge. The Tai-ping leader was a partially educated man, who had been superficially influenced by Christian missionaries at Canton. He became obsessed with fanatically religious ideas and an overwhelming sense of revolutionary mission. The religious societies which he organized developed, as one of their chief activities, the destruction of idols. The movement next took on a political character and became an anti-dynastic rising bent upon establishing by military conquest the "heavenly kingdom of great peace," which was committed to an extraordinarily advanced program of social reforms. The rising showed so much vigor that the Imperial Government was glad to get the help of American and British military experts in quelling the long-drawn-out insurrection.

That a rising which originated in their own Province of Kwangtung should have gone so far before being suppressed would make its own appeal to the two Southern boys. What seemed even more to interest them was that it began as a movement against superstition with iconoclasm as its method. This fitted perfectly into Sun Yat-sen's Hawaii-derived ideas about the necessity of driving superstition forcibly out of men's minds in order to make an entrance for new ideas.

The two youths had not far to look to observe superstition. They could see members of their own households frequenting temples and prostrating themselves before idols of lacquered wood. On any feast day Sun Yat-sen could go with his father to the village temple and be expected to do likewise. These young men knew all too well how much these gods were feared and placated; to neglect them was to risk bad crops and sicknesses and death. Now that the two youths themselves were enlightened, they felt that they must attack the superstition that was degrading their fellow-villagers. They went deliberately about this with a religious sense of mission.

Some reports say that the act occurred at a village festival, when every one went to the temple; others that the youths chose a time when the temple guardians were absent and that they took with them certain of their boy friends. Even in the latter case it was a daring thing to do. At the temple Sun Yat-sen spoke boldly of the error of idolatry: these gods were no gods; they could not even protect themselves; how could they protect the village? He climbed up, seized the hand of the central image and broke off its finger; he also mutilated one of the other images. Nothing happened to him; but the onlooking lads and the crowd that soon gathered were stricken with horror. Evil would surely come upon the village, they said. Sun Yat-sen's father was mortified as well as angry. The village councilors, who were by virtue of their position trustees of the temple, met and considered what should be done. They decided the young culprit must leave the village and that his father must repair the damage; only thus might the gods be appeased and the village saved from their wrath. The people agreed that Sun Yat-sen was acting madly, and that his mind had been poisoned by the foreigners.

There was better luck in the outcome than Sun Yat-sen had expected. The months he had spent at Choyhung had irked him. He began thinking of this period at home as "the wasted year." Now he had a chance to return to school; he suggested Hongkong; his father could not do otherwise than let him go. Who gave him the money for further education is not explained; Ah Mi's prosperity in Hawaii was probably at the bottom of it. Lu Hao-tung returned to Shanghai to try to get back into his position with the telegraph company.

By the late fall of 1883 Sun Yat-sen was in Hongkong; there he did the most natural thing; he applied at the school whose position corresponded with Iolani's in Honolulu—the Diocesan School of the Church of England. Perhaps he had a letter of introduction; in default of that, his Iolani prize would have served as a credential. The school records—so I am authoritatively informed—

show that "Sun Yat-sen joined the School as a Day Boy in November of 1883, and that he left in December of the same year. There is no information as to why he left the School."

When Sun Yat-sen resumed his schooling it was at Queen's College, but he did not enter Queen's immediately upon leaving the Diocesan School, though he may have intended to do so. It would have been advantageous for him to have entered Queen's at the beginning of the new school year, which there falls on January 1st. Instead of this, the first three months of 1884 are empty and unexplained. The Chinese New Year season would account for some holidays, and would make opportunity for a visit home, but this year one would think it unlikely that he would make such a visit unless called home. Perhaps his marriage was planned; perhaps his father was ill and he was summoned.

From other evidence it appears that his father's death took place some time within a year after the idol-mutilating incident, with which he is always associated. The death of a parent is in China more disrupting to a son's life than it usually is in the Occident. The minimum period of mourning is seven times seven days. During these weeks a son would be very unlikely to return to school. Even among the less ceremonious folk in the villages a marriage could not take place within a hundred days of a parent's death. If Sun Yat-sen's father died at the end of 1883 or early in 1884, that would go far toward accounting for the seeming vacuity of the first three months of 1884 and the congestion of important events immediately afterward.

In Hongkong Sun Yat-sen took lodgings in a building that was being used during the week to house a day-school for Chinese boys. There he came to know Charles R. Hager, a young man who had just come to China in the fall of 1883 as a missionary of the American Board of Commissioners for Foreign Missions—the very organization that had been engaged since 1820 in the evangelization of Hawaii. Because Sun Yat-sen could speak English, the newly arrived missionary was able very soon to be on friendly terms with him. Dr. Hager's account of their contacts has escaped the notice of the biographers of Sun Yat-sen. It contains details of great significance. Dr. Hager says:

It was in the autumn or possibly the winter months of 1883 that I first met him and judged him to be sixteen to eighteen years of age. He had returned to China from Honolulu, where he had spent a number of years in study, while his older brother was there engaged in business.

Of course I could not help asking him whether he was a Christian, to which he replied that he believed the doctrine of Christ. "Then why do you not become baptized?" "I am ready to be baptized at any time," he replied; and so after some months of waiting he received the ordinance in a Chinese schoolroom where a few Chinese were wont to meet with me every Sunday, about a stone's throw from the present American Board mission church in Hongkong.

It was a humble building in which the future provisional president of China's first republic received the sacred ordinance. During the week a Chinese boys' school was taught there, while our young friend lived in the second story with some other Chinese, and an American Bible Society's colporter and I lived in the third story. In this way I saw a great deal of Sun, and always liked him.

For a time he attended the diocesan school of the Church of England, but soon changed to go to Queen's College.[4]

It must have seemed surprising to the zealous young missionary, fresh out of America, to happen upon a convert so ripe for the picking. But to us, who now know facts that Dr. Hager could not have known, the sequence of events seems natural. By intention, though not by baptism, Sun Yat-sen had become a Christian in Honolulu along with his Chinese schoolmates at Iolani. His Christian feeling had been strengthened by his friendship with Lu Hao-tung,

whom he thought of significantly as his "doctrinal friend." Together the two youths had put their religious courage to a test in
their bold attack upon the idols of Choyhung. That Sun Yat-sen
had been disciplined by his fellow villagers because of his act would
tend to fix him more firmly in his purpose to become a Christian.
If his father's death had occurred before Dr. Hager knew him
well enough to broach the subject of baptism, that would be an
additional explanation of Sun Yat-sen's extraordinary readiness to
be "baptized at any time."

That Sun Yat-sen acted independently of his family in becoming
a Christian is psychologically of the utmost significance. It would
have meant far less to him (and far less to those of us who interpret
him) if he had become a Christian, as has been so often erroneously
reported (See Appendix A) because his father before him was a
Christian. The fact that he was the first member of his family to
take this step, and the additional fact that his elder brother in
Honolulu and his father in Choyhung had both opposed it, made
of his Christian baptism a cardinal break with tradition and a
revolutionary acceptance for himself of a new order of life.

Sun Yat-sen's entry as a student at Queen's College, Hongkong,
occurred in the same crucial year, 1884. Queen's College is an old
institution with a continuous corporate history that goes back to a
time before Sun Yat-sen was born. In its earliest phase it was known
as the Government Central School, later as Victoria College; since
1887 it has been called Queen's College. Its final examinations are
now given by the University of Hongkong—an institution not yet
in existence when Sun Yat-sen was a student at Queen's. Its courses
now prepare for university matriculation. In American usage
Queen's would be called an academy or a preparatory school, in
European terminology, a middle school. I have the word of Mr. A.
H. Crook, Head Master of Queen's, that Sun Yat-sen entered the
school under the name of Sun Tai Tseung, in April, 1884, and

passed through what were then Classes III and II. "The exact date of his departure," Mr. Crook writes, "is not given, as he obtained no leaving parchment: but he told me himself that he was here for two and a half years." These dates dovetail neatly into other verifiable facts about Sun Yat-sen's education. By entering Queen's in April of 1884, he was probably able to complete Class III by December—the school year corresponds with the calendar year at Queen's. The year 1885 seems to have been given to Class II without breaks other than regular holidays. If in 1886 he made a beginning in Class I, the total would correspond approximately with Sun Yat-sen's report; that is, he would have two completed years to his credit and part of another.

Sun Yat-sen's biographers have never quite done justice to Queen's College as an educating factor in his life. One question has puzzled the Chinese writers: Where did Sun Yat-sen get his education in Chinese? His schooling at the village of Choyhung was at best very brief and elementary. Somewhere, somehow, he got enough Chinese education to write articles in the antique literary style. The fact has been overlooked that at Queen's College the requirement is that the education in Chinese must be on a par year by year with the education in occidental subjects. A boy who fails in Chinese is not promoted, no matter how brilliant he may be in Western subjects. So at Queen's Sun Yat-sen had a discipline in Chinese which supplemented considerably his elementary village education. He also went forward in his Western studies.

Sun Yat-sen's beginning year at Queen's was not only his first year as a professed Christian, it was also his first year of marriage. That traditionally necessary event took place, if we may trust implicitly a statement made by the woman he married, on "the thirteenth day of the fourth moon of the tenth year of the Emperor Kuang-hsu"—which, it appears from a comparative calendar, was May 7, 1884. One wonders why marriage should have been jammed into an already full year. Perhaps his family insisted upon it because they were apprehensive of further alienation by renewed foreign schooling. For Sun Yat-sen marriage seems to have been the fulfillment of a filial obligation. There was not a spark of self-determination in it. The bride had been sagaciously chosen by his parents from circumstances similar to those of the Sun family. By marriage she became a member of the Sun household, where she lived with her mother-in-law and saw her schoolboy husband when he came home for holidays. For eight years after his marriage Sun Yat-sen was still a student and seldom at home. It is not surprising that under these circumstances marriage seems to have lacked for him any degree of romantic flavor.

That Sun Yat-sen was zealous in his new religion is the testimony of Dr. Hager. He had not long been a church member, when he set out with his foreign friends on a tour of evangelism; he escorted them directly to his own native village and to his own home. The courage which this called for can only be wondered at. It may have been Sun Yat-sen's way of announcing as impressively as possible to his fellow-citizens of the Fragrant Hills the new direction he had taken for himself. Dr. Hager tells the story straightforwardly in the language of a true missionary:

It was sometime in 1884 that an Englishman and I accompanied Sun Yat Sen to his home in Heung Shan. We decided to sell a number of Gospels on the way, and in passing through the Portuguese colony of Macao we disposed of a great many Scriptures. Sun Yat Sen took us to a Chinese inn, where a bed and two meals cost us about thirty or forty cents a day. Of course we ate with Chinese chopsticks and slept on Chinese bed boards, just as did our friend. After a day or two we went to his home and for several days enjoyed his hospitality; and if I remember rightly we also saw his wife. I concluded that Sun Yat Sen belonged to one of the more well-to-do families. The house in which we lodged was of a superior type. This was probably due to the elder brother's prosperity in business in Honolulu.

After Sun Yat Sen became a Christian he immediately began to witness for Christ, and such was his earnestness that in a short time two of his friends accepted Christianity. This was at a time when few converts were made and when many feared to identify themselves with Christians. But so great was the influence of Sun that he won these men to the truth. It was the same power that he has always had of making men accept his opinions.[5]

It was an upstanding and promising youth that Dr. Hager came to know and grow fond of: a typical schoolboy with long cotton gown and black, skull-fitting cap below which hung a smoothly braided black queue. An attractive photograph of him at eighteen shows a face more than ordinarily candid and eager. He was a youth studious with his books, yet stirring up his fellows with questionings about religion and about affairs. It was to this healthily developing young man that there came in 1885 the prick of war and the sting of national defeat, which loosened in his expanding mind the first thought of revolution. But of that more later.

The elder brother in Hawaii cut short the Queen's College course in 1886. He summoned Sun Yat-sen to Honolulu to sign certain legal papers necessary to the sale of property in which both brothers had an interest. School was given up and the journey made. Chinese who live in Honolulu have told of this visit and of the ensuing quarrel between the brothers. A lucid account comes from Dr. Hager, who had the story at the time from Sun Yat-sen himself:

Sun Yat Sen has learned many lessons in the hard school of adversity. No sooner had his brother at Honolulu heard that the young man had become a Christian than he sent word home that unless he gave up his Christianity he himself would no longer send any money home; and an elder brother in China, in case of the father's death, has almost unlimited authority and power. This dire threat had no effect upon our young, enthusiastic Christian, who did not cease promulgating his views on the Christian religion and the falsity of idols. Finding his threats unavailing, the elder brother sent for Sun Yat Sen to come once more to Honolulu, as he wanted to effect a certain sale to which the younger man's signature was necessary. This was, however, a mere subterfuge to get him away from China. After his arrival in Honolulu, his brother not only threatened him, but absolutely refused to give him any money; at length the Chinese Christians contributed the funds to send him back to China to study for the ministry; for at this time he had a strong conviction that he must become a preacher of the gospel.

The above incident was told me by Sun Yat Sen himself after his return to China.[6]

In his difficulties in Hawaii Sun Yat-sen was also befriended by leaders of the Christian denomination with which he was now affiliated—the Congregational Church. Among these was the Rev. Frank Damon, Superintendent of the Chinese Mission in Honolulu. When Sun Yat-sen reached China again, some time in the summer of 1886, his year's work at Queen's was ruptured beyond repairing, and he was straitened financially. It was Dr. Hager who helped him, as his account shows:

Perhaps if there had been a satisfactory theological seminary at that time in Hongkong or in Canton, and some one to support him, Sun Yat Sen might have become the most famous preacher of his time, by the magnetic power of personal contact with men in winning them to Christ. After several months of inactivity he decided to take up the study of medicine, which has always been held in high esteem and next to the ministry by the Chinese. At his personal request I gave him a letter to the venerable Dr. J. G. Kerr, asking him if he would not remit a part of the medical fees, which were at that time about twenty dollars a year.[7]

Dr. Hager's narrative clears a major question which Sun Yat-sen's life raises: Why did he study medicine? The use that he made of his medical training in later life proved to be so little that it would be difficult to believe that he had an irresistible affinity for the practice of a physician. Dr. Hager makes it clear that Sun Yat-sen had no field for choice. One cannot say that in taking up medical studies he followed the path of least resistance; he followed the path that did not offer insuperable resistance. Driven by his thirst for Western learning, which seems to have been unquenchable, he went into medical study—a field particularly alluring because of its large offering of scientific subjects.

Dr. John G. Kerr was already past sixty years of age when Sun Yat-sen carried a letter of introduction to him. He had spent more than thirty years of his life in China as a missionary of the Board of Foreign Missions of the Presbyterian Church in the United States. In coöperation with an international body known as the "Canton Medical Missionary Society," Dr. Kerr had built up in Canton an extraordinary hospital, called in local speech *Pak Tsai.* Through this hospital Dr. Kerr's reputation waxed great and his surgical practice became phenomenal; indeed, it may be doubted whether in certain aspects it has ever been paralleled. As far back as 1879 Dr. Kerr had begun conducting classes in the Chinese language for the training of young men in medical knowledge. It was in one of these that Sun Yat-sen worked for the year 1886–87, paying his way in part by assisting in the routine work of the hospital.

IV. THE MAKING OF A REBEL

Changes were multiplying for Sun Yat-sen himself. First he had exchanged a Chinese village for a new world of travel. Then from being a Chinese schoolboy he had become a British schoolboy. By revolting against an idol-worshipping community he had branded himself an iconoclast. After breaking with his village he had cultivated the friendship of missionaries in British-ruled Hongkong. Contrary to the tradition of his family he had become a Christian. Estranged from Chinese studies, he was embarking upon the study of foreign medicine. Out of an old civilization, he was emerging, avid for a new. Still another change was impending—that from a peaceable citizen of the Chinese Empire to a plotter against it.

"More than a thousand times," Sun Yat-sen once remarked, "the question has been put to me, when and how I got my revolutionary ideas." To this question he seems to have varied his answers. When he was speaking to fellow Christians, he emphasized the liberating influence of his Christian schooling and of his association with foreign missionaries. When he was making an address at the University of Hongkong, the inciting force of the revolution was the sharp contrast between the efficient British government of that colony and the malgovernment of the Chinese Empire. When he was speaking to Chinese audiences, the urge to revolution was attributed to the economic and territorial encroachment of foreign powers, which the Manchu emperors failed to resist. Doubtless all these causes and others, too, must be combined to account adequately for the turning of Sun Yat-sen into a revolutionist.

In written narratives of his own life Sun Yat-sen always associates the germination of his revolutionary purpose with the Franco-Chinese War, which broke out in 1884 and was not ended until June, 1885. This war was the result of France's territorial ambition to possess and develop Tongking—the link between what she already held in Indo-China and the rich Chinese province of Yunnan, which she coveted as a sphere of influence. At the time the war broke out Sun Yat-sen was about eighteen years of age, a middle-school student at Queen's. Watching the war, as he did from Hongkong, he saw his own nationals make a creditable and effective resistance on land, only to have it neutralized by a raid of irresistible French warships up the coast as far as Foochow and Formosa. The Franco-Chinese War rankled in Sun Yat-sen's memory, and he alludes to it many times in his writings. The loss of territory to foreigners was only a fraction of his grievance. He turned against the Manchu rulers most bitterly because he was convinced that while the Chinese armies were winning the war by brave fighting on the frontier, the Emperor's ministers were making a craven peace. As a matter of fact the long distance between Peking and Annam and the difficulties of communication do not fully excuse what seems to have been a serious lack of coördination between the negotiating government and its own military forces.

At the Canton Hospital School in 1886–87 Sun Yat-sen's embryonic revolutionary impulses met with encouragement from youths of like mind. His "doctrinal friend" Lu Hao-tung had also turned up as a student of Dr. Kerr's; it is said that the friends roomed together. They talked freely as before, and this time they discussed the idea of revolution against the ruling dynasty. Lu Hao-tung had come to Canton in company with a wealthy son of a Shanghai merchant, named Cheng Shih-liang. This young man's father had suffered in a lawsuit at the hands of a magistrate and in chagrin had pined away and died. His son, as a result, hated officialdom and was ripe for rebellion. At Dr. Kerr's medical school Cheng Shih-liang was an outstanding leader, full of initiative, and well-liked by his fellows. The other two young men drew him into their clandestine talk about revolution, and found him very responsive. It was he who told Sun Yat-sen about the strength of certain anti-Manchu secret societies that had existed for many scores of years among lower-class people. He suggested that their resentments might be appealed to and the secret societies enlisted on the side of a revolution. Cheng Shih-liang was himself a member of high ranking in one of these societies, known among Occidentals as the Triad.

They were only three young students in a foreign missionary medical school! That they dreamed of revolution and talked of revolution was interesting in itself, even if it had never got beyond talk. It did get beyond talk, but not until eight years later. Sun Yat-sen was soon separated from the other two.

At that time a movement was afoot in Hongkong for the opening of a medical school in connection with the newly erected hospital of the London Missionary Society—the Alice Memorial Hospital. Typical of the Hongkong of those days, this hospital was the gift of a wealthy Chinese, Dr. Ho Kai, whose father had been one of the early converts to Christianity. Ho Kai was himself an M. D. of Aberdeen, and the hospital was given as a memorial to his English wife. The community contributed toward its equipment, and physicians of the colony gave their services. Among those active in the establishment of a medical school in connection with the hospital was Dr. Cantlie, afterwards Sir James Cantlie, F.R.C.S. Somehow Sun Yat-sen had got the money for a new venture in education. Probably by that time he had made his peace with Ah Mi. Perhaps the plan for the study of medicine appealed to this affluent Hawaiian brother as other plans had not. Remittances of the necessary money must have been dependable. Dr. Cantlie tells how Sun Yat-sen was the first student to register in the new medical school in October, 1887; five years later he became one of its first graduates. Inasmuch as Dr. Cantlie saw Sun Yat-sen through his whole course and into the actual practice of medicine, his book, *Sun Yat Sen and the Awakening of China,* contains one of the most dependable pictures we have of Sun Yat-sen as a young man. He says:

Dr. Sun Yat-sen, whilst yet a boy, saw and understood the uselessness and senselessness of education in Chinese schools, and knew full well that an intimate acquaintance with the Chinese classics led to nothing. He longed for instruction in science, and it was this desire that brought him to the medical college in Hongkong the moment it was opened;

he was the first student and the first graduate. The sciences of botany, chemistry, zoölogy &c., with which all medical teaching commences, opened new worlds to him, and every branch of study served to satisfy this son of intelligent China. . . . Sun studied medicine as he has studied everything else, ardently.[8]

By taking his medical course in the British colony of Hongkong Sun Yat-sen gave himself an environment in which his revolutionary ideas could grow with little check. In Hongkong he found three friends with whom he talked so freely about revolutionary changes that they got the nickname of "the Four Big Rebels." It was while he was still a medical student that Sun Yat-sen's first child, a son, was born on Oct. 18, 1891, at Choyhung. He is now known as Sun Fo.

After five years of uninterrupted medical studies Sun Yat-sen was graduated in 1892 with a Certificate of Proficiency in Medicine and Surgery. He began his professional life in Macao, the large city nearest his native village. Dr. Cantlie had encouraged him to go on with surgery. Sun Yat-sen found in Macao an old-fashioned Chinese hospital that allowed him the use of a building for surgical work to be conducted according to his newly acquired foreign methods. In those days Dr. Cantlie made the water trip from Hongkong on certain occasions to assist Sun Yat-sen in major operations. "Why did I go this journey to Macao to help this man?" Dr. Cantlie answers his own question: "For the same reason that others have fought and died for him, because I loved and respected him." Dr. Cantlie describes the great interest which these operations aroused:

Surgical work is not conducted in China with the privacy that attends similar work in Britain. At Sun's operations the lay committee of the hospital came and seated themselves near the operating table, and the relatives and friends of the patient stood around watching the proceedings attentively. Especially did the manipulations in cutting for stone interest the onlookers.[9]

Sun Yat-sen's professional career in Macao was shortly brought to an end by the enforcement of a regulation which required a Portuguese diploma for the legitimate practice of medicine in this Portuguese colony. Sun Yat-sen removed to Canton, but his practice was not enough to deter him from seeking a position in the North. It was in 1893—probably in the warm months—that he set out with his friend, Lu Hao-tung. This trip seems to have been one of the turning-points in Sun Yat-sen's career. He was twenty-six years old and was still professionally ambitious.

Those were days when the dominant figure in the North was the old Viceroy, Li Hung-chang, a statesman whose name was known around the world by reason of his influence with the Manchu rulers and also because he had become personally known to the Occident through extensive travels. In his own viceroyalty—the area in which Peking is situated—he had been the practical exponent of such progressive policies as China had then dared to venture upon. Among the advance steps which he was taking was the creation in Tientsin of a group of modern institutions of higher learning. One of the foundations was a medical college. It is said that Sun Yat-sen's trip was made to apply for a medical position in Tientsin. What would be more natural than that an ambitious early graduate of the British Medical College at Hongkong should aspire to some connection with the new medical college in the North? And Li Hung-chang was the official patron of the school.

The two young men fancied they could get an interview with the Viceroy in Tientsin. Sun Yat-sen was a budding reformer as well as a physician seeking a position. Even at the beginning of his medical practice—according to his own statement—he had carried on revolutionary agitation in Macao and Canton, but had to do it secretly. This may have been no more than the kind of radical talk that any young man can do any time in China. He and his radical young friends had been thrashing out their ideas in many discussions; these bore fruit in a memorial—very carefully prepared —which Sun Yat-sen carried with him to Tientsin, and planned to deliver to Li Hung-chang. It must have been a bitter checking of his sanguine enthusiasm, when he found he could not get access to the Viceroy. And there was no medical position forthcoming for Sun Yat-sen. Who can say how different the course of Sun Yat-sen's life might have been, if he had secured that position and had been received by the Viceroy? Li Hung-chang knew how to develop the talents of younger men. A promising protégé named Yuan Shih-kai was coming on under his patronage at this time: his interest had been enlisted in the development of a modernized army, and he was being trained also in efficient civil administration at a very difficult post in Korea. If the ardent force of Sun Yat-sen's youth had chanced to receive direction from a man of Li Hung-chang's experience, if the young man's plans for his country had been given some practical outlet, he might have become, for a while at least, a promoter of a slower process of change for China. He might have found himself among the reformers instead of among the revolutionists.

There could scarcely be a more vivid revelation of Sun Yat-sen's youthful thinking. The memorial advocated large but eminently sane policies—not in the least calculated to raise alarm against their author as a revolutionary. Sun Yat-sen urged Li Hung-chang to develop to the utmost four elemental requisites of national progress: the talents of men, the produce of the soil, natural resources and the circulation of commodities. For the attainment of these ideal ends he advocated—and this is not a complete list—free public education and vocational training, the scientific development of agriculture and improvement of farming methods, the discovery and exploitation of natural resources, the introduction of machinery into industry, the removal of barriers to trade and the creation of new systems of transportation and communication. Among these reforms he felt the scientific improvement of agriculture to be the most pressing—more important even than schools; he reasoned characteristically that food is the most fundamental need of the people.

Surely it was open-minded and adventurous in a young man to envisage such a future for a nation so fixed in habit and so set in its own civilization as China then was. Such an omnibus attack upon social problems is not infrequently characteristic of youthful reformers. In the unfolding of Sun Yat-sen's life it will be seen whether he outgrew the method which began in this memorial. Its thought is cast in the form of a program, comprehensive and ambitious, but disregardful of the practical problems that would arise for Li Hung-chang or any other administrator who would undertake to make any part of the program effective for China.

Unable to deliver his ideas in person, Sun Yat-sen had, apparently, to put the document back in the pocket under his long Chinese tunic. The two disappointed young men went on to see the capital. It is characteristic of Sun Yat-sen that, in writing about this trip in his *Autobiography,* he does not tell the whole story. He does not mention Li Hung-chang or the memorial. He represents the trip north as having been revolutionary in purpose and says that he and Lu Hao-tung visited Peking to learn for themselves how strong the Manchu dynasty really was, and that they returned by way of Wuchang and Hankow to observe conditions in the Yangtze Valley. The trip may easily have become revolutionary in feeling after his disappointment. If ever Sun Yat-sen traveled in the romantic fashion told of him, preaching revolution to the common people in disguises, it must have been on some such trip as this. Under the circumstances the two young men could be as vagabond as they wished. Slow traveling would give them better opportunities to observe the temper of the people as well as the power of the government.

Sun Yat-sen's heart was not in his Canton medical practice when the war with Japan broke out in the summer of 1894. To him and to his revolutionary-minded friends in the south it seemed that national defeat was certain: Japan was equipped with modern armaments and China was not. They were of the opinion that a losing war would offer an opportunity for a revolution. But anything that was undertaken would cost money. That he proposed to get in Hawaii and America. It could not have been many weeks after the declaration of war by Japan on August 1st, when Sun Yat-sen again saw his old friend, Dr. Hager, who writes vividly of the meeting:

Not long after my return to China, in 1894, Sun Yat Sen called upon me with a former pastor of the London Mission. He seemed the same kind and respectful young man that he always was; what surprised me was the remark of the native pastor, who had just returned from a three years' sojourn in Germany as a teacher of Chinese in Berlin. "How were you able," he asked, "to persuade such a man to become a Christian?" Today it seems clearer to me than ever before that even at that time Sun Yat Sen had already impressed himself upon the most progressive element of Chinese society, so that they were following him as their leader. [10]

Evidently Dr. Hager did not know at the moment upon what an audacious adventure his convert was setting out, else he would not have been so surprised at the remark of the pastor. Perhaps Sun Yat-sen himself did not realize what his trip might lead to. He was off for Honolulu. Meanwhile his reform memorial, which had failed of delivery to Li Hung-chang, was being published in Shanghai in September and October, 1894, in *Wan Kuo Kung Pao,* a progressive journal which was getting a hearing among the educated classes.

There are Chinese still living in Hawaii who remember the organization there in 1894 of Sun Yat-sen's first society, the *Hsing Chung Hui* (Prosper China Society). Its objects as stated in its regulations were "To associate progressive Chinese—in China and abroad—in an organization whose purpose shall be to make a study of wealth and power in order to promote and prosper China." The reasons for its creation are passionately stated in rhetorical phrasing:

Affairs in China are going wrong. The old loyalties and virtues are corrupted every day. Our strong neighbors look down upon us and despise us for the reason that we are not one at heart. Our people are striving for selfish and immediate ends, and are neglectful of the situation in the large. They do not realize that when China is one day dismembered by other people, their sons and grandsons will be enslaved and their families will go unprotected. There can be no urgency more urgent than this. Selfishness was never more selfish. The whole nation is confused. Nobody understands. There is nobody to save the situation. How then is calamity to be averted? If we do not make an effort to hold our own, if we do not rouse ourselves in time, our thousands of years of fame and culture, our many generations of traditions and morals will be destroyed, utterly ruined. Who must be responsible in this situation? Who else but the good and intelligent men who know what the situation is? [11]

It was the plan of the organization to promote all sorts of things that might help China—to establish newspapers to teach the masses, to establish schools to educate the talented, to develop industry to improve the livelihood of the people, and anything else that would promote the prosperity of China's four hundred million people. Initiates were required to take an oath before the meeting. Sun Yat-sen was the first to place his left hand on an open Bible and with right hand uplifted swear allegiance to the Prosper China Society and its aims. Then he signed its register. Others followed his lead; it was not a large group; all were young men, some mere youths. By this memorable meeting Sun Yat-sen and a small body of overseas Chinese bound themselves together to work for the modernization of China. Branches of the society were to be established in any place where as many as fifteen might be gathered together to form it. Its head office was to be in China. The first thing needed for its promotion was money. Members were invited to buy ten-dollar shares with a hope of getting them back some day with interest. Funds were also solicited from well-to-do Chinese in Hawaii. Among those who responded was prosperous Ah Mi.

DOCUMENTATION OF QUOTED PASSAGES

[1] Interview by Rev. William Carter, D.D., *New York Herald,* Sept. 10, 1922. [2] *Honolulu Diocesan Almanac,* 1877, p. 25. [3] *Honolulu Diocescan Magazine* Vol. III, No. 3, p. 43. [4] Appendix B, p. 382. [5] Ibid., p. 383. [6] Ibid., p. 383. [7] Ibid., p. 384. [8] Cantlie and Jones: *Sun Yat Sen and the Awakening of China* (New York, 1912) p. 202. [9] Ibid., p. 32. [10] Appendix B, p. 385. [11] Direct translation from the Chinese text, to be found in Sun Yat-sen's Collected Works.

SOURCES AND AUTHORITIES: See Appendix C, p. 395.

CHAPTER II

Adventurers for Change

I. CONSPIRACY AND EXILE

THE war with Japan was going very badly for China, so badly that a letter followed Sun Yat-sen to Honolulu urging him to return to China and launch a revolution at once. The message came from a Shanghai friend of the would-be revolutionaries, surnamed Soong. Many years earlier, while Sun Yat-sen was still a schoolboy in Honolulu, another adventuring Chinese youth of little more than his own age had turned up at Wilmington, N. C., on board the U. S. cutter *Colfax* in 1880. The kindly disposed Captain of the ship made an effort to find friends for the boy and, at some one's suggestion, put him in touch with the pastor of a local Methodist church. Shortly afterward the youth was converted in revival meetings and baptized as Charles Jones Soong, taking as a foreign name that of the friendly Captain. Next he was hopefully provided with a financial patron, who sent him as a special student to Trinity College, North Carolina, where he spent a year, easily making friends, and uniting with the college church. Afterwards he was given a three-year course, 1882–85, in the Theological Department at Vanderbilt University, Nashville, Tenn. On returning to China he located at Shanghai, where, after trying other activities, he found himself in business. He married a talented girl who had been educated by a Christian mission. As the years went by, both he and his wife became more and more prominent in the Christian community, and were highly respected as promoters of many good causes. Charles Soong was already the father of five, when Sun

38

Yat-sen became his friend, played with his children and enlisted his help in the first revolutionary planning. (Anticipatory as it is, it may be remarked that it is the affiliation of several of his children with the present Nanking Government that has brought upon it the nickname of the "Soong dynasty.")

Sun Yat-sen had planned to go on from Hawaii to America to further his revolutionary preparations there. Instead, he returned to China, taking with him some of his "sworn brothers" from Honolulu. China's war with Japan shortly came to an end with the Treaty of Shimonoseki, April 17, 1895, by which China was forced to cede Formosa to Japan and to recognize the independence of Korea, which, as the sequel proved, was only a step toward its annexation by Japan. A disturbed period followed in China. Soldiers who had served in the war with Japan roamed the country, dangerously unattached and idle. There was more than one outbreak of rebellion, even in the south. Sun Yat-sen and his fellow-conspirators felt keenly the national disgrace as they went about their plotting. The immediate objective they set for themselves was the capture of the headquarters of the provincial government at Canton. Sun Yat-sen in his own revolutionary *Autobiography* tells how they laid their plans and worked hard at preparations for a half year. To screen their plotting and to furnish themselves with a working center they organized a "Scientific Agricultural Association" in Canton. In Hongkong they opened a shop, which was really a sub-office. They then proceeded with the risky business of buying ammunition and enlisting. In Hongkong they bought pistols, rifles, even dynamite. There also they recruited men. A consignment of six hundred pistols, shipped as casks of cement, was discovered by the Maritime Customs at Canton, and the secret was out. The central conspirators at once took to flight, burning incriminating papers. Their headquarters were raided Sept. 9, 1895. The casualties Sun Yat-sen puts at three men executed; more than seventy were arrested. The first to give his life for the revolution was Sun Yat-sen's "doctrinal friend," Lu Hao-tung. The fact that this young leader was a Christian and had been a student in a missionary school made the incident keenly felt in local Christian circles. Some of the doomed man's co-religionists attempted to intercede for him, but he himself would ask no mercy of the Manchus. He went bravely to his death after publishing a "Confession."

For several days Sun Yat-sen was hidden by friends in Canton. Then he made his escape and wandered southward through the labyrinth of inlets and canals that makes the Pearl River Delta a haunt of pirates. He took his way gradually to Macao, sometimes in a boat, sometimes afoot. In that city he saw a posted notice offering 10,000 taels for his capture. From Macao he got away by steamer to Hongkong where he sought out his medical professor, Dr. Cantlie. In *My Reminiscences* Sun Yat-sen says:

At Hong Kong my safety was hardly more assured, and on Dr. Cantlie's advice I went to see a lawyer, Mr. Dennis, who told me that my best protection was instant flight.

"Peking's arm, though weaker, is still a long one," he said, "and in whichever part of the world you go, you must expect to hear of the Tsung-li-Yamen."

Fortunately friends provided me with funds. . . .

At Kobe, whither I fled from Hong Kong, I took a step of great importance. I cut off my cue, which had been growing all my life. For some days I had not shaved my head, and I allowed the hair to grow on my upper lip. Then I went out to a clothier's and bought a suit of modern Japanese garments. When I was fully dressed I looked in the mirror and was astonished—and a good deal reassured—by the transformation. Nature had favored me. I was darker in complexion than most Chinese, a trait I had inherited from my mother, for my father resembled more the regular type. I have seen it said that I have Malay blood in my veins, and also that I was born in Honolulu. Both these statements are false. I am purely Chinese, as far as I know; but after the Japanese war, when the natives of Japan began to be treated with more respect, I had no trouble, when I let my hair and moustache grow, in passing for a Japanese. I admit I owe a great deal to this circumstance, as otherwise I should not have escaped from many dangerous situations.[1]

It was a momentous hair-cut; like the change of raiment, it was symbolic of an already accomplished inward change. The queue was something which Chinese of those days did not carelessly part with. Because the custom of wearing the hair in the long hanging braid had been introduced into China by the Manchu dynasty, the queue had become the universal symbol of peaceable acceptance of Manchu rule. To cut off one's queue was a rebellion against custom sufficient to arouse suspicion and to create a public sensation. Wherever Chinese might travel or colonize, whether they were laundrymen or diplomats, they carefully cherished their queues in preparedness for the always-hoped-for return to the homeland. When Sun Yat-sen cut off his queue he did more than disguise his appearance; he accepted as final his break with the old China; he sealed his own resolve nevermore to be subject to the Manchus.

From this point on we shall no longer visualize him as the long-robed, black-queued Chinese student, proudly conscious of having climbed from the level of the land to the Aristocracy of the Educated. It is with an admittedly foreignized Chinese that we shall keep company—a rather small, darkish man in European clothes, wearing a collar a little too large, which, however, sets off a neatly knotted tie; his luxuriant black hair naturally grows low over his brow, but is parted at the side, brushed back and well pomaded to train it in the new way. To this ensemble there is added a very self-conscious young mustache, with the help of which Sun Yat-sen will slip in and out of many a scene, conveniently taken for a Japanese.

One of the conspirators remained in Japan. Sun Yat-sen decided to go back to Hawaii, where he had a brother to give him asylum. He remained in the Islands for six months. Some time during his stay the *Hsing Chung Hui* was called together; some new members joined, but the general feeling was one of discouragement.

What must have been the excitement at Choyhung when news of the discovery of the plot reached the Fragrant Hills! The Lu family and the Sun family were alarmed for themselves, and with reason: the Manchu government had a well-understood practice of visiting punishment upon the families of notorious offenders. This was founded upon the Chinese philosophy of the family's responsibility for the conduct of its members. A great-uncle of Lu Hao-tung, who was at the time head elder of Choyhung, fled for his life and escaped. It happened that a young scion of the family, who like Sun Yat-sen had emigrated to Honolulu at an early age, was at home on the important errand of marriage. He was about to return to Hawaii with his bride when Sun Yat-sen's whole family was placed in his care and by him escorted to Honolulu. Thus the revolutionist's widowed mother, his wife and his three children—a boy of four years of age and two daughters of more tender years—all became fugitives in Hawaii.

Ah Mi, the elder brother, assumed the responsibilities laid on him by Chinese tradition and received them into his household. For many years they remained members of his family, while Sun Yat-sen lived the life of a revolutionary vagabond. In 1895 Ah Mi was no longer in business near Honolulu, but was a cattle rancher on the Island of Maui near Kula, where there was a growing Chinese settlement. In Hawaii the old mother, harshly uprooted from her native soil, found difficulty in striking new roots. It is reported that she would bemoan her fate and reproach her younger son, saying, "Oh! Why did you bring all this trouble on your family?" That the flight from Choyhung had more than panic at the back of it is shown by the pitiable fate of one who remained behind—the father of the young man who got Sun Yat-sen's family away to safety. This reputable villager knew he was innocent, although he had heard some of the talk of the hot-headed young men; he remained in the village, only to be arrested and cast into prison. His Honolulu son spent about six thousand dollars in persistent efforts to get him released, and succeeded only after six years by enlisting the influence of Wu Ting-fang, the Chinese minister at Washington.

Sun Yat-sen had already made plans for leaving Hawaii when a fortunate incident occurred, which by linkage of events resulted in the saving of his life in a crisis. In Honolulu he met by chance Dr. Cantlie, who was returning with his family to England in 1896 by way of America. From the time he had sent Sun Yat-sen to the lawyer in Hongkong, Dr. Cantlie had been ignorant of the young rebel's whereabouts. He tells how he and his wife were driving through the streets of Honolulu; with them in the carriage was their little son in the charge of a Japanese nurse. They were hailed by an Oriental wearing European dress and a mustache; he lifted his hat, smiled and put out his hand. Even the nurse mistook him for a fellow-national and instinctively addressed him in Japanese. He shook his head and introduced himself as Sun Yat-sen. Without his queue and his Chinese costume it was very difficult for his good friends to recognize him. The meeting was casual and brief. Sun Yat-sen showed them about Honolulu and promised to visit them in London—little did he know under what circumstances.

Sun Yat-sen left Honolulu in June, 1896, sailing for San Francisco. Inasmuch as the Geary Exclusion Act was then in force against Chinese immigrants, one wonders how he managed his landing—whether a through-ticket to England sufficed, or whether he was able to enter as a Japanese, a possibility that he hints at. Because of his rebel status, a Chinese passport would have been impossible for him to secure. He says that he stayed a month in

San Francisco and three months altogether in the United States. In San Francisco he sat for a photograph, with mustache and European suit—a hazardous bit of vanity for a man whom the Chinese government considered an escaped criminal. We infer that Sun Yat-sen thought well of his occidentalized appearance. About his trip through America he makes a restrained statement in his *Autobiography:*

> I found the Chinese in America even more conservative than the Chinese in Honolulu. I traveled from San Francisco to New York, and stopped at a good many places—sometimes for a few days, sometimes for a couple of weeks. Everywhere I preached to the Chinese about the crisis in the mother-country, the corruption of the Manchu government, and the necessity of a fundamental national reconstruction in order to bring about national salvation. I also pointed out that it was every one's duty to participate in the reconstruction. Though I worked hard, there were very few who paid any attention to me. There were only a few individuals, at most a dozen or two in each city, who were favorable to my ideas of revolution.[2]

Sun Yat-sen's presence in America became known to the Chinese minister at Washington, who kept a detective's eye on him and got accurate descriptions of his foreignized appearance and also copies of the San Francisco photograph. The Washington minister wrote in advance to the Chinese minister in London about Sun Yat-sen, and later gave notification by cable of the date of his sailing. On Sept. 23, 1896, Sun Yat-sen sailed from New York on the *S.S. Majestic,* arrived at Liverpool on the 30th and at London on October 1st. He put up at Haxell's Hotel in the Strand, and on the next day called on Dr. and Mrs. Cantlie at 46 Devonshire St., Portland Place. These friends helped him to find lodgings at 8 Gray's Inn Place, Holborn, and he became an almost daily caller at their home. One day Dr. Cantlie drew Sun Yat-sen's attention to the fact that the Chinese Legation was located also in Portland Place, quite near by, and jokingly suggested that Sun Yat-sen call there. With maternal alarm Mrs. Cantlie remarked: "Don't you go near it; they'll catch you and ship you off to China."

II. DETENTION AND DESTINY

The Chinese minister in London had been notified by a letter from Washington that a political criminal, known in China as Sun Wen, was traveling through America for England. The orders were that he should be watched by detectives and that the British government should be asked to extradite him. After Sun Yat-sen's arrival in England his movements were followed, but the request for extradition was refused by the Foreign Office on the ground that no extradition treaty with China existed and that extradition arrangements with Hongkong would not apply in this case.

For ten days Sun Yat-sen enjoyed London without any untoward incident; he called frequently at the Cantlie home and spent much time reading in the Doctor's study. Chinese report has it that he even visited at the Chinese Legation under an assumed name, and became friendly with a Cantonese interpreter there. This is a detail that Sun Yat-sen never related to the Cantlies. He gave them to understand that the first contact came on Sunday morning, October 11, when he was on his way to join the Cantlies and go to church with them. A Chinese accosted him on the street, engaged him in conversation, and drew him into the Legation building. There he was treated cordially and shown around the place. When he reached a room on the third floor a door closed ominously behind him, and he was confronted by the English adviser of the Legation, Sir Halliday Macartney, who told him that word had come from America of a political criminal, named Sun Wen, who had taken passage for England; since he was undoubtedly the man, would he be kind enough to remain with them until they could communicate with Peking?

The Legation then tried to get instructions from the Chinese government as to what to do with Sun Yat-sen now that he was in custody. The only method of getting him back to China that would be secret enough to avoid interference seemed to be the chartering of a vessel specially to take him; but that would be expensive, so the Legation applied for authorization of the plan or other instructions. Peking's reply was so long delayed that the situation grew warm in London.

A prisoner on the top floor of a London house, with Chinese watching lest he should escape, and English servants bringing him food and tending his fire, Sun Yat-sen was a most unhappy young man. His fellow-Cantonese—the interpreter—increased his anxiety by letting him into the Legation's plan to ship him back to China. Then Sun Yat-sen's imagination busied itself painfully with all the horrors of criminal torture and execution practiced in his native land; the old régime was far from humane in its punishments. (This is the one time in Sun Yat-sen's life that the curtain of reserve parts enough for us to see him cowering with fear.) There was plenty of leisure to imagine what his fate might be. His sleep was scanty and troubled. The week dragged by, day after long day. He wrote frantic letters which never reached his friends; out of the window he dropped notes weighted with coins; he tried without success to get a message to Dr. Cantlie. Then with inspired resourcefulness he used his religion in an emotional appeal to one of the English servants, "telling him that just as the Sultan of Turkey wished to kill all the Christians of Armenia, so the Emperor of China wished to kill him because he was a Christian, and one of a party that was striving to secure good government for China." "My life is in your hands," he told the servant. "If you let the matter be known outside, I shall be saved; if not, I shall certainly be executed." To this appeal the man responded, and notes passed the guarded door hidden in the coal scuttle.

Sun Yat-sen's religion had to do more for him in this crisis than work upon the sympathies of an English servant; Sun Yat-sen's own terrified spirit was in need. His Western religion was being deeply tested by the grilling experience. In his own narrative, *Kidnapped in London,* his state of mind is described, in the language, however, of the unnamed English friend who composed for him the vivid little book:

My despair was complete, and only by prayer to God could I gain any comfort. Still the dreary days and still more dreary nights wore on, and but for the comfort afforded me by prayer I believe I should have gone mad. After my release I related to Mr. Cantlie how prayer was my one hope, and told him how I should never forget the feeling that seemed to take possession of me as I rose from my knees on the morning of Friday, October 16th—a feeling of calmness, hopefulness and confidence, that assured me my prayer was heard, and filled me with hope that all would be well.[3]

A letter written shortly after the incident to one of Sun Yat-sen's Chinese Christian friends in Hongkong gives a more revealing account of the crisis:

While I was in the Chinese Legation in London I prayed constantly for relief. For six or seven days I prayed without ceasing. At the end of the seventh day fear left me: this I thought of as an answer to prayer. . . . Although I realized the gravity of my situation, I believed God would send a man to save me. The next day I succeeded in getting a servant to carry a letter to Dr. Cantlie. . . . Although the Manchu dynasty had planned to transport me to China, I was saved by God. . . . Now I believe in God more than ever. I am like the prodigal son and the lost sheep: I owe everything to the great favor of God. Through the Way of God I hope to enter into the Political Way. I hope you will not cease to write to me about the Way of God.[4]

These statements reveal a man, not merely in terror of an excruciating death, but undergoing a major crisis in his inner life. We cannot be far wrong in judging that it was Sun Yat-sen's religiousness—in the large sense, not his particular brand of pious Christianity—that saved the event from being just a hairbreadth escape, and made of it something for him to interpret significantly.

At eleven-thirty at night on Saturday, October 17th, the doorbell of Dr. Cantlie's house was rung and a letter pushed under the door. The messenger was gone when the ring was answered. The letter read:

There is a friend of yours imprisoned in the Chinese Legation here since last Sunday; they intend sending him out to China, where it is certain they will hang him. It is very sad for the poor young man, and unless something is done at once he will be taken away and no one will know it. I dare not sign my name, but this is the truth, so believe what I say. Whatever you do must be done at once, or it will be too late. His name is, I believe, Sin Yin Sen.[5]

It was learned later that the letter had been written by the wife of one of the English servants of the Chinese Legation. Dr. Cantlie lost no time; he went that very night to the detectives at Scotland Yard. They told him that they could not consider it any of their business. The next morning, Sunday, Dr. Cantlie called on his friend, Sir Patrick Manson, also formerly of Hongkong. At Dr. Manson's he found the English servant from the Legation with cards from Sun Yat-sen; one of them had written on it:

I was kidnapped on Sunday last by two Chinamen, and forcibly taken into the Chinese Legation. I am imprisoned, and in a day or two I am to be shipped off to China on board a specially chartered vessel. I am certain to be beheaded. Oh! Woe is me! [6]

Together the two physicians went to Scotland Yard, but were courteously advised to drop the matter. Dr. Cantlie, however, had no intention of doing so. He bethought him of the power of the press, and decided to give the story to the newspapers. At ten o'clock Sunday night he called at the *Times* office and made a careful statement, but for some reason the *Times* saw fit to pigeonhole the news. Sunday had not ended, however, before one thing had been accomplished: a detective was posted to watch the Chinese Legation from a hansom cab.

On Monday Dr. Cantlie took the case to the Foreign Office. There it moved slowly through the red tape. An attempt to get a writ of *habeas corpus* was thrown out by a judge at Old Bailey, but a *Globe* correspondent got wind of it and interviewed Dr. Cantlie. The story was published in Thursday evening's issue of the *Globe*, and within a very short time the Chinese Legation was more than busy dealing with representatives of the press. The English counselor to the Legation realized that the game was up, and admitted the presence of Sun Yat-sen in the house. The next morning all the newspapers carried the story, and no one who read them could be in ignorance of the plight of the Chinese revolutionary. The Legation became the object of much criticism. By that time the case had progressed through the Foreign Office and had reached the Prime Minister, Lord Salisbury. He despatched a message to the Chinese minister politely explaining that the action taken and the action proposed were infringements of British law, and diplomatically advising the release of Sun Yat-sen. On Friday afternoon, October 23rd, Sun Yat-sen was handed over to messengers from the Foreign Office. After a group-interview with newspaper men and a stop at Scotland Yard for the filing of a statement, Dr. Cantlie was allowed to take his rescued protégé home. The day after Sun Yat-sen's release the long-delayed money was cabled from Peking, six thousand pounds with authorization to spend it on shipping Sun Yat-sen to China.

Men have come out of less difficult experiences defiant of God and man. Smaller frights have made slinking cowards of others. From this detention there might have emerged a bitter derelict or a more furtive adventurer. Sun Yat-sen got out of the event, not discouragement or defeatism, but a sense of singularity that seemed to designate him for some high mission. His religion had taught him to think of his life in relation to a power controlling and directing it, called God. When, in a crisis, he found himself craven and powerless, and there suddenly appeared both Control and Direction, he felt that God had laid His hand upon him. From out of the Legation's door he went seeking "the Political Way" for China by renewed devotion to "God's Way." The Sun Yat-sen who emerged from the harrowing experience was becoming conscious of Destiny; he was on the way to being significant for his own generation.

Not quite thirty years of age, Sun Yat-sen is henceforth a marked man. Wherever he may hide himself or wherever he may travel, the Manchus will spy him out, never forgetting that he made a sensational escape from punishment as a rebel. A flattering price remains on his head—a surprisingly large sum considering the futility of the plot and the moderate amount of attention that it attracted at the time.

Among the overseas Chinese, wherever they labor or trade or colonize the world over, in Malaysia, Japan, Hawaii, America or Europe, Sun Yat-sen will need no introduction; his notoriety will be introduction enough. No one will need to say, "This is Sun Yat-sen, the revolutionist." Chinese everywhere will know the story of his London escape.

The episode has also lodged Sun Yat-sen in the consciousness of the Occident. People who know no other Chinese name will remember his. And the press which made him famous will catch up his name whenever it appears in a news despatch and play with it as with something familiar.

For men who feel the deep currents running through affairs Sun Yat-sen has become a man to watch. It is almost startling to read such words as these, published in the *China Mail* at Hongkong, Dec. 3, 1896:

Sun Yat-sen, who has recently been in trouble in London through the Chinese Minister attempting to kidnap him for execution as a rebel, is not unlikely to become a prominent character in history. . . . It may be safely said that he is a remarkable man, with most enlightened views on the undoubtedly miserable state of China's millions. . . . Last year's attempt was not likely to succeed, but it was likely to bring success a stage nearer, and in that sense it was well worth the effort to an ardent patriot. Dr. Sun was the only man who combined a complete grasp of the situation with a reckless bravery of the kind which alone can make a national regeneration. . . . He is of average height, thin and wiry, with a keenness of expression and frankness of feature seldom seen in a Chinese. An unassuming manner and an earnestness of speech, combined with a quick perception and resolute judgment, go to impress one with the conviction that he is in every way an exceptional type of his race. Beneath his calm exterior is hidden a personality that cannot but be a great influence for good in China sooner or later, if the "Fates are fair. . . .[7]

III. OTHER DREAMERS, OTHER DREAMS

The Chinese have a proverb remarking quaintly that men may sleep in the same bed and have different dreams. While Sun Yat-sen was working at his ill-fated revolutionary plot of 1895, a patriotic alarm of another kind was being sounded by a virile scholar

whose name China will never forget, Kang Yu-wei. Unlike Sun
Yat-sen, this man had gone through the treadmill of the old Confucian training. He had already made a stir in the intellectual
world by publishing in 1891 a critical work arguing for the spurious-
ness of certain texts previously accepted as the work of Confucius.
This assault by "higher criticism" was felt as a deadly blow to Confucian "fundamentalism." A man of impelling dignity combined
with a piquancy of face and a jolly kindliness of the eye, Kang Yu-
wei was not at all the ascetic and abashing type of intellectual, but
the much rarer teacher-sort that makes even scholarly contacts warm
and stimulating, and thinks of all learning in human terms. One
look at a photograph of him is to understand why a school which
he conducted at Canton attracted some remarkable students. Among
these was an extraordinarily promising young man, Liang Chi-chao,
who at the age of sixteen had competed successfully at the provincial
examination. Kang Yu-wei, finding himself with a pupil who had
taken a degree, went up and took the examination himself and became *chü jen* also. China's reverses in the war with Japan stirred
these men, just as Sun Yat-sen had been stirred. They, however,
thought not of revolution but of reform. Kang Yu-wei began in
Canton an agitation for reform, both by writing pamphlets and
by lecturing.

Characteristic of the old China that is gone was the trip made in
1895 (the year of Sun Yat-sen's first conspiracy) by master and
pupil together to Peking to compete in the highest examination
given in the Empire. Kang Yu-wei carried off the coveted honor.
In the hour of his success he did a spectacular thing: he published
a brilliantly written memorial to the Emperor, begging him to *Reform China and Save Her*. Once the distinguished lead was given,
hundreds of degree-holding *literati* united in a notable petition to
the government asking for reform. This created far more public

interest in 1895 than Sun Yat-sen's callow conspiracy. Kang Yu-wei also organized a society for the promotion of Western learning, and for a while edited a journal for it. A group of his followers, including Liang Chi-chao, began issuing at Shanghai in 1896 a newspaper on modern lines. One of its popular features was the serial publication of a Chinese translation of *Sherlock Holmes*. In the same year the educational reform gave birth to a little-noticed institution which, as the years passed, became an ally of incalculable value—the now world-famous publishing house, the Commercial Press of Shanghai. But it had yet to win its place. Its earliest publications met with scant approval—either for substance or for form—from men of Kang Yu-wei's class. Novelty learning was not for them.

In his zeal for progress Kang Yu-wei published in 1897 another extraordinary book, *Confucius as a Reformer*. In this he took the position that Confucius was first of all interested in reform, and that he was not the conserver of the antique past that he was held to be; that his interest in history was merely as a book out of which to instruct men how to live in the present; that he appealed to legends of the past, not because he believed them historical but because he thought that stories of model emperors in a golden age would make men better citizens and better rulers. This book of Kang Yu-wei's not only struck a body-blow at the orthodox interpretation of Confucius; it assaulted fundamental positions long held by the Chinese as to the value of antiquity; it took issue with ideas which kept them looking backward instead of pressing forward, and opened their minds to historical progress.

In the winter of 1897–98 Kang Yu-wei was back in Peking. Things were going from bad to worse with China. In rapid succession four Powers, each using a pretext of its own, exacted from China the lease of strategically located harbors: Germany got Tsing-tao; Russia, Port Arthur; England, Weihaiwei; and France,

Kwangchow-wan. The popular foreign talk was about spheres of influence and a possible partition of China. The Emperor at that time was a young man, who after fifteen years of subordination to regents had come to his majority and had become actually the ruler of his people. The Empress Dowager had retired to the Summer Palace, on which she had squandered a huge fund collected for the purpose of building a modern navy.

It was becoming known that the young Emperor was interested in studying foreign institutions and foreign industries, and was an eager borrower of foreign books. Kang Yu-wei sought access to him, and through the Imperial tutor an audience was arranged. The Emperor was attracted by the famous scholar who soon acquired great influence over him. A coterie of reformers gathered around the Emperor, and from June to September, 1898, edicts of radical reform were issued so fast that the nation was almost breathless.

The reform movement was given added prestige by the coöperation of an older man of very high position. Unlike the young advisers of the Emperor, Chang Chih-tung had climbed all the rungs of the official ladder and was at that time the Viceroy of Hunan and Hupeh, two great provinces converging in the upper Yangtze Valley. He had previously lent his influence on occasion to the young reformers. In 1898 he set China agog with a little book carrying in Chinese the unassuming title, *A Charge to Learn*. The young Emperor gave the book his Imperial endorsement, and its vogue became as sensational as the reforms themselves. With a secure anchorage in Confucian philosophy and Confucian ethics, Chang Chih-tung advocated vigorously the study of Western institutions and Western learning, expressing opinions such as these:

In no period in China's history has there arisen an emergency like the present. It is a time of change and His Imperial Highness, the Emperor of China, has accepted the situation by altering somewhat the system of civil and military examinations and by establishing schools.[8]

In order to render China powerful, and at the same time preserve our own institutions, it is absolutely necessary that we should utilize Western knowledge. But unless Chinese learning is made the basis of education, and a Chinese direction given to thought, the strong will become anarchists, and the weak, slaves. Thus the latter end will be worse than the former.[9]

The strength of foreign countries and the weakness of China have been clearly demonstrated to us within the past three years. The *literati* at the ports have been reading the *Wan Kwoh Kung* Pao [*The Review of the Times,* a monthly published in Shanghai] studying certain works translated by foreigners, and associating with the foreign missionaries. Gradually we have found out that the knowledge possessed by the Chinese cannot compare with that of Western people.[10]

If we do not change soon, what will become of us? European knowledge will increase more and more, and Chinese stupidity will become more dense. We shall be marked as the sure prey of the West; foreigners will still trade with us as before, but China will play a losing game and get only chaff, whilst her competitors garner the wheat, and we shall really, if not openly, become the slaves of Westerners.[11]

A clarion call, such as this, was bound to echo from one end of China to the other. The copies of the book distributed before 1900 are estimated at fully a million. This influential little volume is worth citing to show the progress made by public opinion before Sun Yat-sen had got fairly into action. Even sentiment in favor of a republic was abroad. Chang Chih-tung deals at some length with it:

There is a class of Chinese in the country just now who have become impatient and vexed with the present order of things. They chafe at the insults offered us by foreigners, the impotency of the mandarins in war, and the unwillingness of high officials to reform our mercantile and educational methods: and they would lead any movement to assemble the people together for the discussion of a republic. Alas! where did

they find this word that savors so much of rebellion? A republic, indeed!
There is not a particle of good to be derived from it. On the contrary
such a system is fraught with a hundred evils.[12]

The Viceroy takes the position that neither the officials nor the
people understand anything about the intricacies of such a form
of government, and he insists that the advantages urged for a republic can be had under the present form of government.

If this republic is inaugurated, only the ignorant and foolish will
rejoice, for rebellion and anarchy will come down upon us like night.
. . . Let us wait until our educational institutions are in full swing,
and the capabilities of our men are tested by daily experience, and then
consider the matter. The present is not the time.[13]

All the world knows that the conservative element of the Manchu
régime took alarm at the rapidly progressing reform movement.
The Empress Dowager accomplished her swift *coup d'etat* before
the end of September, 1898. The reform edicts were annulled; the
adventurous young Emperor was shorn of all power and became
a luxuriously detained political prisoner within one of the most
easily guarded palaces of the Forbidden City. Of the reformers six
were caught and executed. Kang Yu-wei is said to have escaped
aboard a British gunboat. All the reform newspapers were promptly
suppressed by the reactionary government. Liang Chi-chao saved
his head by living in Japan, where he edited other journals that
gained great influence over the rising young Chinese intellectuals.

The Empress Dowager never forgave these men. When she celebrated her seventieth birthday (in 1904) she proclaimed a general
amnesty to political offenders exempting only three, who, she said,
could never be forgiven; these were the three men—Kang Yu-wei,
Liang Chi-chao and Sun Yat-sen.

IV. THE SOBERING OF SECOND THOUGHTS

During the high tide of the reform movement Sun Yat-sen was living obscurely in Europe. After the thrilling hazard of detention in the Chinese Legation at London, life for him had flattened. Romance was, for the time being, exhausted. From 1895 to 1900, Sun Yat-sen, then in his early thirties, a political exile from his native land with no prospect of going home, lived through what he later characterized as the hardest period of his life. He spent two years in Europe, very much cut off from fellow countrymen. At that time (he says in his *Autobiography*) there were no Chinese students studying in Europe, and the number of Chinese merchants and laborers there was very small. A group of thirty government students had been sent in the '70's to England and France, but they had returned to China before this time. Under such circumstances Sun Yat-sen could scarcely have made any practical use of his medical training. Enforced frugality one reads plainly between the lines of his acknowledgment of the loyalty of friends: "They have never failed me. But then, fortunately, apart from traveling my wants are few. I have often for weeks together lived on a little rice and water, and I have journeyed many hundreds of miles on foot."

But not even a Chinese can live in England and on the Continent of Europe for two years on rice and water only. Without visible means of support, Sun Yat-sen must have had an invisible supply. It is curious that among all the wildly romantic stories told about him there is none that represents him baffled by an empty purse. Orientals, as well educated as he, have in a pinch done work that they would have felt *infra dig* at home; but there is no story of a stranded Sun Yat-sen forced to earn food and lodging by cutting grass or washing dishes or hiring out as a butler. We never hear of him turning his physical strength or mental abilities into an earning occupation. Doubtless his economic competence was very modest, but it seems to have been dependable, and for that, history must chiefly thank the loyal elder brother in Hawaii.

Sun Yat-sen seems to have made use of his leisure in industrious reading. Dr. Cantlie says:

When residing with us in London, Sun wasted no moments in gaieties; he was for ever at work, reading books on all subjects which appertained to political, diplomatic, legal, military and naval matters; mines and mining, agriculture, cattle-rearing, engineering, political economy, &c., occupied his attention and were studied closely and persistently. The range of his opportunities for acquiring knowledge has been such as few men have ever had.[14]

So it was the libraries that saw most of Sun Yat-sen in those outwardly colorless days. In one of the London libraries he made some acquaintances whom he had reason to recall in later years: he fell in with a group of Russian exiles who asked him questions and won his confidence; together they talked of their common interest, revolution, and compared their prospects of success. And in the libraries he met other revolutionaries in books, notably, Henry George and Karl Marx. *Das Kapital* had been done into English by Moore and Aveling and published in 1887. *The Students' Marx, an Introduction to the Study of Capital* by E. A. Aveling appeared in 1892. Henry George's death in 1897, in the midst of his second mayoralty campaign in New York City, called world attention afresh to his theories, which made a permanent impression on Sun Yat-sen. Contacts with the socialistic movements influenced his mind profoundly in this still-formative period. He traveled to the Continent and spent time in Paris, and later recorded his impressions of conditions in Europe in his *Autobiography:* he observed that in spite of power and wealth and democratic government, the people of Europe were not happy, and that the progressives among them wanted to establish a new social order and were in some cases thinking in terms of revolution. Thus for Sun Yat-sen's mind the idea of democratic revolution had not had time to mature before there was added to it the ferment of socialism. For Europe there had been a spread of several generations between the struggle for democracy and the emergence of socialism; but democracy and socialism came upon Sun Yat-sen together. With characteristic optimism he conceived the possibility of a social revolution and a democratic revolution going forward simultaneously in China.

Whether Sun Yat-sen returned to the Orient by traveling eastward or by turning westward is not quite clear. There is the tradition which Dr. Cantlie reports that "as a spectacled pedlar with knick-knacks in his wallet he traveled through the Malay Peninsula and the Straits Settlements, attracting not only the laboring coolies in the plantations but the masters as well." If that was ever done so picturesquely, it must have been as early in his career as this. On the other hand, to return by way of Honolulu would have given him a visit with his own family and a chance to see his growing children. His first reunion with his family after the risk and notoriety of the London detention must have been a great occasion, and it would have been natural for Ah Mi to have made something of it and to have had a photograph taken. Such a photograph exists: a very prosperous-looking family appears in it, with foreignizing influences most evident in the occidental clothing of the men and boys. It could have been taken nowhere but in Hawaii, and if we may judge by the sizes of the children, it must have come out of this period.

It was in the cloud-strewn afterglow of the reform movement of 1898 that Sun Yat-sen left Europe and went to Japan. That he was in Japan by the fall of 1899 is clear from the belated publication in Chinese of the London Legation's side of the detention story, dated the "eighth moon" of that year. This narrative states that the British Foreign Office, in response to the requests of the Chinese minister at London, had taken steps to hinder the hatching of revolutions in Hongkong, and that for this reason Sun Yat-sen was no more able to return to Hongkong than to Kwangtung, and had therefore taken refuge in Japan. That country now seemed to Sun Yat-sen a practicable base for operations against the Manchu dynasty for the reason that all foreigners residing in Japan had lost in July, 1899, the privileges of extraterritoriality which they had previously enjoyed. As a matter of fact the Chinese had lost their special status four years earlier, at the end of the Sino-Japanese War. After 1899, however, they were not different in this respect from English, French, American or other foreigners living in Japan. Consular representatives of China could not arrest or deport their nationals; Sun Yat-sen was as safe in Japan as in England. He settled in the foreign quarter of Yokohama at 121 Yamashita Cho, only a short distance from the Chinese Consulate, and there began again his plotting against the Manchus. There were at that time about twenty-five hundred of his countrymen in Yokohama, mostly Cantonese. In Nagasaki there were Chinese from Ningpo. Foochow Chinese had clustered in Osaka and Kobe. Altogether, Sun Yat-sen estimates, there were in Japan as many as ten thousand Chinese. He admits that he found them very unresponsive to his revolutionary propaganda. Among them less than one hundred were won to his cause.

This was Sun Yat-sen's first opportunity to study Japan at leisure. After the collapse of his revolutionary conspiracy he had stopped in Japan long enough to grow a mustache and acquire European clothing, but he had never lived there until 1899. Among the Japanese he found some friendliness. The Liberal Party was just at that moment becoming powerful, and it was by certain of its leaders that Sun Yat-sen was cultivated and encouraged. It was Inukai (the same who, while Premier, was assassinated in May, 1932) who took the initiative by sending two men to meet Sun Yat-sen in Yokohama and to bring him up to Tokyo, where he met the Japanese Liberal leaders—not only Inukai himself but later Okuma also. Sun Yat-sen tells of their meeting in his *Autobiography,* and says: "We talked about our affairs as if we were old and intimate friends."

V. AN OLD GRUDGE AND A NEW RESENTMENT

How far was Sun Yat-sen's genuinely patriotic movement to better his country reinforced or subconsciously motivated by an inherited grudge against the Manchu dynasty? The passage of more than two centuries had gone far toward removing Chinese racial resentment of the Manchu rulers. By no means as alien to Chinese culture as is sometimes represented, the dynasty was fortunate in producing early in its history two conspicuously able Emperors, each of whom reigned sixty years—Kang-hsi and his grandson, Chien-lung. They adopted a wise policy of identification of themselves with the Chinese, not only conforming themselves to Chinese custom, but becoming munificent promoters of all Chinese arts. So effectively did the absorption of the dynasty progress that the fourth Emperor, Chien-lung, considered himself so much a Chinese as to forbid any literary reference to a distinction of racial stock between the throne and the people. Loyalist uprisings, which had sporadically appeared in the earlier years of the dynasty, gradually ceased, and the defeated rebels retreated toward the southeast and into Kwangtung Province. Sun Yat-sen himself tells how, after having lost the spirit to rebel, loyalist societies were perpetuated secretly in order to keep Ming traditions alive and to serve as rallying points if any opportunity should come for a restoration.

Because the patronage of the Emperor meant everything to the literary and official classes, they would not ally themselves with such societies, which consequently found their members more and more in the lower levels of the people. In his *Autobiography* Sun Yat-sen describes briefly the workings of such a fraternity. It had to be secret. Officials and local gentry, who were the natural tools of the government, were excluded from membership. Because it was thus restricted to the common people, its methods became popularized. Dramatic performances were associated with initiation. The secret signals were vulgar words or even bad language, chosen with the intention of repelling the cultured and throwing them off the scent. Gradually through lapse of time the true purpose of the organization dropped out of sight. But even in periods when its anti-dynastic origin was forgotten it continued as a mutual-aid fraternity. Sun Yat-sen found it flourishing among the Chinese in America, where it had the social functions of a lodge.

The idea of utilizing such societies in a republican revolution had early been suggested to Sun Yat-sen by the popular schoolmate of his Canton year, Cheng Shih-liang. This young man had worked with Sun Yat-sen in the first conspiracy and had fled with him to Japan. He possessed intimate knowledge of the old loyalist organizations. He is said to have held a position of high rank in the Triad Society. Instead of prolonging his security in Japan, he took the risk of returning to China to promote revolutionary intrigue among the secret societies. The awakening of the old grudge against the Manchus does not seem to have been difficult in China. The Triad had not had time to forget the important rôle it had played in the Tai-ping Rebellion. It is an interesting fact that in the very year of Sun Yat-sen's first conspiracy an anti-dynastic rising, fostered by the Triad Society, appeared in the Canton region. This attracted more attention in the contemporary press than Sun Yat-sen's plot, nipped as it was in the bud. Sun Yat-sen is candid about the use made of these societies in the republican conspiracies. In a treatise entitled *China's Revolution* he says:

> When I first began to think about revolution in 1885, only a very few of my friends and relatives were interested in my ideas. The official upper classes could not be interested, but among the lower classes there was an organization called the *San Ho Hui* (The Triad Society) which originally had been a loyalist society opposed to the Manchu dynasty. From very long lapse of time the original purpose of the society had been forgotten. These people could, however, be appealed to with the idea of revolution better than the official-gentry class. To begin the revolution I worked to attach them to the cause.[15]

In this period Sun Yat-sen's movement was altogether as plebeian as the use of these societies suggests. It was quite apart from the movement among the intellectuals which made such a stir in 1895 and in the reform year. The movements were at the two poles: One was utterly plebeian, the other was extremely intellectual. True, the revolutionary movement was led by a small group of students; but chief among these were early mission-school students, peculiar in the possession of a little Western learning. Because they were among the earliest to receive Western education, they were pushed ahead of, or off-side, the stream of intellectual life in China, and thereby separated from the very intellectuals who were crying aloud for the Westernization of Chinese education.

Events were moving toward another national crisis. There was plenty of matter for criticism of the government. Foreign aggressiveness was receiving no check. Railway and mining concessions were being lavishly given away. Russia had obtained in 1896 concessions in Manchuria for the eastern division of the Trans-Siberian Railway. A French and Belgian syndicate was in 1900 constructing the trunk line from Peking to Hankow and considerable work had been done at each end. The Germans had Shantung railway projects in their hands. A line from Tientsin to Peking had been open to traffic since 1897. Other arterial lines had been projected and partly surveyed, numbering thirteen routes by 1900. With railway concessions were associated extensive mining rights. These rapid developments of foreign enterprise disturbed the intelligent conservative element in China. The ignorant masses formed an easily inflammable body. The torch was applied by the Boxers, a fanatic semi-military organization whose watchword was "Exterminate the foreigners." Encouraged by high officials and by the Empress Dowager herself, the Boxers worked havoc in North China. Within a few months in the summer of 1900 fully two hundred Americans and Europeans were massacred and many more Chinese Christians perished with them. Allied troops of eight nations marched on Peking for the relief of their besieged nationals. As the armies approached, the entire court fled across the mountains, a long journey, to the ancient western capital, Sianfu. The final stringency of the settlement which exacted an enormous indemnity ($330,000,000 gold) formed a punishment from which China has been suffering ever since. To the reformers it must have seemed that China had reached the nadir of humiliation.

Sun Yat-sen reacted to the Boxer war as he had reacted to the war with Japan: he felt that the humiliation of the court offered an opportunity for revolution. Instead of risking a direct attack on Canton, an insurrection was planned at Waichow, about a hundred miles east of Canton. All the preliminary work seems to have been done by Sun Yat-sen's fellow medical student, Cheng Shih-liang, who had been enlisting the support of the secret societies. It is claimed that he had ten thousand men in his following. When Sun Yat-sen went to Hongkong with the intention of getting to China from there, he was refused landing; in response to requests from the Chinese government Great Britain had put him on a proscribed list. Sun Yat-sen then went to Formosa, which since 1895 had been Japanese territory. The Governor, he says, welcomed him and promised help. Japanese military experts were employed; ammunition had been ordered in Japan. Thinking everything ready, Sun Yat-sen authorized his friend "to start the revolution and capture the coast cities of Kwangtung and Fukien." A notable beginning was made in the fall of 1900, only to have ammunition give out and supplies fail to arrive. How completely Sun Yat-sen was depending on Japanese help is shown by the singular fact that the rising came to grief, not as the result of overpowering by Chinese officials, but because of a change of government in Japan. Sun Yat-sen says that less than two weeks after the rising began, his friends, the Japanese Liberals, were out of power. And the new Prime Minister's policy did not include the aiding of rebellions in China. Orders were sent to the Governor of Formosa to let the revolutionists alone and not to supply them with ammunition. Even the messenger whom Sun Yat-sen despatched to report this reverse to the waiting commander was a Japanese, who spent more than thirty days in getting through with the message and was seized and executed as he attempted to return. Cheng Shih-liang immediately disbanded his forces. A coöperating attempt to bomb the Viceroy's *yamen* at Canton failed also and the leader was caught and executed. Sun Yat-sen returned soon afterward to Japan and seems to have spent most of the next three years there.

This "second revolutionary attempt," although soon snuffed out, was felt by Sun Yat-sen to have been creditable rather than otherwise. Thanks to occidental journalism, there exists a vivid record of his state of mind at the time. On March 23, 1901, George Lynch published in the *Outlook* an article on "Two Westernized Orientals"; the second half of this contribution describes the already aged Japanese Liberal leader, Count Okuma, while the first half is about the young Sun Yat-sen. Although the details of the rebellion must be supplemented by franker narratives of later years, there is much in the article that is worth quoting for its sympathetic exposition of Sun Yat-sen's aims and hopes:

When I went through southern China in October for the purpose of seeing something of the Rebellion, which was in progress near Canton, I was perpetually hearing of Sun Yat-sen. He was the organizer, the invisible leader, the strange, mysterious personality whose power was working it all. Yet no one could tell his exact whereabouts. Sometimes one heard that he was in Formosa, sometimes that he was in Hongkong in disguise, sometimes that he was in a district close to that in which the Rebellion was in progress and which would shortly also flare up in insurrection. . . . It was only after I reached Japan, after having given up all hope of meeting him, that I learned that he was then living in Yokohama, under an assumed name. In reply to a request for a personal interview, I had a courteous reply written in perfect English, making an appointment for that evening. He was living in a house in the Chinese quarter. Passing through a strange labyrinth of lanes, I stopped opposite a gloomy-looking house in a dark street. No lights were visible in front of the house, but on knocking I found Mr. "Nakayama" was expecting me. I followed a tall, well-built Chinaman down a dark passage and passed several doors which were closed behind us. I was shown into a brilliantly lighted room, and as I entered, a short young man, dressed in European clothes, stepped forward, from a table around which were seated a number of Chinamen in native costume, with outstretched hand to greet me. At first sight one would take him for a Japanese, slightly built, with pointed black mustache and bright, dark eyes. His manner was brisk, and the grasp of his lithe, shapely hand was firm, with a lingerage of Oriental caress in it. The room was plainly furnished with European chairs, tables and bookcases which were well stocked with English and French books and periodicals. They all related to warfare, munitions of war, history or political economy. He had all the latest publications on these subjects— the last edition of Block's book on "Modern Warfare and Weapons," Clery's "Minor Tactics," apparently every book that has been written on the Boer War, besides several technical works on explosives and projectiles. He had no reluctance to speak about the rebellion which he had lately organized. He brought down maps and pointed out the places where engagements were fought, and the line of march of the rebels. He explained that they had failed only for want of ammunition. . . .

"We are not in the least depressed," said Sun Yat-sen, "over the result. Quite the reverse, in fact, as it shows us how easily the Imperial troops can be defeated, as soon as our men are properly armed and prepared for a great effort." . . .

I asked him if he saw no prospect of reform in China short of a revolution. He replied that "any one who knows the Chinese Court, and knows the people by whom the Emperor is surrounded and influenced, must know that he is powerless for effectively carrying out the drastic reforms necessary." Sun Yat-sen's ambition, and that of his friends, is to carry out a revolution similar to that which took place in Japan thirty years ago. The Japanesing of China is what they want. He talked earnestly on this subject, with complete conviction. To my inquiry as to whether the people of China would be as ready to change as the Japanese, he replied that they certainly would, if they were led and directed by their natural leaders. The great mass of the people would do as they were bid; and then he waxed almost enthusiastic, despite his reserve of manner, on the superiority of his countrymen over the Japanese—their superior intelligence, their capability of copying and learning new things and picking up new ideas. "What the Japanese have taken thirty years to accomplish would not take us longer than fifteen." . . . He talked long and interestingly of his aims and projects. He has a good following of what he calls modernized young Chinamen, who have been educated in England, in Honolulu and in Japan, and among them men who are sufficiently wealthy to supply the requisite funds when the time comes for what they believe to be the only salvation of their country. . . .

"It is certainly a great ambition," I remarked.

"Yes," he said slowly, puffing out a great cloud of cigar-smoke and beginning to pace the room. "It is worth giving one life for." Then he went on to speak of China, its vastness, its immense population, its undeveloped resources, and the possibilities that the future holds for it, if there comes a great awakening like that which came to Japan. . . .

Seldom have I met a more interesting personality. There was that inexplicable something about him that stamped him as a leader of men, a personal magnetism about him that affected one strangely, a singleness of purpose to the end for which he was devoting his life that compelled admiration. . . . A federal or a republican form of government is what Sun Yat-sen wishes to substitute for the Imperial rule; and, as he said, the times are ripening for the change, when the foreigners have looted the capital, outraged the gods, and when the Imperial prestige has been shattered and the sacred precincts of the palace itself in the heart of Peking desecrated by the feet of invaders. . . .[16]

From all these varied events one cannot fail to get the impression of stirring days in China, days of insurgent intellectualism, of rabid resentment and of heroic sacrifice. Currents swirled wildly in different whirlpools. Among the adventurers there was disunity of ideal and of method. About one thing only were all agreed—that China was in imminent danger and that some change was necessary if she was to be saved. Concerning the causes of the crisis there was much disagreement. The reform party said it was because the Westerners were superior in knowledge and could therefore overpower China. Sun Yat-sen's party said it was because the Chinese rulers were corrupt and their government bad. The Boxers said it was because foreigners had increased in China and were preying upon the Chinese like wolves. Each movement had its own policy for the crisis. The reformers said: "We must change our method of education so that we shall no longer be inferior in any way to the Westerners." The revolutionists thought the first and chief remedy was to overthrow the dynasty and set up a government like foreign governments. The Boxers said: "The foreigners are at the bottom of it all; exterminate them!"

What were the results as they appeared about the end of 1900?

The reformers had been defeated; some executed, others exiled. The revolutionists had been defeated; some executed, others exiled. The Boxers had been defeated, and the courtiers who had backed them were refugees from their own capital. The Adventure for Change was at a standstill. But not one of these movements was dead.

DOCUMENTATION OF QUOTED PASSAGES

[1] Sun Yat-sen: "My Reminiscences," *The Strand Magazine* (London, March, 1912) Vol. 43, p. 303. [2] "Autobiography of Dr. Sun Yat-sen," translated by Leonard S. Hsü, *China Tomorrow* (Peking, Sept. 20, 1929) Vol. 1, p. 151. Also Hsü: *Sun Yat-sen His Political and Social Ideals,* p. 50. [3] Sun Yat-sen: *Kidnapped in London* (Bristol, 1897) p. 55. [4] Direct translation from the Chinese text found in *The Young Companion* (Shanghai, November, 1926) *Kuo Fu* Supplement, p. 7. [5] Cantlie and Jones: *Sun Yat Sen and the Awakening of China* (New York, 1912) p. 42. [6] Sun Yat-sen: *Kidnapped in London* (Bristol, 1897) p. 66. [7] Quoted among press comments at the back of *Kidnapped in London.* [8] Chang Chih-tung: *China's Only Hope,* trans. Woodbridge (New York, 1900) p. 19. [9] Ibid., p. 63. [10] Ibid., p. 87. [11] Ibid., p. 85. [12] Ibid., p. 55. [13] Ibid., p. 58 and 62. [14] Cantlie and Jones: *Sun Yat Sen and the Awakening of China* (New York, 1912) p. 202. [15] Direct translation from the Chinese text: Sun Yat-sen: *Chung Kuo chih Ke Ming* 3:1. [16] Lynch: "Two Westernized Orientals," *Outlook* (March 23, 1901) Vol. 67, No. 12, pp. 671–673.

SOURCES AND AUTHORITIES: See Appendix C, p. 397.

CHAPTER III

The Crumbling of the Old and the Vigor of the New

IN the years after 1900 the already awakened intellectual movement showed a vigor that would not be denied. Reforms that were quashed in 1898 demanded reconsideration. The court, conscious of humiliation and disgrace, took a more conciliatory attitude toward requests for the encouragement of Western learning. The Empress Dowager, whether changed at heart or not, displayed a new toleration of reform, even becoming something of a progressive. To many this has seemed a desperately shrewd attempt on her part to save the Imperial régime. Yet to have ignored the exasperated intelligentsia of China at that stage would have been stupid indeed; and, whatever we may think of the Empress Dowager, we cannot think her a fool.

The court did not venture to return to Peking before it had dealt the old educational system a smashing blow in the three edicts of August and September, 1901. The first of these struck at the educational qualifications for public office by doing away with the particular accomplishment then required by the examiners, a highly formalized composition on a theme chosen from the ancient classics. This antiquated curiosity, picturesquely dubbed an "essay with eight legs," met its demise in this edict. The other two edicts provided for schools of Western learning and for sending students abroad to study. From this time educational reforms went on logically step by step. Within five years the whole system of education was revolutionized. In 1903 a commission was sent abroad to study Western school systems; a year later a national educational system was formulated for China; another year, 1905, saw the old civil-service examinations finally abolished and a National Ministry of Education created, at the head of which was none other than the Viceroy who had written *A Charge to Learn*. One more year passed and the first Imperial examinations were held with Western learning as a subject; in this only thirty-two candidates were successful. All these were reforms that lasted.

The wave of reform had left as a deposit a few rudimentary government colleges. The first group of these higher institutions appeared at Tientsin, promoted, shortly after the war with Japan, by that early progressive, the powerful northern Viceroy, Li Hungchang. This group soon included schools for military, naval, medical and telegraphic studies, and, in addition, a college of liberal arts. Nan-yang College was established in Shanghai soon afterward, especially to provide administrators and civil engineers for railways. The reform year, 1898, brought forth the edict creating an Imperial University at Peking. It was to such institutions as these that sons of officials and youths of the gentry went in increasing numbers for the study of Western learning. Wu Chih-hui, who taught at Tientsin and later at Shanghai, tells vividly (in his outline of Sun Yat-sen's life) how intellectual discussions flourished among the professors. He says that at Tientsin a group of brilliant professors who were opium smokers used to lie comfortably on their smoking couches with opium lamps beside them, leisurely discussing—between pulls at the long pipes—the relative merits of Eastern and Western learning. One of these opium-smoking *literati* was Yen Fu, the translator of Huxley's *Evolution and Ethics,* which was published in 1898, ran through many editions and had a great influence on the minds of both young and older men.

It was impossible to create schools and colleges fast enough to take care of the numbers that were soon clamoring for Western learning. Schools founded by foreign missions, which for two or three decades had been the only institutions in China offering Western studies, found their capacity suddenly overtaxed. Old China was a country with an enormous student class flowing constantly through the old channel of education—the only opening to recognition and position. This student body was co-extensive with the country. Every province had its highly articulated portion of the system of education for civil service. When the old educational system was abolished, the great student river was cut off from its accustomed channel; it was bound to break a new channel somewhere. It found an outlet into other lands. Then began the migration of Chinese students for study abroad. The history of this migration alone is worthy of a book. It is a story of ambition and romance, of struggle and disillusionment that should be written before its thrill is forgotten. Its place is important here because of the new strength it brought to the movement for which Sun Yat-sen stood. Japan, being the most accessible country, received the first student overflow. In the year of the reforms (1898) about twenty students were sent by the government to Japan. By 1903 there were over six hundred Chinese students in Japan. Then the stream flowed faster; in 1904 students were going over at the rate of a hundred a month, and the tide was not yet at its height.

What Sun Yat-sen was doing in Japan in the years 1901 and 1902 is not reported in detail. He was living quietly in Yokohama and gaining in personal influence. After 1900 he himself noticed a new attitude in those with whom he came in contact: he was no longer treated as a traitor and an outlaw. The reaction against the Manchu rulers after the international punishment of Peking in 1900–01 was throwing the balance of feeling over on the side of Sun Yat-sen. Wu Chih-hui, writing of the cultural history in which he had an intimate share as a college professor and organizer of new institutions, tells of being in Japan early in 1901 and of how three of his Chinese friends went to Yokohama to hunt out Sun Yat-sen and call on him. Wu Chih-hui himself had not then a high enough opinion of this revolutionary to wish to go with them, and he was very much surprised at the report brought back to him that Sun Yat-sen had the appearance and the temper of a great man.

By his background and academic history Wu Chih-hui was affiliated with the most progressive men among the intellectuals. He was keenly alive to the brilliant writing which Liang Chi-chao was putting out from Japan. Although an intellectual from the dome of his long head to the tips of his sensitive fingers, Liang Chi-chao was no recluse of a bamboo grove. Usually to be found in the mid-current of affairs and of movements, he managed— even when caught in a backwater—to make lively currents of his own. Commanding a distinguished literary style which has given him a secure place in Chinese letters, he was yet one of the most eagerly read journalists of his period. With artistic sense of expression he combined the discriminations of a critic; and he applied his critical acumen and his powers of expression to the championship of the reforms. He and Sun Yat-sen were contemporary exiles in Japan. They are said to have had many talks together about China's problems, but always with disagreement. The issues between the two were doubtless complicated by differences of temperament. Sun Yat-sen's less subtle and more categorical mind could have found little real delight in Liang Chi-chao's incisive brilliancy. Moreover, such perfected Chinese culture could scarcely have escaped the subconscious envy of Sun Yat-sen, who both by breeding and schooling had missed it and had taken something foreign in its place. Liang Chi-chao, on the other hand, was a reformer who believed in continuities of development rather than in harsh breaks; he could have had no admiration for Sun Yat-sen's policy of breaking down the old before beginning on the new. He was working as hard as Sun Yat-sen to free the people for new developments, but he was attempting it by illuminating their minds rather than by smashing their institutions. That his work was effective is the testimony of many men who were young at the time. Hu Shih, for instance, was profoundly affected by Liang Chi-chao's writings and does not hesitate to pronounce him "the most powerful writer of the age," testifying that he took away from the rising generation in China the complacency that had characterized the older generation. He introduced his readers to great Western thinkers, pointedly comparing Chinese and European culture, and insisting upon the superiority of Occidentals in many traits of character. In political policies Liang Chi-chao was an advocate of developments well rooted in Chinese habits of thought and action rather than drastically plucked away from them. Although he had no more reason than Sun Yat-sen to love the rulers then in power, he did not relinquish hope of a reformed and constitutional monarchy as the stabilizer of a new age. But a constitutional monarchy had no place in Sun Yat-sen's plans, and the advocates of a constitutional monarchy seemed to him enemies of his cause. So, to Liang Chi-chao's influence Sun Yat-sen remained impervious. Only in one respect did he possibly learn a lesson from Liang Chi-chao: the vogue of his writing may have been influential in bringing Sun Yat-sen to a realization of the potentialities of the new journalism. Before 1900 the revolutionists took to publishing their own daily paper, *Chung Kuo Pao,* at Hongkong for the diffusion of their revolutionary ideas.

The temper of the new students was soon felt in Japan, and became the subject of many protests from Peking. Wu Chih-hui and a friend of his were banished from the country for picking a quarrel with the Chinese minister. This pushed Wu Chih-hui into the company of disturbers of the status quo, and doubtless prepared his mind for more radical actions. There is record of another typical case—a youth who was expelled from his school because Peking objected to a fiery speech he had made against the Manchus.

At Shanghai, also, the students were becoming revolutionary, not through Sun Yat-sen's influence but by a kind of spontaneous combustion. Very early in its history Nan-yang College became a center of patriotic insurgency; it staged the first of all the modern student strikes as far back as 1902. The protesting students were supported by certain sympathetic professors; among them were Wu Chih-hui and a man who became famous later as the Chancellor of the National University at Peking. Seceding students and teachers hived off and began a new college which they called "Love-your-country College." Taking advantage of the International Settlement, in which it had located itself, this college went so far as to have public lectures on revolution, and the Settlement authorities were finally forced to take cognizance of the plotting of rebellion on Chinese soil. The group edited also a revolutionary journal, which the government finally brought to book by suing the editors in the Shanghai court. As a result two brilliant men were put in prison and remained there for two or three years. Wu Chih-hui saved himself by flight to England.

II. OVERSEAS FOR THE REVOLUTION

While the students were developing their own revolutionary ideas, Sun Yat-sen took his ideas with him and set out wandering the world again. In 1903 he made a trip to Annam, ostensibly to attend an exposition at Hanoi. Invitations had been pressed upon him by the French Legation at Tokyo, which was beginning to take a political interest in him. At Hanoi he not only met French officials, but came to know wealthy Chinese merchants who joined his *Hsing Chung Hui* and helped him financially. On returning to Japan Sun Yat-sen felt encouraged by the indications that the number of revolutionary-minded Chinese was growing. After an interval in Yokohama he set out on a much longer tour. On Oct. 5, 1903, he arrived at Honolulu on the *S.S. Siberia*. In Hawaii he spent almost six months, much of the time visiting with his family on the Island of Maui, where Ah Mi was then a well-to-do cattle rancher. Sun Fo was more than twelve years old and the little daughters were of an appealing age. Among the Hawaiian Chinese Sun Yat-sen continued his propaganda for revolution and solicited funds. When the *Hsing Chung Hui* was called together in Honolulu, a new enthusiasm was felt. "At that time," Sun Yat-sen reports, "wherever I went, the overseas Chinese gave me a hearty reception, and their attitude toward me was totally changed." But the overseas Chinese were not all of one mind. An outstanding experience of this second long tour of Sun Yat-sen's was the opposition he constantly met from those who favored reform rather than revolution. Of this recurring clash Sun Yat-sen reports no details in his little revolutionary *Autobiography*. As a matter of fact, the issues that had sharpened between himself and Liang Chi-chao in Japan cleft all the Chinese communities wherever Sun Yat-sen might visit them throughout the world. At this time the monarchist reformers were much ahead of Sun Yat-sen in propaganda and influence among the overseas Chinese. This was due not only to Liang Chi-chao's pen, which could reach Honolulu and America as well as Peking and Shanghai, but also to the personal influence of Kang Yu-wei in the extensive travels of his exile.

Much too distinguished a figure to remain long concealed anywhere, Kang Yu-wei had been tossed about the fringes of China for a few months after the collapse of the reforms of 1898, evading the Manchu secret service and keeping out of the way of would-be assassins. Pushed out of Japan by an uneasy government, he came to America and found asylum on the Canadian Pacific coast. Accompanied by a servant and by a Japanese who professed to be an interpreter, he was interviewed as the boat called at Seattle on April 8, 1899. But the correspondent could get little by route of the interpreter except that the famous scholar was in a pessimistic mood about what had happened in China and had come to America to learn. Considering that Kang Yu-wei had no Western language then at his command, it is a marvel that he came to be the world-traveler that he did. He lived only two years longer than Sun Yat-sen, and he visited thirty-one countries and circumnavigated the globe four times, whereas Sun Yat-sen had three world-girdlings on his books.

For work among his fellow-nationals Kang Yu-wei needed no new language and no introduction. Reform influences radiated from him, and reform societies sprang up not only in his footprints but in the path ahead of his honorable feet. He was the head of the society that went by a dignified Chinese name meaning literally "Protect the Emperor Association" (*Pao Huang Hui*). Back of it was the hope that the progressive young Emperor Kuang-hsu, who had yielded so readily to the influence of Kang Yu-wei in 1898, would be somehow at some time rescued from the degradation put upon him by the aging Empress Dowager and be made again the center of a progressive movement for China. The objects of the society appealed strongly not only to the intelligentsia among the overseas Chinese but to the substantial and stable merchant class in the Chinese communities.

It was not until December 13th that Sun Yat-sen addressed a public meeting in Honolulu. The Hotel Street Theater was filled with Chinese. The reporter for the English-language press was caught by the foreignized appearance of the speaker with his suit of linen and his short-cut hair; his listeners wore Chinese clothes and the long queues. To this newspaperman Sun Yat-sen did not seem a fanatic, but an impressive speaker, punctuating his words with forcible gestures. His main contention was that nothing short of a revolution would save China. About a week later the *Pacific Commercial Advertiser* made a concise statement of his position:

Arousing a spirit of nationalism in the empire of China among the Chinese people who are not Manchus, will be the life work of Dr. Sun Yat Sen, the Chinese revolutionist, now in Honolulu. Once this spirit can be awakened in the dormant minds of the conquered Chinese race which has submitted to the Manchu yoke for centuries, Dr. Sun believes that the Chinese nation will rise in the might of four hundred millions of people and overturn the Manchu dynasty forever. It is his hope also that upon this Far East revolution a republic will be erected, for Dr. Sun likens the vast provinces of the Chinese Empire to the States of the American Union, needing only a president to govern all alike.[1]

With Sun Yat-sen's unqualified radicalism contrast the concerned liberalism of Kang Yu-wei:

A republican form of government is too advanced for China . . . her whole social system is built upon the knowledge of a monarch living in Peking. . . . It is quite true that . . . there was much democracy among the people, that the power of the Emperor was not felt acutely in inland towns and cities, and that life was ordered on a very free and democratic basis. But isn't that true in other countries which are constitutional monarchies? Is it necessary for a ruler to oppress his people in order to demonstrate that his country is a monarchy? . . .

There will come a day when every country will be a republic. But that is far ahead for China. The majority of the Chinese people are illiterate, uneducated, with no knowledge of national affairs. Democracy is a system of government for the educated. . . .[2]

Before Sun Yat-sen got away from Hawaii, Japan declared war on Russia Feb. 10, 1904. It is noteworthy that during the whole of this war Sun Yat-sen was absent from Japan. When he began to plan his trip to the United States, he realized that he would have to face a very strict application of the Exclusion Law against the Chinese. A way of making an entry possible occurred to him, or was suggested by his Hawaiian friends. Hawaii had been annexed to the United States in 1898. By virtue of that fact Chinese born in Hawaii, even before 1898, might have the privileges of American citizenship. If provided with a proper certificate of Hawaiian birth, a Chinese could not be excluded from the United States. To facilitate his revolutionary travels Sun Yat-sen made, March 9, 1904, a deposition of Hawaiian birth, and somehow hoodwinked the United States officials into certifying it. It reads as follows:

I, Sun Yat Sen, being first duly sworn, depose and say that to the best of my knowledge and belief I was born at Waimanu, Ewa, Oahu, on the 24th day of November, A.D. 1870; that I am a physician, practicing at present at Kula, Island of Maui; that I make my home at said Kula; that my father, Sun Tet Sung, went to China about 1874 and died there about eight years later; that this affidavit is made for the purpose of identifying myself and as a further proof of Hawaiian birth; that the photograph attached is a good likeness of me at this time.

(Signed) Sun Yat Sen

This act of Sun Yat-sen's has been a stumbling-block both to moralists and to biographers. Curiously enough there was documentation available for his claim, which, if it was cited, would have seemed plausible to a busy immigration officer. (Errors of fact as to Sun Yat-sen's life got into print early and lasted late.) A statement to the effect that Sun Yat-sen was born in Hawaii had been made in a Hongkong newspaper, *The China Mail*, as early as 1896; and the communication in which it occurred had been reprinted in the little book, *Kidnapped in London*, published in 1897 in England. For a short time about 1912 it was believed in the United States that Sun Yat-sen was legally an American citizen. But the position was not very long tenable. That he deliberately misrepresented facts to serve his ends gives the biographer a lessened sense of security in using Sun Yat-sen's statements about himself and makes it obligatory to check them with more than ordinary care. The incident makes other misrepresentations, when discovered, seem not altogether out of character.

It was on March 31, 1904, that Sun Yat-sen sailed on the *S.S. Korea* for San Francisco with his certificate of Hawaiian birth in his pocket. But Fate had a humorous punishment waiting for his perjury. "Are you a Chinese or a Japanese?" used to be the first question asked of Orientals by immigration officials at an American port. Reporting this on one occasion in an address, Sun Yat-sen went on to say that if the answer was "Japanese," entry was easy, but if the answer was "Chinese," the examination proceeded very strictly. Once, he said, he was detained by the immigration authorities for three weeks; but he felt himself fortunate that he had not been deported. In 1904 Sun Yat-sen was entering neither as a Chinese nor as a Japanese, but as an American citizen. *The San Francisco Examiner* reported colorfully and sensationally his arrival April 6th aboard the *Korea,* featuring a small picture of him in a fedora hat, and describing him in the headlines as "Manchus Foe":

His arrival in the city yesterday caused a flurry of excitement in the local Chinese quarter and many were the harsh denunciations uttered by the members of the merchant class. . . . When he leaves the Pacific Mail steamer *Korea* today, Sun Yat Seen will go into hiding for a time. . . .

He travels extensively in first-class style and assumes a number of aliases. On the *Korea* yesterday he first stated that he was a Japanese, but later he admitted his identity.[4]

Immediately, Sun Yat-sen dropped out of public notice. Eleven days after his steamer came to port, the prominent picture on the front page of the *Examiner* was of a Manchu Prince-of-the-blood, who—with his suite—was arriving on the *Gaelic* to represent China at the St. Louis Exposition. Prince Pu Lun did not drop out of sight. The Secretary of State had arranged to have him met and furnished with an escort during his stay. A millionaire merchant of Chinatown, himself the head of the local branch of the Constitutional Reform Society, met the Prince in person, supported by a troop of Chinese cadets. Only after Prince Pu Lun had got far away to the east to be received by the President did Sun Yat-sen emerge from his hiding. The "hiding," as it turned out, was an enforced stay of three weeks in the detention shed of the Immigration Department. Not until April 28th was he released. The report in the *Examiner* of April 29th is explicit:

He came on the steamer *Korea* and was denied a landing by the Chinese bureau, notwithstanding the fact that he had papers showing that he was a native born of Honolulu and had taken an oath of allegiance at the time of annexation. The refusal was made on the ground that when he went to China he took out a Number 6 certificate, which is issued only to foreign born Chinese.[5]

The details of this story have special interest because of the paucity of other information as to the devices and subterfuges used by Sun Yat-sen in crossing inspected boundaries and passing ports of entrance. One report—not to be too lightly dismissed—is that the *Pao Huang* party instigated this particular trouble. Not wanting Sun Yat-sen's rival propaganda in America, these monarchist reformers would have been glad to see him deported. Another explanation—possibly only another facet of the same story—was suggested at the time in the *San Francisco Examiner:* The real trouble was not with his papers but with his reputation. The American government did not wish any untoward incidents during the visit of the Manchu Prince; assassination was a possibility to be avoided by whatever precaution might suggest itself. It was felt that a Manchu Prince and a notorious revolutionist were better kept apart. The Immigration officers received their orders:

When Sen Yat-sen was about to leave his ship something wrong was found in his papers. He was placed in the detention shed and kept there for three weeks, being given his liberty only after Prince Pu Lun had been gone from the city fully a week. He went to Chinatown and took up his headquarters in the Chinese Society of English Education.[6]

III. PROTAGONIST OF THE PEOPLE

Such overseas Chinese as were inclined to adventure for change at all were presently divided into revolutionists seeking a republic, and liberals seeking a reformed monarchy. To many it seemed safer as well as saner to follow Kang Yu-wei than to follow Sun Yat-sen, although both men were in exile with prices on their heads. The reforms which Kang Yu-wei had championed were showing surprising alacrity in coming to life after having been left for dead. And the Empress Dowager herself had sponsored many changes after the humiliation of Peking by the Powers in 1900. So why should one not be of the reform party? And why resort to revolution if reform would accomplish the desired end? A revolution might become another Tai-ping Rebellion, drawn out for many years only to be quelled in the end. There were many who reasoned this way. In San Francisco the merchants, by and large, were opposed to Sun Yat-sen. Their opposition sharpened when, about a week after he completed his entry, he addressed a public meeting in the Washington Street Theater. He spoke with such effect that the Chinese consul-general immediately posted Chinatown with a warning:

There is a revolutionary leader in our midst, who is arousing people by his false statements. The educated element can easily understand that his aim is to collect money, which he will afterwards squander, and I fear the ignorant people will become his victims. As the chief—the general Consul here—it is my duty to protect them. I advise the elder people, who will not be turned by his false utterances, to caution their younger brothers and sons to beware of this man. He will squander your money and get you in trouble.

May 6, 1904   (Signed) Consul-General Chung [7]

Speculating about the reason for such alarm, the *Examiner's* reporter said:

Many of the Chinese have been calling to mind his visit here about eight years ago, when he collected a fund ostensibly for revolutionary purposes. Since then he has been living with his wife and brother in Honolulu, making frequent trips to Japan and even once venturing into Hongkong. It is evidently the intention of Consul-General Chung to prevent him from collecting another fund.[8]

Whereas Kang Yu-wei was an intellectual of the intellectuals—the learned man is the aristocrat of Chinese society—directing his efforts toward influencing foreign opinion and reaching the better informed and weightier members of the Chinese settlements, Sun Yat-sen was always ready to look for a following in the lower levels of the people. He set out to get the help of petty shopkeepers, laundrymen, gardeners, and other laborers. Wherever there was a city or town with a colony of Chinese, thither he made his way, stopping in cheap hotels or lodging with Chinese friends. Wherever he went there was propaganda for revolution and solicitation of money. Where he could he addressed audiences of his fellow-countrymen, as he had done in Honolulu and San Francisco. But any group, however small and humble, was large enough to talk to. He added members to his Prosper China Society.

In one respect Sun Yat-sen had an advantage which the ardent Confucian, Kang Yu-wei, did not have; he was a Christian, and that well-understood fact gave him a strong hold on an element among his fellow-countrymen that was more than ordinarily progressive. Chinese pastors were hospitable to him, and Chinese mission services were his sure resort. But his Christianity was not his only resource; again he used the secret societies to open the door; he had used them in China in connection with his "second attempt"—the insurrection of 1900. Chinese secret organizations have long been intriguing to our Western imagination, not only because they flourish perennially among the Chinese, but because they are often influential with the mysterious sort of effectiveness that Occidentals associate with the traditionally romantic Orient. Occasionally, however, some Occidental forgoes colorful fiction-building about "tongs" and "tong-wars," and collects some information about these societies. Mr. Stewart Culin read an informing paper about them in Philadelphia before the Antiquarian Society as early as 1887—when Sun Yat-sen was a first-year medical student in Hongkong. Later published by the society, this paper is entitled *The I Hing or "Patriotic Rising"*; it describes clearly the antidynastic character of certain of these societies in China, their power in the Straits Settlements, and, in greater detail, deals with their functioning in America, where they were sometimes known as the Patriotic Rising, a league which included nearly two-thirds of all the Chinese in the country. He says:

It was instituted in San Francisco between 1850 and 1860, during the time of the Tai-ping rebellion, when many of the emigrants were refugees from the outbreak which then occurred in the southern provinces. At present there are branches of the original society in most of the American cities in which there are Chinese colonies. They are known by different names, but are united in policy and object, and are in constant communication with each other.[9]

As far back as 1887 this society had flourishing lodges in San Francisco, St. Louis, Chicago, New York and Philadelphia.

All members are brothers, relieving each other in distress, and aiding each other in business and in every laudable enterprise. . . .

Sunday, a holiday with the Chinese in America, is selected as the day for assemblies of the brotherhood. None but members and candidates for admission are permitted to enter the meeting room, where much ceremony is observed. . . .

Every social relation must be forsworn and eternal fealty pledged to the brotherhood before an altar on which is some burning incense and a drawn sword. . . . The new member now receives a book, a bulky Chinese volume in which are contained instructions for secretly making himself known to fellow-members and a vocabulary of the secret language. . . . Lifting the cup with the thumb and two fingers, or shaking it thrice over the bowl when drinking are among the many methods employed. To advance one foot within the doorway of a house, leaving the other without and place an umbrella on the sill is a signal for assistance given by a fugitive from the officers of the law. The secret language or slang is formed by substitution of one Chinese word or phrase for another. . . . It is from one of . . . the romances . . . the Shwui hu chuan ("The Story of the Banks of the River" . . .) that some of the Chinese here say that the plan of the present society is derived—an account of the lives and adventures of a band of one hundred and eight chivalrous robbers. . . .

Of the political significance of the *I hing* it is difficult to speak with certainty. Opposition to the Manchus and the re-establishment of the Chinese dynasty of the Mings form part of its propaganda. . . . There is little discussion of Chinese politics among the people here, and few know or care about anything that concerns their country beyond the village in which they were born. Occasionally one hears revolutionary talk, but the better class of immigrants, who regard the secret order with hatred and contempt, express themselves well satisfied with the present government, and deplore all attempts to revive here an agitation from which many of them have suffered so bitterly in the past. . . . The

I hing, nursing the spirit of discontent, may some day play no unimportant part in the revolution, political and social, which contact with foreign civilization must inevitably bring about in China.[10]

Respect for Western observation of Chinese manners mounts as one realizes that this was written just about the time that Sun Yat-sen's popular medical chum was first opening his eyes to the revolutionary possibilities of the secret societies. When Sun Yat-sen began serious work in the United States, he found the Patriotic Rising awaiting his use. That he created a ferment in the lodges is certain—enough to attract the attention of the diplomatic representatives of the Manchu régime. Before long Sun Yat-sen was protesting—in a pamphlet printed in America—

. . . the proclamation issued recently by the Chinese Minister at Washington prohibiting the Chinese in this country from having anything to do with the Patriotic Society under the severe penalty that their families and distant relatives will be arrested and beheaded in China.[11]

In this connection Sun Yat-sen describes the Chinese Patriotic Society as commonly known in the United States as "the Chinese Freemasons," and says, "About eighty per cent of the Chinese in this country belong to this league."

A little knowledge—and a little more ignorance—concerning Sun Yat-sen's relations with the secret societies is probably accountable for the popular picture of him as a kind of supersleuth. "Sun Yat-sen has allied himself with one of the most powerful tongs" was the report that got around among press correspondents; and "tong" suggests to a Western mind mysterious intrigues and ruthless enmities. Even as late as the Revolution Sun Yat-sen was characterized (in the New York *Sun,* Dec. 31, 1911) as the "hidden spirit of strange secret societies, whose ramifications have made moletracks through every land where Chinese men are." He is reported as emerging from "underground passages of plot and intrigue the nature of which no Occidental could hope to understand."

Sun Yat-sen was too much of a propagandist to be a first-rate sleuth. He found the tong useful; it would get him an audience, either in the lodge hall, or better still, in a public theater. A hearing was what Sun Yat-sen wanted, and money contributions afterward. He seems to have had some degree of success in raising money in the United States. In *My Reminiscences* he says:

All over the world, and particularly in America the legend has grown up that the Chinese are selfish and mercenary. There never was a greater libel on a people. Many have given me their whole fortune. One Philadelphia laundryman called at my hotel after a meeting, and, thrusting a linen bag upon me, went away without a word. It contained his entire savings for twenty years.[12]

Sun Yat-sen was not as secretive as revolutionists are supposed to be. Witness what he would put into print over his own name! Evidently with the hope of reaching the American public—led astray, as he felt, by Kang Yu-wei's ideas—he put out a pamphlet in English in 1904 bearing the title, *The True Solution of the Chinese Question*. This small, red-covered treatise of eleven printed pages affirms at the outset that those who are thinking of the war between Japan and Russia as likely to clear the Far Eastern Question are mistaken. "The war raises more difficulties than it solves," is Sun Yat-sen's opinion; the only solution of the Chinese question is the overthrow of the Manchu government, whose weakness and corruption threaten to disturb the political equilibrium of the world. The ruling dynasty is arraigned in convincingly Chinese English:

Since the Boxer war many have been led to believe that the Tartar government is beginning to see the sign of time and to reform itself for the betterment of the country, just from the occasional imperial edicts for reform, not knowing that they are mere dead letters made for the express purpose of pacifying popular agitations. It is absolutely impossible for the Manchus to reform the country, because reformation means detriment to them. By reformation they would be absorbed by the Chinese people and would lose the special rights and privileges which they are enjoying. The still darker side of the government can be seen when the ignorance and corruption of the official class is brought to light. These fossilized, rotten, good-for-nothing officials know only how to flatter and bribe the Manchus, whereby their position may be strengthened to carry on the trade of squeezing.[18]

The listing in this pamphlet of Ten Wrongs suffered under the Manchus is neatly contrived to impress the Occidental; most of the evils existed before the Manchu dynasty began, and not a few of them still blacken the history of the republic. The most interesting feature of the treatise is Sun Yat-sen's report of the widespread reaction against the dynasty and the crumbling state of the old régime:

Those Chinese who favor revolutionary ideas may be roughly divided into three classes. The first class, the most numerous of the three, comprises those persons who cannot even obtain a bare livelihood because of the extortions and exactions of the officials. To the second belong all those who are provoked by racial prejudice against the Manchus, while to the third class belong those who are inspired by noble thoughts and high ideas. These three factors, co-operating together in different directions, with increasing force and velocity, will ultimately produce the desired result. It is evident therefore that the downfall of the Manchu government is but a question of time. . . .

The Manchu Dynasty may be likened to a collapsing house; the whole structure is thoroughly rotten to its very foundation. Is it possible for any one to prevent the house from falling just by supporting the walls collaterally outside with a few beams? We fear this very act of supporting it might hasten its tumbling. The dynastic life in China, as shown from history, is much the same as an individual; it has its birth, growth, maturity, declining and dying. The present Tartar rule has begun to decline since the beginning of the last century and is dying fast now. . . .[14]

That must have seemed over-optimistic to many readers in 1904. Every one would now admit that it showed acute prevision. Would that as much could today be said of Sun Yat-sen's equally vivid optimism as to the possibility of a republic:

Now it is evident . . . that a new, enlightened and progressive government must be substituted in place of the old one. . . . There are many highly educated and able men among the people who would be competent to take up the task of forming a new government, and carefully thought-out plans have long been drawn up for the transformation of the out-of-date Tartar Monarchy into a "Republic of China." The general masses of the people are also ready to accept the new order of things and are longing for a change for better, to uplift them from their present deplorable condition of life. China is now on the eve of a great national movement, for just a spark of light would set the whole political forest on fire to drive out the Tartar from our land. Our task is great but it will not be an impossible one. . . .[15]

The publication ends with a direct appeal to the people of the United States for "sympathy and support, either moral or material," and the final sentence is: "We hope we may find many Lafayettes among you."

By the irony of events Sun Yat-sen's Lafayette-to-be was at the moment Lafayetting for his rivals, the constitutional monarchists. Undersized and a hunchback, an eccentric American youth, named Homer Lea, early developed a marked interest in military theory. By physique disqualified for any military school, he attended Stanford University, where he made a hobby of collecting military maps and studying military strategy. There he also showed another eccentric enthusiasm—an interest in Chinese wherever he might find them, whether as fellow-students, or as house-boys and cooks employed in dormitories. After completing the Sophomore year Homer Lea had a trip to China at the expense of the China Reform Association of San Francisco, which, at his suggestion, sent him out as a foreign agent. But his itch for publicity, and a consequent article about him in the San Francisco *Call,* published just on the eve of his sailing, frustrated his secret service completely. He went nevertheless. But after exhausting his funds and getting nowhere in his errand either at Hongkong or at Macao, he was furnished with money to return to California. He retired to Los Angeles to write a novel called *The Vermilion Pencil.* But he kept in touch sufficiently with Chinese Reform Societies to drill cadets for them. It was at this period that a fervor for military training spread among overseas Chinese. The following seems an informed account of the development:

Lea was made General of the Reform Cadets, who were Chinese youths of San Francisco fitted out with uniforms and guns and taught to do the hay foot straw foot in hired halls night after night.

The idea spread to other cities in the United States and to Manila. The Reform Cadets became a widespread organization. American drill masters were hired to coach them; they had target practice and they gave exhibition drills.

Out in San Francisco the agents of the Chinese Government once tried to prevail upon the city and state authorities to break up the organization because it was technically an armed band of aliens on American soil. The effort failed.[16]

Sun Yat-sen's visit to America lengthened to about a year. His missionary friend, Dr. Hager, who had seen him on the Pacific

Coast, saw him again on the Atlantic Coast, and gives a convincing and graphic touch to the picture:

I conversed with him for a little time at San Francisco. He told me that nothing less than a change of dynasty was needed in China. I tried to show him that the reforms which he formerly advocated were being adopted, to which he replied merely by saying that the Manchus must be ousted. During the same year (1904) I met him once more in a Chinese mission service in New York. He had lost much of the vivacity of his youth, and seemed careworn and oppressed with anxiety, but he was still loyal to the Christian faith.[17]

In that Chinese mission in New York City Sun Yat-sen had tried friends and true, particularly in the Chinese pastor and his intelligent occidental wife. The Huies had seen Sun Yat-sen on a trip west, and had given him a cordial invitation to make the Chinese mission his stopping-place when he came to New York. This he gladly did, spending some weeks there in 1904. In this bi-racial home, with children playing about him, Sun Yat-sen seemed to be more than ordinarily at ease. He let himself go in talk with the sympathetic pastor about his plans for China, and cultivated the friendship of two Christian students holidaying from their studies at Yale and Columbia. The mission became a germinating place for ideas. The brothers Wang, one of whom has since become a distinguished jurist, talked with Sun Yat-sen for many days about the ideal constitution for the republic of China, then only a revolu-tionist's wild dream. In many ways the republican ideas were benefited by the stimulus of the sharply antagonistic propaganda of the monarchist party. So strongly were the monarchist currents moving in New York's Chinatown that the mission was threatened with a Chinese boycott for harboring Sun Yat-sen. But the pastor stood his ground and refused to oust Sun Yat-sen or any other man

for his political coloring. Yet no one knew better than good Pastor
Huie what his rebel guest was up to. In his *Reminiscences* there is
this little telling sketch of the way Sun Yat-sen was working:

A fascinating and fluent speaker . . . Dr. Sun could hold his audiences spellbound for hours at a time, whether they numbered by the
hundreds and thousands or only a handful. He was at his best when
in the quiet of the night, with a small group of followers gathered about
the lamplight, as often happened in the back-rooms of the little laundries
in New York City, he spoke to them about the military reverses and
diplomatic failures of China and expounded his programme for the
liberation and self-rule of the Chinese people. He often appeared weary
and worn in body, but always enthusiastic for his cause and never down-
hearted.[18]

It was not about the Emperor that Sun Yat-sen was thinking as
he moved from city to city, seeking out his humble nationals in little
rooms back of laundries and missions; his concern was for the people. Government by a monarch? No, "government of the people, by
the people, for the people." Possessed by the spirit of Lincoln's
great phrase, he tried to put it into words so simple that no scholar
would be needed to explain their meaning. His first rendering—
turned back into our language—was: "The people are to have, the
people are to control, the people are to enjoy." On bits of memo-
randum-paper he set down the Chinese characters, and then tried
to turn the three desiderata of the people—which, abstractly expressed, are their national solidarity, their political control and
their economic welfare—into catchy Chinese phrases, balanced, easily remembered and meaningful for China. When he had completed
them to his satisfaction, no one with whom he talked them over—
laundryman, pastor or any other friend—knew that Sun Yat-sen
had brought forth what was to become the most famous formula
in modern China—the Three Principles of the People.

Sun Yat-sen had his thoughts in order and his democratic slogan in his pocket when he left New York for Europe in the spring of 1905. He had not been many weeks gone, when Kang Yu-wei swept eastward on an almost triumphal tour. He, too, was bound for Europe to cultivate public opinion. At Washington he was received by President Roosevelt. At Philadelphia he had a splendid reception, reported in detail in the next day's *Public Ledger*. Descending from the train in a maroon-colored robe, he was met by a welcoming committee of Chinese merchants. He was escorted by two companies of Reform Cadets smartly uniformed in blue, carrying the dragon flag as well as the Stars and Stripes. To the music of a hired military band Kang Yu-wei and his suite were paraded past Independence Hall, then to a reception in Race Street, and then to the Hotel Walton, where he and his suite were to put up during their stay. He was accompanied, so the report states, by "Lieutenant General Homer Lea, his military adviser." That night Philadelphia's Chinatown celebrated in his honor with fireworks. The next day he addressed a mass-meeting in Odd Fellows Temple, and in the evening the whole Chinese colony feasted with him.

At New York he had a similarly enthusiastic reception. And all this was the finish of about a year that he had spent visiting Chinese colonies in the United States. Who would have ventured to say that Fate and the Future were not with the honored silken-robed scholar but with the easily overlooked, foreign-dressed Chinese, who had slipped away to Europe with the Three Principles in his pocket?

IV. THE STUDENT STREAM FLOWS INTO THE REVOLUTION

It was in Europe in 1905 that Sun Yat-sen got his first thrilling response from the modern Chinese student. He had not been working much with students in the United States. In the earliest years of the century Chinese students were few and far between in America. Dr. Alfred Sze has said that in 1901 he was one of five Chinese students in all the United States. The remission of the Boxer Indemnity by the Roosevelt Administration was what incited the big migration of students to America. In Europe Sun Yat-sen had found no Chinese students on his former visit. In the spring of 1905 he found them not only in England but also in Brussels, Paris and Berlin. To the students at Brussels he made the first speech of his life on the "Three Principles of the People," and it was to students he first expounded his conception of a government with five component powers instead of the usual triple formation of legislature, executive and judiciary. The students were so interested that in each of the continental cities mentioned he was able to organize branches of the *Hsing Chung Hui* (Prosper China Society) which up to that time had drawn its membership from people lower down. In Brussels the branch had about thirty members, in Berlin about twenty, and in Paris more than ten. Some of these students were receiving stipends from the Imperial Treasury in Peking, yet saw no inconsistency in registering in Sun Yat-sen's membership book.

In one of the Chinese sources a diverting incident is told of two government students who became thoroughly frightened when a Manchu fellow-student pointed out to them that they would surely lose their income from the government, and perhaps also their heads, if it were reported to Peking that they had joined Sun Yat-sen's revolutionary society. To save themselves they made their way into Sun Yat-sen's lodgings when he was out, and searched until they found the register of the society on which they had enrolled their names. With this book in their possession they made off to the Chinese minister at Paris, and on their knees begged him to help them out of their predicament. This diplomatic servant of the Empress Dowager had no desire to become involved in any such publicity as had befallen the Legation at London in 1896, and he was rather liberal himself. So he gave the two students a sound rating, not for joining the society, but for committing the indiscretion of stealing the membership book; he told them Sun Yat-sen might be sending the French police after them. In no uncertain tones he commanded them to take the book back to Sun Yat-sen, warning them that if there was any delay about it he would have their stipends cut off. Worse frightened than ever, the two culprits went to Sun Yat-sen, fell on their knees before him, confessed everything, and begged his forgiveness. Fortunately for them, Sun Yat-sen was of a forgiving temperament.

Amusing as this episode is, it is indicative of the temper of the students of the period and of their undeliberative readiness to espouse the cause for which Sun Yat-sen stood. As he traveled on eastward, he had a sense of the potentialities of a student following, if it could be won for the revolution.

The return journey to the Orient was by way of Singapore. This gave Sun Yat-sen the opportunity to establish branches of the *Hsing Chung Hui* among the prosperous Chinese colonies of the Straits. Whatever may have been the adventures of his youth, he was not traveling this time "as a spectacled pedlar with knick-knacks in his wallet." A Singapore photograph taken in 1905 shows him jauntily dressed in a foreign tropical suit set off with white shoes. He seems the personification of the modernism he was trying to promote, as he sits at his ease among his supporters in the garden of a wealthy Singapore merchant.

By the summer of 1905 Sun Yat-sen was back in Japan. It was a victory-stirred Japan, whose schools and colleges were congested with Chinese students; during that year, they were crowding to Japan at the rate of five hundred a month. At the climax of the migration, which came a little later, the number rose to a thousand a month. Impetus had been given to the migration by the triumph of Japan over Russia. That war had an effect upon China greater than any of her own recent wars, and it was of an opposite kind. After a period of depression China was able again to find hope. That Japan, which China thought of as a small, young nation, should be able to defeat a giant nation of the West took away in some degree the sting of China's own defeat by Japan, and gave little Nippon a few years of prestige in Chinese eyes. It gave China also a new confidence in herself. Typical of Chinese feeling about Japan's rise to power was Sun Yat-sen's reaction. He puts it this way in one of his lectures:

A new Japan, transformed into a first-class Power, has arisen, and Japan's success has given the other nations of Asia unlimited hope. . . . Japan has been able to learn from Europe and, since her modernization, to catch up with Europe. . . . Because Asia possesses a strong Japan, the white races now dare not disparage the Japanese or any Asiatic race. So Japan's rise . . . has raised the standing of all Asiatic peoples. We once thought we could not do what the Europeans could do; we see now that Japan has learned from Europe and that, if we follow Japan, we, too, will be learning from the West as Japan did.[19]

For Sun Yat-sen, as for most Chinese, modern Japan was explained by the adoption of science and by modernization. So students rushed to Japan, eager to learn by the miracle of a moment this wonderfully potent science and this method called "modernization." In 1905 about six thousand Chinese were congested within a radius of a mile and a half in the student quarter of Tokyo. Most of them were young; the average age was found to be twenty-three. Fully half were supported by the government. Many of them were hot-headed; all of them were patriotic, with a patriotism accentuated by sojourn in a foreign land where they felt themselves strangers and among a people with whom they did not find perfect compatibility. When Japan emerged victorious from her spirited war with Russia, the contrast between China and Japan was provocative. The students were feverish with discussion.

Japan had become increasingly the refuge of exiled reformers and rebels; year by year their number was increasing. There were men who had displeased the government by radical journalism; there were plotters and insurrectionists. While Sun Yat-sen was in America, a rather brilliant revolutionary rising had been fomented in the Province of Hunan; some of its escaped leaders were in Japan when Sun Yat-sen reached there, notably, a military man named Huang Hsing and a civilian, Sung Chiao-jen. They cooperated with Sun Yat-sen in calling a patriotic meeting of students in Tokyo in September, 1905, shortly after the conclusion of the Treaty of Portsmouth which ended the Russo-Japanese War. It was largely attended, and is said by the Japanese to have been the most enthusiastic meeting of Chinese students ever held in Japan. After the purpose of the meeting was stated, Sun Yat-sen made an address. With the general consent of the audience an organization was created on new lines and given the name which may be roughly rendered the Revolutionary Covenanters or the Revolutionary Brotherhood. From motives of common prudence the word "revolutionary" was usually dropped from the name, which was shortened to *Tung Meng Hui*—literally, the Together Sworn Society. Although in inception it was a combination of already existing revolutionary organizations, no such word as "alliance" or "league" is colorful enough or stern enough to stand for this organization. The members of the *Tung Meng Hui* were pledged together by an oath, whose exact content was one of the secrets of the society. In this respect the organization followed an ancient practice among Chinese secret societies, whose members were usually sworn in and regarded one another as "sworn brothers." To the better-bred members of the new society, the use of the oath seemed a plebeian practice; nevertheless the following pledge was required for admission:

I swear under Heaven that I will do my utmost to work for the overthrow of the Manchu dynasty, the establishment of the Republic and the solution of the agrarian question on the basis of the equitable redistribution of the land. I solemnly undertake to be faithful to these principles. If ever I betray my trust I am willing to submit to the severest penalties imaginable.[20]

In spite of the radical character of the pledge and the terrifying penalties—which were specified—several hundred members were enrolled at the initial meeting. Among them seventeen out of the eighteen provinces of China were represented. The only province which had no members was the wild western Province of Kansu, and at that time it had no students in Tokyo.

Sun Yat-sen's earlier organization (*Hsing Chung Hui*) had been, on paper at least, a moderate patriotic society that sought the welfare of China by all means within its power, under which revolution could be and was subsumed. The new Brotherhood was an out-and-out revolutionary and radical organization. Others collaborated with Sun Yat-sen in drafting its objects which were boldly defined:

1. To overthrow the Manchu Government.
2. To establish a republic.
3. To conserve world-peace.
4. To favor the nationalization of land.
5. To favor coöperation between citizens of China and Japan.
6. To entreat other Powers to act favorably toward China's revolutionary movement.[21]

Four compact slogans were also adopted:

1. Drive away the Tartars!
2. Recover China for the Chinese!
3. Establish a republic!
4. Equalize land-ownership! [22]

The appearance in this platform of anti-dynastic and republican planks is not surprising, but it is surprising that so early in the history of the revolutionary movement a radical socialism should have been accepted. This shows how seriously Sun Yat-sen had taken Henry George and Karl Marx. The redistribution of land is the feature in which the now famous socialistic "Principle" is anticipated.

In signing the oath all members accepted this radical program. Wu Chih-hui tells how, when he was first confronted with the membership pledge and invited to sign, he laughed it off as a mean way of exacting loyalty. That was an excuse to cover his doubts. Because he was a gentleman, it meant something to him to put aside his class pride and prerogatives and swear to support a program of land-equalization; but he did it, and joined the *Tung Meng Hui*.

Sun Yat-sen was elected president of the Brotherhood. The vice president was Huang Hsing, who had led the rather brilliant revolutionary failure in Hunan. The success of the great meeting was very encouraging to Sun Yat-sen, who wrote: "On the day of the organization of the Brotherhood at Tokyo by intellectuals representing the whole of China, I began to have confidence that my revolutionary work might be completed in my lifetime."

The Tokyo offices of the Brotherhood were the headquarters of the revolutionary movement. A survey of every province in China was undertaken, and within a year there were ten thousand enrolled members; there was not a province without a branch. The membership included, according to Sun Yat-sen, the educational class, the working class, merchants, soldiers and politicians. This progress exceeded any one's expectation. Branches were also organized in the Straits Settlements and in America.

The Brotherhood began immediately publishing a newspaper for propaganda of its ideas, the *People's Paper* (*Min Pao*). On its editorial board were two able men, both still living: Hu Han-min, a member of the Nanking Government of 1928, and Wang Ching-wei, a peculiarly persuasive radical, who is frequently in and out of politics, and always has a following among the young students of China. Both were themselves young students in Japan at the time of the organization of the Brotherhood. To this day Wang Ching-wei is distinguished in the Kuomintang for the fluency with which he speaks Japanese. It was the effective writing in the *Min Pao* which made the revolutionary ideas known among the educated. The revolution had passed from the status of an organization among the lower classes to one commanding the support of intellectuals also. It had entered a new epoch.

DOCUMENTATION OF QUOTED PASSAGES

[1] *Pacific Commercial Advertiser* (Honolulu) Dec. 21, 1903, p. 3. [2] Finch, Percival: "A Chinese Sage Speaks to the World," *New York Times Magazine*, June 21, 1925. [3] Prefixed to the American edition of Cantlie and Jones: *Sun Yat Sen and the Awakening of China* (New York, 1912). [4] *San Francisco Examiner*, April 7, 1904, p. 5. [5] Ibid., April 29, p. 7. [6] Ibid., May 7, p. 1. [7] Ibid., May 7, p. 1. [8] Ibid., May 7, p. 1. [9] Culin: *The I Hing or "Patriotic Rising"* (Philadelphia, 1887) p. 2. [10] Ibid., pp. 4–7. [11] Sun Yat-sen: *The True Solution of the Chinese Question*, p. 5. [12] Sun Yat-sen: "My Reminiscences," *The Strand Magazine* (London, March, 1912) Vol. 43, pp. 305, 306. [13] Sun Yat-sen: *The True Solution of the Chinese Question*, p. 5. [14] Ibid., pp. 7 and 9. [15] Ibid., p. 9. [16] Feature article on Sun Yat-sen, *The Sun*, New York, December 31, 1911. [17] Appendix B, p. 385. [18] Huie Kin: *Reminiscences*, p. 71. [19] Sun Yat-sen: *San Min Chu I*, trans. Price (Shanghai, 1927) p. 15. [20] T'ang Leang-li: *The Inner History of the Chinese Revolution* (New York, 1930) p. 49. [21] Direct translation from the Chinese text found in *Chung-shan Hsien-sheng Nien P'u* under the year 1905; also to be found in Sun Yat-sen's Collected Works. [22] Ibid.

Sources and Authorities: See Appendix C, p. 398.

CHAPTER IV

The Dream That Came True Too Soon

I. HOW THE REVOLUTION WAS NOT WON

THE Chinese Revolution was not won by military insurrections. The story of their failure is written in Sun Yat-sen's *Autobiography;* therein with unemotional conciseness ten "revolutionary attempts" are listed one after another. And these are only the ones in which Sun Yat-sen himself had a share. Others broke out sporadically here and there; the Chinese sources mention them so frequently that a reader gets the impression that, for every rising sponsored by Sun Yat-sen, another could be listed. An Occidental reads the records with amazement, that it should ever have been supposed that by such amateurish outbreaks anything could be accomplished against the coördinated military and official system of the Empire. The wastefulness of failure seems to us tragic. But the Chinese are close to nature in being "careless of the single life." Their point of view is expressed by a recent Chinese historian:

These immature armed attempts had one wholesome effect: they served to arouse the people to the necessity of revolution.[1]

Another Chinese writer remarks:

These rebellions, if they served no other purpose, did keep alive before the Chinese people the revolutionary idea and converted many thousands to the revolutionary cause.[2]

Before any plans could be coolly made for a rising, the first blood of the Brotherhood was shed in an enthusiastic but unofficial rebellion on the border of Hunan Province (at Pinghsiang). Breaking out early in 1906 under the leadership of men who were of the "together-sworn" brothers, this venture appealed strongly to many of the Tokyo members. Sun Yat-sen tells how students came daily to the headquarters of the Brotherhood, clamoring to be sent to reinforce the revolutionists. Some of the more ardent spirits set off without permission, but before they could get to the scene of the rising the Manchus had quelled it.

This early experience was not without a lesson for the young organization: better coördination and central control of revolutionary projects seemed imperative. Supreme authority was placed in the hands of a special committee at the headquarters, and the decision was immediately made to restrict operations to the southwest borders of China, where French territory could be used as a base, and sanctuaries could more readily be found for refuge in defeat. This policy was not altogether popular with those members whose native provinces were in the Yangtze Valley or farther north. The committee also supervised the collection of necessary funds, chiefly from overseas Chinese.

Sun Yat-sen seems to have had a large share in both these forms of service. In the first half of the year 1906 he traveled for funds; and he had more than a finger in the preparations for a rising at Canton—again with the Viceroy's *yamen* as the objective. This is listed as the third of Sun Yat-sen's unsuccessful attempts. The fourth has been definitely dated April, 1907; but to the third Sun Yat-sen does not vouchsafe an approximate date or a single descriptive detail in his *Autobiography*. Perhaps it was a particularly inglorious failure.

In the early months of 1906 an American Circuit Judge in the Philippine Islands was asked by his Cantonese cook for a leave of absence. On being pressed for a reason the cook revealed his great secret—that he had been summoned to China to help Sun Yat-sen. For a few months he was absent and unaccounted for. When he returned to his master, before the end of the summer of 1906, he was badly crippled for life and had a story to tell of having been caught, mangled and left for dead, but by strange chance coming to and escaping. His ardor for the revolution was so intensified that he won Judge Linebarger to an interest in Sun Yat-sen's cause, and very shortly brought about a personal meeting between him and Sun Yat-sen in Manila. That was before the end of the summer of 1906.

A vivid narrative of participation in the "third attempt" (it is so designated, although wrongly dated) comes from Honolulu. One of Sun Yat-sen's sworn brothers was summoned from Hawaii to report for service at the headquarters in Japan. He responded at once and was sent on to China in company with some students who were also joining the rising. Unlike the Philippine recruit the Hawaiian-born Chinese came through the exploit unscathed and returned to the Islands, where a dozen-or-so years later he told his story to Bishop Restarick of Honolulu. He said that he had found Sun Yat-sen at the secret headquarters in Canton personally directing the plot. Since Sun Yat-sen was a banished man with a large price on his head, this seems extraordinarily venturesome. But the Hawaiian Chinese asserts that he himself slept in the same room with Sun Yat-sen and acted as his personal aide. He observed, as best a young and inexperienced man could, the hazardous organization of secret groups committed to coöperation at a time to be appointed. But the government got a clue to the conspiracy and the assault on the *yamen* never matured. It was with the Hawaiian Chinese that Sun Yat-sen fled to the river, where they hired a boat handled by women. After being pulled out into the stream, they offered the women money for their work-clothes, and Sun Yat-sen and his companion made their escape from the opposite shore disguised in the cotton pants and head-kerchiefs of Cantonese boat women.

After this third failure Sun Yat-sen seems to have taken again to money-raising—his habitual recovery from disaster. It was probably on a financial mission that he visited Manila and met Judge Linebarger, who became henceforth in his own way a Lafayette to Sun Yat-sen. The second half of 1906 was spent by Sun Yat-sen in Japan, according to the circumstantial account of a Japanese pastor who was later transferred to Honolulu, where he also told his story to the Bishop. He tells of his acquaintance with Sun Yat-sen in Yokohama:

Sun was frequently at my house and we became good friends. He trusted me and was grateful to me and we had long talks about his affairs. He was very hopeful and said he was sure of success in the end, by the help of God. Those were the very words he used, for he had told me that he was a Christian. I do not think he went to church in Yokohama for he could not have understood what was said.

He moved to Tokyo where he became friends with many of the professors of Waseda University, and during his stay there he met Count Okuma, who, of course, could not express sympathy but was interested in him. The Japanese Christians, especially, were in favor of Sun because they believed that he stood for the rights of man and was opposed to oppression and cruelty, as shown in the policy of the Manchus.[3]

Judge Linebarger himself was in Tokyo, Oct. 12, 1906, while his ship for America was making the port-call at Yokohama. Whether he actually saw Sun Yat-sen there or not, he remembered to jot down somewhere this note:

Several times this afternoon I have heard expressions of disappointment that Dr. Sun did not address the students in a series of lectures as they wished.

This is not Dr. Sun's fault . . . there are other matters even more important than this. . . .[4]

Sun Yat-sen was right in not risking the publicity such lectures would have entailed. Trouble overtook him swiftly when, on Jan. 16, 1907, he addressed an audience of Chinese students in Tokyo on the occasion of the first birthday of the revolutionary journal, *Min Pao*. The speech, which attracted an audience of five thousand, was on the lately gestated Three Principles of the People. It brought him into such prominence that the Manchu government was able to press Japan to banish him.

Leaving the headquarters and the *People's Paper* in the hands of unproven men, he took with him Wang Ching-wei and Hu Han-min and went to Annam to make his new headquarters at Hanoi. Whereas in an earlier stage the revolutionary cause had received help from Japan, there was now expectation of French help. On one of Sun Yat-sen's returns to Japan by way of Shanghai an incident had taken place which he records in his *Autobiography*. A French officer called on him while his boat was at Woosung (the exit of Shanghai to the sea), and offered him the help of French experts. As a result eight retired French army officers were distributed over South China and the Yangtze Valley, where with the help of Chinese revolutionists they investigated military conditions and made secret overtures to officers of the provincial armies. The lengths to which they went are illustrated by what happened at Wuchang. There the revolutionists held a large secret meeting, selecting, Sun Yat-sen says, a church as the place for it. Revolutionary speeches were made, one of them by a French officer. It happened that the General commanding the Imperial Army at Wuchang was in the audience; he had heard of the meeting and came in disguise; so he was able to report the proceedings to the Viceroy. The Chinese leaders were arrested and executed. A foreigner was engaged to spy on the French officer. By pretending to be favorable to the revolution, he easily drew the officer out in talk about the revolutionary plans. These were duly reported to the Viceroy and then to Peking. Protests were lodged with the French government but resulted in no action.

In Annam French military men were engaged for the training of a Chinese revolutionary army. Guns and ammunition were ordered through the Brotherhood's headquarters in Japan. Unfortunately this was a period of intrigues and disunity within the organization itself, with the result that secrets leaked out and ammunition was detained. The Annam campaign was seriously hampered by this central disorganization.

The attempt to invade China over the French border was probably Sun Yat-sen's most ambitious revolutionary undertaking. It grew to the dimensions of a campaign and extended from July, 1907, into the year 1908. Although the accounts of it are very sketchy and scattered through the Chinese chronicles, the campaign may be briefly described as exhibiting Sun Yat-sen's insurrectionary method at its best. He had the coöperation of Huang Hsing, the vice-president of the Brotherhood, who had taken a military course in Japan.

It seems to have been mainly with the help of Huang Hsing that a certain code of bravery was developed among the revolutionary soldiers, who were given the stimulating name of "Dare-to-dies." In its popular form the appeal to these men was to die for the revolution in order that their descendants through endless generations might enjoy a redeemed and prosperous China, and that their own spirits in another world might be blissfully aware of the happy results of their good deeds.

Opportunely to Sun Yat-sen's plans there had broken out a popular insurrection against taxes in the hilly region which forms the border between the most sparsely populated province of southern China, Kwangsi, and Annam. The Manchu government sent

two generals and several thousand soldiers to put it down. Sun Yat-
sen despatched two of his ablest supporters into the Manchu camps
to carry on revolutionary propaganda, and sent others to work for
the support of gentry and peasants. Even the two generals listened
and gave the plotters to understand that they would support a
revolutionary rising. Everything looked easy then to Sun Yat-sen.
He tells how much he expected:

Though I had to be in French territory, I could conveniently direct
operations in Chinese territory. I calculated that we could form two
thousand troops without any difficulty as soon as the ammunition arrived from Japan. Should we consolidate the volunteers in the Ch'in
district, we could get another six thousand troops. When our troops
combined with the . . . armies . . . , we should have a very powerful
army; and with additional training we could easily occupy Kwangtung
and Kwangsi. From there we could proceed to the Yangtze Valley and
join with the modern armies in Nanking and Wuchang. It would not
be difficult at all to occupy the entire country.[5]

Contrasted with these hopes, what actually happened was a petty
story. Sun Yat-sen's forces invaded the tax-rioting district in July,
1907. But the expected ammunition did not arrive from Japan. The
Manchu generals saw this, and they remained loyal to the government. The revolutionary troops were defeated and beat a retreat
into the "Hundred Thousand Mountains" that form the border.
A second invasion was organized, in which Sun Yat-sen himself
participated. A fortified town was taken, and several vantage points
were seized; but the invaders were outnumbered by the Imperial
forces, and were ejected after a few days and nights of resistance.

The Manchu government had meantime negotiated for Sun
Yat-sen's banishment from French territory. He sailed for Singapore, leaving his colleagues to carry on. Huang Hsing was sent to
make another incursion over the border. With only about two hun-

dred revolutionary soldiers he was able to hold out in this wild country for several months. When finally there were no more bullets, he returned to Annam.

In 1908 a man with no military training to boast of made a more successful raid on the Yunnan border at Hokou. The commander of the frontier defense was killed and several thousand soldiers taken prisoners. But the revolutionists could not long hold out; Sun Yat-sen's attempt to send Huang Hsing to their aid was foiled by the French authorities who would not let him through. Isolated, the revolutionary commander in Yunnan had to retreat; but he came back to Annam with six hundred soldiers instead of something over a hundred with which he had set out.

Such was the campaign on the Annam borders. The net result of French training, of many months of effort, and of much money was nothing but retreat, retreat, retreat, retreat—four more failures for Sun Yat-sen to list.

The Yunnan episode apparently wakened the French rulers of Annam from their indifference. They put an end to the operations in their territory by banishing the leaders and deporting six hundred revolutionists to Singapore. The English authorities there had no desire to receive them; the ship was detained and objections made. Finally, however, they were reluctantly admitted—men out of occupation, out of house and home, facing the difficulty of settling in a strange land. Their discontent helped the general feeling of pessimism that got the better of the revolutionists at this time.

The remaining two reverses in the tale of ten were attempts to capture Canton and the government *yamen*. One, in January, 1910, was badly bungled; some one acted prematurely. This failure was the more distressing because it was the hopefully trained "new army" which disappointed the Brotherhood. The attempt of March 29, 1911, was costly in life; seventy-two of the very flower of the Brotherhood lost their lives; many of them were of the intellectual class. This was an undoubtedly brave but very reckless assault by Huang Hsing and about a hundred of the sworn-brothers on the Canton *yamen*. The coöperating units failed to keep the date set for rising, and the central group acted alone. Using pistols and small bombs they dislodged the *yamen* guards, destroyed buildings, and, for about five hours, resisted the attempts of government troops to regain the *yamen*. When the battle was over, forty-three of the revolutionists were dead on the field, and twenty-nine were captured —to be promptly executed. The remaining few, including Huang Hsing, made their escape. This most sensational of all the revolutionary failures goes now by the name of the "Martyrdom of the Seventy." A monument at Canton commemorates their sacrifice, and Nationalist China keeps the date, March 29th, as a memorial holiday.

These will serve as illustrations of the methods of the revolutionaries. An "attempt" was managed by a central group with a small corps of inadequately trained amateur soldiers at its disposal. Coöperating with them was the inchoate thing which came to be called the "People's Army"—affiliated usually through the secret societies. Its function seems to have been irregular reinforcement of the armed group and disintegration of local resistance. In the Annam campaign support was expected from insurgents already in revolt against the government. In the later attempts intrigue was carried on within the Manchu armies in the hope of their going over to the revolution after an initial success. Ammunition depots and strategic defenses were designated for capture. The plan was to get control of some district and work out from it. Over and over the Viceroy's headquarters at Canton were the objective. By invasion over the French border it was hoped to take Canton indirectly and also to work northward to the Yangtze Valley. All these seem naïvely ambitious projects, considering the very small force of amateurs undertaking them. Faultiness of coördination was the commonest cause of disaster; some one acted prematurely, failed to keep an appointed date or divulged secrets. Shortage of ammunition was perennial. When we think of the great bulk of China stretching northward over fourteen hundred miles to Peking, we wonder what these men could have been thinking of, when, gathering a hundred or two zealots together, they went forth to storm some stronghold or to beat out a few months in border warfare. It seems the very wooing of futility.

The reply to such criticism comes readily; the eleventh attempt succeeded. Why? Before attempting to answer that question, it should be recorded that another violent method was used, about which some of the most startling stories of the revolution are told, namely, assassination. Encouraged as a terroristic policy calculated to break the morale of the supporters of the dynasty, it was also frankly used with an eye to spectacular effect. Access to the designated official was attempted in various ways; sometimes by lying in wait in a frequented place, sometimes by entering the household as an employee—a cook or a house-servant in default of anything better. Not always was the official killed; but whether the attempt succeeded or failed, Sun Yat-sen has ardent praise for it. In *China's Revolution* he enters a list of some who attempted this kind of service to his cause; among them are revered "martyrs" of the Republic.

The most spectacular of the failures in assassination was the throwing of a bomb Oct. 15, 1905, at the constitutional commission of five distinguished men, just as they were boarding their train at Peking to go abroad for observation of constitutional government. Bystanders suffered but the commission escaped. Occurring as it did very soon after the organization of the *Tung Meng Hui,* this attempt seems to have been electrifying in effect. But it is the most ironical act of the chapter—that Sun Yat-sen should have set his revolution at cross purposes with the very movement which was buoying it up. The constitutional commission was an incident in the reform wave. Without the reform movement there would have been few students studying in Europe or in Japan. Without the students abroad there would have been no Revolutionary Brotherhood.

Another notorious attempt was made by Wang Ching-wei, one of the early editors of the *People's Paper*. In 1909 he became so disheartened over the repeated failures of the Brotherhood's plots and insurrections that he determined to act desperately. He attached to himself some kindred terrorists—a young woman among them—who traveled with him by stages northward. After considering other plans, they decided that nothing short of an assassination at the capital would be sufficiently sensational. Early in 1910 they foregathered at Peking and plotted to kill the Prince Regent (the Emperor was then a small child). Their dynamite and mechanism were discovered on March 28th. Not until April 16th was Wang Ching-wei apprehended with one of his accomplices. He created the sensation of his life by stating his name and explaining exactly what he intended to do. He and his mate were clapped into prison and lucky to keep their heads until the Revolution brought them release.

The considered use of assassination by the Revolutionary Brotherhood should not be forgotten when, a little later, the method shows a robust survival under the Republic.

II. HOW THE REVOLUTION WAS FOUGHT

The Revolution of 1911 by which China cast off the Empire and put on a new form of government was accomplished by a conjunction of efforts, no two or three of which could have effected the change.

The earliest of all directed efforts, one that persisted patiently and with growing enthusiasm, was the assistance financial and spiritual, of overseas Chinese. Among them the first revolutionary organization arose, and among them Sun Yat-sen was at work when he got word of the first revolutionary success. When everything was going against the revolutionists the overseas Chinese did not slacken their support. Sun Yat-sen tells how, after the Canton fiasco of January, 1910, he returned from America by way of Honolulu and Japan to the Straits, and summoned several of his chief supporters to Penang for a conference. All of them had suffered defeats; they looked sorrowfully at one another for a while and could say nothing. Sun Yat-sen rallied them and they set out on a money-raising campaign. This was in October or November, 1910. In one night in Penang they got eight thousand dollars (Chinese currency) and within a few days had secured over fifty thousand. They toured the cities of the Straits and everywhere met generous support from the Chinese. It was Sun Yat-sen's wish to go on working among the Chinese of the South Seas, but by this time all the colonial governments were alive to his activities, and he was effectively excluded, not only from Hongkong, Japan and French Indo-China, but also from Siam and from the British and Dutch colonies of the South Pacific. No country conveniently near China would any longer harbor Sun Yat-sen, so he had no choice but to go farther off. He went to Europe—this time approaching bankers for a very large loan, rumored to have been as much as £100,000. He caused some interest, and continued his journey to America. If he anywhere secured a large loan, the fact has not been revealed. In the United States he traveled widely, and with his customary inconspicuousness and inexpensiveness, stopping with friends or choosing dingy rooms for lodgings, and eating in cheap restaurants. His gift of public address served him well in these prolonged efforts to secure financial backing. Moreover, he had courage that would not accept reverses; and he evidently created confidence in his judgment and in his integrity. Generously his countrymen gave—from the humble Philadelphia laundryman, who brought Sun Yat-sen his savings in a linen bag, to a prosperous curio dealer in Paris who sold out his business to give the proceeds amounting to over sixty thousand Chinese dollars. This money represented more than generosity; it represented a deep faith in the future of China, and a strong desire, more or less untutored, to see China realize herself.

The enlistment of certain secret societies in the cause of the revolution was a capital stroke of policy, to which reference has been already made. The revival, particularly in the Triad Society (*San Ho Hui*), of its almost forgotten anti-dynastic purpose was the strategy of the revolutionists. European governments came in contact with this society in their Eastern colonies and came to know its strength. In the English and Dutch island possessions the Triad proved to be so powerful as to interfere at times with colonial administration. Although in some places it had degenerated into lawless groups—bandits and pirates—in other places, Singapore for instance, the society included practically the whole Chinese population in its membership and could act very clannishly in resisting the government. In Hongkong and the Straits Settlements ordinances were finally enforced in the effort to uproot the Triad Society. A secret society is, however, no easy thing to extirpate. That the Triad was very useful to the revolution cannot be doubted. Sun Yat-sen's success among overseas Chinese was due in considerable measure to the openness of this group to anti-Manchu appeals. In China the society was strong in the South. The Province of Kwangtung was its birthplace. It had Grand Lodges in each of five southern provinces.

Another secret society which played a rôle in the revolution was the *Ko Lao Hui* (Brothers and Elders Society). It was definitely anti-dynastic in purpose. Dyer Ball, writing in the early '90's, says:

An Association which has attracted some attention lately is the Kò-lò-wui, which has its headquarters in the province of Hunan, the army being quite honeycombed by this political Association which, like the Triad, has for its object the overthrow of the present dynasty. It is said to have its emissaries in every province, who travel under the assumed character of doctors, disseminating news and gathering in members as they go. . . . An elaborate initiation ceremony is said to be employed. It is described as resembling Freemasonry, and not essentially seditious. . . . It took its rise at the time of the T'ai-p'ing rebellion.[6]

Of this society Sun Yat-sen seems to have been himself a member. According to Dr. Cantlie he formed in 1894 a branch of the *Ko Lao Hui* in Canton. In Sun Yat-sen's *Reminiscences* reference is also made to close relationship between himself and this society.

If no more than these two secret societies were interested in the revolution a useful entrée was made. The five Grand Lodges of the Triad Society were in Fukien, Kwangtung, Yunnan, Hunan and Chekiang. The *Ko Lao Hui* had a distribution over Kiangsu, Anhui, Hupeh, Kiangsi and Kwangtung. Geographically supplementing each other, their scope included all of southern China and most of the Yangtze Valley. It was in just these regions that, Sun-Yat-sen tells us, his organizers worked to turn the restoration fraternities into active revolutionary societies. The *Ko Lao Hui* is said to have gained influence also in the extreme west and northwest, particularly in Szechuan, Shensi and Shansi.

A third effective method of forwarding the revolution was the work done surreptitiously among the Imperial armies. The *Ko Lao Hui* did its share of this. Military students in Japan were by no means overlooked. Some of them joined the Revolutionary Brotherhood, and then returned to China to take military posts with the Imperial army. They were thus in a position to help the revolution when the crisis came. Personal agents worked also among the officers in China, not only investigating conditions, but alienating men from the government to the revolution. We have already noticed this kind of work directed by French officers; Sun Yat-sen touches upon it in his *Autobiography*. The armies in Nanking and Wuchang, he says, were found to be particularly favorable toward revolution; he makes the large claim that secret understandings in Nanking included all military officers above the rank of captain!

A fourth effort, one which yielded very great results, was the winning of intellectuals to the revolution. That has been recorded fully in the preceding chapter. The intellectuals of China are always thought of as the leaders of the people. It is because they take this responsibility seriously that they become effective agents in any political movement. In the revolution students and teachers worked at hazardous plotting and organizing; some even attempted assassinations, and some assumed military duties. They all helped in word-of-mouth dissemination of ideas and in the circulation of tracts, books and newspapers. Because in old China all the officials belonged to the educated class (without educational standing, no office) to win the intellectuals was to undermine officialdom.

III. PROPAGANDA AND PREJUDICE

"One newspaper is worth a hundred thousand soldiers" is a saying popularly attributed to Sun Yat-sen. The revolutionists were among the pioneers in modern Chinese journalism. The reform movement had demonstrated the power of the newspaper, especially when written by as able a man as Liang Chi-chao. The Empress Dowager's reactionary measures of 1898 had included the suppression of newspapers. We have seen how Liang Chi-chao then continued his journalism from Japan. An alien habitat was desirable for any journal which at that time undertook to criticize the government. Sun Yat-sen had the first of his revolutionary newspapers edited safely in Hongkong, the *China Daily* (*Chung Kuo Pao*), which got under way some time before 1900. The next one to be heard of was the organ of the Revolutionary Brotherhood, the *People's Paper* (*Min Pao*), edited in Tokyo. That became "the tongue of the party." It lavished much ink in controversy with the reform societies, especially with the constitutional monarchists.

In addition to the circulation of newspapers much use was made of pamphlets and small books—openly overseas, but more or less surreptitiously in China. Their appeal to the literate classes was widespread. Occasionally they were copied by hand to increase their availability.

The broad lines of the propaganda are fairly clear: the urgency of learning from the West, of which Japan was a shining example; the corruption and extravagance of the Imperial régime; the insincerity of its promulgated reforms; the stupidity of its dealing with foreign nations; the humiliating wars; the alienation of territory and the imposition of indemnities; the peril of the partition of China; and the advantages of popular government.

But the appeal was not so dispassionate as this would suggest. Prejudice is mightier than reason in stirring people to action. The passion to which most effective appeal was made was racial prejudice. As revolutionists Sun Yat-sen and his co-workers made use of persistent propaganda, both oral and written, to inform the people that their rulers were foreigners. What was euphemistically called the doctrine of racial solidarity was promulgated for the purpose of pitting the Chinese against the Manchus. It is not too severe a criticism to say that in the name of racial solidarity the revolutionists preached racial antagonism. A passage may be cited from an admirable book by a Chinese, *The Kuomintang and the Future of the Chinese Revolution*, by T. C. Woo:

THE DOCTRINE OF RACIAL UNITY.—As far as the Revolution of 1911 was concerned this doctrine was the chief weapon of the revolutionists used against the Manchu Government. It was a sharp wedge driven between the Manchus and the Chinese, and was the corner stone of the theory of revolution preached in the early years. There were at that time a host of revolutionary writers who daily inculcated in the minds of the Chinese people the racial distinction between the governing and the governed classes. These men published dailies and pamphlets on the central thesis of racial distinction; they exposed the corruptions and degenerate conditions of the Manchu royal household and of the Manchu officials in order to destroy the respect of the people for the Government. That was the one point on which they concentrated their energy; it was the point on which the Revolution of 1911 depended. The success or failure of the movement relied on whether or not the revolutionary leaders were able to bring home to the people the idea of racial unity or solidarity of the Chinese.[7]

Prepared beforehand and ready for use in the event of an initial success, a Revolutionary Manifesto had been lying for some time among the papers of the Brotherhood. It had been formulated within a year or two after the organization of the *Tung Meng Hui* in 1905. Then imagining a *fait accompli,* Sun Yat-sen, Huang Hsing and the others had put into militant expression their aims and their program. A succinct statement of what the revolutionists planned to do and to stand for, it is also full of the passion and prejudice without which no revolution would ever have been brought about.

It is headed, "The Manifesto of the Military Government of the Revolutionary Brotherhood." The purpose of the revolution is set forth: to throw off the Manchu rule, to restore China to the Chinese, and to promote the welfare of the whole population. It is urged that in fighting against foreign rulers the Chinese are following a noble and ancient tradition, but that in this revolution there is a new element:

The revolutions of earlier history were hero-revolutions wrought by a few brave men. The present revolution is of the people as a whole.

This means that all should possess the spirit of liberty, equality and fraternity, and that all should share the responsibility of the revolution. The Military Government is nothing but the headquarters of the move-ment.[8]

The aims of the revolution are identical with the four slogans of the Brotherhood already reported in an earlier chapter, but the exposition is so militant that the passage is worth quoting:

1. To drive away the Manchus.

The present Manchuria was originally a territorial possession of the outer barbarians. During the Ming dynasty these barbarians were a constant menace to China. Finally they took advantage of our internal chaos, entered China at Shanhaikwan and conquered us. By force they made us their slaves, killing hundreds of thousands of those who refused to obey them. Chinese have now suffered under a foreign government more than two hundred and sixty years. The Manchus have done us enough cruelty. Now is the time to raise an army and overthrow the Manchu government and regain the sovereignty of our country. Such Manchus and such Chinese in the Manchu army as repent themselves and surrender to us will be pardoned. We will kill those Manchus who oppose us, and also all Chinese who traitorously help the Manchus.

2. To restore China to the Chinese.

The Chinese state belongs to China; her political institutions should be administered by Chinese alone. We must drive away the Manchus and restore our China to Chinese. If any are bold enough to support the foreign tribe—like Shih Ching-tang and Wu San-kuei of old—it is the duty of all Chinese to see that they are killed.

3. To establish a republic.

Our revolution is based on the principle of equality, therefore we shall have a republican form of government, in which all citizens will be equal and have equal opportunity and equal right to participate in the affairs of government. The president will be elected by the mass of the people. A parliament will be made up of men elected by the citizens. A constitution will be promulgated for the Republic and every citizen will be obliged to obey it. If anybody plots to restore despotism in China, we must kill him.

4. To equalize the land-power.

All benefits resulting from social improvements should be shared equally by all citizens. Improvement of our economic condition will be made: first, by fixing the price of land; that price will be reckoned the property of the owner; any later increase in value due to social progress must belong to the state and be equally shared by all citizens. We shall establish a socialistic state that will ensure to all citizens a decent living. If any one ventures to monopolize the economic resources which are the property of all he must be got rid of.[9]

After this forcible statement of the objects in view there follows a description of the steps by which they are to be attained, similar to, yet differing from, the reconstruction program of today. Progress is to be made in three definitely marked stages.

The first is to be a period of military government in which the soldiers must be supported by the people. In this introductory period the country is to throw off the evils of the monarchical régime—oppression, official "squeeze," cruel punishments, heavy taxes, and that badge of subjection, the queue. Slavery, footbinding, opium smoking and ignorant superstitions are all to be prohibited.

After three years of military rule every district (*hsien*) is to learn to govern itself. Local councils and all local administrative officers are to be elected by the local citizens. A provisional code is to be put into force defining the relations of the district with the central government, which will still be a military government.

When this provisional arrangement has been in force all over China for six years, a permanent constitution is to be promulgated. The citizens will elect their president and the members of parliament. The military government will retire and the constitutional government will be completed.

In this nine-years revolutionary program we have a sharpened example of Sun Yat-sen's programizing method. His youthful memorial to Li Hung-chang was a plan, but not a schedule. The Manifesto ends with a fervid appeal to the four hundred millions of China to support the revolution.

IV. THE INCIDENCE OF THE REPUBLIC

When all the converging revolutionary forces have been described, they still seem inadequate to account for the events which followed one another rapidly in the autumn of 1911. For further explanation it is necessary to observe what was happening within the Imperial régime.

Though Sun Yat-sen would never have admitted as much, it may be pointed out that the progress of constitutional reforms under the Empress Dowager made no small contribution toward the success of the revolution. Under the guidance of a shrewd and able group of progressive minds the reforms had gone great lengths, not only in the organization of education and of an army, but in advances toward constitutional government. The constitutional commission which escaped the revolutionary bombing in 1905 returned from abroad in 1906 and recommended steps toward new forms. In that year there appeared the Imperial edict promising a constitutional government; it was followed by other decrees concerning the proposed reorganization. The plan was to move gradually toward a full-fledged parliament by first developing provincial assemblies with powers of free discussion and advice, later a national assembly with similar powers; after the members had been developed by experience, full legislative rights were to be granted. On Aug. 27, 1908, an articulated Nine-Years Program of Constitutional Reform was promulgated, which in its thoroughness and scope was a great credit to the Imperial statesmen. To each of the nine years was allocated a very full schedule of civil and military changes in the provinces and in the central government. These were to lead up to the climax—parliamentary control.

Two months and a half later, Nov. 15, 1908, the enigmatic Empress Dowager, Tzu Hsi, died. She did not pass away without making sure that her palace prisoner, the tragically thwarted young Emperor Kuang-hsu, was beyond the reach of political plotters. His death, the day before her own, took away the center around which the *Pao Huangs* might have most enthusiastically rallied. His successor was a very small child whose father assumed the regency. Almost at once the Regent dismissed the strongest statesman-soldier of the Imperial following, Yuan Shih-kai. In the Occident this dismissal was deplored as a reactionary move. But the *Pao Huangs* spoke out in protest against the Western estimate of Yuan Shih-kai as the foremost exponent of modernism. Kang Yu-wei cabled from Penang to take to himself the credit for the fall of Yuan Shih-kai, and openly charged him with having been the agent of the deceased Empress in effecting the death of the Emperor on whom the Reform Party had built its hopes. The Regent professed to be a patron of reforms, but he created disaffection among Chinese officials by certain of his acts, and by others offended the "modern army" which was largely of Yuan Shih-kai's making. Many people then were able to see what Sun Yat-sen had dared to assert in 1904 —that the old régime was rotting. With its line of strong rulers exhausted, and with petty men in high places thwarting the rising will of the people, the dynasty was obviously crumbling. And nowhere in the world is it truer than among the Chinese who made the proverb that "Every one knocks a piece from a crumbling wall."

In spite of the Regent's feeble reactionism the Program of Constitutional Reform remained in force. In October, 1909, the Provincial Assemblies convened for the first time according to the Program. Although only advisory in power, they furnished opportunity for debate, criticism and recommendation. These met once a year on the first day of the ninth month for a session of forty days. (It was the Provincial Assembly of Hupeh which in October, 1911, turned the first province over to the revolution.) On Oct. 3, 1910, the first National Assembly met according to the Program in Peking. One of its first actions was to petition for a real parliament at an early date. In response to this, the nine years of the Program were cut down to five years, and the first parliament with legislative power was set for 1913. The National Assembly was not satisfied with this concession and renewed its demands, but obtained nothing more. It finished its session with considerable petulance and disorder. However, it met again the next year; then the revolution broke out. The combative attitude of this Assembly toward the Regent, and its renewed insistence upon immediate legislative organization, psychologically abetted the revolution against the dynasty.

It will be seen that in regard to constitutional changes the psychology of China had reached a crisis favorable to the revolution. Constitutional development had not gone so far as to produce any disillusionment or shock to faith; it had advanced just far enough to whet the appetite for more. Those who had tasted parliamentary power, even the limited power of debate, were now impatient of a wise, slow program of discipline and learning. They wanted an immediate consummation. Anything that suggested restraint from headstrong progress was construed as an obstructionist policy.

A synchronizing event of another kind proved helpful to the revolution—the conflict which had become apparent between national interests and provincial interests in the new enterprises of railway development. The provincial spirit, always strong in China, developed in certain areas considerable opposition to the Peking Government's policy of nationalizing the railways. This conflict became acute over the railways projected into western China, particularly in the Province of Szechuan, which raised a revolt over the railway policy in the summer of 1911. The disaffection easily traveled from the upper Yangtze to the middle stretches of the river. The outbreak of the revolution some months in advance of the date planned was doubtless due to the railway insurrection, which also determined the place where the revolt erupted. Indeed, at the time, the railway contention seemed to make a very large contribution toward the Revolution of 1911. It became a matter of violent disagreement between the National Assembly and the rulers. As the occasion of their troubles it bulked hugely in the minds of the Manchus, who assigned it a disproportionate place as a cause of the turn to a republic. When the revolution is seen as a long-planned movement, the railway contention dwindles into an incident. It aroused the final criticism of the rulers, toward whom feeling had gradually risen to such a pitch that confidence was no longer possible. No wonder that a revolution which awakened popular faith swept everything before it.

Events were precipitated by the accidental explosion of a bomb in a secret ammunition depot within the Russian Concession in Hankow, Oct. 9, 1911. This led to the discovery of a revolutionary plot. The Viceroy at Wuchang (no longer Chang Chih-tung) arrested over thirty and made seizure of ammunition and documents, among which was the register of the local Revolutionary Brotherhood. So many people were incriminated by the register that it was felt to be too late to withdraw. At the same moment trouble broke out in the provincial garrison over the execution of eight soldiers for stealing a field gun from an ordnance park. The Imperial artillery and engineering corps, which had been secretly won over by revolutionists, openly mutinied, bombarded the Viceroy's *yamen* and burned it. The Viceroy fled, the military commander also, and the Imperial armies were left in a state of confusion. Wuchang fell to the revolutionists on October 11th. They selected as their commander a Japan-trained officer who was Colonel of one of the Imperial brigades, Li Yuan-hung. The next day they captured the city of the steel mills across the river, Hanyang, and got possession of the arsenal. On the following day the Provincial Assembly of Hupeh joined them and proclaimed the secession of the province from Imperial rule. Hankow was also captured. With the triple cities and the province in their hands the revolutionists issued their Manifesto and called on other cities and provinces to rise and drive the Manchus out. Provincial assemblies were at that time in session all over China.

When the government at Peking bestirred itself, its first act was to recall Yuan Shih-kai to become Viceroy of the disaffected area. He did not hasten to the help of the Regent, who was forced to raise his bid first to supreme military and naval command, and later to the premiership. Even then Yuan Shih-kai considered and refused, and reconsidered and laid down his own conditions. When he took hold of the military situation, what he really wanted was not the suppression of the revolutionists but an understanding with them, a compromise, if possible, on a limited constitutional monarchy—in any case, scope for his own ambitions.

Meanwhile the Regent was making frantic efforts to retrieve the situation by issuing in the name of the child Emperor an edict of abject apology and by making promises to limit and constitutionalize the monarchy. The Imperial armies had been concentrated in an attempt to recover the Wuhan cities; there had been some success in counter attacking, and Hankow had been burned. But the revolution had been spreading down the Yangtze Valley where city after city went over. By the time Yuan Shih-kai was persuaded to take up the premiership, the capitals of a great block of provinces of the Yangtze Valley and southern China were in the hands of the revolutionists, including Canton. The most stubborn resistance to the revolution was at Nanking which was not won until December 2nd. In all these capitals the Manchus were turned out of official buildings and garrisons and the governmental areas in which they lived. The "Tartar city" in Nanking was razed to the ground —reduced to a mass of rubble. In Wuchang an attack broke out against the Manchu people but was checked. In Sianfu, Shensi, the massacre of Manchus was terrible beyond words. It was only after the awakened race fury had done some tragic work that it was realized by certain of the leaders that the sympathy of the world would be alienated by such cruelties; then a different tune began to be heard—equal treatment for all, including Manchus.

The amazing fact, which Yuan Shih-kai took note of in a memorial to the throne, was that within a month thirteen provinces had been lost to the Empire. More followed. Early in December the Regent was forced to resign and Yuan Shih-kai was given a free hand. He favored a settlement by a peace conference and appointed as his chief representative a vigorous, American-educated Cantonese—Tang Shao-yi by name—born in the same district as Sun Yat-sen. Although this man had been a subordinate of Yuan Shih-kai's, he was known to have republican leanings; possibly he was sent for that very reason. Representing the revolutionists was another Cantonese, Wu Ting-fang, who had been for many years the affable Chinese minister at Washington. When these men met in Shanghai, December 15th, the question was still open as between a constitutional monarchy and a republic. There were sections of the revolutionists who would have accepted the former, but Wu Ting-fang and the Southern group insisted on nothing short of a republic. Tang Shao-yi saw that a republic was inevitable and agreed to refer this recommendation to Peking. Yuan Shih-kai was the powerful man there, and he knew how to retard settlement until he could turn it to his own advantage.

V. THE ROMANCE OF BEING OUT OF IT

While the revolution was spreading in China, Sun Yat-sen was away in America soliciting money. He had been traveling most of the time since 1909—his third prolonged tour. After a journey to America he had returned to the Orient by way of Honolulu in 1910. He stopped off in disguise in Japan, but was discovered and ejected. Then he went on, as we have already noted, to meet defeated and disheartened colleagues in Malaysia. He helped them to recover courage, got them new financial backing, only to find himself vigilantly excluded from the colonial possessions in the South Pacific. He went then to Europe and America.

An encouraging episode, which probably belongs to this American sojourn, was the appearance in one of the revolutionary meetings of an undersized, pale-faced, delicate-looking American, a stranger to Sun Yat-sen, who took him for a student or a missionary. (He tells the story himself in *My Reminiscences*.) After the meeting the stranger came up and spoke to Sun Yat-sen:

"I should like to throw in my lot with you," he said. "I should like to help you. I believe your propaganda will succeed."

Sun Yat-sen thanked him, wondering who he might be.

"Who was that little hunchback?" he asked a friend afterward.

"Oh, that is Colonel Homer Lea," was the reply. "One of the most brilliant—perhaps *the* most brilliant military genius now alive. He is a perfect master of modern warfare."

"And he has just offered to throw in his lot with me!" Sun Yat-sen was much stirred.

Homer Lea had, since his association with Kang Yu-wei and the reformers, published a book in 1909 that had brought him considerable fame—*The Valor of Ignorance*. Sensational as it was, this amateur book met with some approval from military men both for its technical mastery and for its argument, which was a protest against the military unpreparedness of the United States, especially in view of the rapid rise of Japan. Homer Lea seems to have been almost as antipathetic toward the Japanese as he was cordial toward the Chinese; and the possibility of a Japanese invasion of the Pacific Coast became an obsession with him. The book was illustrated with topographical maps to show just how readily Los Angeles, San Francisco and the Puget Sound would lend themselves to invasion.

Sun Yat-sen sought out Homer Lea the next day and called on him. He promised to make him his chief military adviser, if ever he should have the official power to do so.

"Do not wait until you are President of China," Lea answered. "You may want me before then."

And so Sun Yat-sen had his Lafayette, but with small prospect of making practical use of him.

That Sun Yat-sen was not thinking of himself as indispensable to the cause in China seems to be clear from an episode reported by J. Ellis Barker, who in 1911 had been visiting Chinese settlements in the United States and Canada, and had met Sun Yat-sen in Victoria. There he spent "several afternoons and evenings in his company."

I found him at a fourth-rate hotel, a kind of lodging-house for working men, occupying a bare and miserable little room. His dress was modest and his luggage scanty. . . . One night, when we had been discussing Chinese affairs till past midnight at my hotel, I wished to accompany him back to his hotel, a distance of about three-quarters of a mile, partly from courtesy, partly in order to protect him if he should be attacked. Although he was alone, he absolutely refused my repeated and pressing offers. At last I told him, "With a reward of £100,000 on your head, you should not go alone through the deserted streets of a strange town. If you have no fear for yourself, you should at least spare yourself for your cause and your country." He replied with a quiet smile which was half sad and half humorous: "If they had killed me some years ago, it would have been a pity for the cause; I was indispensable then. Now my life does not matter. Our organization is complete. There are plenty of Chinamen to take my place. It does not matter if they kill me." [10]

Somewhere in the western States Sun Yat-sen was handed a cablegram in code from Hankow. That he was not anticipating any urgent message is clear from the fact that he had packed his code-book in his trunk which he had sent on much ahead of himself to Denver, Col. Not able to read the cable he put it aside. When he reached Denver a fortnight later, he deciphered the message and found it to be a request for the remittance of money, and a statement that the Wuchang revolutionists were ready to rise. He decided to have a night's sleep before answering and he took a long one—until eleven o'clock the next day. On his way to a restaurant for breakfast he bought a morning paper and read the headlines: "Wuchang occupied by revolutionists." After the long series of ten miserable failures such news must have been exciting. We can picture the solitary unrecognized Chinese in foreign clothing poring over a too-scanty despatch. What should he do under the circumstances? He might go directly westward to China; he could reach Shanghai in twenty days. He concluded his service was not on the battlefield, and bought a ticket for New York. At St. Louis he saw another newspaper which carried the statement that the revolution had broken out at the order of Sun Yat-sen, that the revolutionists were going to set up a republican form of government, and that the first President would be Sun Yat-sen. Was there ever news more personally significant read by an unrecognized traveler? If any one on the train had discovered who he was, newspapermen would have been hot on his trail for interviews. He did not divulge his identity.

Sun Yat-sen's thoughts were on the international relations of the projected republic; it would need friends among the nations. American public opinion, he knew, was favorable to China. It was the United States that had championed the "open-door policy" and had brought the other nations to a new way of thinking. American sympathy was instinctively with the republican venture. In France both the government and the people were friendly. Germany and Russia were pro-Manchu, and in these countries Sun Yat-sen had no entrée to either people or government. In Japan he had found friendly people, but the government was not favorable toward the Chinese revolution. Japan's power to act was not, however, unrestricted; the Anglo-Japanese Alliance had been recently renewed. Clearly Britain was the key to the diplomatic future of the yet unborn republic. There the people were sympathetic; of the government's policy Sun Yat-sen could not feel sure; it would be bound up with the policy of Japan. So he decided to go on at once to England and there do what he could for the emerging republic through diplomacy.

As he traveled he avoided publicity, knowing well the inconveniences of it. He, the arch-revolutionist and potential President of China, slipped out of America quietly. He was helped no doubt by his Chinese friends who knew how to keep him hidden.

When he reached London, he came into public notice. His good friends, Dr. and Mrs. Cantlie, were anticipating his arrival; telegrams had been coming for him in their care for some weeks, and they had been instructed to open them. One telegram in cipher addressed "Sun Wen, London," had been marked "Try Chinese Legation" and delivered there. After being opened, read and annotated with certain Chinese characters, it was sent to the Cantlie home with the inquiry whether the person to whom it was addressed was stopping there. Mrs. Cantlie, to whom the telegram was carried, fearing some evil intention on the part of the Legation spies, warily made a copy of the telegram, and then returned it with the word that Sun Wen was not with them. Two hours later Sun Yat-sen walked in. Mrs. Cantlie gave him the copy of the ciphered telegram, which he glanced at with a smile and put in his pocket. Next day she learned that it was an invitation to him to return to China with the prospect of becoming President of the Republic.

Sun Yat-sen's concern in England was chiefly over fiscal matters; he also wanted to hinder Japan from going to the assistance of the Manchus, and to get a revocation of his own exclusion from British colonies. The policy of making political loans to China through international banking groups had begun in 1908. In 1911 a Four-Power Consortium Loan for railway construction had been concluded. The bonds were already issued, and the cash was ready to be paid before Sun Yat-sen arrived in London. Another loan to the Manchus had not progressed so far. Sun Yat-sen put in a plea for diversion of this loan to the Republic. The president of the Consortium replied that a regular government recognized by foreign powers would receive consideration.

It was while he was in London that Homer Lea made another junction with him. This military theoretician had gone to Europe a few months earlier to better his health. When he heard that an adventure was on for China he was eager to be part of it. It was soon bruited about that Homer Lea was to be Sun Yat-sen's Chief Military Adviser. When the little that could be done was accomplished in London, Sun Yat-sen went, on November 11th, to Paris, where he met cordiality—notably from Clemenceau. He sailed from Marseilles on a P. and O. boat; Homer Lea was aboard, a passenger also for China. He is mentioned in more than one of the press despatches by which the world was kept in touch with Sun Yat-sen en route. This trip was to be the last adventure of this oddly adventurous man. At Singapore a crowd was waiting on the wharf to welcome Sun Yat-sen. He was taken ashore to spend the night with a wealthy Chinese friend. At Hongkong Sun Yat-sen was able, for the first time in sixteen years, to land freely; the press interviewed him about his hopes for China.

DOCUMENTATION OF QUOTED PASSAGES

[1] Woo: *The Kuomintang and the Future of the Chinese Revolution* (London, 1928) p. 24. [2] T'ang Leang-li: *The Foundations of Modern China* (London, 1928) p. 147. [3] Restarick: *Sun Yat Sen, Liberator of China* (New Haven, 1931) p. 100. [4] Linebarger: *The Gospel of Chung Shan* (Paris, 1932) p. 43. [5] Sun Yat-sen: *Tzu Chuan,* See Hsü: *Sun Yat-sen,* p. 67. [6] Ball: Things Chinese (Hongkong, 1892) p. 362: "Societies, Secret." [7] Woo: *The Kuomintang and the Future of the Chinese Revolution* (London, 1928) p. 51. [8] Direct translation from the Chinese text found in Wang Tien-hen: *Sun Chung-shan Chih Shih.* [9] Ibid. [10] Barker: "Dr. Sun Yat Sen and the Chinese Revolution," *Fortnightly Review* (London, November, 1911) Vol. 96, p. 779.

SOURCES AND AUTHORITIES: See Appendix C, p. 399.

CHAPTER V

The Defeat of Optimism

SUN YAT-SEN was never more admirable in personality and character than at the time the revolution was realized. His better self speaks without hesitation from every picture of the period. An unsuspicious optimism softens the face, whose strength is struggle-born. The slightly pompous but determined tilt of the head backward suggests that what he had won he had fought for, and meant to preserve. The weakness of his mouth is a secret in the keeping of his twirled mustache. His countenance is suffused with ethical earnestness, a little too consciously cherished. Stubborn of jowl but beneficent of expression; of good will toward men but stiff-necked toward misguided men; his qualities are at their best balance.

An impression of him, penned in 1911, describes him as

A man of medium height, slight but wiry . . . forty-five years old. He speaks good English. He is very quiet and reserved in manner, and extremely moderate, cautious and thoughtful in speech. He gives the impression of being rather a sound and thorough than a brilliant man, rather a thinker than a man of action.[1]

A large deputation of admirers met Sun Yat-sen at the steamer when he arrived at Shanghai on Dec. 24, 1911. They were photographed with him on the ship before his landing. His third and last world tour was over. For the past three years he had been seeking out his overseas countrymen wherever they could be found in groups; he had been patiently indoctrinating them with his revolutionary ideals and plans and gathering them into the Revolutionary Brotherhood. What money he raised seems to have been despatched from time to time to the headquarters instead of accumulating in his keeping. The first question the reporters asked him at Shanghai was about the large sum which rumor said he was bringing to the new republic. This rumor he had to deny over and over. He said he was bringing only one thing, the revolutionary spirit.

One can imagine his inward elation on being told that the peace conference between the North and the South seemed to be working out favorably for a republican government; proposals had been forwarded to Peking and were being considered there. Furthermore an important gathering was on the point of meeting at Nanking, a Council, the summons for which had been issued more than a month earlier, of representatives of all the provinces that had declared their independence. On December 29th this body met, and, without waiting for the consummation of parleys with the North, elected Sun Yat-sen Provisional President by sixteen out of seventeen votes.

New Year's Day, 1912, he was inaugurated President at Nanking in Western style by taking an oath of office—an innovation in the history of Chinese government. He issued an edict proclaiming the Republic, and characteristically combined with it an adoption of the Western solar calendar in place of the ancient Chinese lunar system. In consequence all the subsequent "years of the republic" are reckoned from January first. To change by proclamation an age-old system of government and an ancient tradition of reckoning time was, indeed, the assumption of power! But to Sun Yat-sen, and to the revolutionists generally, all things seemed possible at the moment. In his revolutionary *Autobiography,* which is cut short at this point, the final words are: "On that day I saw the successful accomplishment of the great ambition for which I had struggled during thirty years, the restoration of China, and the establishment of a Republic."

Sun Yat-sen's American "military adviser" saw his hero made Provisional President; but before the North and the South could see things eye to eye, Homer Lea was critically ill in Shanghai—an illness from which he never recovered. Early in the spring he was taken home to California in a helpless state, and died before the first "year of the republic" was over. Exit Sun Yat-sen's futile Lafayette! With all his strategic acuteness Homer Lea seems never to have grasped the significance of party cleavage among the Chinese: he became the champion in turn of two parties that were antagonistic in their purpose and policy. He served the monarchist reformers first, and later allied himself with the most irreconcilable anti-Manchu republican; thereby he endeared himself to neither side. He is not so much as mentioned in Sun Yat-sen's Chinese *Autobiography*.

In January the Provisional President formed his Cabinet and made some progress in organization at Nanking. To reassure the world, edicts were issued promising protection to foreigners and regard for China's existing diplomatic and financial contracts. One matter Sun Yat-sen could make little headway with—the financing of his government. Since his presidency was by definition temporary, European financiers would not make loans to him. He got some funds, however, from Japan, giving the security which the Japanese required: a mortgage on the iron works, which had been established opposite Hankow by the enterprise of Viceroy Chang Chih-tung, the man who wrote the sensationally successful pamphlet, *A Charge to Learn*. The Japanese were acute enough to see that, whatever might become of the loan, they would be assured of a supply of iron, a product Japan lacked and greatly needed for modern developments.

Religious toleration was promised by the new Republic. To the always friendly Dr. and Mrs. Cantlie Sun Yat-sen wrote from Nanking:

> I thank you for your earnest prayers offered on my behalf. I am glad to tell you that we are going to have religious toleration in China, and I am sure that Christianity will flourish under the new régime.[2]

Sun Yat-sen's conception of religious toleration seems to have been protection for the religion of the West. He made a simultaneous attack upon what he covered by the word "superstition," issuing orders encouraging the destruction of idols and idol temples. An outbreak of iconoclasm resulted, during which many ancient images were burned or thrown into the rivers. Temples were in some cases taken over by the civil authorities to be used as schools. Missionary-minded people everywhere were congratulating themselves that Sun Yat-sen was a Christian. A biographical sketch, which had a large sale in China in 1912, referred to Sun Yat-sen's Christian training, to his belief in God, his habits of prayer and his friendship with Dr. Cantlie. It was a matter of comment that there were not a few Christians among the leading spirits of the new Republic. *The Missionary Herald* of Boston published the statement that Sun Yat-sen's "private secretary, his son, at least three of his cabinet members, the president and the vice-president of the Assembly at Nanking and twenty-five per cent of the members were professing Christians." In Sun Yat-sen's own province, Kwangtung, sixty-five per cent of the new officials were said to be Christians.

But what about the North? The Emperor was still on his throne. A National Assembly, constitutionally created, had made Yuan Shih-kai Premier, and the Premier had sent his representative to Shanghai to conduct a peace conference. The revolutionists had then taken the bit in their teeth and had elected a president and made a republic. A deadlock resulted. The North was not willing to accept a republic with Sun Yat-sen as president. His revolutionary history made him unwelcome to the remnant of the monarchists. Besides, he was a Cantonese. Regional jealousy—always to be reckoned with in Chinese affairs—was a real element in this situation. Moreover, Sun Yat-sen was totally inexperienced in government. The revolutionists, on their part, did not wish to fail of their end—the overthrow of the Manchus. A republic that was not complete might come to much grief. Unless a settlement could be found civil war was inevitable and the outcome by no means certain. Sun Yat-sen had to make a choice between the failure of his revolutionary ambition to overthrow the Manchus, and the obliteration of himself in favor of a China united around Yuan Shih-kai. He does not seem to have hesitated. If he had any inward battle over the renunciation it never came to light. On January 15th he telegraphed to Yuan Shih-kai offering him the presidency; the offer was conditioned upon abdication of the Emperor, and, on Yuan Shih-kai's part, a complete break with the Manchus and acceptance of the Republic.

Yuan Shih-kai held out a little longer for a more orderly decision by a national convention properly summoned and constituted. But as disorders increased in many quarters, and the treasury of the Empire ran low, the time element became important. To get a national convention together was a long process. On January 28th a neatly timed memorial came to the Throne signed by all the Imperial generals and commanders outside of Peking urging abdication for cogent reasons:

The People's Army has announced its readiness to provide for the Imperial Family. It offers them splendid treatment and glorious honors. . . . Why not accept these conditions? The Imperial Army can no longer be reinforced, while the People's Army is being reinforced daily. All China is now in favor of a Republic, including a majority of the Princes. Only a few of the younger Princes object, and they do not produce money to carry on the struggle. The morale of the soldiers is being destroyed, because they are not being paid. Therefore we think the National Convention ought not to be waited for. Its results would be a foregone conclusion. We think it best for the Throne to accept the terms now offered and to abdicate immediately.[3]

This opportune memorial made it easy for Yuan Shih-kai to advise the then ruling Empress Dowager—a compliant woman compared with her famous predecessor—that abdication was unavoidable. On February 12th Imperial edicts consummated the retirement. Their wording shows the state of public opinion and the compromise of the factions:

It is now evident that the majority of the people are in favor of a Republic. From the preference that is in the people's hearts the will of Heaven is discernible. How could we oppose the desires of millions for the glory of one family? Therefore we, the Empress Dowager and the Emperor, hereby vest the sovereignty in the people. Let Yuan Shih-kai organize with full powers a Provisional Republic and confer with the Republicans as to the methods of union that will assure peace to the Empire, thus forming a great Republic by the union of Manchus, Chinese, Mongols, Mohammedans and Tibetans.[4]

At once Yuan Shih-kai sent a telegram announcing the inception of the Republic. It was addressed to President Sun, the National Council, and the Cabinet at Nanking. He says:

A Republic is the best form of government. The whole world admits this. That in one leap we have passed from autocracy to republicanism is really the outcome of many years of strenuous efforts exerted by you all, and is the greatest blessing to the people. . . . Henceforth, forever, we shall not allow a monarchical government in our country. . . .[5]

The saying of it could not have been handsomer. Yet one thing about the edicts did not please the Nanking group. They did not like the Republic to be a gift from the Throne, nor the power of its executive to be derived from appointment by the Emperor. This point Sun Yat-sen contested. "The Republican government cannot," he said, "be organized by any authority conferred by the Ching Emperor. The exercise of such pretentious power must surely lead to serious trouble." Yuan Shih-kai assured him that he did not intend to construe the edicts in this way, but would follow the wishes of the republicans. On February 13th, Sun Yat-sen submitted his resignation to the Nanking Council in a formal message:

Today I present you my resignation and request you to elect a good and talented man as the new President. . . . The abdication of the Ching Emperor and the union of the North and the South is largely due to the great exertions of Mr. Yuan. Moreover he has declared his unconditional adhesion to the national cause. Should he be elected to serve the Republic, he would surely prove himself a most loyal servant of the State. Besides, Mr. Yuan is a man of political experience, upon whose constructive ability our united nation looks forward to the consolidation of its interests. . . .[6]

The next day the National Council at Nanking elected Yuan Shih-kai Provisional President. If Yuan Shih-kai's nomination for the Presidency can be said to have come from the abdicating Imperial family, it came equally from Sun Yat-sen; and his constitutional election was the work of nobody but the republican revolutionists themselves, assembled in their own National Council at Nanking. If in this their judgment was bad, that must appear in the developing history. If they had not chosen Yuan Shih-kai, who else was there to choose? He was the outstanding candidate for the office. Sun Yat-sen was retiring—as he was in honor bound to do when the abdication became a fact. He was a theorist pure and simple. He had never administered so much as a county; how could he be expected to administer a country? On the other hand Yuan

Shih-kai had a long and brilliant record of official life. He had proved himself a strong Governor and Viceroy. With equal ability he could assume the command of armies or be Prime Minister. There were few men in practical politics as progressive as he. And there was no other progressive who had the confidence of the Manchu rulers in sufficient degree to lead their reluctant steps along the road to abdication. He seemed the man of the hour—one whose career had specially fitted him for the responsibility of steering China through the transition from a monarchy to a republic. Although he had served the Imperial family well, circumstances now gave him greater power than his masters. That he was *persona non grata* with the monarchist reformers created a predisposition in his favor among the revolutionists: it is often true that common enmities are the making of alliances. So, when Yuan Shih-kai actually delivered to the revolutionists the abdication they had demanded, the republican National Council repaid Yuan Shih-kai with the Presidency.

II. THE EXALTED MOOD OF SUCCESS

China had become a Republic. The Empire with several thousands of years of glorious history had voluntarily erased itself. The results as Sun Yat-sen analyzed them in *China's Revolution* were these: by the overthrow of the dynasty the country was washed clean of a corrupt political régime and the races were made equal; despotism having been got rid of, democracy had begun.

Everywhere there was congratulation. The young were tingling with patriotic enthusiasm. Talk of reforms and prophecy of rapid change were widespread. Add to all this the decided alteration in the outward appearance of the whole people as the result of cutting off the queues—now condemned as the symbol of Manchu domination—and no one can fail to understand the remark that came over and over to the lips of foreigners and Chinese alike: "We are living in a new China!" Sun Yat-sen was in a mood of great exaltation in which everything was thought of idealistically and hopefully. Of personal ambition he seems to have had little consciousness; his ambition had been attained. What he had been thinking of as the possible culmination of a life's work had fallen into his hands when he was forty-five. At the end of *My Reminiscences* he expresses his feeling:

> I have done my work; the wave of enlightenment and progress cannot now be stayed, and China—the country in the world most fitted to be a republic, because of the industrious and docile character of the people—will, in a short time, take her place amongst the civilized and liberty-loving nations of the world.[7]

It is next to impossible for us, at this date, to recapture the optimism that possessed the Chinese Republic at the beginning. Our perception of the impracticability of its policies has been so sharpened that it is difficult to credit even the leaders with the optimism that their words and actions so clearly expressed. The Kuomintang historians yield to temptation and project backward into the optimistic months the suspicions that were developed in the later conflict, painting as foresights what were actually disillusionments. In this connection it is well to remember what Sun Yat-sen's most extravagant hero-worshipper says: "His only faults were over-credulity and generosity." Against the reading of history backward we must place the evidences of Sun Yat-sen's almost hectic optimism.

On the day after Yuan Shih-kai's election as President, Sun Yat-sen was the central figure in a picturesque procession to the Ming Tombs, which lie on a slope of the imposing hills outside of Nanking. Up the long avenue, lined with stone images of animals and warriors, they went—President, Cabinet, civil and military officials and a large escort of modern-trained soldiers of the Republic. The ceremony they were bent on was a reversion to an old form observed in ancestral worship—a considerate informing of the spirits of the dead concerning events in which they might be presumed to take an interest. This pageantry was the logical conclusion of the anti-dynastic propaganda of the revolution and must have been particularly full of sentiment to those who inherited Ming-loyalist traditions.

Facing the tomb of the founder of the Ming dynasty, himself a revolutionist, buried there a hundred years before Columbus discovered America, Sun Yat-sen addressed to his spirit a rhetorical account of the Republican Revolution. Full of feeling, this so-called "Prayer" had the good fortune to be well translated into English and was published to all the world. To the Western world the incident appeared incongruous with pretensions to an enlightened republic. But to Sun Yat-sen, without a doubt, it was an act of intense emotional exaltation. Looked at from a distance it now seems a symbol, little realized at the moment, of the hold of old tradition upon the men gathered there in smart Western military uniforms and with hearts intent upon "modernizing" China. In the address the Manchu rulers were given a public castigation:

From a bad eminence of glory basely won, they lorded it over this most holy soil, and our beloved China's rivers and hills were defiled by their corrupting touch, while the people fell victims to the headsman's axe or the avenging sword. Although worthy patriots and faithful subjects of your dynasty crossed the mountain ranges into Canton and the far south, in the hope of redeeming the glorious Ming tradition from utter ruin, and of prolonging a thread of the old dynasty's life, although men gladly perished one after another in the forlorn attempt, Heaven's wrath remained unappeased, and mortal designs failed to achieve success. A brief and melancholy page was added to the history of your dynasty, and that was all.[8]

After reviewing various insurrections made against the Manchu dynasty without success, Sun Yat-sen approaches the present:

Although these worthy causes were destined to ultimate defeat, the gradual trend of the national will became manifest. At last our own era dawned, the sun of freedom had risen, and a sense of the rights of the race animated men's minds. In addition the Manchu bandits could not even protect themselves. Powerful foes encroached upon the territory of China, and the dynasty parted with our sacred soil to enrich neighbouring nations. The Chinese race today may be degenerate, but it is descended from mighty men of old. How should it endure that the spirits of the great dead should be insulted by the everlasting visitation of this scourge?

Then did patriots arise like a whirlwind or like a cloud which is suddenly manifested in the firmament. They began with the Canton insurrection . . . rising followed rising all over the Empire. . . . One failure followed another, but other brave men took the place of the heroes who died, and the Empire was born again to life. The bandit Manchu Court was shaken with pallid terror, until the cicada shook off its shell in a glorious regeneration, and the present crowning triumph was achieved. . . . An earthquake shook the barbarian court of Peking, and it was smitten with a paralysis. Today it has at last restored the Government to the Chinese people, and the five races of China may dwell together in peace and mutual trust. Let us joyfully give thanks. How could we have attained this measure of victory had not your Majesty's soul in heaven bestowed upon us your protecting influence? . . .

I have heard that in the past many would-be deliverers of their country have ascended this lofty mound wherein is your sepulchre. It has served to them as a holy inspiration. As they looked down upon the surrounding rivers and upward to the hills, under an alien sway they wept in the bitterness of their hearts, but today their sorrow is turned into joy. . . . Your legions line the approaches to the sepulchre: a noble host stands expectant. Your people have come here today to inform your Majesty of the final victory. May this lofty shrine wherein you rest gain fresh lustre from today's event and may your example inspire your descendants in the times which are to come. Spirit! Accept this offering! [9]

III. TRIUMPHAL PROGRESS

Not until April was Sun Yat-sen able to lay down the government and leave Nanking. There were formalities to be gone through. It was fitting that distinguished representatives should go from Nanking to Peking to inform Yuan Shih-kai of his election and to escort him to Nanking for inauguration. The plan was that Nanking should be the scene of the inauguration and the seat of the government. The move was frustrated by a serious riot in Peking, which Yuan Shih-kai has been strongly suspected of having adroitly staged to prove the impracticability of his withdrawal from the north. In the north he could better conserve his power. The republicans yielded the capital temporarily to Peking, and on March 10th Yuan Shih-kai was inaugurated there. On the same day the National Council at Nanking adopted a Provisional Constitution which at this time was expected to be only short-lived. Sun Yat-sen and his Cabinet laid down the seals of office on April 1st and the transfer to Yuan Shih-kai was complete.

Sun Yat-sen had his plans made to return to Canton; he mentions them in a letter to Mrs. Cantlie dated at Nanking, March 12, 1912, from the President's office:

It is true that the Tai Ching dynasty is "a thing of the past," but the dethronement of the Manchus does not mean the complete salvation of China. We have an enormous amount of work ahead of us, and it must be accomplished in order that she may be ranked as a great power among the family of nations. . . .

I am going to Canton shortly and there try to convert the old city into a new and modern one.

My family is in Nanking with me. My son will return to America for his education, and I am contemplating sending my elder daughter along with her brother for the same purpose.[10]

Wherever Sun Yat-sen went in the succeeding months he was received with enthusiasm. Many receptions were given him and he did much public speaking. He was in Foochow on April 21st, and there addressed large popular and student audiences. He also consented to preach a sermon, and his theme was "The Mission of the Church in Rebuilding the Nation." Among the photographs of the spring of 1912 are several quite different groups taken on various occasions when he was the guest of honor. One shows him at a gathering in Canton, April 29th, of the "Model Army" organized by Chinese overseas members of the Revolutionary Brotherhood. Very smart soldiers they look, in their modern uniforms—several hundred of them—banked behind the row of distinguished guests. Another shows Sun Yat-sen and his wife at a reception on May 9th given by an international group of Christian missionaries in Canton. In a third photo he appears as the guest of the Oriental Medical Association at Hongkong.

After many years of speaking to Chinese abroad Sun Yat-sen now entered upon the career of an influential public speaker in China. This was an ultra-modern rôle and one in which he had few rivals; such public speaking does not derive from elder Chinese custom. Sun Yat-sen in his youth contemplated the career of a Christian preacher. He became, instead, China's preacher-at-large, and his flair for addressing audiences never left him. Two descriptions of him as a speaker may be quoted, the first from a British observer and the second from an American.

He does not care to use the dramatic eloquence which appeals to the imagination and the passions of the masses, and which is usually found in political and religious reformers of the ordinary kind. . . . I have heard Dr. Sun addressing a meeting of his own countrymen. He spoke quietly and almost monotonously with hardly any gestures, but the intent way in which his audience listened to every word—his speeches occupy often three and four hours— . . . showed me the powerful effect which he was able to exercise. . . .[11]

Dr. Sun is a short, stocky man, deliberate in his movements and very gentle in his manners. He was dressed in a plain white duck suit, with no ornaments or orders. When he began to address the audience, he did not make a gesture; as he proceeded he made a few, but spoke with moderation, showing that he was not at all puffed up by his success. In his address he briefly outlined the steps he believed necessary to ensure a stable government.[12]

Certain foreign books and journals of the period report that Sun Yat-sen was advocating a socialistic program for China. The Chinese sources say that he spoke on the Three Principles of the People. Few, indeed, were the Occidentals who, at this time, had taken notice of the Three Principles. Even the better informed among them knew little about the basis of the Revolutionary Brotherhood. They could not well understand how socialistic Sun Yat-sen actually was.

The climax of Sun Yat-sen's popular reception was his visit to Peking at the invitation of Yuan Shih-kai in the summer of 1912. General Huang Hsing, who was to have accompanied him, turned back even after going aboard the ship, because of reports fresh from the press of the summary execution at Peking of two prominent visiting revolutionists from Wuchang. Sun Yat-sen's friends urged him not to go. He scouted their fears and went.

Things had been going none too smoothly for the young Republic, which was operating ostensibly on the basis of the Provisional Constitution framed at Nanking. Yuan Shih-kai had chosen as Premier a man thoroughly acceptable to the republicans, Tang Shao-yi, who had by this time become a member of the

Revolutionary Brotherhood. The transferred legislature—the National Council with an enlarged representation from each province —had been opened at Peking in the meeting-place of the now superseded National Assembly; ministerial policies were reported and a flag was adopted for the Republic—the five-barred symbol of racial union.

But friction and factions developed very quickly. There was friction between the President and the Premier. Three main factions appeared in the Council, not one of them with a majority. The Cabinet was a coalition body chosen to represent South and North and all parties. First, the Premier came to grief over the negotiations for foreign loans and resigned. Being of his party, a large group of Cabinet members resigned also, protesting that a coalition Cabinet was impossible, that it must be a party cabinet or they would have nothing to do with it. Yuan Shih-kai pleaded for coalition and harmony until the government could be got running, and chose for the new Premier a non-party man. Then a new coalition Cabinet was submitted to the legislature for approval, but every name was voted down. It was only the pressure of outside opinion which brought the Council to the point of accepting a substituted list of ministers.

On Aug. 13, 1912, an important event took place which was really a strategic move to form a party that could control the national legislature. The Revolutionary Brotherhood (*Tung Meng Hui*) was amalgamated with one of the other main factions and with several smaller societies. The group was reorganized as a political party under the name of the Kuomintang—National People's Party. The prime mover in this was the revolutionist who had presided at the founding of the Brotherhood in Tokyo, Sung Chiao-jen, a "modernized" young man, who—like Sun Yat-sen— set tradition at nought and wore a mustache. He had taken a large part in forming the Provisional Constitution. The Kuomintang issued a manifesto setting forth its aims. It is interesting to observe how it digested the socialistic program of the Revolutionary Brotherhood. It was reduced to this statement of object:

To adopt the principles of social service to prepare the way for the introduction of socialism in order to facilitate and better the standard of living, and to employ the powers and strength of the Government quickly and evenly to develop the resources of our country.[13]

The execution, already referred to, of two prominent revolutionists on August 15th caused a great storm in the National Council; it was not over when Sun Yat-sen arrived in Peking before the end of August.

Yuan Shih-kai received Sun Yat-sen and entertained him with royal honors. Luxurious lodgings had been prepared for him in one of the government buildings. The child Emperor's mother, through whom the abdication had been consummated, took thought for Sun Yat-sen's comfort and sent messages. Prince Pu Lun, as her representative, gave him a great feast. This Imperial host was the very prince for whose safety the arch-plotter, Sun Yat-sen, had been held by United States Immigration officers in the detention shed at San Francisco for three weeks in April, 1904. Surely this was a triumphal entry for the rebel into the courts of the Manchus! In addition many societies and clubs entertained him, and he made innumerable speeches.

A meeting was arranged at which he could address his fellow-Christians. In the centrally located grounds of the American Board (Congregational) the church people assembled on September 5th. From all over the city they came and from all the Protestant denominations. Admission was by ticket, yet three hours before the time announced people were arriving. The large church was packed to its limit and crowds gathered outside the gates. An account of the occasion was despatched to America the next day by Dr. Henry S. Martin. He wrote:

Since the establishment of the Republic the Chinese Church has not let an opportunity go by to show its loyal support of the new government. Yesterday's reception to Dr. Sun Yat-sen, given by the united churches of Peking, is added evidence of the fact. The meeting was a happy conclusion of Dr. Sun's complete capture of Peking. . . .

Sun Wen, as he is commonly called in China, is known throughout the country as a loyal believer in the principles of Christianity. His attitude in becoming the guest of the churches and his speech at the reception further confirm this belief. . . .

Dr. Sun's speech . . . the people listened to with the keenest interest. He spoke in southern Mandarin, but was quite easily understood by those who are accustomed to the northern dialect. "Men say" he began "that the revolution originated with me. I do not deny the charge. But where did the idea of the revolution come from? It came because from my youth I have had intercourse with foreign missionaries. Those from Europe and America with whom I associated put the ideals of freedom and liberty into my heart. Now I call upon the church to help in the establishment of the new government. The Republic cannot endure unless there is that virtue—the righteousness for which the Christian religion stands—at the center of the nation's life." [14]

With Yuan Shih-kai, Sun Yat-sen spent much time in conference. It was their first personal acquaintance. Day after day they talked together, the astute mandarin of the old school in his high-soled black satin boots and silken robes, and the dapper little revolutionist, whom we cannot be far wrong in visualizing in an English tropical suit in the August weather. If Yuan Shih-kai felt himself at any disadvantage with this product of Western education and world travel, we may be sure he never showed it, unless the more gracefully to flatter his guest. He agreed so affably with the earnest

expositor of republican ideals and republican technique that Sun
Yat-sen went out of his gate proclaiming him a great man, well
fitted for the presidency. When Sun Yat-sen prepared a report of
the visit for the Western press, he said:

I told him very frankly my ideas upon many important matters that
were then to the fore. We discussed at length the six-Power loan, as
it had been called, and the terms upon which it should be made and
accepted. We also went into the matter of the relief of distress, the
organization of political parties, the teaching of civil science to the
people, the disposal of government mines and lands, the project of
opening vast tracts of agricultural lands for settlement and other matters
of import.

At the same time President Yuan gave out a very complete statement
of his views on many of these questions, and while his expressed opinions were his own, they embodied very largely my own views on the
various topics. Almost to the last word of that statement my own views
were in accord with those of the President.[15]

The subject which Sun Yat-sen had most upon his mind was railway development. He took advantage of the visit to present a great
scheme of railway extension, proposing to construct 75,000 miles of
government railway in ten years at a cost of three billion dollars
gold. He advocated the solicitation of foreign capital. Yuan Shih-kai
gave the project his approval, and appointed Sun Yat-sen head of
railway development for the whole of China, and instructed him
to draft plans, submit them to foreign financiers and then report
to the government for approval. An appropriation of 30,000 Chinese
dollars a month was granted him on which to make this beginning.
Yuan Shih-kai may have thought of this appointment as a sinecure
—a sop to his rival—or, as some have suggested, a bribe for his
support. But there is no trace of that construction by Sun Yat-sen;
he took the position very seriously. The testimony from more than
one source is that at this time he had made up his mind to leave

the political field to Yuan Shih-kai and devote himself to the economic development of his country. He partially revealed his idealistic purpose in an article in the *Independent* Sept. 19, 1912:

At present I am more interested in the social regeneration of my country than I am in questions of party and politics. Having finished the task of bringing about a political revolution, I am now devoting my thought and energies to the reconstruction of the country in its social, industrial and commercial conditions. I have seen enough of the discord between capital and labor in Western countries, and the misery that besets the multitudes of the poor, that I am desirous of forestalling such conditions in China. With industrial development there will come an increase of manufacturing, and with the change of conditions there is a danger of widely separating the working classes and those who possess the capital. I wish to see the masses of the people improved in their conditions rather than to help a few to add power to themselves until they become financial autocrats.[16]

Sun Yat-sen's Peking visit continued into September, and contributed much toward better feeling in the Republic. He made visits also to Kalgan, Taiyuanfu, Tsinan and Tsingtao. It was as a result of the trip north that he addressed a communication "To the Friends of China in the United States of America," which was intended to remove the impression—by no means unfounded—that disruptive forces were already at work in the new Republic. This was published in the New York *Sun,* Sept. 24, 1912. Parts are worth quoting to show the high altitudes to which Sun Yat-sen's optimism could soar:

I wish to go on record once and for all as saying that in spite of the efforts, past or future, of the enemies of the Chinese Republic there will be no civil war in our country. . . .

Foreign ill-wishers may as well understand first as last—perhaps better now—that the men who are at the forefront of Chinese affairs are a unit for the Republic as established and cannot be brought, individually or in factions, to oppose the onward march of the Chinese nation. Neither flattery, fear, intrigue, nor gold has the power to make the leaders of the new China, nor any one of them, turn back the hopes, wishes and aspirations of our people. . . .

President Yuan Shih-kai is the head of the nation, the strong, worthy leader of his people, and I am not authorized to speak for him, for his Cabinet or for the National Assembly; but I believe I am voicing the sentiment of a united and unanimous people when I warn trouble-makers at home or abroad, that the Chinese Nation has joined the great family of republics to remain a member thereof at whatever cost or sacrifice. . . .

Perhaps it is almost superfluous for me to say that the most pressing need of China today is her establishment upon a sound financial basis. The country is in need of a large sum in order that the wheels of government machinery may revolve without friction. . . . It is but a question of time—six or eight years perhaps—that, even without a great national loan, the affairs of the country will be upon a satisfactory financial basis. . . .

Now that the country is again at peace, excepting in certain remote and unimportant districts, I look for a big increase in commerce, domestic and foreign, with consequent well being in agriculture, manufacturing and the various other industries. With the people everywhere working, with peace at north, south, east and west, the country is bound to be prosperous and the Government stable and substantial.[17]

Was there ever an optimist so utterly mistaken? Kuomintang historians would have us believe today that Sun Yat-sen mistrusted Yuan Shih-kai from the beginning. What does evidence such as this mean? Surely Sun Yat-sen was not trying to gull the Western public into believing something he knew to be false! He may have had his lapses from the truth, but he was no such ignoble charlatan as that would make him. When, later, he knew he had a quarrel with Yuan Shih-kai, he kept the cables hot with advertisement of the conflict. No! The Sun Yat-sen of 1912 was not the suspicious and sometimes vituperative Sun Yat-sen that the Kuomintang remembers best. The Sun Yat-sen of the first year of the Republic was magnanimous to a fault, and pathetically trustful. With him it was a point of honor to believe; and in whom would he be more likely to believe than in Yuan Shih-kai—a man of much experience in the affairs of government, tested administrator of great areas, disciplinarian of modernized armies? Something deep in Sun Yat-sen's own heart would have been happier, and China's history would have been unrecognizably different, if he could have affirmed the same experience and ability of himself. The wording of the press despatch may be the facile English of some deft collaborator, but the too-great-faith of it was Sun Yat-sen's.

IV. A FLATTERING FRIEND

Sun Yat-sen's side-trips while in the north were associated with observation of the railways for whose development he now became responsible. And the railways were worth seeing. China's great railway expansion had taken place in the decade preceding the Republic; comparatively little railway-building has been done since. Sun Yat-sen was able to travel over hundreds of miles of regularly operating roads. The line to Kalgan was opened in 1909. Shansi was connected with the Peking area in 1907. Through trains connecting Tientsin and Nanking had been put on in June, 1912. Tsingtao, which he also visited, was a striking example of harbor development under German enterprise. After about a month of travel and observation Sun Yat-sen returned to central China and set up his bureau of railway development in Shanghai, instead of in Peking as might have been expected.

While still in Peking Sun Yat-sen had spoken publicly on railway policies at a function given in his honor by the National Railway Union, advocating far-flung arterial lines running out much beyond the bounds of the eighteen provinces. Characteristically he thought in terms of a glamourous program; ten ambitious years, two of which were to be spent in negotiating loans, three in surveys, and five in construction. He figured that, with two million laborers and five-years time, 75,000 miles of track could be constructed at a cost of three billion dollars gold.

How far these plans became concrete during the months when he was Director-General of Railway Development can be judged only indirectly: they seem never to have reached the formulation of a report. Their nature, however, can be inferred from the projects which Sun Yat-sen later published in Chinese periodicals and collected in an English volume, issued in 1920, under the title *The International Development of China.* In forty-nine pages he there presents maps and plans for five huge railway systems with an estimated length of 100,000 miles. Yuan Shih-kai's instructions were to draft plans, approach foreign financiers, and report to the Chinese government. With the liberal appropriation of 30,000 Chinese dollars a month Sun Yat-sen could work without handicap.

Though not publicly stated, it was probably in pursuance of the railway program that Sun Yat-sen set out for Japan in February, 1913. There he traveled in a private car furnished by the courtesy of the Imperial Japanese Railways. "I am here to study industrial conditions and the people, as well as to observe other things," he told a reporter. Inasmuch as Sun Yat-sen had spent years in Japan, in may be presumed that he was already well-informed about industrial conditions and the people. It is more probable that he wished to sound financiers about the capital for developing railways in China.

It should be recalled that ever since his first flight from China in 1896 Sun Yat-sen had been experiencing in one way or another the friendship of the Japanese. After he had cut off his queue and had donned European clothes, he had added another touch which was in effect a Japanese disguise—a mustache. That his Japanese appearance was serviceable has already been noted elsewhere.

From 1899 to 1903, Sun Yat-sen had lived almost continuously in Japan. This period of obscure exile was his major opportunity to observe and study the "modernization" of an oriental people. Moreover, the Japanese helped him from time to time in his revolutionary attempts by furnishing him money, military experts, ammunition. After his second world-wandering he returned to Japan in 1905, organized the Revolutionary Brotherhood there, and left only when the notorious activities of his organization made the Manchus insistent that Japan should not harbor him any longer. Even after his expulsion in 1907 he could slip quietly back into Japan for short periods. In a reminiscent mood Premier Inukai said in 1932:

For a time Sun Yat-sen lived with me. My house was a secret meeting place for the revolutionists. Often they shared my food and clothes and even my meagre income. None could have been more jubilant than I was, when the new republic sounded the knell of the Manchu dynasty.[18]

In his *Autobiography* Sun Yat-sen made generous acknowledgment of the help of Inukai and other Liberal politicians, also naming famous Japanese financiers, all of whom had aided and abetted him in his revolutionary attempts. "We must wait," he says, "for the official history of the Chinese Revolution to record in greater detail the invaluable work of our Japanese friends."

It is interesting to note that an alias, under which Sun Yat-sen avoided publicity in Japan, has become his posthumous name in China. An American journalist, George Lynch (already quoted), had found him at the end of 1900 hiding under an assumed name, Nakayama. Two simple Chinese characters, in common use also in the Japanese language, make the name, which is pronounced in Japanese Nakayama and in Chinese Chung-shan. Sun Yat-sen is respectfully referred to in China today as Sun Chung-shan, or simply Chung-shan, not without popular interpretation of the suggestive figure: it is explained that Sun Yat-sen's place in the Republic is like the *central mountain* towering over everything else.

One of the most serious charges against Sun Yat-sen's statesmanship is that during his tenure of the presidency he mortgaged the big iron works six hundred miles up the Yangtze River at Hanyang to Japanese, as security for funds loaned. This has given the Japanese an uncomfortable hold upon the iron industry of China. Sun Yat-sen was in Japan in 1913 for the very purpose of promoting other loans from the Japanese, the outcome of which for China would probably have been just as regrettable. It is fortunate that what he accomplished did not correspond with what he aimed to do.

In Japan Sun Yat-sen was given such an ovation as must have made him wonder how the hunted exile could have changed to a glorified visitor in so short a time. Three thousand Chinese students, including hundreds of girls, met him at the Tokyo railway station, February 14th, and gave him a rousing welcome. From that moment on he was kept busy—in Tokyo and in other cities—with a full program of entertainments, meetings, receptions and feasts, given him by boards of trade, banks, public bodies and organizations in variety. At these he was a speaking guest. He left Moji, March 18th, expressing regret that the hospitalities in his honor had prevented his inspection of the Japanese railways. Yet his visit was felt to have been significant. Some thought Sun Yat-sen had come as a personal envoy from President Yuan Shih-kai seeking official recognition for the Chinese Republic. All agreed that the enthusiastic reception everywhere given was expressive of good will toward the new Republic. Speculation was rife as to the true and inward purpose of the visit. A *Reuter* despatch of March 2nd from Tokyo said:

Dr. Sun Yat-sen leaves Tokio on the 5th instant. Owing to the non-recognition of the Chinese Republic by the Powers, Dr. Sun's visit was unofficial and was made ostensibly to thank the Japanese for aid which they rendered during the Revolution. Dr. Sun is generally regarded, however, as representing President Yuan Shih-kai and it is considered that his real intention, which is hardly concealed, is the initiation of a commercial understanding between Japan and China and the development later of a political *entente* between the two countries. In his numerous speeches Dr. Sun Yat-sen emphasized the dependence of China upon Japan for the maintenance of peace in the Far East, for preserving the integrity of the territories of the Republic, for the creation of an efficient administration, and for the development of industries and commerce.

Great results are anticipated as a result of numerous conferences between Dr. Sun Yat-sen and Japanese capitalists, to whom important concessions were offered. The Japanese press is unanimous in regarding Dr. Sun's visit as potential of vast commercial and political developments in the future.

Yesterday the initial meeting took place of the leaders of the proposed Sino-Japanese Commercial Trust Company. Among those present were representatives of the First Bank, the Hundredth Bank, the Yokohama Specie Bank, the Yasuda Bank, Messrs. K. Okura and Co., The Mitsu Bishi Company, and the Mitsu Bussan Company. The proposed company will have a capital of £1,000,000 and will interest itself principally in railway construction.[19]

Exactly contrary to the policy that underlies such activities is the *Reuter* report of sixteen days later (March 18th) that at Moji, when about to leave Japan, Sun Yat-sen "stated that he was determined to finance Chinese railways by means of domestic loans only, and advocated the reclamation of rights for railway construction and control which had been granted to foreigners in various treaties."

How account for what looks like a reversal of policy on Sun Yat-sen's part? Had his negotiations with Japanese capitalists so disappointed him that he took this way of dismissing them? The policy announced at Moji does not agree with Sun Yat-sen's life-long stand in regard to foreign capital. As late as 1920 he was ad-vocating the use of foreign capital not only for railway construc-tion but for the creation of harbors, for road-building, and for industrial expansion on a very large scale. The query arises: Did Yuan Shih-kai approve of Sun Yat-sen's proposals to Japanese financiers? What had the President been feeling about Sun Yat-sen's policies and popularity in Japan? Was the Director of Railway Development taking his prerogatives too seriously to please the President? For months Yuan Shih-kai's government had been negotiating with an international Consortium for a huge loan—styled the Reorganization Loan—and Japan had joined the bank-ing group. The Consortium had been brought into existence for the purpose of reducing rivalries for concessions by substituting inter-national loans for loans from competitive nations. Moreover, Yuan Shih-kai knew a great deal more about Japanese cunning than Sun Yat-sen did. He had watched Japan's policies in Korea and had learned wariness. In the days when China and Japan were at logger-heads over Korea, Yuan had made difficulties for Japan. Li Hung-chang, then Prime Minister of China, had sent this oncoming young protégé of his to Seoul to hold out for China's interests there. This he did with tenacity and ability, and he thwarted Japan at so many turns that the Japanese never forgave him, and even charged him with having brought on the Sino-Japanese War. Such are the throws of fortune and the self-determinations of strong men that about twenty years later, Yuan Shih-kai, sitting at Peking as President of the Republic of China, was hearing of the ovation given by Japan to a revolutionist who had plotted his first callow conspiracy against the Manchus at the time of the Sino-Japanese War, when Yuan Shih-kai was making an enemy of Japan by serving the Manchus all too well.

V. A QUARREL THAT CAME TO BLOWS

Peking was under a lowering sky. Old enmities were not slow in reappearing, and with them a recrudescence of assassinations. Wang Ching-wei had hardly been released from prison after the Revolution when he took again to terroristic activities—"so as to impress the Peking Government." (The quotation is from a Chinese exponent of Wang Ching-wei's policies.) On Jan. 17, 1912, an attempt had been made on Yuan Shih-kai's life on the streets of Peking. "His morale was temporarily shaken." (Same Chinese authority.)

After Sun Yat-sen's visit of 1912 to Peking, previously described, the National Council did not quarrel; it lapsed gradually into inactivity. Business could not be attended to properly, because too many members were absent. Many went off electioneering to secure their return to the forthcoming fully constituted National Assembly, which was summoned to meet at Peking in March, 1913.

On March 21st the country was startled to hear that the chief organizer of the Kuomintang, previously prominent in the Revolutionary Brotherhood, Sung Chiao-jen, had been shot dead at the railway station in Shanghai just as he was about to board the train for Peking. At that time Sun Yat-sen had not got back from Japan. If, while there, he had been affected by Japanese criticisms of Yuan Shih-kai, and if in addition he had himself come to some clash of policy with the President, the situation he found developing in China on his return was enough to complete the alienation. When he reached Shanghai on March 25th, he received an almost hysterical popular welcome, and the police of the International

Settlement took special precautions for his safety. The Kuomintang newspapers, which had lost no time in accusing the Peking Government of the murder of Sung Chiao-jen, published documents which implicated an official in the Ministry of the Interior. It was a stormy prospect with which the National Assembly convened April 8th with two houses totalling 860 members. The Kuomintang fell short of a majority, but had more members than any other party. The Assembly at once fell to quarreling, first over the election of speakers, then with the government over the Five Power Loan, which Yuan Shih-kai, after many difficulties, was bringing to a conclusion. This was for $125,000,000 gold.

The storm over this so-called "Reorganization Loan," which broke in the National Assembly and presently rocked the country, had not blown up overnight. Money matters had been troubling the Republic since its pre-natal days. The first step toward such a foreign loan was unofficially taken by Sun Yat-sen himself in December, 1911. No sooner had he heard of the success of the Wuchang revolutionists, than he traveled directly from America to London, there to confer with the President of the International Banking Consortium which was handling loans for China. As yet there was no republic; of course there was no provisional president; yet Sun Yat-sen made an effort to deflect the Consortium's loans from the Empire (not yet overthrown) to the republic that was yet to be.

The months that intervened between the Wuchang Revolution of October, 1911, and the inauguration of Yuan Shih-kai, March 10, 1912, were hard months financially for both the old régime and the one struggling to birth. Naturally, the International Banking Group was chary of giving funds to an unaccepted revolutionary government. This tightness toward his administration Sun Yat-sen resented, and he turned to Japan—with an unhappy sequel. No sooner was the abdication of the Emperor completed and Yuan

Shih-kai elected President, than negotiations for a large "Reorganization Loan" were begun with the Consortium: that was on Feb. 27, 1912, while Sun Yat-sen was still in the President's chair. At once the Consortium advanced funds for the current needs of the Republic, not waiting for the completion of a contract. The first advance was for two million taels—more than that many gold dollars. When ex-President Sun Yat-sen visited President Yüan Shih-kai at Peking in August, 1912, the proposed international loan was one of the subjects discussed between them, and it was one of the matters concerning which Sun Yat-sen reported that they saw eye to eye.

For more than a year after Yuan Shih-kai's inauguration the negotiation for the loan dragged on. Many disturbing incidents occurred, and much feeling was aroused. The banking group had its own internal differences. Over and over, its functioning was interrupted by interloping syndicates which secretly made large loans to the Chinese government. When China could not get advances as fast as she wanted from the Consortium, she accepted other offers. But, in spite of notorious competition, the Consortium held out stiffly for difficult terms.

The history of all modern loans made to China is a recital of anomalies. Under the Empire, China's foreign credit had actually to be created by foreigners. Being a uniquely organized nation, China had no conception of the financial technique of the West. Working under Chinese Imperial authorization, an able Briton, Sir Robert Hart, built up for China an efficiently administered and financially productive Maritime Customs Service, which was the very foundation of China's international credit. The Customs Service, under foreign administration, furnished satisfactory security for loans, until the enormous demands made upon it for the Boxer indemnity exhausted what it was then producing. It could not be used for securing a large loan to the Republic. The Consortium made it known that the national salt taxes—commonly referred to as the salt gabelle—would be satisfactory security provided they were brought under the administration of the foreign-controlled Customs Service, or some new service similarly supervised by foreigners. The young Republic was proud and self-confident, and believed that China should, in virtue of the Republican Revolution, be treated as a modern nation. Terms which had been pragmatically accepted by the Empire seemed derogatory to the Republic. Idealists, like Sun Yat-sen and Huang Hsing, came out flatly against foreign supervision of the salt taxes. Agitation against the Consortium grew warm. Some efforts were made to raise funds by domestic subscription. Enthusiasm brought results for a while, but it was realized before long that the total fund obtainable that way was not sufficient for the needs of the new Republic. Other schemes were proposed; they, too, brought in some money, but not enough.

The Consortium continued advances, with an option on the future contract. Nine million taels were advanced within about one month's time in the spring of 1912. In sessions of the National Council (the acting legislature) the whole loan policy was severely criticized. A Cabinet crisis resulted, and the Prime Minister left Peking. In spite of agitation and appeals the Consortium did not soften the terms. It was not until December, 1912, that Yuan Shih-kai's government and the Consortium agreed upon a contract to be submitted to the legislature, the now languishing National Council, which was to be superseded in a few months by a regular parliament. In a secret session of this unsatisfactorily functioning body the contract was passed with amendments. This action Yuan Shih-kai held to be a constitutional authorization of the loan. More hitches occurred in the early months of 1913. (This was the time when Sun Yat-sen was visiting Japan over railway promotion.) On March 11th the Chinese Minister of Finance sent a protest to the Consortium over the delays. Suddenly, a sensational diversion was created on March 16th when President Wilson announced that the United States Government would not approve the participation of American bankers in the loan, on the ground that its conditions compromised the independence of China. This was very gratifying to those who had been protesting the hard terms. As a result the American bankers presently announced their withdrawal from the Consortium. What had been planned as a Six Power Loan became a Five Power Loan.

Public feeling was tense over the loan, and shocked by the assassination of the leader of the Kuomintang, when the unwieldy National Assembly opened at Peking on April 8, 1913. In early sessions the loan was criticized, and its submission to the Assembly was insisted upon. Yuan Shih-kai held that it had already been approved by the preceding legislature. He pushed it through its final stages.

In the precincts of the Hongkong and Shanghai Banking Corporation within the Legation Quarter the signatories met April 26th, for the final transaction of the contract. In a dramatic moment C. T. Wang, one of the leaders in the Assembly, broke in on the group and hotly denounced the loan in the name of the Chinese nation. When Yuan Shih-kai announced that the loan was concluded, feeling ran high in the National Assembly, where the President, of course, had supporters. Sessions became so disorderly that other stormy sessions ensued to deal with offenses against order.

Early in May Sun Yat-sen despatched a telegram to London attempting to persuade the Five Power Banking Group not to carry out the loan. He denounced it as "suddenly and unconstitutionally concluded." The telegram reports:

At present time fury of people is worked up to white heat, and terrible convulsion appears almost inevitable. . . . If Peking Government is kept without funds there is prospect of compromise between it and people. . . . Immediate effect of liberal supply of money will probably be precipitation of terrible and disastrous conflict.[20]

This protest accomplished nothing. The loan was oversubscribed on May 21st.

Although it is, in a sense, futile to question an event which has historically wrought irretrievable havoc, it is pertinent to an understanding of that havoc to raise the question whether the Kuomintang might not have bettered its position by other tactics. The Kuomintang made a constitutional issue of a loan whose urgency few questioned, and about the hardship of whose terms parties agreed. Might not the results have been much healthier and happier for the infant Republic, if the Kuomintang had accepted the long-contested loan as an accomplished fact, regretted though its terms were by every patriotic Chinese, and had devoted the party's constitutional zeal to the direction of its expenditure? By the construction which was put upon the loan the party read itself out of any show of right to control appropriations and disbursements. The Kuomintang actually denounced it as a personal loan made to Yuan Shih-kai himself—than which a more corrupting interpretation could scarcely have been devised. The result was that the loan got away without control and without accounting. Already cut in half by advances and other obligations, the remainder of the money vanished in the maw of current expenses with no demonstrable "reorganization" to show for it. The loan became the subject of endless recriminations, the root of enduring bitterness, and the precedent for many financial irregularities.

Opinions may differ as to whether the dispute over the loan was the cause of cleavage, or whether cleavage was inevitable in the very nature of the differences between Yuan Shih-kai and the modernists. The incident, in any case, was evidence enough that cleavage was already a deplorable fact. Yuan Shih-kai and the modernists had parted ways.

Before the summer of 1913 the Yangtze Valley was showing much unrest. By the end of June rebellion broke out at Wuchang, but was severely repressed by Li Yuan-hung. The dismissal in June and July of three provincial governors who were Kuomintang men led to other revolutionary outbreaks. On July 2nd Sun Yat-sen sent a public telegram to Yuan Shih-kai calling on him to resign:

. . . Formerly you were invited to the Presidential office to bear the heavy responsibility of the country, and now you should leave it in order to save the country from being involved in trouble.

. . . If you can follow my advice, I will persuade the soldiers and the people in the South and East to lay down their arms. . . . If you reject my sound advice . . . I shall adopt the same measures against you as those used against the absolute monarchy. I have made my mind up now. This is my last advice, and I hope you will consider it well.[21]

This ultimatum had no effect; Yuan Shih-kai did not resign. On July 12th an attack was made on the government garrison at Kiukiang. The military-minded Huang Hsing proceeded to Nanking, which declared its independence on July 14th. A bombastic proclamation was issued announcing a "punitive expedition" against the President, and calling for his destruction as the betrayer of the nation. Four provinces joined the revolt—Kiangsu, Kiangsi, Anhui and Kwangtung. On July 20th the insurrectionists tried to seize the telegraphs in Shanghai. The International Settlement then took measures to protect itself; for three weeks a military cordon was thrown round the Settlement. On July 23rd Sun Yat-sen was deprived of his post as Director of Railway Development. It was freely charged that the funds which had been entrusted to him for railway planning had been used for financing the rebellion. On the other hand it was asserted that Yuan Shih-kai was able to act promptly and vigorously because he was well supplied with funds by the newly concluded loan. In August his troops made steady gains against the revolt, and the leaders were fleeing for their lives. The press reported Sun Yat-sen's arrival in Japan on August 8th, and the arrival of Huang Hsing and others very soon after. The one notable insurrectionary effort took place after these leaders had left China; Nanking made a very stout resistance under a truly brave young officer, but the city was taken September 1st.

Yuan Shih-kai celebrated his triumph by being constitutionally elected President by the National Assembly for five years, and by a brilliant inaugural ceremony on the Revolutionary anniversary, October 10th. This was attended by the Diplomatic Corps, and the formal recognition of the Republic by the Powers was made complete. Sun Yat-sen's defeat was crushing.

But Yuan Shih-kai was not yet through with his struggle with the Kuomintang. The committee that had been drafting a permanent constitution for the Republic was sitting in the Temple of Heaven at Peking. In this there was an influential Kuomintang element. On October 26th the committee finished its work. Yuan Shih-kai objected to certain provisions which were designed to curtail the power of the President. He sent a representative to discuss his objections with the committee, but he was refused a hearing. Thereupon he turned to the governors of the provinces and other high officials, many of whom were indebted to him for their rise to power. A flood of telegrams came in denouncing the constitution, some demanding the dissolution of the National Assembly. On October 31st eight Kuomintang members of the Assembly were arrested and sent south for trial. Protests from the Assembly resulted. On November 3rd the final blows came in Presidential mandates countersigned by the Premier, ordering the immediate dissolution of the Kuomintang throughout the country as a seditious organization and the unseating of all Kuomintang members in the Assembly.

Both these measures were rigorously enforced. Over three hundred members of the Assembly were thus expelled. The remainder could not constitute a quorum. No steps were taken to fill the vacancies. It became clear that the National Assembly was to come to an end. In January it was indefinitely suspended. Yuan Shih-kai at the same time ordered the dissolution of the Provincial Assemblies. He constituted at Peking a Political Council, a smaller advisory body, which met December 15th. One of its first acts was to advise another representative assembly, but of smaller size. So China continued further experimentation in parliamentary government. The history of the period is strewn with wrecks of experiments, and with constitutions and regulations on paper—a bewildering exhibit of futility.

The story of the first two years of Sun Yat-sen's Republic is not a brilliant one, nor a gratifying one to report. The present orthodox Kuomintang interpretation of its unhappy events is, in brief, that it would have succeeded except for the treachery of Yuan Shih-kai, who accepted the Presidency after Sun Yat-sen's magnanimous withdrawal in his favor, then betrayed the Republic. The Kuomintang finds no words too hard to apply to Yuan Shih-kai; "the Judas of the Republic" is the most Westernized form of execration. "Yuan was never human; he was all fiendish," is the description in a recent publication of the Kuomintang. He is habitually pictured as a coldly calculating traitor, who from the beginning was ambitious for himself only, who at every turn diabolically thwarted high-minded patriots and the patriotic party (the Kuomintang), who resisted constitutional limitations of his power, got himself financially backed by intriguing imperialistic Powers, and with the help of their money was able to put his military machine into action, defeat the "Second Revolution" and demolish the Kuomintang and the parliament.

For one who surveys the course of events as an outsider another interpretation emerges. Yuan Shih-kai was no aureoled saint; no such man as he would ever be canonized by any people. He was as self-seeking as ambitious men usually are, and he was—with one glaring lapse—clever enough to turn circumstances to his own advantage. In the light of his career he seems to have been nothing worse and nothing better than a strong ruler of the elder Chinese tradition, securely grounded in the belief that the business of a ruler—whatever his office might be called—was to keep things in hand even at the cost of ruthlessness. He was not a Western-educated man with a mind crammed, like Sun Yat-sen's, with the theories of Western government. His ideas of what a republic might be were doubtless as unformed as the ideas of others who had grown up in the Chinese governmental service. In the development of modernized armies he had been an outstanding progressive, but in clear intellectual grasp of the technique of republican government he was unsophisticated. But so were all Chinese in 1912; there were as many callow ideas of what a republic should be as there were republicans; there were hazy ideas, and doctrinaire ideas, and fantastic ideas, and ideas that were sheer emptiness with a name. The only postulate which everybody agreed on was that the Republic was not the Manchu dynasty. Nor was Yuan Shih-kai different from hosts of others in being ready to adventure into the glamourous state called republican. The republican ideal intrigued him as an unexplored country intrigues a traveler, or as an era of enlightenment intrigues the ignorant. He did not shrink from the responsibilities of an untried office, any more than any other ambitious Chinese would have done if he had had Yuan Shih-kai's opportunity. What is equally to the point is the fact that Sun Yat-sen and his fellow-revolutionists raised Yuan Shih-kai to the presidency, not because he knew anything about republics but because he was a strong administrator whose ability had been proven under the old régime. That he could change by a ceremony of inauguration into a president of the European or American pattern was taken for granted, just as it was taken for granted that China could make a swift alteration of all her governmental ways with the casting off of a dynasty and the writing of a republican constitution.

Although the government in which Yuan Shih-kai was experienced, and in which his habits were deeply set, was the authoritarian rule of a strong man entrusted with large powers, he was not a bad sport—so it seems to some outsiders—in taking on the vesture and the ritual of republican government; he gave cabinets and parliaments a trial; and he experimented with republican forms and functions. But, whenever the experiment threatened disaster instead of order, whether through hampering relationships, impracticable constitutionalism, treasonable plottings, quarrelsome legislatures, outright fomentation of rebellion, or any other difficulty, Yuan Shih-kai's habitual reaction was—rather than wait for things to clear themselves—to reassert the strong rule which the old régime had trained him to exercise. The Republic—it will bear repeating—had put Yuan Shih-kai into the presidency because he was a strong man experienced in strong government; but to Yuan it surely must have seemed that the republicans had no sooner raised the strong man to the presidency than they made it their first and foremost business to sheer him of power, not only by devising constitutions to restrain him, but by vetoing his choice of cabinets, hampering his financial policies, organizing parties to oppose him, and all too soon raising outright rebellion. With appalling immediacy China presented to the observing world the situation of a strong man in conflict with an inchoate but tempestuous group of republicans, characterized by no emergent group consciousness, unable to agree among themselves or to discover ways of working together cohesively, but nevertheless urging changes and yet more changes. This nebulous chaos of idealistic republicanism stood no chance against an able exponent of a coördinated old order. When Sun Yat-sen had attained years of more sober objectivity, he admitted as much himself. It is in one of the lectures on "Democracy" that this statement occurs:

> The southern provinces, which were enjoying some of the left-over glory of the Revolution of 1911, displayed great enthusiasm on the surface, but the party within was split to pieces and could not agree upon orders. As for Yuan Shih-kai, he had the old six-army defense organization of the Peiyang Party; the divisional commanders, brigadier generals, and all the soldiers in these six armies were under splendid discipline and subject to one command. In a word, Yuan Shih-kai had a firm organization while we in the Revolutionary Party were a sheet of loose sand, and so Yuan Shih-kai defeated the party.[22]

The failure of the Chinese Republic in its earliest years was the result of the unforeseen, but speedily manifested, incapacity of both the President and the legislature to function in the unaccustomed pattern called a republic. There is no need to postulate a treasonable Yuan Shih-kai to account for the events; and it is unrealistic in the extreme to assume that the infant, christened the Kuomintang, could have made a success of the Republic in 1912 and 1913, if only there had been no Yuan Shih-kai.

With the villain cut out of the play what is left is an unheroic story. Granted! It is the story of a quarrel in which now one party, now the other, schemed for advantage, created an incident, or retaliated. It is the sordid story of mutual suspicion, plotting and counter-plotting, accusation and vilification, assassination and revolt—in short, a story that reflects little credit either on Yuan Shih-kai or on Sun Yat-sen, either on the conservatives or on the Kuomintang. It is the story of antagonism tightening until it came to blows in the short war now given the flattering sobriquet of the "Second Revolution."

No, the final word on the period has not been spoken by the

Kuomintang—nor yet by any one else. This book is not the place to attempt the tedious disentangling of threads and the analysis of tortuous motives. It was a deplorable mêlée in which Chinese parties were springing at one another's throats, while foreign diplomacy threw financial barbed-wire entanglements over the field. But it was more than that. It was a great social tragedy, in which a nation with deeply set habits of action, and an amassed heritage of cleavages and craftiness, attempted to become something which it inherently was not. Some day we may have imaginations equal to grasping the tragedy of this people. When that day comes, the exchange of blame among parties will be purged away in emotions of pity and terror. As the tragedy moves to climax after climax, the stage is piled with the slain, not alone the blood-slain and the politically slain, but the spiritually slain. With the changes in Yuan Shih-kai himself some other author will one day wrestle. Among the spiritually slain we have to reckon the believing Sun Yat-sen, magnanimous and sure of his fellow-men: him we shall never see again. Sun Yat-sen passes into a new phase of character as well as of life.

DOCUMENTATION OF QUOTED PASSAGES

[1] Barker: "Dr. Sun Yat Sen and the Chinese Revolution," *Fortnightly Review* (London, November, 1911) Vol. 96, p. 778. [2] Cantlie and Jones: *Sun Yat Sen and the Awakening of China* (New York, 1912) p. 65. [3] *China Year Book for 1913,* ed. Bell and Woodhead (Shanghai) p. 480. [4] Weale: *The Fight for the Republic in China* (New York, 1917) p. 395. [5] *China Year Book for 1913,* ed. Bell and Woodhead (Shanghai) p. 485. [6] Ibid., p. 487. [7] Sun Yat-sen: "My Reminiscences," *The Strand Magazine* (London, March, 1912) Vol. 43, p. 307. [8] *The Times* (London), April 3, 1912. [9] Ibid. [10] Cantlie and Jones: *Sun Yat Sen and the Awakening of China* (New York, 1912) p. 65. [11] Barker: "Dr. Sun Yat Sen and the Chinese Revolution," *Fortnightly Review* (London, November, 1911) Vol. 96, p. 779. [12] Nelson: "Dr. Sun Yat Sen in Canton," *Missionary Herald* (Boston) August, 1912, p. 355. [13] *China Year Book for 1913,* ed. Bell and Woodhead (Shanghai) p. 670. [14] Martin: "Peking Churches' Reception to Dr. Sun," *Missionary Herald* (Boston) November, 1912, p. 512. [15] "China is United, Declares Dr. Sun," *The Sun* (New York) Tuesday, Sept. 24, 1912, p. 1. Also in American edition of Cantlie and Jones: *Sun Yat*

Sen and the Awakening of China, pp. 241–252. [16] Sun Yat-sen: "The Chinese Republic," *Independent* (New York, Sept. 19, 1912) Vol. 73, p. 664. [17] "China is United," *The Sun* (New York) Sept. 24, 1912, p. 1. [18] Inukai's Introduction to Kawakami: *Japan Speaks* (New York, 1932). [19] *The North China Herald* (Shanghai) Vol. 106, p. 664. [20] Ibid., Vol. 107, p. 620. [21] Ibid., Vol. 108, p. 736. [22] Sun Yat-sen: *San Min Chu I,* trans. Price (Shanghai, 1927) p. 211.

SOURCES AND AUTHORITIES: See Appendix C, p. 400.

CHAPTER VI

The Fall into Obscurity

SUN YAT-SEN'S was not a personality that remained always the same. It was undoubtedly his education as an adolescent in Honolulu that bred skepticism about tradition and set him on the long pursuit of modernization. His acceptance of Christianity, first sympathetically at Honolulu and later openly in Hongkong, was in itself a cardinal rebellion against tradition and a commitment to a new order. This overturning of his own life gave him a strengthened moral urge and a decided altruistic bent. As a student he was eager, open-minded, ingenuous and adventurous. He was only a schoolboy in Queen's College at Hongkong when revolutionary ideas first took root in his mind. During his professional study he was a rebel in embryo; after graduation he began plotting in earnest. The shock of defeat and the flight from Canton in 1895 tightened his determination to play the rebel for a cause. On their heels came a psychological crisis in the harrowing days of detention in the Chinese Legation in London in 1896. From this peril he seems to have emerged with a profound sense of designation for a mission. The sensational publicity of the incident itself placed him in the world's eye as a rebel against the Chinese Empire. This would have been a stigma upon his whole life if he had not chosen to continue to be a rebel until the consummation of a revolution. Because he accepted rebellion as a distinction it became such, and his notoriety was serviceable in making entrée for his propaganda among his own people in overseas settlements. His brother's affluence, together with the

172

Chinese tradition of the elder brother's responsibility when the father is deceased, relieved Sun Yat-sen of the economic support of his own wife and children, and left him free to shift for himself and move from place to place during the sixteen years of exile and propaganda from 1895 to 1911. The risks of the conspirator were many, yet in these he seems not to have lacked courage or persistence. The years of exile, however, had a pronounced effect upon him in that they isolated him from his native environment and tended to make him think unrealistically of China's problems. His habit of rationalizing solutions and of defining far-off objectives began in this long drawn-out banishment from his native land. Continued years of plotting undoubtedly sobered him and made him graver, quieter and less unsuspicious.

The effect of the realization of his life-purpose sooner than he anticipated was that he was lifted for a while to the heights of optimism for China. He planned for the renunciation of the presidency with a degree of will-resistance to natural pride that is not lightly to be accounted for. China has never forgotten this act of self-effacement. The overwhelming popular receptions given him after his retirement, culminating in regal honors at Peking and an ovation in Japan, apparently did not spoil him. As far as human judgment can see into a man's heart, Sun Yat-sen up to the suppression of the so-called "Second Revolution" was an unproud man. And he was a religious man. He not only fraternized with Christians among his own people, but was unashamed to be known as a Christian wherever he went. He responded to invitations to speak in churches and made strong declarations of his indebtedness to Christianity.

The experience that changed Sun Yat-sen, indeed, temporarily wrecked him, was not honor and public acclaim; it was the abysmal fall from public esteem that resulted from his participation in the ill-fated rebellion against Yuan Shih-kai in 1913. Never was there a hero of whom it was truer that he "dropp'd from the zenith like a falling star." The incalculable "loss of face" brought to consciousness the hidden pride which he had known nothing about; a growing egoism was the form taken by his obstinate resistance to despair.

It is sad to picture Sun Yat-sen in those days of eclipse. Many of his friends had not followed him into the rising against Yuan Shih-kai; not a few stuck to their posts under the government. For their personal safety his former followers in China had to repudiate both him and the rebellion. Sentiment, moreover, was quite generally against him; even the Christians became critical. The missionaries suffered a diminution of faith in him; at their summer resorts in 1913 they were asking: What has gone wrong with Sun Yat-sen? To the northern summer colony at Peitaiho, came a traveler fresh from Japan—Rev. E. W. Thwing of the International Reform Bureau. He had visited Sun Yat-sen in Japan as he came through, and he made the following statement about the defeated patriot:

A year ago he had been accorded a place second to no Chinese in the world. But since his visit to Japan he has become a changed man. His attitude toward China has changed. He is the sworn enemy of President Yuan Shih-kai and all his policies. He has pledged his support to the overthrow of President Yuan. His ideals for a great China, undivided and unified, have evidently gone. He said: "It makes no difference if China is divided into ten parts—each would still be as big as Japan." [1]

In the *Peking Gazette* a letter appeared late in October which was an attempt on Sun Yat-sen's part to set himself right with a Christian friend. It is interesting as showing the religious interpretation of his life, as he then saw it. He cites his rescue in London in 1896, and his subsequent narrow escapes from many dangers in Canada, the United States and elsewhere as due to Divine protection and not to luck. He says he accepted Christianity when young and has always been convinced of the existence of God who is unseen and supreme. He reviews his own history since his return to China in December, 1911. "He reverts to the scenes of his early childhood when he lay awake at night grieving for the sufferings of the poor and pondering over methods for their relief. He expresses the belief that rebellion will prevent Yuan Shih-kai from continuing his Napoleonic policy. Finally he leaves posterity to judge whether he has been the real offender."

Sun Yat-sen's wife was not with him in Japan, as she had been in Nanking. She was not accustomed to travel the world with her fugitive husband. True to Chinese custom she had been a member of the household rather than the companion of a wandering son. She had lived first in her mother-in-law's house at Choyhung while Sun Yat-sen pursued his studies at Hongkong; at Choyhung she bore him three children. After Sun Yat-sen's first revolutionary plot failed in 1895, the family in fear emigrated to Hawaii, and there his children grew up and received their earlier education. Sun Fo, the only boy, did journalistic work while attending school in Honolulu, where he was graduated from St. Louis College (Roman Catholic). Sun Fo entered the University of California as a Freshman in 1911, but his studies were broken off by the exciting news of the Revolution in China and of his father's election to the presidency. He and a group of other young Hawaiian Chinese hastened to China to offer their services to the new government.

The rest of the family was involved in changes of residence made by Ah Mi. When he was about sixty years of age and had accumulated what to a Chinese was a tidy little fortune, he sold his properties in Hawaii and returned to his native land in 1909. He took with him as part of his patriarchal family, his mother and Sun Yat-sen's wife and two daughters. They settled at Kowloon across from Hongkong. Ah Mi's house there became such a rendezvous for revolutionists that the British authorities asked him to leave. He moved next to the French concession at Kwangchowwan, and shortly afterwards to Macao.

When Sun Yat-sen went to Nanking to be President, his family joined him. Some of them followed him when he returned south in the spring of 1912. Mrs. Sun appears in photographs of certain great functions given in her husband's honor in that year—by no means an unattractive figure. (She has been grossly caricatured in some of the biographies.) When in 1912 the excitement of the presidency was over for the family, Sun Fo returned to his education in America, accompanied by both his sisters. They stopped long enough in Honolulu for Sun Fo to be married at the home of his friends, Rev. and Mrs. Frank Damon of the Chinese mission. Then with one more member the party continued the journey to America. In the fall of 1912 Sun Fo re-entered the University of California and in due course was graduated in 1916. The sisters entered Snell Seminary, also at Berkeley. They appear in a snapshot taken in the fall of 1912, with their brother and sister-in-law and their father's friend, Dr. Hager.

When Sun Yat-sen opened his offices as Head of Railway Development for all China, he and Mrs. Sun appear to have taken up residence in Shanghai in 1912–13. His memorable visit to Japan in February and March, 1913, was quietly observed by his wife who traveled thither incognito, accompanied by Miss Soong, the eldest daughter of Charles Soong—remembered at Trinity College and at Vanderbilt University—who was at this time prospering in Shanghai. Miss E-ling Soong had finished a course at Wesleyan College, Georgia, in 1909 and, leaving a younger sister there with four years of college life ahead of her, had returned to China. It is reported that E-ling did some English secretarial work for Sun Yat-sen during his brief presidency. Being well-educated and a cosmopolitan traveler, she was a suitable companion for the less experienced Mrs. Sun Yat-sen on the trip to Japan. In spite of the effort of the two women to travel unrecognized, they came into public notice through an automobile accident in which both were hurt, Miss Soong the more seriously. Some time during that spring Sun Yat-sen's elder daughter, Sun Yen (Annie) returned to China. She was very sick at the time of the "Second Revolution," July, 1913. Mother and daughter were cruelly harassed by searchers for Sun Yat-sen. When, as the penalty of insurrection, Sun Yat-sen was again an exile in Japan, Mrs. Sun returned to Macao. The sick daughter, Annie, died some time during that ill-fated year, 1913.

This exile was a time when newspaper men found Sun Yat-sen very hard to get at. More than one journalist can tell a story of frustration, of being put on wrong clues, or going to a given address only to be passed on to another misleading address in a tiresome series. Not until June 7, 1914, did a correspondent of the *New York Tribune* report being finally taken to Sun Yat-sen's hiding-place in a suburb of Tokyo built of frail foreignized houses. There he found the exile in Japanese dress and talked with him in a room whose tables were littered with periodicals and whose walls were well ranked with books. The man who spoke in that interview was not the magnanimous and self-effacing Sun Yat-sen, but one bitter with sectional hatred, and hot with resentment, not only against Yuan Shih-kai and his followers, but against the foreign bankers who had furnished the new Republic with a handsome sum of money that it might get on its feet and go forward. Here we have the interpretation of the Five Power Consortium Loan that is taught in books and schools of Nationalist China today. It derives from Sun Yat-sen himself:

Not our own people, not our own mistakes, drove us from China, but foreign money power, deliberately employed for the breakup of our country. The foreign bankers of the five-Power group held the balance of power between the North and the South for three years. When we were in power they starved us of the credit, except on the most humiliating terms. . . . Last year's personal loan of one hundred and twenty-five million dollars to Yuan Shih-kai, fought to the last ditch by every constitutional party in China, simply put a club in the hands of the North with which they straightway smashed our cause. That huge bribe, and that alone, is the reason why we are here today.[2]

II. MODERNIZATION MADE FLESH

To Sun Yat-sen at the very nadir of his life solace came in unexpected guise. Before the tired eyes of the discouraged revolutionist, "modernization" suddenly became flesh in the person of an attractive girl graduate just returning from America. Soong Ching-ling Charles Soong's second daughter, had been studying at Wesleyan College, Macon, Ga., for five years and had finished with a diploma and an A.B. in June, 1913. There she was known also as Rosamonde Soong. Her father, it will be recalled, had been one of Sun Yat-sen's earliest supporters; he had helped him with money in the rising of 1895, when Ching-ling was a small child. Being himself a product of modernization, and a man of some means, he had been sending his children to America for higher education. He had made a modest competence in business relations with foreigners in Shanghai. Both he and his wife were very prominent Christians there.

As a college undergraduate in America Ching-ling had been thrilled by the despatches reporting the success of the Republican Revolution in China. In the patriotism of her young heart she had written an English article about it in 1912 for the college magazine. She mentioned no Chinese leaders in the article, not even Sun Yat-sen, but she expressed an exalted faith in her people and unbounded satisfaction that they had rid themselves of their Manchu rulers. Before Ching-ling could get back to the Orient in 1913, the Republic in which her faith had been so buoyant was already splitting upon rocks. How deeply her own family was involved in the wreckage she could not have known before she got to Japan. Her father had helped his old friend, Sun Yat-sen, by acting as treasurer of the revolutionary funds. On the collapse of their venture he also was a fugitive in Japan. He was living with his eldest daughter, E-ling, in Tokyo, and there Ching-ling joined them and became one with the group of disappointed revolutionaries in exile. Her sister had been doing some English secretarial work for Sun Yat-sen (how much or how regularly does not appear). When E-ling's hand was won in a thoroughly modern courtship by H. H. Kung, then a Y.M.C.A. secretary working among Chinese students in Tokyo, Ching-ling took over the secretarial tasks for Sun Yat-sen.

This is how it came about that when Sun Yat-sen was lonely and down-hearted, living in discreet obscurity among Japanese friends, Soong Ching-ling walked into his life, young, and modern, and—if we may trust a photo—wearing foreign clothes and a large "picture hat." One can imagine them talking together, the man with his wounded pride and the girl with her worshipful faith. She romanticized and comforted the defeated leader, and for her faith in him when he was down, China now romanticizes her. Sun Yat-sen's temperament reinforced his response. Although the possibility of divorce—and that without court proceedings—was recognized by elder Chinese custom, divorce was as a matter of fact very seldom resorted to. Society approved secondary marriages instead. Furthermore, except for certain definitely understood causes, divorce was impossible; none of these causes could have been cited against Mrs. Sun Yat-sen. The fact that she had borne her husband not only daughters but a son was in itself a powerful social protection of her status. If Sun Yat-sen could have obtained a divorce in the easy American fashion, he might have made everything seem to Western eyes more reputable. Perhaps he felt that not much of a ceremony was necessary to be the moral equivalent of an occidental divorce. Certainly everything has been done to give the world the impression that a divorce took place. Unfortunately authorities differ as to the date of the marriage—Chinese sources saying 1914, others, 1915. The details of that event are as well hidden as Sun Yat-sen was in Tokyo, where he was living under an assumed name, said to have been at this time Hayashi. His second marriage did not come to public notice until after Yuan Shih-kai's restoration of the monarchy and the beginning of the open revolt against him. Then the news appeared in the Japanese press early in January, 1916. New York newspapers got it a month later. The *World* published it February 16th, together with a despatch from Berkeley, expressing the skepticism of Sun Fo, who was then a student at the University of California, and knew his mother was still living.

Loyal to Chinese marriage traditions, Mrs. Sun Yat-sen conceded her husband another wife possessed of the modern education and social accomplishments which she herself lacked. But, although set aside and thrown upon the financial support of her son, she has never to this day in mind or heart relinquished the proud position of the first wife undisplaced. She lives in a house given her by Sun Fo, with portraits of Sun Yat-sen hanging on the wall. She spends her time in friendly services to the poor and sick. She, too, is a Christian, but of a much later date than her husband, and of a different denomination. She finds help in the religious exercises of the church to which she belongs, and some solace, also, in tending—as a loyal Chinese wife should—the graves of her husband's ancestors. She has overcome the illiterate state of most women of her class, and takes great delight in being able to read. If China had a Rembrandt, he would want to paint her portrait. In her lined face all the tragic strength of old China seems to be depicted.

The rearrangement of Sun Yat-sen's domestic life, which would have caused no comment whatever if it had been consistently carried out according to Chinese traditions, became a subject of un-happy comment because the principals were Christians. That fact in itself is not without significance as to the impression Christianity has made upon the social traditions of China. Doubtless there are Westerners who would have respected Sun Yat-sen more, if he had not resorted to the rationalization of a thin divorce. But, modernized to the extent that he was, he could not have respected himself with-out it. So he put away, as best he could, the first wife before taking the second. But Ching-ling, a Christian of a Christian family, stepped into difficulties.

A divorce that is revolutionary is sure to be put on the defensive; Sun Yat-sen's divorce lay all the more open to attack because the second marriage, whatever form it actually took, was most ob-scurely consummated in Japan. Ching-ling's first appearance with Sun Yat-sen in Canton several years later created an outburst of criticism; public opinion by no means conceded her the status she desired. She had to face the moral disapprobation of the mission community, to which both she and Sun Yat-sen were intimately bound, not only by church membership but by education in mission schools. The more worldly business element among the foreigners cynically scouted a divorce without legal proceedings and court record. Fully as obnoxious to Ching-ling's modernized spirit as either of these reactions was the inevitable Chinese interpretation of her status as that of a secondary wife, although in this they meant no disrespect.

Sun Yat-sen's unconformable action had its effect upon his re-lations with the church, although the matter was not brought to any church court or judiciary. His long revolutionary career had so detached him from the Hongkong church into which he was re-ceived at baptism that it felt no responsibility for inquiry into his conduct. It should be recalled that for sixteen years before the Rev-olution Sun Yat-sen had been unable to reside in Hongkong, because the Manchus had influenced the British to banish him also from that colony. During this long period of repeated plots and insurrections his membership was a liability upon the church rather than a status for Sun Yat-sen. Opposite his name on Dr. Hager's church roll was written in English the one word "Banished." Shortly after the Revolution Sun Yat-sen is said to have spoken in the church once, but he never again lived in Hongkong, and his relations with the church became even more tenuous. Careful investigation of the facts makes it possible, here and now, to send to the discard another myth about Sun Yat-sen—the frequently circulated report that he was excommunicated from the Christian church. His name was never stricken from the roll of the church into which he was baptized.

So, whatever alienation may have resulted from Sun Yat-sen's second marriage, criticized as it was by both Chinese and foreign church people, it was not due to ecclesiastical discipline. But neither Sun Yat-sen nor Ching-ling could have been unaware of disapprobation; a sense of maladjustment with the Christian community was inevitable. Moreover, there were real changes that must have been felt sooner or later. Sun Yat-sen was no longer sought as a speaker in churches and missions; he ceased to be used for Christian propaganda; his name dropped out of missionary journals. In China uncertainty grew as to whether Sun Yat-sen any longer thought of himself as a Christian. Newspaper men had it that he was bitter toward "missionary Christianity." A little later, and he was echoing in his own speeches the current criticism of missionaries as advance agents of imperialism. A well-informed Chinese gives what is doubtless the right interpretation of this:

In Sun Yat-sen's later years his hatred of Western imperialism led him to link missionary enterprises with foreign exploitation and caused him to make public utterances that were interpreted as anti-Christian.[3]

In spite of this he seems never to have lost his valuation of Christianity as a developer and stabilizer of character in men. And both he and Ching-ling retained personal friendships with missionaries. On several occasions near the end of his life he was invited to speak on national issues from Christian platforms. He addressed a Y.M.C.A. National Convention in Canton in October, 1923, and in the same fall gave an address at Canton Christian College (*Lingnan*).

Ching-ling was, in spite of temperamental shyness, in every way a modern woman. Through her, Sun Yat-sen attained a modernization of his domestic life, in character with his foreignization in other respects. She at once took an active part among the revolutionaries living in Japan. She acted constantly as her husband's most trusted secretary. After Sun Yat-sen's return to public life in China she became a familiar figure at public functions, sometimes sitting on the platform when he was making an address. She also had activities of her own and was sought as a patroness of modern projects. She finally became, in effect, a liaison-officer between Sun Yat-sen and the youth movement. That she had real influence upon the direction of his later years cannot be doubted.

III. JAPAN'S DREAM OF A NIPPONIZED CHINA

No sooner had China overthrown the Manchus and cast the die for modernization than Japan began to dream more vivid dreams of industry, commerce and power extending westward into the rich realms of her vast neighbor. If Sun Yat-sen was thoroughly discouraged and in need of any prodding to renewed revolutionary activity, the Japanese were eager to give it to him. The readiness for an economic entente which had appeared during Sun Yat-sen's visit to Japan in February and March, 1913, came to expression again with the "Second Revolution." In the issue of the *Japan*

Magazine for August, 1913, the agitation and the motive for it are set forth:

The more radical politicians in Japan have been attempting to influence the government to show a more decided preference for South China in the dispute, as that section of the Republic is Japan's best customer, taking nearly three-fourths of the total exports to China; but the Japanese government has all along remained strictly neutral as regards the dispute between North and South China, and intends adhering to this policy.[4]

The same magazine in November, 1913, contains this statement:

The leaders of the southern faction in the abortive rebellion in China are reported to have taken refuge in Japan, though their exact whereabouts appears to be a matter of speculation. As enormous sums of head-money are said to have been placed upon them by the Peking authorities, it is just as well that the place of their hiding should be unknown. . . . Dr. Sun Yat-sen and his compatriots show abounding trust in their Japanese friends in thus throwing their lives into Japanese hands. . . . There appears to be some doubt in press circles abroad as to whether Japan can grant refuge to the plotters against Peking and still maintain her neutrality, but Japan takes the stand that England or America would, if the refugees should claim protection in these countries, and holds that political refugees are entitled to humane treatment. . . . Considering the large degree of sympathy entertained by Japanese for the southern cause in China, the Japanese government must be given credit for the efficient manner in which it has been able to maintain inviolate neutrality. . . .[5]

Yuan Shih-kai's drastic efforts in the fall of 1913 to suppress his Kuomintang opponents by expelling them from the National Assembly and ordering the dissolution of the party throughout the country were met by Sun Yat-sen with a reorganization in Japan in 1914 of a more compact Ke-ming-tang—the "Revolutionary

Party"—in place of the Kuomintang, whose post-revolutionary expansion into a political party he had not approved. Concerning this phase of Sun Yat-sen's revolutionary activities the current policy is to say nothing. So it is refreshing to discover in an English publication by a Kuomintang writer a guarded but vivid criticism of the autocratic tightening of Sun Yat-sen's revolutionary technique:

The new organization was not satisfactory. Candidates for membership were required to take an oath of loyalty to Dr. Sun personally, signing a pledge to that effect with . . . finger-print as seal. Sun was to become the single head of the Party, and to him all Party officers were to be responsible. These arrangements kept from participation in the new Party many of his adherents who in principle agreed to the necessity of reorganization, such as Wang Ching-wei and Huang Hsing, but who objected against the oath of loyalty and the finger-print. Out of deference to the leader they did not, however, raise their protests in public but merely adopted a negative attitude, when Sun insisted on his scheme. Thus, Wang went to France, and Huang Hsing to America. . . .

The reorganization of the Party failed to revivify the revolutionary spirit in China.[6]

When Sun Yat-sen reverted to the revolutionary this time, he did no traveling abroad to appeal again to the overseas Chinese. He sought help chiefly in Japan. One of his fellow-participants in the ill-fated rising of 1913 reports:

His plan was the following: first of all, an alliance with Japan. This alliance was to weaken the forces of Yuan-Shih-Kai and strengthen the forces of our Party, as Japan is an Eastern Power and a neighbour, and friendly relations with her would be a blessing for our country. "If Japan helps me, victory will be on my side: if she helps Yuan-Shih-Kai, he will conquer"—these were the very words of Sun-Yat-Sen.[7]

The designing temper of the Japan of these years seems to have completely eluded Sun Yat-sen; some other Chinese were equally blind. The nature of the plans which the Japanese already had afoot for the exploitation of China's resources may be judged by the hold they gained, as we have already reported, on the iron industry of the Yangtze Valley in return for the loan made in Sun Yat-sen's presidency. A similar agreement had just been made with the Province of Hunan in 1913. Stimulated by the risings in other provinces, Hunan declared its independence on July 26, 1913. That was no sooner done than the Provincial Assembly accepted a loan of 15,000,000 yen from a Japanese syndicate, in return for which the very rich mining rights of Hunan were bartered away. These are instructive episodes because they show how short-sighted the young reformers of those days could be in dealing with an ambitious foreign power. In Hunan, subsequent events saved the province from the consequences of a major mistake; the province could not make good its rebellion against Peking and the contract perished with the insurrection.

While Chinese revolutionists were showing almost incredible naïveté in international finance, the Japanese seemed suddenly to develop a precocious astuteness and daring in their projects for national advantage. Nothing could be more likely than that the Japanese would make overtures to Sun Yat-sen in his exile, and under the circumstances they would ask hard terms. Sun Yat-sen, on the other hand, was too deeply in their debt for past friendliness and too desperate in his humiliation to do otherwise than lend an ear. Even in his most alert moments he could never be described by the phrase "wise as a serpent." Apparently it had never occurred to Sun Yat-sen that Japan would do China any wrong. His philosophy was that Japan was China's natural friend, and that their interests coincided. What could be better than to have Japanese loan China money and develop her natural resources? The Western nations would like to partition China, but Japan, he believed, would stand for her integrity. Therefore he desired Japan and China to be closely interlocked economically and in league politically—thus able to stand against the rest of the world. From this it will be seen that desire for revolutionary money was not the only thing that lured Sun Yat-sen into the trap; his quixotic international idealism laid him open to Japanese intrigue.

There are two documents which, if actually assented to by Sun Yat-sen, implicate him in policies charged with extreme corrosiveness to China. It was in the month of June, 1914, that what had been a secret document leaked out into the press. In Shanghai it was published in the *North China Daily News* as a "Letter alleged to have been written by Dr. Sun Yat-sen to a high personage in Japan." I cannot easily be persuaded that this document was Sun Yat-sen's composition. It does not seem to be in his form of statement or his mold of thought. Yet I cannot lightly dismiss the possibility that he gave it his approval, signed his name to it and sent it on its way as from himself. We have already observed that Sun Yat-sen was no stickler about what he signed. The letter is in substance a request for help for the Chinese revolutionaries in return for which they would agree to throw China open without reservation to Japanese industrial and commercial exploitation. To quote from it is important:

As Japan is close to China, and the prosperity or ruination of one affects the other, it is but natural that the revolutionaries should first seek aid from Japan. . . . Considering that Japan and China are nations of the same race and same literature, there are weighty reasons for the revolutionaries to look for help from Japan. After Japan has assisted China to reorganize her administration and religion, and to develop her potential resources, the Governments and peoples of the two countries will be on much more intimate terms than between other countries. China will throw open all the trade centers in the country to

Japanese labour and merchants, and enable Japan to monopolize the commercial field of China.

When the time comes, China will desire to free herself from the restrictions imposed by former international dealings and to revise unfair treaties. She will need Japan's support in handling diplomatic questions. She will also depend upon Japan's advice to reform her laws, judiciary and prison system. Moreover, Japan can facilitate the abolition of extraterritoriality by giving her consent first. This will be beneficial to the Japanese because it will enable them to live in the interior of China. By the time China regains her control over customs she will enter into a commercial alliance with Japan, whereby Japanese manufactures imported into China and Chinese raw materials imported into Japan will be exempted from paying duties. The prosperity of Japanese commerce and industry will go hand in hand with the development of the natural resources of China. . . .

Japan could, therefore, without incurring the trouble and expense of stationing troops, as Great Britain did in India, acquire big commercial marts in China. . . . She will leap to the forefront of the world's greatest Powers.

Japan could, however, never aspire to such a position if she continues her present policy toward China. The reason is this. In governing China, Yuan ignores the trend of general affairs in the Far East. Outwardly he appears to cultivate the friendship of Japan, but he indulges in antagonism against her surreptitiously. . . . When China is stronger it is needless to say that Japan can only expect to get even worse treatment. Should Japan refuse to support China, the antagonism toward Japan will always be great while Yuan is in power. Even after that Government falls of its own accord, Japan cannot inspire the confidence of the Chinese people. . . .

Speaking from another standpoint, if the Chinese revolutionaries are devoid of the support of a strong nation in connection with their campaign, longer time will be needed to achieve success, and after success is achieved, they will fail to reform the administration and improve diplomatic relations. On this account the revolutionaries are now anxiously looking for support, and Japan would reap enormous benefit if she were to give this support. . . .

It is my firm conviction that China can never have peace unless the governmental powers are in the hands of the Mintang. The reasons are that the Chinese are roughly divided into three classes, to wit, the official class, the Mintang and the masses. The last take no active part in politics. The official classes make energetic efforts to protect their personal interest, but their energy only lasts as long as they are in power. . . . Such was the conspicuous example of Yuan himself. . . .

The Mintang, however, is composed of persons of different type; its members are fearless and determined to attain the end they have in view. . . . Any one who has studied the conditions in China will realize that, as long as the Mintang fails to attain its object, China will never have peace. . . .

Though it is an extraordinary matter for a Government to support the people of another country to overthrow their Government, yet extraordinary men accomplish extraordinary deeds in order to attain extraordinary results.

. . . It is scarcely necessary to mention that, in order to prevent diplomatic complications, secrecy and adroitness are necessary for carrying the matter to a successful issue.

Yours, etc. etc.,

(Signed) Sun Wen [8]

It is very difficult to think of this document as a product of Sun Yat-sen's mind—with the possible exception of the paragraphs about the *Mintang*. It has many signs of being a Japanese-wrought composition. It would be hard to believe that a Chinese would put in such a proposal as that exemption from tariffs should apply to Japan's manufactures when entering China, while only China's raw materials should enter free into Japan. There are many rather bad give-aways; such as the suggestion of assistance to China in reorganizing her religion, the "monopolizing" of the commercial field of China by Japan, the invidious suggestion that the revolutionaries in event of success would still be unable to reform China's administration and improve her diplomatic relations, and the final urging of secrecy to prevent "diplomatic complications."

The letter is undoubtedly first of all a revelation of Japanese thinking, but none the less it may contain some revelation of Sun Yat-sen's measure of agreement with Japanese thinking. If we can overlook the Japanese idiosyncrasies in the statement, the document does not seem to be inconsistent with the involving kind of international coöperation which Sun Yat-sen more than once advocated in later years.

IV. JAPAN'S DEMANDS AS SERVED ON SUN YAT-SEN

More disconcerting to a biographer is a detailed agreement purporting to have been made by Sun Yat-sen and his fellow-revolutionists with certain Japanese who undertook to finance them. This did not come to public knowledge until the furore broke out in China over Japan's Twenty-one Demands; then it appeared in the press in April, 1915. There is no reference in this document to the World War. At the end there is a statement that the "articles have been discussed several times between the two parties and signed by them in February." If it is a genuine contract, its date, one would infer, was February, 1914. It comes from the same phase of Japanese psychology as the Twenty-one Demands, yet it must have preceded them. It is incredible that Sun Yat-sen or any other Chinese revolutionist would have dared to conclude such a contract as late as February, 1915, when the whole of China was aroused by what Japan was attempting at Peking. The alleged agreement may fairly be said to embody Japan's demands as served on Sun Yat-sen. It is an attempt to gain economic foothold in South China by giving military aid to the revolutionists. It begins with this paragraph:

In order to preserve the peace in the Far East, it is necessary for China and Japan to enter into an offensive and defensive alliance whereby in case of war with any other nation or nations Japan shall supply the military force while China shall be responsible for the finances. It is impossible for the present Chinese Government to work hand in hand with the Japanese Government, nor does the Japanese Government desire to co-operate with the former. Consequently, Japanese politicians and merchants who have the peace of the Far East at heart are anxious to assist China in her reconstruction.[9]

It is stipulated that certain Japanese named will provide funds, not exceeding 1,500,000 yen, and rifles not exceeding 100,000 pieces. This loan is to be secured by 10,000,000 yen worth of bonds to be issued by Sun Yat-sen. "It shall, however, be secured afterwards by all the movable properties of the occupied territory." The Japanese are not only to furnish military advisers with real power, but also a Japanese "volunteer force"; they are also to supervise expenditure of the money. Details are stated as to pay and compensation of soldiers, terms of employment of officers and other matters. The funds are definitely restricted to military operations in the provinces south of the Yellow River. Invasion of any of the northern provinces must be done jointly by Japanese and Chinese. In return for such assistance, it is stipulated that after the occupation of territory "all industrial undertakings and railway construction and the like, not mentioned in treaties with other foreign Powers, shall be worked with joint capital together with the Japanese." It is further agreed that as soon as a new government is established, it will recognize all of Japan's demands on China as settled and binding. At the end of the document it is definitely stated that the articles were signed in February and that the first installment of 400,000 yen had been paid.

The decision as to whether this was an agreement actually entered into by Sun Yat-sen will have to wait upon further historical inquiry into these obscured years of Sun Yat-sen's life. This period of exile in Japan, 1913–16, is ignored by the heroizing biographies; that in itself is a suspicious circumstance. Some burden of proof should rest upon those who would raise doubts about Sun Yatsen's having entered into such an agreement. I find any other hypothesis difficult. That the document was forged to discredit him I do not believe. It was not a moment when any one would be likely to forge Sun Yat-sen documents; he was already disgraced and down. That Yuan Shih-kai's secret service could have produced this document is unbelievable; no Chinese could have so consistently interpreted the secret ambitions and plotting of Japan at this time. The Japanese, friendly as they were toward Sun Yat-sen, would have had no motive for producing such an agreement except as a secret paper for Sun Yat-sen to sign secretly. With such considerations in mind a historian cannot dismiss the agreement as irrelevant.

In the light of what we know of Sun Yat-sen's guileless internationalism, does this alleged agreement seem to represent a credible transaction? Only as a contract made prior to the notoriety of the Twenty-one Demands. What Sun Yat-sen would conceivably agree to a year before the Twenty-one Demands would be very different from what he could consider after the upheaval of anti-Japanese feeling in China. If such a contract was entered into, it must have become impossible of performance after the popular anti-Japanese resentment had been aroused among the Chinese. If the revolutionists had attempted to invade China then with the military support of Japan, the tables would have been turned, and Yuan Shih-kai would have become the popular hero for resisting them. The contract, if made, must certainly have been allowed to lapse.

That Sun Yat-sen was deep in plotting and in the financing of plots before the middle of 1914 is proven by a presidential mandate of midsummer. A press despatch of July 18, 1914, says:

A Presidential mandate dated July 15th, at Peking, orders authorities to execute on the spot every one who takes in payment notes circulated by Sun Yat-sen and alleged to be secured by an interior loan, or notes of an alleged military administration bearing the picture and the signature of Huang Hsing and Chen Chi-mei. The notes are circulated especially amongst the troops, and attempts are being made to incite the troops against the Government.[10]

This development is dramatically consistent with the agreement already discussed. Perhaps in retaliation for this, a statement was issued from Tokyo, in September, 1914, criticizing Yuan Shih-kai's loan policies and concluding thus:

The Kuomintang after holding several meetings now states that all loan bonds whether issued by the central government or by the provinces, and all notes issued by its banks or official money offices will not be recognized by the New Government when established.[11]

The outbreak of the European War in 1914 had the effect of intensifying the ambitious plotting of Japan for aggrandizement at the expense of China. In the preoccupation of the European Powers the Japanese saw an opportunity. A group of politicians, who were particularly interested in Chinese relations, had formed what they called the "Black Dragon Society." In the early months of the World War these men drew up a memorandum to urge certain policies, which, as the sequel proves, were very acceptable to the government. The document shows so much ability and astuteness that it is impossible to decry its significance. What it has to say about the encouragement of Chinese revolutionaries is the portion that here concerns us:

After the gigantic struggle in Europe is over, leaving aside America, which will not press for advantage, China will not be able to obtain any loans from the other Powers. With a depleted treasury, without means to pay the officials and the army, with local bandits inciting the poverty-stricken populace to trouble, with the revolutionists waiting for opportunities to rise, should an insurrection actually occur while no outside assistance can be rendered to quell it, we are certain it will be impossible for Yuan Shih-kai, single-handed, to restore order and consolidate the country. The result will be that the nation will be cut up into many parts beyond all hope of remedy. . . .

For Japan to ignore the general sentiment of the Chinese people, and support Yuan Shih-kai with the hope that we can settle with him the Chinese Question is a blunder indeed. . . . We should induce the Chinese revolutionists, the Imperialists and other Chinese malcontents to create trouble all over China. The whole country will be thrown into disorder and Yuan's Government will consequently be overthrown. We shall then select a man from amongst the most influential and most noted of the 400,000,000 of Chinese and help him to organize a new form of government and to consolidate the whole country. . . .

For us to incite the Chinese revolutionists and malcontents to rise in China we consider the present to be the most opportune moment. The reason why these men cannot now carry on an active campaign is because they are insufficiently provided with funds. If the Imperial Government can take advantage of this fact to make them a loan and instruct them to rise simultaneously, great commotion and disorder will surely prevail all over China. We can intervene and easily adjust matters. . . .

This opportunity will not repeat itself for our benefit. . . . Why should we wait for the spontaneous uprising of the revolutionists and malcontents? Why should we not think out and lay down a plan beforehand? When we examine the form of government in China we must ask whether the existing Republic is well suited to the national temperament and well adapted to the thoughts and aspirations of the Chinese people. From the time the Republic of China was established up to the present moment, if what it has passed through is to be compared to what it ought to be in the matter of administration and unification, we find disappointment everywhere. Even the revolutionists themselves, the very ones who first advocated the Republican form of government, acknowledge that they have made a mistake. The retention of the Republican form of government in China will be a great future obstacle in the way of a Chino-Japanese alliance. . . . We must take advantage of the present opportunity to alter China's Republican form of government into a Constitutional Monarchy which shall necessarily be identical, in all its details, to the Constitutional Monarchy of Japan, and to no other. . . . Shall we, in the selection of a new ruler, restore the Emperor Hsuan T'ung to his throne, or choose the most capable man from the monarchists, or select the most worthy member from among the revolutionists? We think, however, that it is advisable at present to leave this question to the exigency of the future. . . .[12]

One is left to imagine how that document would have angered Sun Yat-sen, if he had seen it in 1914 or early 1915. How little he would have relished the juxtaposition of republican revolutionists with those seeking a restoration of the monarchy as "malcontents" —all alike potentially serviceable to Japanese intrigue! One would suppose, too, that, however discouraged Sun Yat-sen may have been, he would resent the expressions of misgiving about the republican form of government, and particularly the report of loss of faith and reversal of opinion on the part of "the very ones who first advocated the republican form of government" for China. But Sun Yat-sen did not see the "Memorandum of the Black Dragon Society" early enough to awaken his misgivings. One wonders whether he had any suspicion that the help almost thrust upon him in Japan was only a move in one of the most daring political games ever played by a nation for the absorption of another. Japan's hand had been behind her back, and Sun Yat-sen, I think, had not seen it. The hand was shown plainly enough on Jan. 18, 1915, when the so-called Twenty-one Demands were personally presented to Yuan Shih-kai by the Japanese minister at Peking.

That China did not concede the most humiliating of the Twenty-one Demands was the result of the fighting spirit of other patriots than Sun Yat-sen; among them was Liang Chi-chao, whose pen was mightier than the sword against Japan. Some feel that Yuan Shih-kai was never more of a statesman than in this crisis. China escaped with her sovereignty, but with a degree of compromise that has left a wake of trouble. The fateful treaties were signed May 25, 1915, after more than four months of spirited resistance.

Who was served with the more ignominious demands, the President of China or the exiled ex-President? The differing character of the two men is nowhere more apparent than here. Yuan Shih-kai knew that China was being outrageously imposed upon; he resisted, and the country with him. Sun Yat-sen believed that China was being befriended; his eyes were not opened until he saw what was happening to Yuan Shih-kai.

Chinese refugees in Japan found themselves, early in 1915, the subjects of vigorous criticism from angered patriots in China. A few of them took this to heart and issued a statement with twelve signatures (Sun Yat-sen's name is not among them). The translation given to the English press is excessively naïve in form; the vigor of the little manifesto is apparent, nevertheless:

. . . We see that the present Government is bad and of this we are exceedingly sorry. But who is there that could fight his own country by means of another country's strength, or who will invite one wolf to drive away another one? . . . In the present crisis we wish to put the interests of our country first; and wish to put our party differences in the background. . . . Although we would like to change the Government, we will not do anything which will endanger the country. We believe our people will understand this. With regard to the present trouble with Japan which is exciting the whole country, we must admit that our country is weak through being divided. But we must insist that the present Government is responsible for that. Therefore, we prefer to leave them to clean up their own mess. . . .[13]

This appeared in February. It was not until April that the alleged secret agreement between Sun Yat-sen and certain Japanese was made public. Measures to discredit Sun Yat-sen were then only to be expected. It was at this juncture that Yuan Shih-kai's officials promoted the circulation of two scandalous biographies of Sun Yat-sen. It goes without saying that these are difficult to get at in China at the present time; if they pass from hand to hand, it must be secretly; they are outlawed books. One entitled, *A Small History of Sun Wen* (*Sun Wen Hsiao Shih*), is a pamphlet of only about 3300 characters. The other is said to be over 10,000 characters long; *Sun Wen, Thief of the Nation* (*Kuo Tsei Sun Wen*) is reported to have been written by one of the most distinguished pens of the Empire.

The cumulative effect of these extraordinary documents—if the following interpretation of them may be considered as a historical hypothesis—is very striking. First, certain able Japanese agents persuade Sun Yat-sen that he and they are in agreement in regard to the ideal relationships between Japan and China; namely, economic interlocking and intimate political coöperation. The Japanese draw up a letter embodying the desired policy, combining with it an argument for help to be given to the Chinese revolutionary party in return for which Japan is to be granted commercial monopoly and political mentorship in China; this they persuade Sun Yat-sen to sign and despatch to "a high personage."

Wheels move secretly. Before long there is submitted to Sun Yat-sen an agreement drawn up in detail, by which the revolutionists are to receive not only money and arms but military assistance and guidance in exchange for almost unlimited industrial and railway concessions. The contract is secretly signed in February, 1914; Sun Yat-sen then issues the required bonds; and the first payment of 400,000 yen is made. There is also an issue of revolutionary currency in the form of notes which agents circulate surreptitiously among troops in China as prepayment for desertion to the cause.

In June, 1914, the secret letter to which Sun Yat-sen had attached his name is unearthed and published in China, and very soon thereafter his notes are found in the hands of soldiers, and a prompt presidential mandate orders any one found accepting them to be shot at sight. To this the revolutionists in Japan reply with an audacious manifesto repudiating the Chinese governmental and provincial bonds and the notes of the government banks. The antagonism is thus tensely drawn by the fall of 1914, when the European War breaks out.

Next comes the serving by Japan of the Twenty-one Demands upon Yuan Shih-kai in January, 1915. China is hot with resentment. Certain of the less involved refugees in Japan are disturbed that they are coming into criticism. They issue a naïve manifesto proclaiming their patriotism and innocence of responsibility. Then the secret agreement of Sun Yat-sen and the Japanese is unearthed and made public.

But all this must be understood to be a tentative piecing together of a not yet fully revealed historical sequence. Further research into related evidence remains to be done by those who can gain access to the secret history. What is done here amounts to the assembling of accessible documents, and an attempt to suggest a plausible interpretation of them. The one thing that cannot be done is to ignore them. While leaving full scope for further proof or disproof, it should be clearly observed that there are certain large facts in the situation which are indisputable. And they are significant facts which should not be clouded by doubt over details.

What Japanese were at the time thinking and planning *vis-a-vis* China is not a matter of conjecture. It is true that when Sun Yat-sen fled for his life to Japan, these facts were not known; they came to light during his stay in Japan, and they are common knowledge today. The negotiations over the so-called Twenty-one Demands of January, 1915, made it clear to China and to the rest of the world that Japan was seeking inordinately large concessions in China and a sequel of political advantage. It is now a matter of history that to gain her ends Japan resorted not only to intrigue but to high-handed diplomatic pressure, taking advantage of a period when European Powers were concentrated upon the World War. Further light was thrown upon the Japanese mind, especially upon the thinking of an influential group of men interested in their country's policy toward China, by the publication of the "Secret Memorandum of the Black Dragon Society." The importance of that document has been pointed out by historians, who see its interest as a revelation of Japanese psychology to be so great that, by comparison, the technical historical question as to whether it was actually presented to the Government of Japan is of minor importance. This Memorandum, as we have already seen, urges a policy of intrigue with Chinese revolutionaries, and the giving of financial aid to them for the purpose of stirring up trouble in China and overthrowing Yuan Shih-kai.

Another group of facts concerns Sun Yat-sen. It was in the Japan whose mind toward China was expressed in the Twenty-one Demands that Sun Yat-sen was living in 1913–16. There he was plotting a further revolution for China with the overthrow of Yuan Shih-kai as one object and the regaining of power by his own revolutionary party as another. In past years Sun Yat-sen had been helped in revolutionary projects by the Japanese, and he had a marked personal entente with them. He had been given a tremendous ovation in Japan in 1913, and had received much evidence of Japanese eagerness to finance economic projects in China, especially railway-building and all the exploitation of resources that may be tied up with it. These also are not surmises but facts.

Other obvious facts concern the documents. They are certainly of the period. One was made public in the press in June, 1914, the other in April, 1915. The first has Sun Yat-sen's personal name as the signature, and in the other he is specifically designated as the one in whose name the bonds are to be issued amounting to 10,000,000 yen.

Surely the facts that are known have a presumptive bearing upon that which remains unrepudiated but unproven. To be perfectly clear, let us summarize the improbabilities.

Attention has already been called to the improbability that the two documents were forged to discredit Sun Yat-sen. With the Japanese mind what it was, and Sun Yat-sen living accessibly in Japan it is highly improbable that he would escape the approaches of intriguing agents. That he would summarily reject such advances is equally improbable; his long record in Japan was against that. A further improbability is that under the circumstances he would be offered any but hard terms. Japan was seeking stupendous benefits for herself, and Sun Yat-sen was at the lowest ebb of his personal career. That Sun Yat-sen would battle for less unfavorable terms or stickle over compromising details will seem probable or improbable according to one's total estimate of his diplomatic skill and wisdom.

The high probability seems to be that a large mortgage on China's future would be required of Sun Yat-sen before any considerable assistance would be given him. Whether the terms to which he finally agreed were as extreme as those set forth in the "Letter Alleged to have been Written" or the "Alleged Secret Agreement" seems less important than the broad fact that he was getting the help of the Japanese at a time when Japan's overweening ambitions boded no good to China. Even if it could be proven that Sun Yat-sen bargained skillfully with the Japanese and got them to trim down their terms—say by fifty per cent—what would then remain would be enough to throw a long shadow over his statesmanship.

By 1915, with China aflame over the Twenty-one Demands, Sun Yat-sen's plotting in Japan must have been stalemate. Huang Hsing had got away to America before the reaction against Japan had set in. He was not coöperating with Sun Yat-sen during this period; a rift had come between them after the "Second Revolution," and each continued plotting in his own way. In early 1915 there was nothing for either of them to do but to hang his head in obscurity. Sun Yat-sen's address continued to be Tokyo, if we may trust *Who's Who in the Orient* for that year.

DOCUMENTATION OF QUOTED PASSAGES

[1] *Missionary Herald* (Boston) 1913, p. 433. [2] Hardy, G. L.: "China's Arabian Nights President," *New York Tribune,* June 7, 1914. [3] Wang, Chi-chen: "China's 'Sun' Marches on," *Herald Tribune,* New York, March 20, 1927. [4] *The Japan Magazine* (Tokyo) August, 1913, p. 240. [5] Ibid., November, 1913, p. 412. [6] T'ang Leang-li: *The Inner History of the Chinese Revolution* (New York, 1930) pp. 121–122. [7] Sun-Yat-Sen: *Memoirs of a Chinese Revolutionary* (London) pp. 151–152. [8] *The North China Herald* (Shanghai) Vol. 111, p. 898. [9] Weale: *The Fight for the Republic in China* (London, 1918) pp. 140–143. [10] *The North China Herald* (Shanghai) Vol. 112, p. 231. [11] Ibid., Vol. 112, p. 971. [12] Weale: *The Fight for the Republic in China* (London, 1918) pp. 132–135. [13] *The North China Herald* (Shanghai) Vol. 114, p. 591.

SOURCES AND AUTHORITIES: See Appendix C, p. 401.

CHAPTER VII

Dream Chaos

SUN YAT-SEN'S return to Chinese public life was due to the dramatic exit of his rival, Yuan Shih-kai, who, if he had planned it, could not have shaped his course of action more favorably for the reëntry of Sun Yat-sen to the political stage. That Yuan was the responsible head of the government while the Republic played out its little game of parliamentary futility relieved Sun Yat-sen of the odium of that failure. After Yuan Shih-kai had rid himself of the republicans and their tempestuous opposition tactics, it was clearly his responsibility to find for the Republic some *modus vivendi*. There were no longer either Kuomintang ministers or Kuomintang parliamentarians to hamper his policies; Kuomintang governors had been displaced; such army units as were formerly pro-Kuomintang had been shattered in the "Second Revolution." Sun Yat-sen, Huang Hsing and other prime movers toward a republic were suppressed or in exile.

For his own proper influence among the Chinese Yuan Shih-kai had become too popular with the foreign element in China, excepting the Japanese, who continued to hate him discreetly. It was foreign advice that speeded his undoing. He had in his service an American constitutional expert, Dr. F. J. Goodnow, a Professor at Johns Hopkins University, who—because he was from the United States—was supposed to have a dependable republican bias. It was he who drafted for Yuan Shih-kai a new constitutional basis—a remarkable instrument known as the Constitutional Compact, which placed great power in the hands of the President, making him a minor Mussolini in a period when no Mussolini had yet emerged for precedent. Yuan strengthened his hold on the administrative machinery of the country through maintaining his own appointees in the provincial governorships and other key positions. He also expanded and developed the modernized army, the beginnings of which in Shantung and other parts of the north in pre-republican days had been early fruits of his enterprise. Under his presidential administration China was not allowed to disintegrate; but centralization was preserved only at the cost of continual repression of republican ideals. Because he found republican institutions obstacles to effective administration, they lost whatever glamour they may have had for his mind. It is conceivable that even he was for a short time carried away by the romance of transforming China into a modernized republican state. If so, he was disillusioned now.

At the winter solstice of 1914 the President offended public taste by reviving the splendid ceremonies at the Altar of Heaven, in which he himself assumed the rôle never before taken by any except an Emperor. This started murmurs about imperial ambitions. What went on behind the scenes in the next seven months is not yet ferreted-out history. The Twenty-one Demands absorbed public attention. In August, 1915, a full-blown monarchist movement appeared with a society to promote it and a pamphlet to make it sensational, *Constitutional Monarchy the Salvation of China.* What created more of a sensation than the pamphlet was a memorandum despatched to Yuan Shih-kai by the objective-minded and disinterested constitutional expert from the great Republic of America, pointing out the advantages of a monarchical form of government in view of China's heritage and development. Then the fat was in the fire. Suspicion and distrust grew rapidly, both among Yuan Shih-kai's enemies and among his supporters. Memorials, petitions and a referendum of sorts pushed the monarchist movement along, until, in December, Yuan Shih-kai "yielded" to his advisers and the new dynasty was announced to begin on Jan. 1, 1916, with Yuan Shih-kai as its first Emperor. But before that day arrived, rebellion broke out.

From Japan Sun Yat-sen renewed his fulminations against the President. On December 5th an abortive attempt was made at the arsenal at Shanghai; among the papers found on the captured men were five documents signed by Sun Yat-sen. Early in 1916 reports were rife that rebel leaders were returning to Shanghai.

The effective revolutionary protest seems, however, not to have originated with Sun Yat-sen. It came from the Province of Yunnan, stimulated by Liang Chi-chao. This man, who crosses Sun Yat-sen's life at so many points, had originally opposed the republican revolution and had advocated instead a reformed and constitutional monarchy. But when the whole country accepted a republic he did not hold off. He went north, became an influence through his journalism, and made brief excursions into public office. He gave Yuan Shih-kai much effective support, notably in resisting Japan's Twenty-one Demands. When, however, Yuan attempted the revival of the monarchy in his own person, Liang Chi-chao opposed him, fled to Yunnan in the extreme southwest of China. With the help of a prominent general, who had once been his pupil, Liang Chi-chao roused the province to revolt. After Yunnan declared its independence of Yuan's authority, six other provinces quickly followed suit. This was the so-called "Third Revolution."

Diplomatic pressure was also brought to bear upon Yuan Shih-kai—first by his old enemies, the Japanese, who opposed his monarchical aspirations. It must have been a bitter pill for him when other Powers, even the most friendly, moved to dissuade him. Recognizing that public opinion was too strongly against him, he gave up the plans for the coronation, renounced the monarchy and reinstated the Republic on March 23, 1916.

On May 9th a despatch from Tokyo reported the arrival of Huang Hsing from the United States. He hastened to Canton to take part in the revolt there, but fell ill and died. A declaration by Sun Yat-sen was published as from "The Intelligence Department of the Republican Government of China, Shanghai, May 15th." It was a verbose apology for himself and an attack on Yuan Shih-kai. Concerning his own last three years he has a little to say:

I have been living abroad, yet my love for my country is as fervent as ever. . . . The state of affairs became so discouraging and heart-rending that I made up my mind to fight single-handed. I organized the *Chung Hua Ke Ming Tang* (Chinese Revolutionary Society) on the strictest principles, with the object of removing all social and political evils and of restoring the supremacy of law. In the course of the last two years I have secured many adherents, including some in the interior of China. All are working unswervingly. . . . We depend not so much on the support of others as on the righteousness of our own cause. . . . The independence of Yunnan and Kweichow has greatly relieved my anxiety, for it is most gratifying to find that we are not the only men who are zealously striving for liberty.[1]

About Yuan Shih-kai, by this time a deeply humiliated man, he says:

On mature reflection I am of the opinion that Yuan's crimes began long before the restoration of the monarchy, and that simply to overthrow him is not sufficient to secure the Republic. The traitor must be brought to justice. . . . As Yuan's attempt against the Republic began with the violation of the Constitution, so the preservation of the Republic must necessarily begin with the maintenance of the Constitution. That Yuan is in the wrong and we in the right is obvious to everybody. . . . We must be firm in our attitude towards Yuan. . . . Yuan overturned the Republic, and for the sake of the glory of his own family, did not scruple to enslave the people. This is why we consider him as the common enemy, who, at any cost, must be vanquished. . . .[2]

Sun Yat-sen was spared the trouble of making his policy effective. On June 6, 1916, Yuan Shih-kai died, chagrined and broken. His presidential term had not expired; he was constitutionally succeeded at once, after the American fashion, by the Vice-president—the General who had been chosen to command the first revolutionists in Wuchang in October, 1911, Li Yuan-hung. The death of Yuan Shih-kai opened the way for Sun Yat-sen to live once more in China. He settled in Shanghai. There he addressed a large private gathering in July in the garden of a wealthy Chinese on a Sunday afternoon, speaking for two hours on "The Republican Form of Government." In August he was addressing audiences in Ningpo and Hangchow on progressive municipal policies. He was reported at that time as being in good spirits and as enthusiastic as ever for his ideas.

Lucky man! Why should he not be in good spirits? He had come back to his own, because Destiny had been playing the game for him, not because of efficiency or statesmanship on his part; in Japan he had shown neither. That Yuan Shih-kai should have attempted the restoration of the monarchy with himself as the Emperor, and that he should have failed in this and lost face forever, that finally he should have come to his end under circumstances which left a suspicion of unnatural death, were all—dramatically considered—the most perfect possible playing into Sun Yat-sen's hands.

II. THE SHATTERING OF THE PARLIAMENTARY DREAM

In a real sense Yuan Shih-kai was a man without a successor. Among his civil and military protégés there was no one strong enough to take up the power he had wielded. Constitutionalism once more had the field. The new President did not have Yuan Shih-kai's force of character and had none of his craftiness. He was very willing to be constitutional; he reconvened the old Parliament and gave it favorable conditions for realizing itself. For a while it seemed to approach a legislative norm. If it had had no crucial business to consider, it might conceivably have been a moderate success. Although the Republic had already devised for herself three constitutions, this Parliament went hopefully to work on another, using as its tentative frame the constitutional draft made in the Temple of Heaven in 1913.

Difficulties began with the arrival of President Wilson's message of Feb. 4, 1917 to all neutral nations urging them to break off diplomatic relations with Germany as a protest against her announcement of unlimited submarine warfare. China brought herself to the point of handing the German and Austrian ministers their passports on March 14th; but for five months after that the Government was unable to reach a conclusion as to whether or not China should declare war. The Premier, Tuan Chi-jui, was for war. The Parliament was for keeping on its way and making a constitution. The Premier summoned a conference in Peking of the military governors of the provinces. This was the moment when the camel put his head inside the tent; it was the fateful day when the military chiefs of the provinces, who had recently been given the title *tuchun,* made their entry into national affairs. They gathered at the capital, and were easily won over by the Premier to the plan for entering the war. The Cabinet also favored war. When the matter was presented to the Parliament, a mob demonstration was staged outside the building to threaten the members into the war policy. Even as tactics this act was a bad mistake. Immediately the newspapers criticized the Premier for inciting the riot. The Cabinet resigned in protest leaving the Premier standing alone with the military governors as his backing. These *tuchuns* in retaliation began to criticize the infant constitution which the Parliament was tenderly nourishing. Parliament, and public opinion generally, demanded the retirement of the Premier. He would not resign; the

President had to dismiss him. When, on May 30th, C. T. Wang, chairman of the Committee for Drafting the Constitution, made a public statement about its features, a group of the northern military governors made emphatic their protest against the constitution by declaring their provinces independent. These militarists got together and called for the dissolution of Parliament, threatening, if refused, to march on Peking. Then the President, in a weak moment, yielded to the military pressure and dissolved the Parliament. The members fled, some in disguise; many of them found their way to Shanghai. Another parliamentary failure had been added to China's efforts to be a republic. This time the force that crushed the legislature was military power, then on a rapid increase in the country.

Representatives of the militarist party reached Peking June 15, 1917. By the end of the month the uncompromising old scholar and reformer, Kang Yu-wei, arch-monarchist of them all, arrived quietly at Peking. The next day the capital was electrified by the news that the boy Emperor had been restored to the throne. This episode is particularly complicated by wheels within wheels. Like many other Chinese political events it was not just what it appeared on the surface. As a restoration, however, it was futile and lasted less than two weeks. A return to republican forms was brought about, not by the Kuomintang but by the militarist group led by Tuan Chi-jui, who took Peking July 14. President Li refused to resume his office, so the Vice-president was put in his place on August 1st. On August 14, 1917, China declared war on Germany and Austria.

In entering the war China was motivated partly by ambition and partly by mistrust. The ascending militarists were especially jingoistic and especially self-interested. If they did not clearly seek the war in the hope of advancing military control over civilian control in Chinese affairs, this motive was soon suggested to them by the civilian apprehensiveness. Any further development of militarism alarmed the Kuomintang; certain of its leaders—but not all—opposed China's participation in the war, urging this danger, and pointing out the chances for official corruption which would come with war loans; they emphasized also the need of national concentration upon internal development. What cut the nerve of this pacifism and incalculably reinforced the war movement was mistrust of Japan, whose part in the World War had already been conspicuous, and whose influence in the peace-making would be certain to threaten China's territorial integrity. In the earliest months of the war Japan had attacked and captured the German holdings in the Province of Shantung, seizing not only the harbor of Tsingtao, but also the German-built railways flung out into the rich Province of Shantung. Japan would expect these as a permanent reward at the end of the war and China was determined Japan should not have them. So China entered the World War in the hope of having an effective voice in the treaty-making when the war was over.

Sun Yat-sen belonged to the faction that was more interested in establishing a constitutional China than in getting the country into the World War. His sympathies and his public utterances were with C. T. Wang's group struggling at Peking to bring about the acceptance of a new constitutional basis for the Republic. When the contest between the militarist and constitutionalist factions was at its height, and when Great Britain and the other Allies were leaving no stone unturned to influence China to join the war, Sun Yat-sen issued an open letter to Lloyd George that was both patriotic and alarmist.

I owe my life to England. I am grateful to her for it. It is both as friend of England and as Chinese patriot that I have come to point out to you the momentous consequences that the campaign undertaken by agents of yours urging China to go to war, may have for China and for England. . . .

China has always had unbounded confidence in the strength of England and in her ultimate victory, but this confidence has diminished since the campaign was started to make us enter into the struggle, a campaign that has gone so far as to insist upon the sending of Chinese troops to Mesopotamia. All this leads to nothing but the lessening of England's prestige, for the Chinese cannot understand why the Allies should have need of them in order to beat Germany.[3]

He suggests further that China's participation in the war might result in indiscriminate massacres of foreigners, in outbursts of Mohammedan fanaticism, and eventually in such a state of anarchy as would disrupt the Entente itself and bring it to disaster.

Participation in the World War—even though it consisted for China chiefly in supplying labor battalions in place of the shiploads of coolies, already taken to the front, added its appreciable stimulus to the development of the militarism that was abroad in the land. From her entry into the European war until now the history of the Republic has been the disheartening story of internal wars. It is not necessary here to follow the formations and reformations of the military rivals. It is enough to note the general facts. With Yuan's death the military machine had lost its recognized master. Once-subordinated generals developed as regional rulers with armies of their own. The most ambitious of them struggled with one another in wars for the control of Peking. If supremacy could be achieved with an outward show of constitutionalism, they played the game. But they not only chose premiers and manipulated cabinets, they put down and set up the presidents. Parliaments for a little while longer were felt to be desirable as a means of getting a president elected. But when in 1923, a notorious militarist, named Tsao Kun, was reported to have paid five thousand dollars a vote for his own election to the presidency, the disgust of the country was unmistakable. Unfortunately the parliament that proved so corruptible was the re-convened rump of the original patriot's Parliament of 1913. So disillusionment about parliaments was complete and Sun Yat-sen was one of the most outspoken critics. The republican form of government had failed to function in China. The pretense of governing constitutionally became thinner and thinner, until finally it was possible for Chang Tso-lin to settle himself at Peking as dictator in 1927, without even pretending to any constitutional sanction. With this anticipatory summary of the trends in the North we return to Sun Yat-sen.

III. SUN YAT-SEN'S DREAM OF A CONSTITUTIONAL SOUTH

When in June, 1917, the revolutionary general, President Li Yuan-hung, was coerced by militarists into dissolving a properly constituted Parliament with a constitution almost ready to be adopted, the future must have looked hopeless indeed to the patriots of the Kuomintang, who fled as best they could to places safer than Peking. Many of them gathered at Shanghai; Sun Yat-sen was there, and they had their counsels. They felt that Peking had become impossible for patriotic idealists; the old officialdom and the newer militarism made a combination that boded no good to the Republic in that quarter. From Shanghai the members, true to form, issued a manifesto declaring the dissolution of the Parliament illegal, the convening of any other parliament illegal, and announcing their purpose of re-convening themselves at some other place than Peking. They also denounced the monarchist attempt and called for the forfeiture of the financial settlement made with the Imperial family in 1912 (payments were already much in arrears) on the ground that the attempted restoration was treason against the Republic.

After being photographed with his following, Sun Yat-sen started for Canton with the high purpose of setting up a truly constitutional government. He was received at that city with a great demonstration. He made much of his rôle as "protector of the Constitution"—meaning the first constitution of all, the "provisional constitution" made at Nanking in 1912, which, in spite of elaborated rivals, had never been legally superseded. The dissolved Parliament was summoned to reassemble at Canton. By August, 1917, the members had responded in sufficient numbers to constitute a quorum. The arrival on August 5th of a considerable fraction of the small Chinese navy to join the new group was the occasion of a great public reception. At that time it was still hoped that Li Yuan-hung would join the South and resume the presidency. The Parliament organized a provisional military government with Sun Yat-sen as Generalissimo. He issued a fulminating manifesto against the northern militarists and made some show of organizing expeditions to subdue them. Associated with him in the civil administration were some of the ablest patriots of the revolution. Wu Ting-fang, for years the witty Chinese minister at Washington, stood by Sun Yat-sen loyally. Tang Shao-yi, Sun Yat-sen's distinguished fellow-townsman, joined the group. All three men were natives of Kwangtung. Foreign journalists who were watching this latest of Chinese experiments referred to them as the Triumvirate. Sun Fo B.A., University of California, 1916, and M.A. of Columbia, 1917, joined his father and acted as secretary of the "Canton National Assembly."

For a while the Southerners had considerable sympathy from the other provinces. But the outcome was not very different from the Peking failures. Factions inherent in the very composition of the group cleft the legislature, harassed the administration and disputed the military power. A notorious assassination emphasized the resemblance to earlier political tactics. Sun Yat-sen found pitted against him and his policies the formidable western group, known as the "Kwangsi faction." He was neither a cunning man after the old mandarin pattern, nor a wizard at conjuring up the not-yet-understood coöperations of democracy. He had missed even a normal man's experience in working with others; his eccentric revolutionary career had deprived him of the corrective discipline of being obliged to get along with people with whom he developed friction. Instead of becoming more resourceful in coöperating with people, his tendency since 1913 had been to become more and more autocratic. His opponents brought him down from his military dictatorship by putting through the legislature a bill for the organization of the government on a committee plan. Instead of Sun Yat-sen as Generalissimo, there was created an Administrative Committee, in which he was one of seven. It soon became apparent that he was ineffective on the Committee; he considered himself defeated, gave up trying to coöperate, and went back to Shanghai. During 1919 and 1920 he was living at 29 Rue Molière in the French Concession, and was elaborating his theories into books. His son again took up journalism and remained in Canton.

In 1920 Sun Yat-sen instructed one of his Kwangtung followers, Chen Chiung-ming, a man of much military experience, to oust the rival Kwangsi Province group from Canton. With the slogan "Kwangtung for the Kwangtungese" he accomplished his task in November, 1920, and Sun Yat-sen was able to return. The rump of the old Parliament returned also and in April, 1921, elected Sun Yat-sen "President of China." The man who won back his domain for him, Chen Chiung-ming, was made Governor of Kwangtung Province and Commander-in-Chief of the troops. Inasmuch as Sun Yat-sen's entire "Republic of China" consisted at that moment of one province only, and Chen was Governor of that province, the two men were bound to have some clashes of authority.

Always a revolutionist at heart, Sun Yat-sen could not accept so restricted a map of the Republic. First, he despatched Chen Chiung-ming in July, 1921, to win back forcibly the western province, Kwangsi, which even under the monarchy had been coupled in one viceroyalty with Kwangtung. He did this satisfactorily. Next

Sun Yat-sen wanted to launch a military expedition against the
North. This did not appeal to Chen's judgment, but Sun Yat-sen,
with much publicity, set it afoot and led it in person in the winter
of 1921–22. It failed. Sun Yat-sen asserted that it collapsed because
it was not supported with money and ammunition by Chen Chiung-
ming. In April Sun Yat-sen returned to Canton and summarily dismissed Chen from the governorship of the province, putting his
old friend Wu Ting-fang in his place. Of course this made an enemy
of Chen.

Of Sun Yat-sen's three brief tenures of power in Canton this—
the second—was the period in which the South began to attract
the attention of China by reason of certain promising reforms in
both local and provincial government, also in sounder financial administration, and in the modernization of the city of Canton. A
small beginning was made toward a reorganization of the Kuomintang, under which the government ostensibly functioned; but Sun
Yat-sen maintained for the most part a personal and autocratic relationship with his supporters.

When, in 1922, it was the fortune of the Peking Government to
be overturned by that *rara avis* among war lords, a General with
pretensions to classical scholarship, he, Wu Pei-fu, assumed the rôle
of restorer of constitutionalism in the North. He reinstated in the
presidential office the long-displaced second President of the Republic, Li Yuan-hung. At once new hope awoke in the hearts of
old patriots that China was about to find the lost path to constitutional government. Sun Yat-sen was invited to come north to plan
for a re-unified China. He declined to do so, and thereby incurred
criticism. There was no love lost between him and Li Yuan-hung, and
he had grown suspicious with the years. In his refusal the already
alienated Chen Chiung-ming found a pretext. He called for Sun Yat-
sen's resignation from the southern presidency on the ground that
constitutionalism was restored in Peking, and that Sun Yat-sen's

period of "protecting the Constitution" was now at an end. But Sun Yat-sen would not resign. So, on June 16th, Chen attacked the Canton presidential residence and drove the President out. In addition to personal revenge, the hand of Peking was suspected in this, and Sun Yat-sen's resentment of "northern militarists" increased; Wu Pei-fu became a focus of his enmity. Sun Yat-sen fled to a ship of the loyal navy, while his house was burned with his books and manuscripts in it. For fifty-six days he remained on the cruiser hoping that friends would come to succor him. Chiang Kai-shek, then a young military man, was with Sun Yat-sen on the cruiser; he spent the long leisure in writing an account of the whole trouble, which is published in a small book with a preface by Sun Yat-sen. When no help came, Sun Yat-sen finally fled to Shanghai, where Ching-ling earlier had taken refuge. Again he issued a manifesto, August 15th, in which he advocated such idealistic policies as the rehabilitation of soldiers as workers, the development of industries to improve economic conditions, the practice of universal suffrage as a check upon militarists. Where so little had been put into practice, such idealism seems to miss its point. In coördination of power with other men Sun Yat-sen was not superior to his countrymen; he failed as they failed; he, too, lacked experience and skill in democratic group functioning. There was no period in his life when he made such bitter enemies or was so severely attacked with criticism. What he accomplished in practical affairs was an inglorious story. If his life had ended at this time, it is doubtful whether China could have heroized him.

IV. RATIONALIZING IN THE WRECKAGE

The Revolution failed to establish a republic except in name. On occasions Sun Yat-sen admitted this frankly. The Revolution overthrew the monarchy and did very little else except make experiments from which humiliating lessons are deducible. The more recent documents of the Kuomintang, which show in part Sun Yat-sen's hand, account for the failure along two main lines—lack of a well-organized political party, and the fatal compromise with the "counter revolutionists"—meaning by them officials of the old régime, notably Yuan Shih-kai, who inherited ideas of autocratic government which they did not relinquish. It is imputed against them that their motive was the wish to retain privilege and power. These explanations have obviously a Party bias.

A deeper-cutting account of the failure is found in Sun Yat-sen's small treatise *China's Revolution,* written in 1923, after the Canton rebellion had put him out of power. To the question "Did the Revolution create a democracy?" he replies, "No! Since the Revolution everything has been unstable." He affirms that the Revolution failed because the three stages which he considered essential were disregarded, that is, a period of military revolution, followed by a period of teaching the people to govern themselves, and only then a third period of constitutional government. The fatal mistake was the omission of one of these steps. A jump was attempted from the military period into the constitutional period without the intermediate process of preparing the people for constitutional government. Sun Yat-sen reasons that to take such a jump was to make one of three bad results inevitable.

Either, first, all the old bad habits of government would persist without change—in which case democracy would be impossible;

Or, second, the old bad habits would be only modified and called new—which would be the creation of a false democracy;

Or, third, the new democracy would be crushed out and old habits survive—then even the name of democracy would be gone.

After this analysis Sun Yat-sen goes more fully into exposition of the omitted educational stage, teaching the smallest governmental divisions (*hsien*) the practice of self-government. Without the development of local self-government, he contends, democracy has no base to rest upon, the people have no channel for the use of power and no check upon the tyranny of higher officials; manipulation of elections and all the consequent abuses become at once possible.

This is one of the soberest statements I have found in Sun Yat-sen's writings. His recognition of education in self-government as a prerequisite to constitutional government is sound to the core. The difficulty is that when once a revolution has been carried out and the existing government toppled over, it becomes impossible so to programize the development of a nation. Everything has to go forward together, central government as well as local. The old monarchy stood a better chance of enforcing a period of disciplinary learning. But, we have already seen what happened when the Imperial régime attempted this. Nobody wanted to be a learner; every one wanted to be a complete democratic citizen at once. The pressure of radicalism was too strong and the "Program" was first cut down from nine to five years and then discarded. And by whom discarded? By the revolutionists of 1911, who put in its place Sun Yat-sen's three stages and grew impatient of them also. In the words of a proverb which the Chinese often use, they were "wanting to run before learning to walk."

If Sun Yat-sen has put his finger on the real cause of the failure of the Republic, he has indirectly indicted himself, for he was the pivot around which the wrong turning was made. Up to the time when he returned to Shanghai, Dec. 24, 1911, the revolution was still in the military stage, following faithfully the program of the "Revolutionary Manifesto." The jump to constitutional government was made when they elected him President and he proclaimed the Republic. The three years of military rule and the six years of developing local self-government were given up at that moment.

It is easy to forget how much China was misled by the demonstration Japan gave her. The over-confident rush into a republic was an effort to accomplish the coveted "modernization," and to do it more thoroughly, more progressively and more brilliantly than Japan had done it. It was a thoughtless over-confidence, but it apparently possessed very many—even foreign observers. That Japan had done wonders seemed a sufficient reason for believing any miracle of China. But Japan did not ruthlessly destroy its major centralizing forces before attempting to reform its government; it retained certain of the old big loyalties and made them serve the new age. In Japan devotion to the ancient, and unquestionably indigenous, Imperial family was revived and intensified, whereas the Chinese were easily persuaded that their two-hundred-and-sixty-seven-year-old dynasty was upstart and alien.

Moreover, China destroyed, root and branch, one of its most important centralizing and unifying forces in the reform of the educational system for civil service. It was not the Republic that did this; the damage was an accomplished fact before the Republic came into being, although its disintegrating results were not yet apparent. When China destroyed the old examination system and set up in its place a modernized national system of education, she did something more than reform the education of youth. Although the examination system had great influence on education, it was not in itself a system of education; it was an adjunct of government. A change that was not bad as an educational reform proved disastrous as a governmental change. With the abolition of the civil service examinations China destroyed without knowing it one of the strongest cohesives of its national order. It was a Board of the Imperial Government that appointed the examiners who went out into the provinces to conduct the examinations. The very fact that a candidate passed the examinations made of him an aspirant for position and a suppliant to the government. From ministers and viceroys down to district magistrates, all obtained office as a gift of the government. The power of dismissing officials was absolute. Thus the impressively conducted examination system reaching out into every prefecture of the country was the very foundation of governmental control. But, in the passionate demand for Western learning, the system was abolished because its educational tests were archaic. The examination halls crumbled or were torn down. Educational qualification through schools took the place of a highly correlated method of sifting candidates for office. Is it any wonder that, as the old officials have died, the central government has grown weaker and weaker? Is it any wonder that the huge country has disintegrated into regions and provinces?

It would seem that China might have retained the correlating examination system, building up alongside it a system of modern education to feed it, and in due time to change the subjects upon which examination was given. But here again imitation led China astray. Other countries did not find such an elaborate examination system necessary; why should China have it? The reformers doubtless reasoned that China could have postal service examinations, or customs examinations or whatever civil service examinations might later seem necessary—as in America, for instance. Meanwhile she has had chaos. Now that the original cohesive has been melted out, it will be many years before a new welding can take place. Such cohesives as the old examination system are not produced by strokes of constitutional writ—call them "organic law" or "provisional constitution" or what you will.

V. THE NEW TIDE OF YOUTH

To our sweeping Western eyes an account of the Republican period is apt to seem either a chronicle of petty jealousies and revenges, or a story of ideal schemes frustrated by the frailty of quarreling men. The very names of the quarrelers become tiresome read-ing. Yet over these disappointing pages here and there shines a ray of light. It is for these rays that one endures the tediousness.

It is fortunate for the progress of the race that in all chaotic pe-riods nature stands ready to provide a relief: she lets the mistake-making generation pass away, and a new youth supersede it. So in China: in spite of the mistakes of elder statesmen and of middle-aged parliamentarians, in spite even of florescent militarism, a new youth was emerging. Happily a new generation is never a sectional matter. In South and North alike, both in Canton and in Peking, youth was making new ideas felt. Modern China has not seen the equal in creative thinking of the decade that began about 1916. China then experienced a lively and promising ferment. The Chinese name for it, "The New Tidal Wave," is a more exactly expressive figure than the borrowed French word *renaissance*. Like a tidal wave it has receded now, but it was gloriously on-rushing while it lasted.

Particularly in the politics of the South youth was making itself felt. Some who were very young when the Tung Meng Hui was formed became prime movers now: Wang Ching-wei, for instance, and Chiang Kai-shek. Children of early revolutionists were given positions of responsibility. Sun Fo returned from American studies just in time to go back to Canton with his father and become a promoter of modernization. Wu Ting-fang's able son (recently in his father's old position as Chinese minister at Washington) served the South in many ways. Always within reach of the younger group was Sun Yat-sen's wife; being in the confidence of her much older husband, she tended to keep him in contact with youth and youth with him. These three are typical of the younger people who in these years supported Sun Yat-sen and threw themselves into the progressive movements at Canton.

Sun Yat-sen's first term as head of the Southern Government was, as we have already seen, very brief; he was soon leveled to a committee position and then pushed out by the Kwangsi faction. While he was living privately in Shanghai, it was his younger Chinese admirers who helped him to publish, in the English language, in 1920 the startling proposals called *The International Development of China*. When he returned to Canton late in 1920 and became "President," the aggressive young men of his following carried the party with them in a movement to reform the municipal government of Canton and to modernize the city. A new pattern of local government was created, and Sun Fo was made mayor of the city. He lost the position when his father was forcibly ejected from Canton by his alienated henchman in June, 1922, and regained it when his father, in February, 1923, returned for his last Canton period. Changes in the appearance of the old port attracted much attention at the time. The ancient city wall was demolished and the enormous quantity of crude stone thus released was used in building macadam roads and boulevards. Improvement of the bund (the commercial waterfront) and of the business center of the city was accomplished by American methods of expropriation. Public utilities were developed and parks and playgrounds planned. People were saying: Canton is giving a demonstration to China of what modernization may do for a city. It was the energy and faith of youth that was back of the demonstration.

More important than the material modernization of ancient cities was the intellectual modernization that characterized the younger generation. By this time students educated abroad were flowing back to China in a stream of no mean magnitude. Their ultra-modernism may be illustrated by their interest in the Soviet Revolution. After October, 1917, the eyes of China's younger intelligentsia were turned toward Moscow with an eagerness to learn from it, if possible, some plan for bettering the desperate state of their own country. When it became known that Sun Yat-sen had succeeded in getting a telegram of congratulation through to Lenin, the hearts of youth applauded. When Soviet agents began to appear in China about 1920, they found a generation eager to be persuaded.

Peking was intellectually the most vital of all the centers of the new youth. The year before Yuan Shih-kai died, a magazine began publication there in September, 1915, under the title which literally means *The New Youth (Hsin Ching Nien)*, and with a French sub-title *La Jeunesse*. The editor of this monthly, Chen Tu-hsiu, was a born radical and a brilliant publicist. It is quite in his character that when the Communist Party was organized in China about 1920 he was among its earliest members. The position which he held for a while as Dean of the College of Letters in Peking National University added prestige and influence to his publication, which became an outlet for advanced opinions on many subjects. The most famous controversy in which this magazine took part was one which we may characterize as the battle for democratic books.

All the world now knows the story of this spirited fight, which originated among Chinese students in the United States and was carried to Peking by a challenging article sent by Hu Shih to *The New Youth*. In it he brilliantly advocated the use of the language of common speech in serious writing in place of the stilted and formalized book-language, which in the course of centuries had so far departed from the spoken language that it was intelligible to scholars only. The opposition the literary reformers met was a terrible trial of mettle. As Hu Shih and his supporters fought gallantly, journalism went rapidly over to their side. The students also took up the vernacular written language and used it effectively in the propaganda against Japan at the time of the famous patriotic strike and boycott of 1919. It is said that in that year about four hundred new periodicals appeared in China, most of them written in the language of common speech. Novels, also short stories, poetry, drama, serious and learned books began to be written in the vital language of the people. As a result of this victory, primary school children of today no longer have the blind struggle with unintelligible classics that Sun Yat-sen had as a boy; they are taught in the living "national language." A great and creditable revolution this has been; there has been an effective overthrow of the tyranny of an obsolete literature and the development of a literature for all the people.

What was Sun Yat-sen's relation to the movement? All that he stood for profited by it beyond reckoning. But, although he seemed to favor it, his own personal practice must be described by the word with which he used to lash his political opponents: he was "reactionary." As late as 1923 he put out a treatise, *China's Revolution,* in stilted, old-fashioned Chinese. Hu Shih, braving the censorship, has criticized Sun Yat-sen for setting a bad example which the Kuomintang has at times followed. What has saved some of Sun Yat-sen's books for democracy was his habit of public-speaking. When he lectured, he talked quite naturally. Such lectures as the *San Min Chu I,* taken down as they were by shorthand, have been made into easily readable Chinese books; hence their ready popularization.

That the language revolution was an emancipation of mind for China is evident from the fact that in its wake came a marked intellectual renaissance. New freedom in writing brought with it a new freedom in the discussion of ideas, and the discussion was very lively. Hu Shih, who had finished his work for a Doctorate of Philosophy under John Dewey, returned to China in 1917 and joined the staff of Peking National University as Professor of Philosophy. That University was in the process of revivification under a president of marked ability, who knew how to gather able men about him. There Hu Shih and others led the younger generation in a critical scrutiny of China's cultural heritage in arts and letters, in ethics and religion, in scholarship and social custom. An extraordinary open-mindedness toward values to be found in the West coexisted with appreciation of the best that China had thought and felt. To the city of Peking students traveled by hundreds and by thousands. Many of them leaped into the language controversy. A student magazine, written entirely in the common language, began appearing in September, 1918. It was called significantly *Hsin Chao, The New Tidal Wave,* and had for a European sub-title *The Renaissance.* It was a vital and vivid publication.

What brought the students of China into corporate consciousness of their power and significance was, strangely enough, the Treaty of Versailles. By secret wartime agreements certain of the Allies had promised to support Japan's claims to the former German hold-ings in Shantung. But that did not make it acceptable to China, when, as a result, the makers of the peace stipulated that Japan should have the rights in China that had been granted to Germany. The sequel is well known: Chinese students, first at Peking, then all over the country "walked out" of their academic work, when they heard that their own altogether too pro-Japanese Government was on the point of authorizing the signing of the treaty. They did not cease to agitate by mouth and pen, by banners and placards and processions, until Japanese goods were effectively boycotted, the most culpable ministers forced to resign, and the Chinese representa-tives at Versailles had refused to be party to the treaty. Those were heroic days for the young in China. By the time they had won the victory, the students of China were knit together in a nation-wide organization and were conscious of political power.

While these forces were working, Sun Yat-sen was living in the retirement of a defeated politician in the French Concession at Shanghai and editing a magazine of his own. For the second time in his life a new movement among students was preparing for him a new following. After the students had resisted Japan so valiantly, Sun Yat-sen joined in the protests against "the Japanizing of China."

"I do not want my country to wake up some day," he said, "and find itself a Japanese China. The Twenty-one Demands showed Japan's hand." Alas for the inconsistencies required of a revolutionist! Sun Yat-sen's eyes had been blind in 1914.

In yet other fields men were fighting hard battles for the success of the Republic. The movement for mass education has been one of the most heroic efforts to save the day for democracy in China. Fortunately, China has had a few seers who have looked inwardly upon the country's problems. Among them were certain men who saw clearly what Sun Yat-sen never admitted—that in the general level of education China was not yet fit for a democracy; to them it was clear that if she ever was to succeed in any such ideal form of government, something more thorough-going must be done than the political tutelage of which Sun Yat-sen was thinking. How could a republic succeed in a land where illiteracy was so enormous? To show what the actual condition was it is necessary only to cite the first "Program" toward a constitutional government—the "Nine-Years Program" made under the Empress Dowager. By using all the education and reform massed in that plan, it was hoped that at the end of nine years—that is, in 1917—five per cent of the people might be able to read and write. Although illiteracy of the masses cannot be thought of as the cause of the bad functioning of the Republic's governing groups, which were literate enough, it can be readily seen that it made of popular suffrage a dangerous farce.

To the creators of the mass-education movement it seemed that the Republic, having been prematurely established, could not wait for a literate generation to grow up from properly educated children. How far off that desirable end might be no one could tell. For, however optimistic earlier educational bodies may have been, it has become more and more apparent that before education can be made effectively compulsory in China there must be raised up a great corps of teachers, and enormous sums of money must be found for salaries and equipment. It goes without saying that the provision of these has been incalculably retarded by the chaotic conditions that have prevailed in Republican China. Yet in the face of such hard facts men have had the courage to attempt the education of adults. China's urgent need of an intelligent citizenship was to them a compelling motive, and the victory for a democratic written language seemed to open the way.

The very original plan upon which the mass education movement was projected had its suggestion in welfare work done among the Chinese labor battalions sent to Europe in the World War. The men of these units were for the most part so illiterate as to be unable to write letters home. An educational effort was organized for them on a simple plan which had been originally thought of as an aid to foreigners studying the Chinese language, that is, of ascertaining the words most frequently used and concentrating upon them as a reading vocabulary. That was the beginning of the "thousand-character" method now so vigorously promoted by Y. C. James Yen and his associates in mass education. A corollary has been the creation of books in the limited vocabulary. The motive appealed to has consistently been good citizenship. The diploma given for completion of the course confers on the graduate the quaint distinction of "literate citizen."

DOCUMENTATION OF QUOTED PASSAGES

[1] *The North China Herald* (Shanghai) Vol. 119, p. 399. [2] Ibid. [3] *New York Herald Tribune,* Feb. 10, 1929, Magazine Section, p. 14.

SOURCES AND AUTHORITIES: See Appendix C, p. 401.

CHAPTER VIII

Russia and Reorganization

WHILE China was surging with the new tidal wave of thought, Sun Yat-sen was dividing his time between brief tenures of power in Canton and retirement to the home of his own choice in Shanghai. His leisure he spent in writing. The years from 1918 to his death in 1925 cover the most active literary period of his life. He issued from Shanghai a periodical in Chinese called the *Reconstruction Miscellany,* in which he published articles that were afterward collected into books. Thus there is abundance of material to show what Sun Yat-sen was thinking about China at this period of his life. The content of his own mind is particularly worth noticing, that it may be compared with his utterances after Soviet influences began to play upon him.

From these writings it is evident that Sun Yat-sen was still puzzling over the failure of the Republic. Although the Revolution had succeeded in overthrowing the Monarchy, the Republic had failed. Why? Sun Yat-sen had actually thought of the reconstruction of China into a republic as an easy matter compared with overthrowing the Manchus. He says, "When the period of destruction closed, revolutionary reconstruction seemed an easy thing to me."

At first it seemed as if I, as the leader, would be able very easily to give effect to the programme of the revolutionary party, *i. e.* nationalism, democracy, Socialism and the Fivefold Constitution, as well as solve the problems created by the Revolution. If I had succeeded in achieving this, China would have found her place amongst the family of nations and would have entered the path of progress and happiness. But, unfortunately, the Revolution was scarcely completed when the members of our party unexpectedly turned out to be of a different opinion from myself, considering my ideals too elevated and unattainable for the reconstruction of modern China.

These doubts, moreover, were taken for granted, and even some of my comrades began to entertain doubts concerning the realisation of my programme. Therefore it turned out that my programme had less chances of being realised when I held the post of President than when I was the leader of the Party which was preparing the Revolution. Hence the attempt at reconstruction was not successful, and the national tasks, which I put forward, were abandoned after the Revolution.

. . . If we analyse our first promptings to carry out the Chinese Revolution, we shall see that we had in view the salvation of the Chinese people and the country; whereas the result has been quite the opposite, and the Chinese people is becoming more and more oppressed, the country more and more unhappy.

To a considerable extent this results from my inability to influence my party comrades and, apparently, my incapacity to guide them. But, on the other hand, my party comrades also cannot escape the reproach of insufficient conviction and effort in the realisation of our revolutionary ideals and the carrying out of our revolutionary programme.[1]

Many times Sun Yat-sen said to his countrymen in effect: "The failure of the Republic is the result of departing from my plans." He seems never to have attributed the republican fiasco in any degree to faultiness or impracticability in his planning. He admitted no doubt whatever that the program he had drawn up was the right program—even to details. He never conceded that it was too big, or too inclusive, or too difficult, or that it failed to reckon with actual conditions or with the limitations of human nature. He resented the growing opinion that he was idealistic and impractical. Yet, in casting about for explanations, he is far from consistent as to the point of departure from his plans which was the chief cause of the revolutionary fiasco.

In one article he is ready to admit that the political intelligence of the Chinese "is immeasurably lower than that of the French at the time of the French Revolution, just as is their capacity for self-government," but he goes on to say that he dealt with that fact when he planned a preparatory period of education in citizenship (a period, it may be recalled, of only six years). The preparatory period had been omitted altogether; hence the failure of the Republic, he asserted.

But when some one urged the insufficiency of intelligence as an argument for a much longer educational process, Sun Yat-sen would not admit so much:

Someone said to me: "If matters are as you say . . . it is impossible to transform China into a modern State until the whole Chinese people has received education. This follows from your own words, when you say that action or realisation is not difficult in itself, but it is knowledge that is difficult, or, in the words of the ancient sages, 'tens and maybe hundreds of years are required for the diffusion of universal education.' Yet you imagine that China can immediately, by a single jump, reach the position of a powerful and wealthy nation, one amongst the world Powers. Where is the logic of your assertions?"

To this I reply: the pupil first learns, and then knows how to act: yet, without having learned, he can also act. After all, in the days before science flourished nearly everything was first done and then learned later. . . .

In application to nation-building, it must be said that if you are striving for the reorganisation of the State, and moreover by the path of revolution, then to act before your actions are fully understood is a matter, not only of possibility, but also of necessity. The majority of countries whose power has flourished, as for example the Great Powers, first acquired their strength, and only then began organising the education of their people. Speaking of China, we can say that our intelligence is quite sufficient to enable us to take our place, at one bound, in the ranks of the Great Powers. The obstacle to this lies, not in the fact that without learning you cannot act, but in the worthlessness of our Government and our officials. They commit many crimes, the worst of which is that they seek to advance only their personal avaricious interests and do not reckon in the least with the interests of the State or the nation. The tuchuns accumulate millions in a very short time by means of robbery, and none of them takes any heed that he is undermining the vital forces of his country. . . .

If our Government officials did not seek power for selfish ends, and did not commit crimes which hurt the whole people, China too would soon attain greatness.[2]

Sun Yat-sen goes on to argue that the way to national realization is not primarily educational but economic. He urges that salvation will come by enlisting foreign financial and technical help in the development of the resources and industry of China. In this he is re-stating another of his unfulfilled plans. For years he had been advocating the industrial development of China with foreign help. Here he revives his old policies on a larger scale. He castigates "the conceited self-satisfaction" which "cannot understand the benefits of international coöperation, and therefore will not tolerate the thought of any superiority over themselves, or of allowing others to correct their mistakes." He sees in this a narrow-minded China, hindering her own progress.

Chinese aspirations can be realised only when we understand that, to regenerate the State and to save the country from destruction at this critical moment, we must welcome the influx of large-scale foreign capital on the largest possible scale, and also must consider the question of attracting foreign scientific forces and highly trained experts to work in our country and train us. Then in the course of the next ten years we shall create our own powerful large-scale industry and shall accumulate technical and scientific knowledge.

After these ten years it will be possible gradually to pay off the foreign loans and acquire complete independence in our work, possessing a complete equipment of the necessary knowledge. Then our national culture can be made literally the common property of all the Chinese. This will render possible the awakening of the slumbering forces and possibilities of China. Remember the Chinese proverbs. . . . "When you heal a sick man, always begin with the worst disease," . . . and "Only a man who has been fed and clothed can observe all the ceremonies." If industry is developed, the full development of the economic resources of China is possible, and only then will it be possible to carry out the universal education of the people.[3]

In yet another essay Sun Yat-sen takes the position that "the cessation of the ceremony of the oath, that foundation of law, was one of the chief reasons for the failure of revolutionary construction." The value of the public oath was one of Sun Yat-sen's fixed ideas. The members of his first society had been sworn in; his second society was called the Together Sworn Society (*Tung Meng Hui*) and required a rigorous oath. Sun Yat-sen felt that an oath of allegiance should be a condition of citizenship in the Republic. With journalistic publicity he revived this proposal and published, under the date Jan. 12, 1919, a new oath with his name attached, and capped it with the exhortation: "Chinese patriots, follow my example!"

I, Sun-Yat-Sen, truthfully and sincerely take this public oath that from this moment I will destroy the old and build the new, and fight for the self-determination of the people, and will apply all my strength to the support of the Chinese Republic, the realisation of democracy through "the three principles," and to carry into effect "the Fivefold Constitution," for the progress of good government, the happiness and perpetual peace of the people, and for the strengthening of the foundations of the State, in the name of peace throughout the world.[4]

II. RATIONALIZING AND PROGRAMIZING

In China the most famous of all Sun Yat-sen's rationalizings about the failure of the Republic is his psychological theory. This revolves around a controversial problem that may be turned over and over by philosophers in a harmless sort of debate. The magazine articles that contained the analysis were issued in a Chinese volume, *Sun Wen Hsueh Shuo* (Sun Wen's Philosophy). This was later forced into a schematic relationship to his *magnum opus* on Reconstruction. The development of his thesis that action is really easy and that only the knowing-how-to-act is difficult—is not what concerns us. The exposition progresses with a characteristic and pedantic display of Western learning; it is vulnerable at a hundred points, and the illustrations often seem to an Occidental unconvincing to a degree. The experience and state of mind which made Sun Yat-sen develop the theory is what concerns a biographer rather than a criticism of its substance. The Preface to these curious essays is revelatory. Already quoted from, it will bear further quotation:

When the first revolutionary wave went by, and organic reconstruction had to begin, I could not help being agitated and delighted, because at last I had united the ideal which had long matured within me with my plan of revolutionary action, in a programme of national reconstruction for China. I desired immediately to give effect to my programme, in the hope of leading China up the steps of progressive modern science. But there were already people to say to me: "We all recognise that your ideal is lofty and full of merit, and your plan is profound and all-embracing. But do you know that actions are always difficult, while knowledge is always easy?"

When I first heard this I was dumbfounded and much confused, because I myself, like other Chinese, believed in this theory, and considered it indubitable that our ancient scholars taught us the truth. . . .

The theory of the difficulty of action and the easiness of knowledge came to us two thousand years ago, and was accepted all over the country. In the minds of a people of 400 millions it has struck such deep roots that they cannot be torn up without great effort. . . .

The theory . . . is my enemy, a thousand times more powerful than the authority of the Manchu dynasty. The power of the Manchus could achieve only the killing of our bodies, but it could not deprive us of our will. . . . When I was agitating for the Revolution, I could hope for progress, but in the days that followed the establishment of the Republic my plans for the reconstruction of China could in no way be carried out. My thirty years' faithfulness to my ideal was almost crushed by this blow, my iron will almost killed. It was terrible and hateful.

. . . While we believe in our minds in the practicability of any plan, be it to remove mountains or to fill up the sea, it can be easily accomplished. But when we are convinced in the impracticability, even of such simple acts as to move our hand or to break a twig, they cannot be carried out. Truly, great is the power of mind.

. . . Just at the beginning of the victory of the Chinese Revolution, the revolutionaries themselves became the slaves of the theory of the difficulty of action and the easiness of knowledge, began to look on my plan as a Utopia and empty words, and renounced responsibility for the reconstruction of China. . . . Seven years have passed since the foundation of the Chinese Republic, and literally nothing has been done in this direction. On the contrary, the affairs of the Chinese Republic have become more and more complicated and the difficulties of the Chinese people have grown with every passing day.

When I think of this, day after day, my heart aches. . . .

. . . When I saw that my teaching was again coming to the surface as a new current in modern thought, and might become a plan for the national building-up of China, I conceived the purpose of writing a book about it under the title *A Programme of National Reconstruction for China*. . . . Perhaps the Chinese still hold the opinion that actions are difficult but knowledge easy? If so, they will look on my plan, on my programme for the reconstruction of China, as a Utopia.

However I still begin the writing of this book, first of all for the purpose of . . . leading the thoughts of my Chinese fellow-countrymen out of the blind alley in which they are at present. Then they will not look on my programme as a Utopia, and millions of them will be my sympathisers, will fight for the reconstruction of China, will consolidate the Republic, and will create a Government by the people, of the people and for the people. I believe in this, since I believe in the Chinese people.[5]

Against the traditional aphorism Sun Yat-sen pitted one of his own, and insisted that to do is easy, to know is difficult. Looked at in one way his aphorism might seem to be a return to what was fundamental in the Confucian estimate of man—that man is essentially a reasonable being, and that if he sees clearly what is right to do, he is not going to resist it stubbornly, but will act according to the light of his reason. Even the converse was accepted, that if a man does not act ideally, it is because his mind has not clearly grasped the right line of conduct. But this was not at all what Sun Yat-sen was driving at. Nothing was farther from him than the feeling that people must be better grounded in their thinking in order that they might spontaneously act. As regards China's problem, he felt that the thinking had been already done. Had not he himself drafted sound plans for China's reconstruction? Nothing remained but to put the plans into effect. Instead of turning criticism on his own plans, he found an "escape"—from his sense of being sorely thwarted—in the idea that the Chinese people were suffering from paralysis of action as the result of a traditional emphasis of long standing on the difficulty of action. A more realistic mind would have seen that to over-elaborate plans was to kill them. Instead of giving people plans for a few years Sun Yat-sen outlined plans for centuries and expected people, uncowed, to rush zestfully into their execution. Because of this, occidental sympathy naturally goes out to those who turned on Sun Yat-sen with the ancient saying, which politely told him that making plans was not so hard as carrying them out. Sun Yat-sen brooded over this reply, until he convinced himself that a terrible force was fighting against him. This he finally ran down to his own satisfaction in popular slavery to the belief that "to know is easy and to do is difficult." Thereupon he set about preaching that the Chinese must reverse their thinking and accept the doing as easy. He produced a learned-sounding, quasi-philosophical, quasi-scientific argument to "prove" that action is easy, citing cases in which action is possible without any conscious knowledge, and other cases in which ignorant people can act effectively through technical methods furnished by scientists, and so on. His purpose was to release people for action, and thus to bring about a speedy accomplishment of national reconstruction.

It is dangerous to attempt a digest of any of Sun Yat-sen's major writings, because our Western impulse to make a consistent digest is very likely to misrepresent the original. Sun Yat-sen was by no means always a consistent writer, and he was never more inconsistent than in these psychological articles. Popular aphorisms are slippery argumentative material. Sun Yat-sen's reversal of the popular aphorism became in his hands a conveniently flexible thing to use. It could be easily turned first this way and then that way, and given new slants to suit new purposes. Occasionally Sun Yat-sen seems to have forgotten altogether that action was what he wanted to stimulate; then he slipped off into extolling knowledge as difficult, and the making of plans as requiring a high kind of intelligence. This was a defense—not very far subconscious—of the project to which he was giving his energies. Incidentally he reveals what he really thought about the intellectual basis of democracy.

If we divide people according to their individualities, we shall find three groups: first, those who create and invent (they are called pioneers and leaders), the second, those who transmit or disseminate new ideas and inventions (these are called disciples), and the third are those who carry out what they receive from the people of the first two groups, without doubting and without hesitating (these are called unconscious performers and people of action). All these three groups are mutually interdependent and closely connected with one another.[6]

Of his own place in this hierarchy Sun Yat-sen had no doubt: he was a creator—the chief if not the sole creator of the only valid plans for China's reconstruction. It was the duty of the people to put his plans into effect, and that without reflection. "Men of action," he says, "do not at all require to be men steeped in knowledge; it is sufficient to be able to carry out what is required."

This way of thinking not only relieved him of the sense of failure in practical politics, but justified him in his characteristic penchant for elaborating programs. Feeling as he did, that China was suffering from paralysis of action, he might conceivably have come to the conclusion that the most heartening thing he could at the moment do for his country would be to demonstrate how easy it really was to do a piece of constructive work. That would have given China new confidence in a period of disappointment. But the circumstances of Sun Yat-sen's life gave him only three or four small periods of a year or two when he dealt directly with practical affairs; and it must be admitted that these held no remarkable accomplishment. The doing did not prove easy for him. Those who hoped that Sun Yat-sen's Canton experiments would set an inspiring example to China must have been saddened by the multiplying of conflicts.

Always underestimating the magnitude of China's undertaking, and never rightly judging his own limitations, he conceived of "knowing what to do" in terms of elaborated programs. It seems not to have occurred to him that "knowing what to do" involved a profound understanding of what group-life is, and the conditions of its growth and change. Looking for the most part away from China, he built up by a process of selection from foreign ideas and foreign institutions his programs for his country.

If I were to characterize Sun Yat-sen's mind in one word, I should not call him a creator, nor should I call him a seer or a prophet. These words connote a kind of imagination which Sun Yat-sen did not possess. Indeed, the word imagination has to be used very carefully if applied at all to Sun Yat-sen. He had not enough imagination to put himself in anybody else's place; this was a limitation in working with men. Nor did he have imagination of the kind that could foresee the probable outcome of a given course of action; this was his limitation as the leader of his people. Consequently he fell back on purely rational processes addressed toward the production of future results. If I may coin a word, I should describe him as a programatist. I doubt whether the world has ever seen another man who dared to programize on such a scale. His penchant for programizing developed into a prodigious abnormality.

This peculiarity began to develop in his periods of enforced retirement or exile. The first of these came when he was thirty years of age, and his mind was still in the making. Directed by studious instincts and a will for industry, his mind went on the adventure of reasoning and systematizing without the check of practical activity, and with all too little contact with minds that could challenge his own.

We have already seen Sun Yat-sen's programizing impulse at work in the Revolutionary Manifesto, and also in the railway scheme presented to Yuan Shih-kai, which projected the building in ten years of a track-mileage sufficient to girdle the earth three times. It was, however, chiefly in the chequered period of thwarted activity and retirement, from 1917 on, that the elaboration of programs grew upon him. He was then upwards of fifty years of age.

He projected a *magnum opus* which gradually absorbed a good many separately published articles as well as lectures: *The General Principles of National Reconstruction* (*Chien Kuo Fang Lüeh*).

This is his all-inclusive program for China. Sections of it were published as separate books. An exposition of the "Three Principles of the People" was originally planned as a major section of the work. That had got no further in 1921 than an address before a Kuomintang Executive Committee meeting in Canton. The section afterward entitled "Material Reconstruction" will serve as an illustration of Sun Yat-sen's monumental planning. The very manner in which it was presented to the Western world reveals the characteristic to which allusion has been made—Sun Yat-sen's inability to judge the outcome of large events and even of his own projects. His plans for the material development of China were put forth in English, as *The International Development of China* (Shanghai, 1920). This was his projected sequel to the World War. He either did not see, or chose not to see (I think the former), that when once the war was ended, all the war-exhausted nations would find themselves plunging in a terrible morass of economic readjustment, in which relief from war-expenditures would be a *sine qua non* of rehabilitation. Without reckoning with the overdrawal of all resources for the conduct of the war, Sun Yat-sen theorizes that in addition to setting their own houses in order, the nations might direct a quarter of the huge total budget of the last year of the war to the development of China, namely, sixty million dollars a day. Enormous as the sum is, one is bound to say that Sun Yat-sen's plans were comprehensive enough to have made use of it. The international war-organization, he thought, could be continued for this project, which presupposes joint action and a unified policy on the part of the capital-furnishing powers. Improbable as such coöperation was, a more improbable feature was the enthusiastic support of the Chinese people and of the Chinese government.

Yet here is the plan! Under the caption "Communications System," the scheme includes 100,000 miles of railways, 1,000,000 miles of macadam roads; and, in addition, canal construction and canal improvement, river conservancy, telegraphs, telephones and wireless. Modernization of cities, water-power development, mineral, and agricultural development, irrigational engineering, reforestation, and colonization of outlying areas are all included in the colossal plan. Three of the elaborated "programs" are devoted to detailed recommendations for coastal harbors, which he subdivides into world ports, second-class ports, third-class ports and fishing harbors. Another "program" is concerned with industries. He says, "I intend to make all the national industries of China into a Great Trust owned by the Chinese people, and financed with international capital for mutual benefit. . . . In a nutshell, it is my idea to make capitalism create socialism in China so that these two economic forces of human evolution will work side by side in future civilization." In his "Conclusion" Sun Yat-sen makes this naïve admission:

During the course of my writing, these programs have been published in various magazines and newspapers time after time and are being spread all over China. They are welcome everywhere and by every one in the country. So far there is not a word expressed in disfavor of my proposition. The only anxiety ever expressed regarding my scheme is where can we obtain such huge sums of money to carry out even a small part of this comprehensive project.[7]

The heaven-storming quality of these plans shows that Sun Yat-sen was still an optimist about China. Even as late as 1919–20 he was hypothecating amazing changes in incredible spaces of time; and he was, one must now conclude, congenitally blind to certain elemental human conditionings of democratic development. He was thinking of programs and of sums of money as necessary, and overlooking that pre-requisite of democracy—coherent group functioning of human beings in the patterns of democracy.

III. ADVISERS WITH A PURPOSE

The Soviet Revolution in Russia was an event whose certain significance for China is not yet coldly calculable. In that memorable "October, 1917" Sun Yat-sen was still in the hopeful flush of the first experiment in organizing a republic with Canton as its capital. But his connection with that experiment was of brief duration—less than a year—and I have yet to find any evidence of Russian influence playing upon him during those months. It was after he had been displaced from leadership and was residing in Shanghai (during the latter half of 1918, all of 1919 and most of 1920) that the threads began to weave back and forth between him and Soviet Russia which were ultimately to secure him in a Russian alliance. This was the period, as we have already observed, when Sun Yat-sen was doing significant publishing of his ideas, and also, ironic as it now seems, it was the period when Judge Linebarger was preparing an authorized biography so prematurely as to fall short of the climax of its subject's life.

Sun Yat-sen's home was a foreign house at 29 Rue Molière, in the French Concession. The foreign furnishing of its living-rooms, its lawn for croquet (a recreation enjoyed by both Sun Yat-sen and Ching-ling), and the charming hostess herself, were noted by correspondents and travelers, who sought out Sun Yat-sen and not infrequently met his young wife also. The piquancy of her semi-foreignized appearance, her ready and intelligent inquiries about English books or the Metropolitan Opera season are remembered and commented upon. In any consideration of the new radical influences playing upon Sun Yat-sen this young wife has a place in the picture. If not a born radical, she was a radical by the complication of circumstances. Her inner championship of Sun Yat-sen, and the place she had so unconventionally chosen to take by his side, put her among the venturers. She was typical, too, of the eager young people who were ready to listen to anything that Russia had to say.

It is worthy of note that Sun Yat-sen himself took the initiative in fraternal relations with Soviet Russia by sending a telegram of congratulation to Lenin. Living as Sun Yat-sen was in the French Concession at Shanghai, he had to take special precautions to get his message past the war censorships. He is said to have sent it by way of America through the agency of Chinese friends living overseas. The message created a sufficient sensation in Russia to set the Communist Party thinking of China as possibly ripening for "world revolution."

As a fellow-revolutionist Lenin could not have failed to interest Sun Yat-sen. As a revolutionist with a socialistic program the fascination of Lenin was irresistible. Those two men had come under the spell of Karl Marx about the same time. Very early in his plottings Sun Yat-sen incorporated socialistic principles in his revolutionary program; that is, by and large, his greatest originality. There has been speculation as to whether Sun Yat-sen had met Lenin in Europe during any period when both of them were eating the bitterness of exile, but no convincing evidence of this has come forth. Nevertheless, Sun Yat-sen did have, even in his earliest exile, some contacts with Russian revolutionaries. Whether they were embryonic Mensheviki or Bolsheviki is not told; they may have been of some anti-tsarist stripe paler than either. It was in an address in Canton in 1924 that Sun Yat-sen recalled the episode:

Once I met several Russians in a library in London while I was doing some reading. After an exchange of conversation we knew that we were all revolutionary comrades. The Russians asked me, "How long will it take the Chinese Revolution to succeed?" Confronted with the question I did not know how to answer. I was then in exile after my first defeat. . . . I did not want to give a casual answer, so I told them my most conservative estimation and said, "Perhaps it will succeed in thirty years." The Russians were surprised, and remarked, "In such a big country as yours, can you succeed in thirty years?" I asked the Russians, "How long will it take your revolution to succeed?" They answered, "If we can succeed in one hundred years, we shall be satisfied, but now we are struggling." [8]

The Russian Revolution of 1917 excited a widespread interest in China especially among the intellectual classes. Lenin had created a new kind of democracy by a new revolutionary method. The Chinese were so conscious of the failure of their own republic, modeled after France and the United States, that Russia's experimentation seemed possibly pertinent to their own problem; they watched it hopefully.

It was this period that saw the escape to China of many dispossessed and unhappy White Russians. In 1919 a Russian Soviet observer named Popoff is said to have arrived at Shanghai. It was also in 1919 (the year of the Chinese student strike) that Moscow made her first ingratiating move toward Peking with the surprising "Manifesto to the Chinese People" dated July 25th and signed by Karakhan for the Commissariat of Foreign Affairs. Because Russia was at that time isolated from the rest of the world, the message was entrusted to wireless transmission; the Peking Government, according to its own report, never received it—even though it was sent also by mail. It was, however, published in the government newspaper in Moscow on August 20th, and from that source came to the knowledge of a few Chinese. How early Sun Yat-sen heard of it, would be a fact interesting to know. It introduced the suggestion that was to become very potent a few years later—that China was a country in bondage to other nations.

If the people of China wish to become free, like the Russian people, and be spared the lot prepared for them by the Allies at Versailles, which would make of China a second Korea or a second India, let it understand that its only ally and brother in its struggle for national freedom are the Russian workers and peasants and their Red Army.[9]

The proposals were renewed in a second message dated Sept. 27, 1920, which was safely transferred by a Chinese commissioner visiting Moscow (along with an authorized copy of the first declaration). By it all the treaties concluded by Tsarist Russia with China were declared annulled; all seized territory and all the Russian concessions were declared restored to China; Russian citizens in China were henceforth to be subject to Chinese courts without any extraterritorial privileges; the Boxer indemnity was renounced; a new treaty was to be worked out covering the Russian-built Chinese Eastern Railway. In return for these relinquishments China was to coöperate with Soviet Russia and to execute new treaties encouraging trade relations.

In 1920 Soviet representatives appeared in China, and the Chinese Communist Party made an almost unnoticed beginning. The earliest Russian agents seem to have been in contact with Sun Yat-sen. From 1920 Russian influences are observable. Certain policies of Sun Yat-sen's progressive second régime at Canton, if not the result of direct Russian suggestion, were indirectly stimulated by what the world was learning about Soviet practice.

A letter from Tchitcherin to Sun Yat-sen dated Oct. 31, 1920, from Moscow must have reached him in Canton very soon after his restoration to power there. "The two men had met in Paris in the old days," says Eugene Chen, "when, though starving, they were rich in visions of a great future based on the destruction of Tsardom and the expulsion of the Manchu and the redress of social injustices and ancient wrongs." While renewing an old acquaintance, the letter (written in English) takes for granted Sun Yat-sen's interest in Russia and expresses gratification at the developing understanding with China. Tchitcherin says:

Your country advances now resolutely, your people enter consciously the path of struggle against the world-suppressing yoke of Imperialism. . . . Trade relations between us must be taken up immediately. No opportunity must be lost. Let China enter resolutely the path of good friendship with us.[10]

So far had the presumption of understanding progressed by the end of 1920!

Within a few months Sun Yat-sen made a statement (March 6, 1921) of his socialistic program; he was speaking before Canton leaders of the Kuomintang on the subject of his "Three Principles of the People." It is significant of the direction currents were then flowing that this address has come into the English language by translation of a Russian book made up of Russian translations from Sun Yat-sen's writings (*Memoirs of a Chinese Revolutionary*). Of his now famous "principles," Sun Yat-sen on this occasion expounded at greatest length the third—the "Principle of Socialism." With his own naïve slant and his peculiar reserves he advocated measures looking toward proportional distribution of land and the control of capital and industry—both of these as provisions against future evils of "modernization" rather than as remedies for existing conditions. He declared himself for a "social revolution" and advocated organized propaganda.

The British and American diplomats are undoubtedly a skilful race, but still the spectre of social revolution is extremely menacing in these countries. Why? Because the principles of Socialism have not been fully realised there.

We must admit that the degree of sacrifice required for the social revolution will be higher than for the political. The Revolution of 1911 and the overthrow of the Manchus only partially realised the principle of nationalism, while neither the theory of democracy nor the theory of Socialism left any impression.[11]

Now there is a committee of the Kuomintang at Canton, where propaganda will be concentrated. In this respect there will be no limitations. We shall soon find that the province of Kwangtung will not only be the soil on which our principles will grow into reality, but will be the birthplace of the idea of democracy and its practical realisation. From here these principles and their realisation will spread all over China. The people of the Yangtse and Yellow River valleys will follow our example. The explanation of the significance of the Republic must be our task.

. . . Now the time is approaching to carry into effect our great principles of nationalism, democracy and socialism. Only by the transformation of all three principles into reality can our people live and develop freely. But the explanation and application of these principles depends very largely on the display of your forces and the degree of energy shown in your propaganda.[12]

If the Russians were hopefully watching Sun Yat-sen, this address must have pleased them. A month afterward Sun Yat-sen was, as we have already stated, elected President of the Southern Republic, and on the fifth day of the fifth month (May 5, 1921) he assumed that office. The government was a party government with the Kuomintang in undisputed control. One is not surprised to learn that in this year a special Soviet representative, whose name is given in the Chinese records as Ma-lin, visited Sun Yat-sen in Canton. T. C. Woo says:

His mission was a double one: to report to Moscow what he observed in Canton, and to inform Dr. Sun of the real economic and political conditions in Soviet Russia. Although nothing definite resulted from that mission, much information had been obtained on the conditions in Russia, especially on the methods of Russian Revolution and on the new economic policy of Soviet Russia. That mission paved the way for the arrival of yet another and more important mission.[13]

It is only fair to the reader to point out, before going further, that the recounting of these events rapidly in sequence makes an impression much more definite than anything that could have been inferred while they were transpiring one by one. What the world noted in these years was the modernization of Canton and the rupture between Sun Yat-sen and Chen Chiung-ming. When in 1922 Sun Yat-sen became a fugitive from Canton some of his correspondence escaped the burning which destroyed his residence. Certain letters published in the *Hongkong Telegraph* about September, 1922, showed that he had been in secret correspondence looking toward an alliance of Germany, Russia and China. These papers were a surprise to some of his admirers, who refused to believe them genuine. Instead of disclaiming them Sun Yat-sen came out in the press with an acknowledgment that they were his, protesting only that in translation they had been garbled. He expressed the opinion that under their changed governments neither Germany nor Russia could be any longer considered menacing to the integrity of China, and therefore he favored closer understanding with them both.

With the seamen's strike at Hongkong in 1922 uneasiness as to what was afoot spread among the commercial settlements in China. People began to speculate as to how far Russian influence might become effective in China. Yet the organizers of that strike, it has been pointed out, were Chinese whose knowledge of labor unions and of strike methods had been acquired in America. It was just at the time when British trade was suffering huge losses from the tie-up of Hongkong that China was flattered by the visit of an able and famous Russian, Adolph Joffe, who had represented his nation at the peace-making at Brest-Litovsk and then as ambassador at Berlin. By that time the new Russian policy toward China was no longer buried in government bureaus. The well-informed knew about it. In August, 1922, Joffe reached North China, where he was hospitably received and honorably feasted. He cultivated with great success the prominent educationists and the intellectual class generally. His speeches against the "capitalistic powers" and "imperialistic nations" met responsive listeners. On one public occasion he pledged Russia's assistance, whenever China thought the time had come to rid herself of "foreign imperialism." The Chancellor of Peking National University thanked him for this, and suggested that Russia's help might be needed.

Whatever one may think of Soviet policy at this time—whether one feels like commenting on its cunning or criticizing its speciousness—it is important to see as clearly as possible China's reaction to it. And that reaction cannot be described as a single state of mind. Those who were ripe enough, or disillusioned enough to be cynical, looked askance and suspected Russian motives. At hand there were Europeans eager to encourage them in their doubt by pointing out that Russia had her own ends to serve in her China diplomacy, whose springs were in her nationalistic struggle made desperate by European enmities. Calm observers even then suggested that Russia, with a grandiloquent gesture, was relinquishing privileges she had already lost, that for revolutionary Russia there was no special status in China unless she was willing to establish heirship to the Tsarist régime, and for her that was unthinkable. If these were the reactions of men to whom life had taught mistrust, there were others, the idealists and the young, who believed in the sincerity of Russia's friendship for China and were fascinated by the ideal of "world revolution." They were stirred that Russia should come at that moment offering in the name of friendship the very thing for which China was hungering and thirsting—generosity in diplomacy. There were still others, the steadily growing group, who may have had their doubts, but came to see what undoubtedly Russia helped them to see, that it was good policy to accept Russia's professed friendship and use it for all it was worth as a lever to gain concessions from other nations. These made the most of Russia's declarations of willingness to give up all the resented special privileges enjoyed by foreigners, to renounce political jurisdiction in railway zones, to give up extraterritorial status, to relinquish former "foreign concessions" in the ports, to remit the Boxer indemnity, and to cancel the "unequal treaties." What they saw in the Russian formulation was not the empty acceptance by a revolutionized people of a *de facto* situation, but a precedent which, if followed by other nations, would create for China a new day. To them the Russian offer was like the gift of a hammer with which to batter to pieces the whole resented group of unequal treaties. So they turned a respectful ear to the Soviet evangel of a "world revolution" and the redemption of "oppressed nations."

After several months in the northern provinces Joffe visited Shanghai in January, 1923. He found Sun Yat-sen there and he made much of him, meeting and conferring with him. If Sun Yat-sen had had any misgivings about Russian influence, they were removed by Joffe's joining him in a long statement issued in the press; one section of it was a reaffirmation of Russia's new policy toward China; another section was about communism:

Dr. Sun Yat-sen holds that the communistic order, or even the Soviet system, cannot actually be introduced into China because there do not exist the conditions for the successful establishment of either communism or Sovietism. This view is entirely shared by Mr. Joffe, who is further of the opinion that China's paramount and most pressing problem is to achieve national unification and attain full national independence; and regarding this great task he has assured Dr. Sun Yat-sen that China has the warmest sympathy of the Russian people and can count on the support of Russia.[14]

It was characteristic of Soviet thoroughness that Joffe busied himself about something more than this gesture. When forced to retire to a resort in Japan for a month of rest and recuperation of health, he made a junction there quietly with one of Sun Yat-sen's trusted friends, a revolutionary co-worker of long standing, Liao Chung-kai. Joffe set about educating this man in the theory and practice of peasant and labor movements and their relation to the revolutionary process. When Liao returned to Canton, he became one of the chief promoters of Russian policies. Rising to the position of Governor of the Province of Kwangtung, he made bitter enemies who, only a few months after Sun Yat-sen's death, brought about his assassination.

Within a month after Sun Yat-sen's conference with Joffe, he was able to return to Canton, in February, 1923. At Hongkong he stopped off long enough to be the guest, on February 20th, of Hongkong University, with which Queen's College is now affiliated. A crowd of cheering students met him at the University gate, and carried him on their shoulders from the automobile to the auditorium, where he addressed a hallful of demonstrative young people. In a deeper sense Sun Yat-sen was being borne to new honors on the shoulders of enthusiastic youth. That he was rising to his final place in the hearts of his countrymen is shown also by a ballot taken at this very time by the *Weekly Review of the Far East* to ascertain the men held highest in public esteem in China. Sun Yat-sen's name headed the list, outranking by many votes the second favorite.

Auspiciously Sun Yat-sen entered upon his last term of office, which proved to be one surcharged with epoch-making events. This time he saw to it that he was supreme in military command; he was elected not president but Generalissimo. He appointed as his chief of staff the young military protégé who had stayed by him loyally in his fifty-six-days banishment on a government cruiser in 1922, Chiang Kai-shek, and in the summer of 1923 sent him to Russia to study Soviet military organization.

Although Sun Yat-sen was moving rapidly toward a Russian policy, an incident occurred which suggests a momentary doubt about the wisdom of it. Late in the spring of 1923 he made one more appeal to other nations. The American Minister, Jacob Gould Schurman, was then visiting Canton. Sun Yat-sen had an interview with him in which he asked the United States to approach England, France and other Powers on the proposal of a joint intervention in China for a period of five years. Sun Yat-sen had the plan worked out with characteristic detail. It involved foreign military occupation of all the provincial capitals, and the lavish use of military and civil experts. The object was to set the provincial and national governments in order, after which elections were to be held, and the foreigners were to train the Chinese administration which was to supersede them.

Was Sun Yat-sen really as desperate at heart as this suggests, or was his tongue in his cheek? It is difficult to think of him as making game of the minister. Sun Yat-sen was not a man who played twisted diplomatic tricks. He was blunt and forthright, if he spoke at all. He was now growing visibly older, and he was in poor health; he had failed repeatedly; he knew that China was not going forward. He was ready to act desperately. The plan called for a degree of foreign intervention which no foreigner would have dared to suggest. The plan, of course, came to nothing. Joint action of the Powers was becoming more and more difficult in matters pertaining to China; disillusioned by a recent experience in Siberia, they knew their limitation.

Sun Yat-sen passed speedily from desperate proposals for foreign intervention to criticism of what he came to believe, and taught China to believe, was foreign intervention of a bad kind. A characteristic interpretation was embodied in what he called "A Manifesto to Foreign Powers" issued early in the summer of 1923. Foreigners were at the time quite out of patience with the "never-ending chaos in China," stirred, as they were, by a notorious bandit outrage on the "Blue Express" north of Nanking. Sun Yat-sen used this psychological moment for his pronouncement. The lawlessness which had made that episode possible he deplored; he attributed it to the spread of militarism and civil wars and the incompetence of the central government. He went on to urge "the disbandment of superfluous soldiery and the establishment of a united and efficient government." Then he threw the onus for disunion and wars on the foreign Powers, who continued to recognize Peking as the government of China, "prompted by the notion that they must have some entity, though it be a nonentity, with which to deal." (That phrasing sounds like Eugene Chen rather than Sun Yat-sen.)

However, by their action, they have given Peking moral prestige. . . . Unconsciously perhaps, . . . they have intervened in China's internal affairs by practically imposing upon the country a government repudiated by it. They have, by supporting a government which cannot exist for a single day without such support, hindered China from establishing an effective and stable government. . . .[15]

Sun Yat-sen was thinking of the most dependable source of national revenue, which was the foreign administration of the maritime customs and the salt gabelle; the income from these had been increasing with the growth of China's prosperity.

The entente between Sun Yat-sen and Russia went forward. By midsummer his mind seems to have settled. In a significant interview given to Fletcher S. Brockman (published in the *New York Times* July 22, 1923), he is reported not only to have expressed radical resentment of the maritime customs situation as it bore on Canton, but also to have set forth the new interpretation of China's ills, which was to be more fully expounded six or seven months later in the *San Min* lectures:

The real trouble is that China is not an independent country. She is the victim of foreign countries. She is really in a worse condition than

Korea or Formosa. They have one master; we have many. Their master
dominates them, but has important responsibilities for the people who
are under their subjection. China is equally dominated by the outside,
but her masters rule without accepting any responsibility.

If the foreign countries will let us alone, China will have her affairs
in shape within six months. . . . The Peking Government could not
stand twenty-four hours without the backing it receives from foreign
governments. . . . Its only revenue comes from the maritime customs
and the salt gabelle. . . . It can collect no taxes in the provinces; it
lives entirely upon foreign-collected money. . . .[16]

Sun Yat-sen's bitterness toward Peking and his determination
to overthrow it, even at the cost of an alliance with the notoriously
autocratic Chang Tso-lin, is bluntly stated, and another alliance
is hinted at:

General Chang and I have the same enemy, and I will take him—or
anybody else who will help me—into the combination to overthrow
Peking.

We have lost hope of help from America, England, France or any
other of the great Powers. The only country that shows any signs of
helping us in the south is the Soviet Government of Russia.[17]

What happened next attracted in due time the attention of the
world. In Eugene Chen's words:

A remarkable Russian arrived in Canton. It was Mr. Borodin. I was
present when Dr. Sun decided to appoint him a high adviser. The appointment was correctly understood as definitely completing Dr. Sun's
Soviet orientation. It was not lightly made. Dr. Sun realized that his
work demanded foreign assistance which, indeed, is the fundamental
thesis of his book on the "International Development of China." He had
tried to secure such from the British but failed, and he knew that the
British attitude would dictate American policy regarding him. He was

forced to look elsewhere. And before death came to him, he was satisfied that his trust in the ability and loyalty of Borodin and his fellow
Russian workers had not been misplaced.[18]

It is said to have been in October, 1923, that Michael Borodin
arrived in Canton. He came ostensibly as the representative of the
Rosta News Agency. Actually he was an agent of the Russian
Communist Party, which he had previously served on similar
missions to Turkey and Persia. How influential he became with
Sun Yat-sen and with the Kuomintang is now a matter of world
knowledge, but at the time no one, whether Chinese or foreign,
could have judged how effectively the Russians were laying their
plans to attack "imperialism" through China and to forward their
ideal of "world revolution" by advising Sun Yat-sen and helping
him to develop a Nationalist Party equipped for revolution.
Furthermore, in 1923 no one, even the most sanguine, would have
ventured to prophesy the success of the Nationalist movement.

It is pathetically characteristic of the inner foreignization of
Sun Yat-sen that he was still looking for some foreign savior of
China. His long hope of an economic alliance with Japan had been
wrecked by popular resentment of high-handed Japanese policies
in 1915 and the anti-Japanese agitation and boycott of 1919. His
quixotic appeal for "The International Development of China"
had fallen flat. He had not found in the United States the influential help for which he had asked. His resentment of Britain
had been deepening for years. It stung him to the quick that
under varying circumstances Britain had supported his rivals; he
became convinced that she was opposing him personally. When
he finally turned to Russia he made no secret of it. Invited to speak
on Dec. 31, 1923, before a meeting in the Y.M.C.A. of Canton he
is said to have fully acknowledged his orientation: "We no longer
look to the Western Powers. Our faces are turned toward Russia."

IV. THE NEW TURNING

Chafing under disappointments, yet longing with undiminished fervor for the advancement of China, Sun Yat-sen was, from the Russian standpoint, an almost ideally prepared collaborator. There was no one in China whose power to arouse youth and to appeal to the masses could be compared with his. He was not in the best of health, but he was still a man of character and force, more than ever inclined to be arbitrary and autocratic, and firmly committed to his theories about China and to his systematized programs. He was not a man who would weakly be made a tool.

An astute and able man was Michael Borodin. Instead of antagonizing Sun Yat-sen he won him. He might have said, "Sun Yat-sen is an impractical idealist; he must be quietly pushed aside." Instead, he recognized the value of an idealistic center in a popular movement. In spirit Sun Yat-sen was a revolutionary; why pick an intellectual quarrel with him over his inflated paper programs? Borodin apparently made no attempt to convince him that his highly rationalized and mechanized republic was still an impossibility in China; Borodin had work to do for the Third Internationale; theories of government could wait.

Borodin had not been in Canton a month before important changes began to take place. It was a momentous day when Sun Yat-sen welcomed the first Chinese communist into membership in the Kuomintang. A distinguished intellectual was admitted to signalize this important event, none less than Li Ta-chao, whose execution for communism in Peking in 1927 created a national sensation. Sun Yat-sen's theory—doubtless arrived at coöperatively with Borodin—was that the Communist Party, because it was also revolutionary in purpose, should work closely with the Kuomintang for the accomplishment of the ends they had in common. Misgiving about this alliance was expressed both within and without the

Kuomintang, but Sun Yat-sen firmly stood his ground, and communists were admitted to his Party just as other members were— and that without any suggestion of curtailing their activities as communists.

The organization of a new army on Soviet lines was at once promoted vigorously. Chiang Kai-shek returned from Russia with ideas and plans. Before 1923 was over, Gallen (this alias is variously anglicized also as Galens or Gallent—his real name is said to be Blücher), an ex-Austrian army officer, who had had experience in training Soviet armies in Russia, arrived at Canton to develop the Whampoa Military Academy and a revolutionary army. During the following six months other military experts came from Russia. By June, 1924, as many as thirty Soviet military men, it is said, were attached to Sun Yat-sen's army. The organization of the army was paralleled by the organization of labor unions and of an ambitious peasant movement under the leadership of Joffe's disciple, Liao Chung-kai.

The foreign powers got the shock of a stiffened radicalism, when Sun Yat-sen demanded for his government the customs surplus from the port of Canton. This was supported by one of the sharpest resentments of patriotic young China—against the anomalous situation of a Customs Service administered by foreigners. However explicable as a historical development, the idea of a foreign-controlled Customs Service has become more and more hateful to informed Chinese. It is an interesting and curious fact that in spite of civil wars, secessions and other disruptions of China, the Customs Service—under foreign administration—has held together in an unbroken system. Sun Yat-sen, as the head of the divisive South, saw the funds collected by the custom-house at Canton forwarded to Peking. He knew—none better—that his own government needed this money. Civil war was still going on in his region, and, what was worse, the rebel leader, Chen Chiung-ming, was cultivating alliances with Sun Yat-sen's enemies among the northern militarists. Sun Yat-sen was not only under the expensive military necessity of keeping Chen in check, but was being entangled in northern wars. As a matter of fact he did take sides in 1924 in a war in the Yangtze Valley and in one at the Great Wall, but in neither of them did he give any effective help; they were fought, and over, before he got into action. Sun Yat-sen's argument concerning the customs was not only that Canton needed the money, but that it was grossly unjust that funds received at Canton should go to Peking to finance his military enemies. Sun Yat-sen's demand was not complied with by officials of the Canton customs, who knew themselves to be part of a large system, not executives of an autonomous local unit. In December Sun Yat-sen threatened to seize the custom-house. Promptly foreign marines were landed to protect it. United States naval vessels joined with British ships in a spectacular demonstration in Canton harbor. This aroused such resentment among the Chinese that congratulations poured in upon Sun Yat-sen for the stand he had taken. Tardily the British, in whose hands the customs administration traditionally rested, came to a compromise with Sun Yat-sen about the receipts.

That Sun Yat-sen's championship of China against the foreign Powers increased the esteem in which he was held by his fellow-countrymen is no occult observation to make. To many Chinese before 1920 he had seemed a man westernized to the point of estrangement; he was so far foreignized as to seem un-Chinese. His part in the Revolution of 1911 might never have brought him any more than conventional esteem, if he had not added to that a final phase of active propaganda for a nationalistic revolution and the militant espousal of China's cause against the world. As a man who understood foreigners well enough to battle with them, Sun Yat-sen acquired a new significance for China.

Important though Borodin's influence was in these matters, it was not in them that he made what is likely to prove his most permanent contribution to Sun Yat-sen and the upspringing nationalism. He left his stamp upon China (who shall say for how long?) in the reorganization of the Kuomintang and the formulation of its political philosophy and policies. A thorough-going rehabilitation of the old party was projected in October, 1923, when Sun Yat-sen (with Borodin advising) created a temporary "Central Executive Committee" for the purpose of summoning a Congress for reorganization. A great deal of thought must have been given to the preparation for this meeting, and there must have been much patient interchange of ideas between Borodin and the Chinese leaders. It was decided that delegates to the gathering should be in part selected by Sun Yat-sen and in part chosen by trusted local branches which had survived the chaos of the preceding years. A ten-days meeting of the Central Executive Committee preceded the Congress to crystallize plans and draft a constitution. Everything was well prepared when the Congress assembled.

In January, 1924, delegates gathered at Canton to the number of 199, representing all the provinces, several outlying dependencies and some overseas groups. "The First National Congress of the Kuomintang" was opened by Sun Yat-sen on January 20th. (It is a curious coincidence that on the next day Lenin died.) The Congress lasted from the 20th to the 30th and held seventeen meetings. It was Sun Yat-sen who made the opening address; it was he who criticized the old party. He said in part:

After the revolution was accomplished, we were at a loss as to the methods we should use for reconstruction. But now we have found the methods. It is for the purpose of presenting these methods for your consideration and adoption that we have assembled our comrades from the different provinces to Canton in this conference. . . . We shall bring up these prepared methods daily in succession. . . . They are not free from imperfections, so it is necessary still to hold this conference, asking you all to study them. After your study we ask you to support them, to put them in practice in different places. . . . There are two things in connection with the reorganization of the Kuomintang this time: Firstly . . . making it again a powerful and organized political party; secondly . . . to use the power of the political party to reconstruct the country. . . .

. . . The reason for the lack of solidarity in our party in former days was not because of any enemy using great power to destroy us; it was entirely due to the fact that we destroyed ourselves; it was because the mind and discernment were too immature, often engendering senseless misunderstandings. . . . There is one thing of the greatest importance in a political party, that is, all members of the party must possess spiritual unity. In order that all the members may be united spiritually, the first thing is to sacrifice freedom, the second is to offer ability. If the individual can sacrifice his freedom, then the whole party will have freedom. If the individual can offer his ability, then the whole party will possess ability. . . . The past failures of the party were due to the fact that while the individual member had freedom, the party as a whole had none, and that while the individual member had ability, the party as a whole was powerless. Herein lies exactly the failure of the Kuomintang of China. Our reorganization today is to get rid of this shortcoming.[19]

This was a wholesome confession of party failings, a great advance on the blaming of others for disintegration in the Kuomintang, a confession, however, so decidedly out of character with Sun Yat-sen's habitual utterances that one must postulate back of it Borodin's analysis of party faults. A new note in Chinese politics is sounded in the philosophy of the functioning group—made effective by the sacrifice of individual freedom. This, too, sounds unlike Sun Yat-sen's accustomed thinking. Some one seems very nearly to have had his finger here on the fatal flaw in the democratic politics of China.

The task of the Congress was two-fold—to create an organization, and to make a public declaration of its policies. Interesting as the declaration is, the organization bids fair to be the more permanent contribution to China. Certainly for our day, no page in Kuomintang history or in Sun Yat-sen's life is more important than this reorganization, which seemed at the time to be only an incident of party politics. The party's new constitution became at once the basis of a new type of government in South China. The pattern was carried by Nationalist conquest to wider and wider areas, until, within five years of the meeting of the Congress which created it, China's national structure had to be rebuilt with the Kuomintang constitution as its foundation. The importance of the Kuomintang constitution is not that it was the reorganization of a party, but that it was the mold in which the Republic was recast. This new governmental pattern introduced into China in 1924 has altered beyond recognition the form of the Republic, which now bears little resemblance to its earlier French and American models. What was done in Canton in January, 1924, has become in the course of events nothing less than a constitutional revolution for China. If this fact is grasped, the importance of carefully noticing the features of the organization will be granted by any reader.

That the Russian brain worked upon the organization cannot be doubted; it is so nearly a replica of the structure of the Russian Communist Party. Its fundamental ideas are a one-party country, ruled by the party, the government of either the country or the party to consist of the smallest practicable group of leaders of real ability. The party secures itself by rigidly guarding the gates of membership, and by strict discipline of the members.

The supreme body is presumed to be the National Congress, which meets once in two years for ten days or more. This Congress is a large representative body to which is assigned the determination of fundamental policies. It appoints a Central Executive Committee which functions for it between the congressional sessions. Certain powers are assigned to the Central Executive Committee which it may not delegate: it must organize, and direct subordinate party organizations; it must control party finances; it must represent the party in external relations. Aside from these functions the Central Executive Committee may create subordinate departments for any sort of vital work, such as propaganda, labor and peasant movements, and work among women. The National Government was created by it, and functions under its control. The Central Executive Committee is required to meet in plenary session at least once in six months. Within it there is a small inner circle called the Standing Committee, which acts in all routine matters between the meetings of the larger committee. The Standing Committee has nine members and meets at least once a week. The Central Executive Committee has created another committee also of great importance—the Central Political Council, which originally included the nine members of the Standing Committee and six others, who are usually ministers of the Government. It has since been enlarged. It meets two or three times a week to consider political problems presented by the ministers and to reach decisions. It is the most powerful political organ of both the Government and the Party. Chiang Kai-shek has held the position of Chairman of the Central Political Council. He has never been, as so many Americans have supposed, President of the Chinese Republic.

Below the central party organization, both created by it and responsible to it, are several ranks of subordinate organizations formed after the same pattern: provincial, district and smaller local units reaching out into the country. The feature of the whole plan most significant to observe is that, according to the constitution, power always descends, it never ascends, through the organization. A provincial organization has no initiative or control in the national organization, but the national bodies direct and control the provincial bodies. The first duty of any unit in the organization is to execute the orders of the body above it. A district may not even summon its own district congress without the approval of a superior body. Another feature that history will have to reckon with is that the character of the supposedly popular assemblies, each of which is presumed to be supreme in its area, is not guarded by the constitution; it is left to the Executive Committee in power at the moment to determine not only the number of delegates, but also their apportionment and their method of election; and when the Congress closes its sessions, the term of office of the delegates ends. This, of course, provides the Executive Committee with an extraordinary temptation to pack a Congress that will reappoint it and otherwise respond to its wishes. Experience already seems to suggest that the National Congresses of the Kuomintang are likely to decline in functional importance, whereas the Central Executive Committee is constitutionally able to gather more and more power into its own hands. The party organization, it will be seen, is not only a dictatorship of the Government when the party is in power, but it is internally organized upon so severe a centralization that it may find itself, as a party, subject to the dictatorship of a small inner group. It should be mentioned in passing that an effort was made by writers of the constitution to provide a check upon Executive Committees by creating Committees of Control coördinate in rank with them, and with powers of scrutiny (such as auditing accounts), powers of censuring, discipline and impeachment. It remains to be seen how effective their powers can be made, and how much incentive they will have to use them.

The Kuomintang Party Constitution became nationally significant with the consummation of the Nationalist Revolution. A truly revolutionary re-organization of the government of Republican China was accomplished at Nanking in 1928. Hope was expressed that in the Kuomintang pattern a new effectiveness and stability would be realized. The possibilities of wreckage from internal disintegration seemed greatly diminished as compared with the unwieldy legislatures and quarreling factions of the earlier republican experiments. Continuity no longer depended upon the cohesive functioning of large groups, but upon the cohesiveness of the small inner group which focussed in itself the actual power. Yet the ground for hope was more than the theoretical simplicity of the administrative pattern; it lay also in the fact that coöperative functioning had been traditionally practiced by the Chinese in patterns similar to the Kuomintang's, albeit not in the field of politics. It was pointed out at the time by Grover Clark in editorials in the *Peking Leader* that, though ostensibly patterned after Russia, the Kuomintang administration was really along lines indigenous to China, just as the Soviet pattern had itself sprung from traditional practices in Russia. Mr. Clark developed the point that committee administration is an ancient practice in Chinese trade-guilds, which are traditionally run on a pattern which amounts to a central executive committee, praesidium, and annual or semi-annual congresses of members. The Shansi Bankers Guild, an organization extending widely over the country, had branch organizations, which from time to time sent representatives to a central conference. In short, the resemblance of the form of organization of the Kuomintang to the Russian Soviet system is not satisfactorily accounted for by conscious imitation, important as that seemed in 1924, but should be thought of as a partly instinctive and partly deliberate return to an already familiar Chinese organization pattern. The likenesses in traditional patterns between China and Russia are yet to be explored.

Having thus anticipated history to point out not only what the Congress did in reorganizing the party but the effects of what it did upon the China of today, let us return to Canton and to January,

1924. In the "Declaration of the First National Congress" Sun Yat-sen's hand is observable, but his is not the only hand. It is inconceivable that even under Borodin's tactful instruction, he should have produced so highly Russianized a document. It is this "declaration" that marks the entrance of Russian ideas into the formulated program of Chinese Nationalism. Although the "Three Principles of the People" are safely enshrined here as China's only hope, there are also ideas that mark a departure from Sun Yat-sen's previously enunciated interpretations and policies. The document is sprinkled with recognizable Russian words and phrases which from this time forth become current in Nationalist propaganda: "comrades," "imperialistic powers," "economic exploitation," "the capitalistic class," "peasants and workers," "the organization of the masses," "exploited workers," and others. There appears here also the yet-to-be-popularized explanation of China's failure to realize herself as a modern nation, namely "foreign imperialism." Here is the beginning of a propaganda that proved to be the most effective single weapon used by the Nationalist Revolution. The chaos of China is ascribed to militarism and "foreign imperialism" and the constant working together of the two to keep China in subjection. China is represented as a country that has lost her independence and must fight for it against "foreign imperialism," which has reduced her to the status of a sub-colony. The platform calls for the canceling of all unequal treaties, and the doing away with foreign concessions, extraterritoriality, foreign control of customs, and all such prejudicial rights of foreigners. "Those of the Powers," it states, "which voluntarily renounce all special privileges and voluntarily abrogate the treaties which infringe on the sovereign rights of China shall be considered the most favored nations."

In true Russian style the party makes a bid for the support of peasants, workers and soldiers. The pungency and militancy of certain sections make the "declaration" one of the memorable documents of recent Chinese history.

We should like to say this to the farmers:

China has been and still is an agricultural nation, and of all the classes of people, the agricultural class has suffered the most from economic exploitation. According to our Doctrine of Livelihood, the state will provide land for cultivation to those farmers who have been deprived of their land or to those who have suffered from their landlords. Irrigation systems will be provided, and colonization schemes will be devised to help those farmers who are without land of their own. Farmers' banks will be established to facilitate rural credits. It is the earnest hope of the Party that everything be done to restore normal happiness to the farmers.

To the workers, the Kuomintang has also a special message.

For centuries, the Chinese government has not done anything to ensure the livelihood of the working class. According to our principles, the state should help the unemployed and pass laws to improve the conditions of the laborers. Systems for the relief of the aged, for the care of children, for providing pensions for the disabled, and for providing education for the mass of the people will also be attended to by the Party in order to better the conditions of the less fortunate classes.

Throughout the length and breadth of China, there is no place where we cannot find destitute farmers and exploited workers. Because their conditions are so difficult, their desire for emancipation is correspondingly great. So the laborers and farmers may be counted among those who will most strongly oppose imperialism, and who will help in our work toward a national revolution. On the one hand, the people's revolution can achieve victory only when the farmers and laborers of the country give it their whole-hearted support. On the other hand, the Kuomintang will do its best to help peasant and labor movements in order to strengthen the people's revolution. Both the farmers and the workers are asked to join the Kuomintang and to give their continuous devotion and efforts to promoting the People's Revolution. Inasmuch as the Kuomintang is opposed to the imperialists and the militarists, who are the most dangerous enemies of the workers and farmers, participation in the struggle of the party is to struggle also for their own interests.

Chinese soldiery has been composed largely of farmers; yet the soldiers themselves are unaware of their duty to serve and to protect the people, the majority of whom are farmers. Although imperialists are dangerous enemies of the people, our soldiers do not know the importance of fighting against imperialism and militarism; they have, on the contrary, been utilized by the militarists to fight against the welfare of the people. The Kuomintang regards these facts as a great anomaly, and perceives that the cause for this state of affairs is that poverty has compelled the soldiers to serve anything or any organization which can provide for them a subsistence or a living. In view of the fact that the Kuomintang is trying its best to educate its own soldiers and to transform them into armies which exist really for the good of the people, the soldiers of the nation should all offer themselves to fight for the cause of the People's Revolution. Those soldiers who have served in the revolutionary army will have the option of returning to agriculture with a grant of a large tract of land, so that they can maintain themselves and their families.[20]

With this bill of allurements the Kuomintang set out upon its great project of national revolution. Surely no one can criticize Sun Yat-sen or the Kuomintang for half-heartedness when once they turned their faces toward Russia. A statement typical of the younger group may be quoted from T. C. Woo's illuminating volume: *The Kuomintang and the Future of the Chinese Revolution:*

The Russian leaders are experts in revolution, so to speak. They are masters of the revolutionary art. They put their experience at the disposal of the Kuomintang.[21]

For years Sun Yat-sen had been calling aloud for the employment of foreign experts to train the Chinese. The expert which he succeeded in attaching to himself was an "expert in revolution." How much of revolution China owes to that expert and his expertness, history will one day summarize in books. This is already clear: what looked at the time to be only expert advice in making a more coherent and effective party organization, has resulted in throwing the nation red-hot into a new pattern of government. The Russian-inspired propaganda against "foreign imperialism"— effective as it was in 1925-27—has lost some of its force; the revolutionary army, into which the resentments of the propaganda were poured like an intoxicant, is now merged with other armies; peasant movements languish and labor movements mark time; but the party organization and the party policies which Borodin persuaded Sun Yat-sen to endorse are, for better or for worse, woven into the very fabric of China's national government.

DOCUMENTATION OF QUOTED PASSAGES

[1] Sun-Yat-Sen: *Memoirs of a Chinese Revolutionary* (London) pp. 5–7. [2] Ibid., pp. 161, 163, 164. [3] Ibid., p. 174. [4] Ibid., p. 145. [5] Ibid., pp. 7–12. [6] Ibid., p. 112. [7] Sun Yat-sen: *The International Development of China* (Shanghai, 1920) p. 160. [8] Quoted by Woo: *The Kuomintang and the Future of the Chinese Revolution* (London, 1928) p. 130. [9] Bau: *China and World Peace* (New York, 1928) p. 130. [10] Chen, Eugene: "Sun Yat-sen: Some Memories," *The People's Tribune* (Peking) Special Memorial Edition, March 12, 1926, pp. 1, 2. [11] Sun-Yat-Sen: *Memoirs of a Chinese Revolutionary* (London) p. 236. [12] Ibid., p. 237. [13] Woo: *The Kuomintang and the Future of the Chinese Revolution* (London, 1928) p. 131. [14] *China Year Book for 1923*, ed. Bell and Woodhead (Shanghai) p. 863. [15] *China Weekly Review*, Vol. 25, p. 232 (July 14, 1923). [16] Brockman: "Foreign Control of Peking Means War, says Sun Yat Sen," *New York Times,* July 22, 1923. Section 7, p. 5. [17] Ibid. [18] Chen, Eugene: "Sun Yat-sen: Some Memories," *The People's Tribune* (Peking) Special Memorial Edition, March 12, 1926, pp. 1, 2. [19] Woo: *The Kuomintang and the Future of the Chinese Revolution* (London, 1928) pp. 38–40. [20] Hsü, Leonard S.: *Sun Yat-sen His Political and Social Ideas* (Los Angeles, 1933) pp. 130–132. [21] Woo: *The Kuomintang and the Future of the Chinese Revolution* (London, 1928) p. 134.

Sources and Authorities: See Appendix C, p. 402.

CHAPTER IX

The Weight of a Patriot's Influence

I. THE MAKING OF THE PARTY BIBLE

NO one can ponder the portentous changes in China in this vital period without returning again and again to wonder at the ways of Michael Borodin. That he succeeded in enlisting Sun Yat-sen at all was an astonishing feat. No one else—either Chinese or foreign— seems to have come so near manipulating China's revolutionary leader. Borodin had doubtless an advantage in not having tried to handle Sun Yat-sen before. He was new to Borodin and Borodin to him. Consequently, Borodin had freshness of vision, and the zest of a new attack. Even so, Sun Yat-sen was at this time of his life a friable personality to handle. Borodin's undertaking was no light adventure. Now that the entire series of events lies before us as a sequence of accomplished facts, it is easy to imagine the process of their accomplishment, but, to forget the hazardous uncertainties of their working out is easy, too.

Borodin found Sun Yat-sen tenacious of his supremacy in the party, but he was wise enough not to trim his power; on the contrary he gave the stanch old patriot assurance of power such as he had never had before. Chapter Four in the Constitution of the Kuomintang stands not only as "a token of everlasting remembrance" of Sun Yat-sen, but also as evidence of the skilful ways of Michael Borodin. Under the caption, "The President," this chapter does not define the functions of the president as such, that is, of any possible president, but only of President Sun Yat-sen:

ARTICLE 21. Dr. Sun, the originator of the Three Principles of the People and of the Five-Power Constitution, shall be the President of the Party.

ARTICLE 22. All members shall follow the direction of the President and work for the advancement of the principles of the Party.

. . . .

ARTICLE 25. The President shall have power to disapprove resolutions of the National Congress.

ARTICLE 26. The President shall have the power of final decision concerning acts of the Central Executive Committee.[1]

Is it any wonder that after Sun Yat-sen's death no successor could be elected to this unlimited dictatorship?

Borodin could see that Sun Yat-sen was a cumulative egoist, continually gathering to himself in public speeches and in writings the credit for whatever significant contributions had been made toward the reconstruction of China. So large did his mission bulk in his own eyes that he could hardly admit the contributions of other men. Borodin understood this egoism; he could see that at the root it was hunger for appreciation; and he gave Sun Yat-sen appreciation. Of course he would point out to him the significance of his having incorporated in the revolutionary program, so long ago, a socialistic principle. It would not be hard to make Sun Yat-sen feel that he had been original and far in advance of his fellows—a born ally of progressive Russia. We can imagine the two men in discussion: Wherein did Sun Yat-sen's Third Principle differ from communism? In essence were they not the same? The only difference would seem to be the practical one: how far might a country go in applying the principle of socialism? Borodin was not pressing China into communism; China was not ready for communism; Joffe also had said it. What Borodin wanted was to get communists admitted into membership in the Kuomintang;

there, he argued, they could be a great force in promoting a revolution. To this Sun Yat-sen agreed and the communists were admitted.

Moreover, Borodin observed in Sun Yat-sen, and in China generally, a deep desire to be an integral part of a world order. Eugene Chen writes vividly of the fascination for Sun Yat-sen of the Confucian ideal of a world in which men will really get together for the common good. He tells of working with him in an effort to translate his favorite classical passage (*Book of Rites* vii, § 1, ¶2) into adequate English, but he does not give us their joint rendering. Much admired and much used by modern Chinese socialists, this ancient statement outlines the ethical principles and the public policies which will characterize the Great Getting-together. Self-interest and family-ambition will then no longer motivate conduct, raise unscrupulous men to power, determine policies of distribution and consumption and provoke wars.

All men everywhere will live for the common good; leaders of worth and ability will be selected; their words will be trusted and they will be makers of peace. Men will not love their own parents to the exclusion of the parents of others, nor their own sons to the exclusion of the sons of others. They will provide sustenance to the aged as long as they live, employment to the able-bodied, opportunity for development to the young, friendly care to widows, orphans, childless men and the disabled; for each man a task and for each woman a home. Not wishing to be wasteful of their possessions, they will nevertheless not keep them for purely personal use; not wishing to be inactive in the application of their strength, they will at the same time not exert it merely in their own behalf. Thus evil devices will cease or fail to prosper, robbers and traitors will be out of work, and outside doors will not need to be closed.[2]

It was a great conception which Confucius deposited in one of his books, there to disturb the complacency of able but greedy men for centuries. Sun Yat-sen warmed his modernized heart at the undying fire.

Deep in the heart of disappointed China there was the craving for international status. Ever since Japan had begun to shine in the galaxy of nations, China had wanted a truly international rôle. Of all nations Russia was at this moment best prepared to offer that to China. Borodin painted for Sun Yat-sen and the Kuomintang a significant share in a "world revolution." The appeal of this rôle to ardent Chinese patriots must not be lost sight of in any attempt to understand the part of Russia in the Nationalist Movement. China and Sun Yat-sen had lost their self-esteem in the abysmal failure of the whole republican experiment. They needed something that would give them back their self-respect. Borodin taught them to think of their own national effort as a contribution to a world revolution against a dread world enemy, called imperialism; to fight against imperialism in China was to fight also for world liberation. This lifted the Chinese struggle above the pettiness of regional wars and gave it the spirit of a world-important crusade.

Borodin did not fail to observe Sun Yat-sen's undiminished power to influence his people by public address and by the written word. Being himself an expert propagandist, he quickly recognized in Sun Yat-sen unusual potentialities as the maker of a propaganda that would be Chinese, not Russian. So he pushed Sun Yat-sen into the light and hid in his shadow. The ideas to go forth must be Sun Yat-sen's ideas, however much Borodin might color them. From the time of the party Congress to the end of his life Sun Yat-sen was kept as busy at public speaking as his failing health would allow. In his *Collected Works,* a whole volume is filled with miscellaneous addresses of this period—forty-four in all, not counting the series known as the *San Min Chu I.* Sun Yat-sen was in his right place once more—as a talking propagandist for a cause. Propaganda and money-raising had been his major contributions toward the overthrow of the Manchus. For the second time in his life, and in the last year of it, he had full scope for his special ability in public address. Opportunities seemed unlimited. Quite impartially he expounded the simple rudiments of democracy to students, bankers, merchants, soldiers on parade, labor unions, farmers' mass meetings, girls' schools, Kuomintang committee meetings, afternoon teas, a missionary college, and a national Y.M.C.A. convention. To Westerners his addresses often seem loose and casual. But he did not fail to say what he wanted to say. He was very blunt, and, although pedantic in a pontifical way, he was utterly unacademic in style. The Chinese describe his public speaking as "heavy artillery fire" (*k'ai ta p'ao*).

It was a fortunate inspiration that set Sun Yat-sen to lecturing on "The Three Principles of the People." For many years the triple formulation had been in his mind. He acknowledges that the suggestion was derived from Lincoln's famous phrase:

The Three Principles of the People correspond with the principles stated by President Lincoln—"government of the people, by the people, for the people." I translated them into *Min yu* (the people to have) *Min Chih* (the people to govern) and *Min hsiang* (the people to enjoy).[3]

This translation is still in use; I have seen it on placards pasted on the reddish stucco of imperial arches in Peking. But more definitive and more frequently used are the three compact topical headings which he devised. By exposition these came to have well-understood meanings: *Min Ts'u*—the racial solidarity of the people, *Min Ch'üan*—the governmental authority of the people, and *Min Sheng*—the economic life of the people. Very roughly, and not quite satisfactorily, we have been accustomed to translate the trio as The People's Nationalism (the analogue of "government of the people"), The People's Democracy (government "by the people"), and The People's Livelihood, or The People's Socialism (government "for the people"). Sometimes also Sun Yat-sen discussed these as counterparts of liberty, equality and fraternity, but with many reservations as to liberty, which he considered a superfluous ideal in China unless restricted to national liberty.

Although Sun Yat-sen had made use of his popular formulation for many years in addresses here and there, he had never published an exposition of the Three Principles. In leisure moments in Canton before 1922, he had been working on such a treatise, and had completed the first section. Materials had also been gathered and some work done on the rest. But in the military attack on his headquarters in June, 1922, his house was burned and all his manuscripts with it; also his library of Western books.

He felt himself at a disadvantage when he was called upon in January, 1924, to deliver lectures every Monday on the Three Principles. Beginning before the First National Congress of the Kuomintang adjourned, the lectures went on until the end of April—six lectures on Nationalism and six on Democracy. Sun Yat-sen had a severe illness in May of this year, brought on, a Chinese authority says, by making five speeches in one day. His death was announced from Hongkong on May 14th; the *New York Times* published an obituary editorial on May 16th. Denials of the reports were disbelieved until Sun Yat-sen was able to give a personal interview to quiet the rumors. In August the lectures were resumed and four were given on The People's Livelihood. These sixteen lectures were taken down by secretaries and rushed into print to be used as Nationalist propaganda. The lectures on Nationalism were being issued as a pamphlet, while the lectures on Democracy were still going on. An apologetic statement dated March 30, 1924, goes with the pamphlet. It is only fair to quote it:

In these lectures I do not have the time necessary for careful preparation nor the books necessary for reference. I can only mount the platform and speak extemporaneously, and so I am really leaving out much that was in my former manuscripts. Although I am making additions and corrections before sending the book to the press, yet I realize that in clear presentation of the theme, in orderly arrangement of the discussion and in the use of supporting facts, these lectures are not at all comparable to the material which I had formerly prepared. I hope that all our comrades will take the book as a basis or as a stimulus, expand and correct it, supply omissions, improve the arrangement and make it a perfect text for propaganda purposes. Then the benefits which it will bring to our people and to our state will truly be immeasurable.[4]

Without this book Sun Yat-sen's claim to the worship of the present generation in China would lack its most important documentation. It is doubtful whether, if there had never been a *San Min Chu I,* there could ever have been a Will or a Cult. The book was the chief firebrand of the Nationalist propaganda in 1926–28, and it is now the most important text in Kuomintang education.

It is an exceedingly difficult book to describe. To a Westerner a complete translation is apt to seem rambling and—over long stretches—dull reading. It is not a book that enlists and holds the spontaneous interest of an Occidental. Consequently, summaries have been attempted for the benefit of those who cannot be compelled by the book itself. I have seen at least a half dozen such, and I am bound to say that the impression the book itself makes has not been caught in any of them. Too many of the summaries have been made for a purpose—either of emphasizing certain ideas which give support to left or right wing opinions, or of creating a favorable impression upon foreigners by a selection of such ideas as make the readiest appeal and omitting such as would antagonize, or, of doing the opposite by selecting the ideas that would most readily antagonize. I have seen yet another variation: an outline that purports to be of the *San Min Chu I*, but presents a schematic conflation with Confucian philosophical ideas. This writer's purpose is to link Sun Yat-sen with the traditional Confucian thinking in the hope of conserving some of the neglected values of the ancient sage.

The Three Principles of the People is a very usable book for *purposes*. Ideas can be selected from it for an impeccable lecture on democratic ideals before an American women's club; and misrepresentations can be found in it to exasperate the respectable foreign business men of Shanghai. One cannot deal fairly with the book and cover up the fact that the misstatements are there as well as the idealism. I should be very much surprised if a synopsis has not been made to the complete delight of Soviet Russia. On the other hand, I know that one has been made thoroughly palatable to the British public. In China, the book is—on the same principle of selection—usable by either the left or the right wing, by communists or Confucianists. A more difficult interpretation for a purpose has come recently from the French. Paschal M. d'Elia, a Jesuit father teaching at Shanghai, has translated and freely annotated the *San Min Chu I* in an earnest endeavor—doubtless forced on him by the required use of the book in schools—to make *The Triple Demism* consistent with Catholic teaching. This is not accomplished without many "conciliatory explanations." The good father says: "With *The Triple Demism* [*San Min Chu I*] in hand, we may tell Sun Yat-sen that, no matter what he says, he is neither a communist nor a socialist, but simply a Demist, and that, once cleared of the obscurity of formulae and the somewhat intentional ambiguity of terms, his Demism can, by means of a few corrections, be presented in such a way that it does not oppose the Catholic teaching."

In its usableness the *San Min Chu I* is an ideal scripture; it furnishes a large range for the selection of ideas and many texts for patriotic sermons. If the usableness of the book seems to make it dangerous, it may be said that its extreme usableness saves it from being too dangerous. Its exponents may readily come to controversies over it, but no party to a controversy can ever produce the only citation of pertinent ideas; all can find some ideas to please them. So I would particularly warn a reader against impressions of the book got from any summary, even my own; for if one should happen upon another summary, it might seem foreign to the impression already gained. Those who have any reason for knowing the book should stick to it and read it through.

From the standpoint of the Western reader, the book is unfortunate in beginning where it does—with the "Principle of Nationalism." Let us make an approach, more likely to be favorable to it, beginning with the lectures on "Democracy." Political theory was presumably the region in which Sun Yat-sen had done most thinking and was most at home. In this section he sets forth the historical trend toward democracy and analyzes its defects with cogency. The West, he holds, is worth learning from in science but not in politics; democracy, in his opinion, has not made much progress in a century, because Western democracy has not worked out a really good method. Here Sun Yat-sen prides himself on an originality and says: "The method which I have thought of is a new discovery in political theory and is a fundamental solution of the whole problem."

This discovery consists in a distinction—which he thinks has been overlooked in the West—between power and ability, that is, between sovereign power and administrative ability. Administration of a government must be done by men of ability, whereas the masses of the people, who cannot rise to this high standard of ability, can hold the power. Government, he says, is like an electric lighting system, in which a child can turn the lights on and off by switches. He reasons that democracies do not develop strong governments because the people are afraid lest the power or sovereignty slip away from them; but, if only the proper method of control is devised, the central government can be strong without any fear. Such a method of control, he affirms, he has discovered. It is just here that his originality evaporates. His only ideas for control of his high-powered government are the Western-derived methods: election, recall, initiative and referendum.

For the parts of his government machine he claims another originality. The familiar Western categories appear here also: legislature, judiciary and executive; to these he would add two more—a revival of China's old Board of Censors with power to criticize the government, and a revival, in some form, of the old Civil Service examinations to pass upon candidates for election or appointment. What then is there original about this? we ask. At most only the combination; the originality consists in putting together two Chinese methods and three foreign ones. Sun Yat-sen thought of this "Five Power Constitution" as one of his major contributions to political thinking.

Some minds will react critically. Suppose we could grant that government is a mechanism; Sun Yat-sen fails to appreciate the genius and the long and patient experimentation which has ultimately resulted in an electrical system, by using which a child can switch on lights; much less does he realize the far more elaborate and nicely adjusted human mechanism that must be perfected before a people can safely manipulate the big control-levers called election, recall, initiative and referendum. If one goes deeper and objects to argument from a mechanical illustration as fallacious when applied to any human grouping, what becomes of his reasoning then? Suppose a government is something more like a living organism, in which tissues may be easily destroyed, but not easily built up, and never actually created!

The section on "The People's Livelihood" (*Min Sheng*) contains the socialistic doctrine which makes the book useful to the left wing. Sun Yat-sen asserts that people have not yet grasped the meaning of this Third Principle. He says they began by grasping only the Principle of Nationalism, have progressed now to some apprehension of Democracy, but still fall short of comprehending the meaning of the People's Livelihood, or the People's Socialism, as others would translate it. The first of the four lectures is a theoretical discussion of socialism, and dissents at some points from Marxism. John Dewey was not slow in observing that this lecture is much indebted to a book to which Sun Yat-sen makes incidental reference, namely, William's *The Social Interpretation of History*. The use of material borrowed from a book that was then but recently published is typical of the avid absorption of Western books by Chinese lecturers. In this case Sun Yat-sen seems to have been characteristically unaware of certain implications of the ideas which he was expounding. Perhaps some communist friend raised a few queries before the next lecture, which came a week later; Sun Yat-sen began it by frankly abandoning the discussion of socialistic theories as confusing. "The more we discuss them," he says, "the less we shall understand them." He observes that Western socialists are at variance—one party advocating revolutionary methods, and another advocating peaceful changes through political action. Which method shall China use? Russia, the advocate of revolutionary methods, has attained success, he asserts, only in her political revolution, not as yet in her economic revolution. From the disputations of socialists Sun Yat-sen turns to a consideration of his own oft-repeated socialistic policies, which he had convinced himself would solve the problem of the people's livelihood: the equalizing of land-ownership by socializing unearned increments, and the control of capital by the development of state ownership of communications and industries. In the third and fourth lectures he discusses, first, the economic problem of food, including the production of it by agriculture and the betterment of the lot of the farmers; and second, the problem of clothing and the production of its raw materials, silk, flax, cotton and wool; on the industrial side of production he advocates state development of industries on a large scale. The consideration of these problems leads him to utter protests against what he calls "economic pressure," particularly the hampering of Chinese industrial development by tariffs favoring the foreign importer; he insists that tariff autonomy must be recovered by China, and that the treaties authorizing these economic disabilities must be canceled. Two other major topics Sun Yat-sen had in mind to lecture upon—housing and communications—but before he could address himself to them, the lectures were interrupted and came to an end.

Economic policies aside, the element in the lectures on Livelihood that has the most historical interest is Sun Yat-sen's attitude toward communism. Inasmuch as he was responsible for admitting communists into membership in the Kuomintang, and in view of their later drastic expulsion from it, this material is historically important.

The men with the keenest minds have taken the world's most valuable materials and have monopolized them for their own profit, making other classes of men their slaves. This has made our age one of fierce human struggle. When can this struggle be settled? Only when we initiate a new period of communism. What is man struggling for, anyway? He is struggling for bread, he is struggling for the rice bowl. In the communistic age, when all have bread and rice enough to eat, there will be no fighting between men, and the human struggle will be eliminated. So communism is a very high ideal of social reconstruction. . . . I can put my distinction today between communism and the

Min-sheng Principle in this way; communism is an ideal of livelihood, while the *Min-sheng* Principle is practical communism. There is no real difference between the two principles—communism and *Min-sheng*—the difference lies in the methods by which they are applied.[5]

At the present time, the most fashionable speakers upon socialism are the ones who indorse Marx's methods. So as soon as social problems are mentioned, most young men rise to champion communism, and want to apply Marx's theories in China. . . . Therefore they are actively organizing a communist party and are beginning to agitate in China.[6]

What is the Principle of Livelihood? It is communism and it is socialism. So not only should we not say that communism conflicts with the *Min-sheng* Principle, but we should even claim communism as a good friend. The supporters of the *Min-sheng* Principle should study communism thoughtfully. If communism is a good ally of the *Min-sheng* Principle, why do members of the Kuomintang oppose the Communist Party? The reason may be that the members of the Communist Party themselves do not understand what communism is and have discoursed against the *San Min* Principles, thus arousing a reaction within the Kuomintang. But the blame for these ignorant and reckless communists should not be charged to the whole Communist Party or to the principles of the party. . . . Since we cannot use the actions of a few persons as an excuse for opposing the principles of a whole group, why has the question arisen among our Kuomintang comrades? Because they have not understood what the *Min-sheng* Principle really is. They do not realize that our Principle of Livelihood is a form of communism. It is not a form that originated with Marx. . . . The first society formed by man was a communistic society and the primitive age was a communistic age.[7]

The great aim of the Principle of Livelihood in our Three Principles is communism—a share in property by all. But the communism which we propose is a communism of the future, not of the present . . . It is a very different thing from what is called in the West "nationalization of property," confiscation for the government's use of private property which the people already possess. . . . Our plan provides that land **now** fixed in value shall still be privately owned.[8]

In working out our principle of Livelihood, we cannot use or apply in China the methods of Marx, although we have the deepest respect for his teaching. . . . Even Marx's disciples say that we cannot use his methods for the solution of all the social problems in China.[9]

Where there are inequalities of wealth, Marx's methods can of course be applied; a class war can be started to destroy the inequalities. But in China, where industry is not yet developed, class war and the dictatorship of the proletariat are unnecessary. So today we can take Marx's ideas as a guide, but we cannot make use of his methods.[10]

We cannot say, then, that the theory of communism is different from our *Min-sheng* Principle. Our Three Principles of the People mean government "of the people, by the people, and for the people"—that is, a state belonging to all the people, a government controlled by all the people, and rights and benefits for the enjoyment of all the people. If this is true, the people will not only have a communistic share in state production, but they will have a share in everything.[11]

That such statements are eminently usable by communists seems a gratuitous thing to say. That they are being used by communists in China today is a fact to be reported concerning their influence. Over and over the communists are saying it; that they are more truly following Sun Yat-sen than the anti-communist group in power at Nanking. But was Sun Yat-sen a communist? It is being argued that he was; it is being argued that he was not. The important thing to notice is that he made statements which can be effectively used by communists; he also made statements which can be cited by those who feel it important to detach his influence from communism. Here again the fruitful controversial method is to select such ideas as please the partisan.

The desire to clear Sun Yat-sen of communism has found expression in America. It is the purpose of a recent book, *Sun Yat-sen versus Communism* by Maurice William, author of *The Social Interpretation of History*, of which Sun Yat-sen made such characteristic and liberal use in his first lecture on the People's Livelihood. Dr. William goes so far as to affirm that Sun Yat-sen was, until near the end of his life, "a convinced Marxist," but holds that, in the three-months interval between the first twelve *San Min Chu I* lectures and the last four, Sun Yat-sen happened to read *The Social Interpretation of History* and was by it won away from Marxism and communism to Dr. William's own social philosophy. I have no desire to combat a conclusion that Sun Yat-sen was not a communist. I should be more inclined to challenge what Dr. William takes for proven—that Sun Yat-sen at one time "accepted Marxism without reservation." Sun Yat-sen was nothing if not eclectic; he was nobody's exclusive disciple; he picked over foreign ideas, chose what appealed to him and conglomerated what he had selected. In his treatise, *China's Revolution,* dated January, 1923, he definitely says that his Third Principle was arrived at by comparative examination of social theories and the selection of the best ideas from among them. That was his method always, but not always with coherent results.

That the reader may think for himself, it should be pointed out that the statements on communism just quoted are all taken from the Lectures on Livelihood, and were made subsequent to the time when Dr. William believes Sun Yat-sen had come to "an ultimate rejection of communism." Reservations as to Marxism are certainly there; but if communism is repudiated, it is done with friendly, outstretched, and welcoming hands.

A nice point of interpretation is involved in any controversy as to what Sun Yat-sen's real position was on a given subject. Communism happens to be the debatable theme with the most important world implications at the present time. It is a question whether any valid results can be got from taking Sun Yat-sen's variable ideas, as if they never varied except on conviction. To understand the nature of Sun Yat-sen's mind is of the essence of the problem. Was it not, after all, the kind and quality of his mental processes, rather than the precise content of his expressed ideas, that opened the way for controversies as to what his opinions were?

The more widely one ranges over Sun Yat-sen's writings the more evident it becomes that inconsistency is not a phenomenon of infrequent occurence. To infer always from inconsistency a well-considered change of opinion would bring one to preposterous biographical conclusions. One has to recognize sooner or later that logical rigidity is an impossible basis on which to live with Sun Yat-sen and come to know him.

It might be cogently argued that, in dealing with an easily absorbent, propagandist mind like Sun Yat-sen's, one should not look to the shifting ideas for his real opinions, but to those formulations which he clung to tenaciously all his life. There is such a central core in Sun Yat-sen's thinking about socialism—a never failing sense of the fundamental importance of a decent livelihood for all the people, and several concrete social changes which he almost naïvely believed would result in a livelihood for all. It is important to remind ourselves that Sun Yat-sen was very much a socialist before the word "bolshevism" had become current among us. The equalization of land-ownership was among his propagated policies from 1905 to his death. State appropriation of unearned increments was tied to his Principle of the People's Livelihood from the earliest expositions of it to the final one. From the beginning of his career to the end, he was determined that rich people should not monopolize wealth, and that capitalism should not be allowed to become the tyranny in China that it had become in parts of the West. The Manifesto of the *Tung Meng Hui,* drawn up soon after the organization of the Brotherhood in 1905, said in no uncertain terms: "We will establish a socialistic state, and cause every citizen to have a decent living. If any one dares to monopolize economic resources that should belong to the citizens as a whole, that man must be got rid of." It was because of Sun Yat-sen's insistence on these socialistic policies that they were so early included in the revolutionary program; not because they were popular policies with his confreres. The story is told of his outburst of anger during the period of his presidency at Nanking, when one of his sworn brothers advised him to talk no longer about the Third Principle. Stirred out of his usual calm, Sun Yat-sen pounded on the table, and said: "The revolution aims at the welfare of the people and the solution of the problem of Livelihood. If we discard the Principle of Liveli-hood, we may as well give up the whole revolution." This was the kind of socialist that Sun Yat-sen was before the Soviet Republic was born.

To show more concretely how Sun Yat-sen's mind functioned under the stimulus of new ideas, it will be instructive, and in this connection pertinent, to notice what he had to say about Russia in these same lectures of 1924 on the Three Principles. It should be recalled that when he began to give these weekly lectures, it was less than six months since he had so much as intimated through an interview given to the *New York Times* that he was about to turn to Russia for help, and it was less than four months since Borodin had come to Canton to advise him. With the short time-interval in mind the quotations will be the more instructive, showing—as they do—how quickly he could absorb a new set of ideas, and how promptly he would pass them on to the public. The statements will also serve to fill in the immediate mental background, out of which the already quoted statements about communism came, and out of which came also the inconsistencies from which Dr. William infers so much. If in these utterances

Sun Yat-sen does not show the independence of a great thinker, he demonstrates the facility that characterizes a propagandist.

Russia was formerly one of the Entente nations; when the Entente Powers were fighting Germany, Russia sent over ten million soldiers into the field—not a puny force. Without Russia's part in the war, the Entente's line on the Western Front would long before have been smashed by Germany; because Russia was embarrassing the Germans on the Eastern front, the Entente Powers were able to break even with Germany for two or three years and finally turn defeat into victory. Just halfway through the war, Russia began to reflect, and she realized that in helping the Entente to fight Germany she was merely helping several brute forces to fight one brute force and that no good results would come of it in the end. A group of soldiers and citizens awoke, broke away from the Entente, and concluded a separate peace with Germany.[12]

This war was a conflict of imperialisms between states, not a struggle between savagery and civilization or between Might and Right. So the effect of the war was merely the overthrow of one imperialism by another imperialism; what survived was still imperialism. But from the war there was unconsciously born in the heart of mankind a great hope —the Russian Revolution.[13]

When, as a result of the Russo-Japanese war, Japan drove Russia out of Korea and southern Manchuria, smashed the Russian dream of world domination, and maintained the integrity of Eastern Asia, a profound change took place in international life. And when, after the European War, Russia overthrew her own imperialism and substituted a new socialist state for her own imperialistic state, another greater change occurred. It is only six years since this revolution began, but in these six years Russia has reorganized herself within and has changed her old policy of force to a new policy of peace. This new policy not only harbors no wild design of world aggression; it aims to check the strong and to help the weak; it advocates justice. But a new fear psychology has developed in the world towards Russia, more desperate than former fears, because Russia's new policy aims not only at the destruction of Russian imperialism, but also at the overthrow of imperialism in the whole world. Furthermore, it aims at the overthrow of the capitalism of the world. For, in every country, although the apparent power is in the hands of the government, real control is with the capitalists; the new Russian policy would smash this control, and so the capitalists of the world are panic-stricken. This is why a profound change has been produced in world affairs by which all future world currents will be affected.[14]

The one hundred fifty million Russians, when their revolution succeeded, broke with the other white races and condemned the white man's imperialistic behavior; now they are thinking of throwing in their lot with the weaker smaller peoples of Asia in a struggle against the tyrannical races. So only two hundred fifty millions of tyrannical races are left, but they are still trying by inhuman methods and military force to subjugate the other twelve hundred fifty millions. So hereafter mankind will be divided into two camps: on one side will be the twelve hundred fifty millions; on the other side, the two hundred fifty millions. Although the latter group are in the minority, yet they hold the most powerful positions on the globe and their political and economic strength is immense. With these two forces they are out to exploit the weaker and smaller races. If the political arm of navies and armies is not strong enough they bear down with economic pressure. If their economic arm is at times weak they intervene with political force of navies and armies. The way their political power coöperates with their economic power is like the way in which the left arm helps the right arm; with their two arms they have crushed most terribly the twelve hundred fifty millions. . . . Lenin . . . advocated self-determination for the oppressed peoples and launched a campaign for them against injustice. The Powers attacked Lenin because they wanted to destroy a prophet and a seer of mankind and obtain security for themselves. But the people of the world now have their eyes opened and know that the rumors created by the Powers are false; they will not let themselves be deceived again. The political thinking of the peoples of the world has been enlightened to this extent.[15]

III. FRIGHTENING CHINA INTO NATIONALISM

"The People's Nationalism," which we have held over to the last, is the section in which there is least of intellectual theory and most of propaganda. The Chinese word *Ts'u,* which is usually rendered Nationalism, is not so political in meaning as our word suggests. It means literally clan, or tribe. *The People's Clan* was Sun Yat-sen's graphic description of the integration of the people as a whole. The idea of racial solidarity is essential to it, and nationality is only its political expression. As a matter of fact "Nationalism" was the one of the Three Principles that had in the course of years proven most variable in interpretation. As has already been reported, Sun Yat-sen's first rendering of Lincoln's phrase "government by the people" was *min yu—the people are to have.* But, to his already revolutionary and anti-Manchu mind, the idea of the Chinese people having the government was inextricable from the idea that the Manchus should not have it; so he seems to have been carried immediately over to the notion of the Chinese people asserting themselves, first of all, for the overthrow of the Manchus. We have already seen in an earlier chapter that before the Revolution of 1911 the First Principle had meant just that— Chinese solidarity against the Manchus who were treated as usurping foreigners. For this meaning the phrase *Min Ts'u,* the People's Clan, was a suggestive formulation.

Immediately after the consummation of the Revolution, nationalism was reinterpreted to mean equality among the races within China, including the Manchus, and their consolidation into a unified Chinese people. The five-barred flag of the early Republic was the symbol of this racial union. When, ten years later, in March, 1921, Sun Yat-sen was interpreting the Three Principles in an address, his thought of nationalism was still much the same: a unified nation created of mixed races (he cited both the United

States and Switzerland as examples of mixed racial strains welded into national unity). He took but a fleeting glance at another aspect of nationalism—the preservation of China's national wholeness against the encroachment of foreign "spheres of influence." In a book finished in January, 1923, *China's Revolution,* Sun Yat-sen's discussion of the Three Principles definitely distinguishes two aspects of nationalism, an internal and an external one: unity and equality of races within China, and China's rights among the nations of the world. Under the latter Sun Yat-sen envisages for China freedom to develop her own civilization, a place of respect among the nations and a share in the promotion of world understanding or world unity. It is worthy of note, that as late as January, 1923, Sun Yat-sen was interpreting nationalism in very moderate terms. In that same month he had his conferences with Joffe, and nine months later Borodin was with him in Canton. One year after the conservative statement just reported, the Declaration of the First National Congress of the Kuomintang appeared, and in it nationalism was interpreted as primarily struggle against foreign imperialism, and secondarily as equality and unity among the racial strains within China. Doubtless there are traces in the *San Min* lectures of 1924 of all the former connotations of nationalism; there are also some none-too-clarifying attempts at definition, and many statements, often inconsistent, about the decline of nationalistic spirit in China; but towering over them all with impressive preëminence is Sun Yat-sen's terrific arraignment of foreign imperialism. The value of this as propaganda was promptly recognized; China's patriotic preacher had surpassed Borodin's most sanguine hope.

Propaganda in the Russian sense is a technique of moving masses of men toward a desired end. With action in view, volition is aroused by an appeal to some strong emotional motive-power, such as self-interest, fear or prejudice. The end in view in this case was to awaken China from an inertia of disillusionment and despair to a combined effort for national unification. Sun Yat-sen made his appeal to an emerging national consciousness, strongest in its racial form of prejudice against foreigners; he appealed also to fear.

He held up before his people a terrible bogey of racial extinction—nothing less. To any one who knows the fecundity of the Chinese and the unnecessary wastage of human life in China, any fear of extinction seems utterly unnecessary. Sun Yat-sen, however, makes such of it. For example: on the basis of unscrutinized figures of population he reasons that one hundred years hence the population of the United States will have become one billion and that China's population will remain at what it now is—four hundred million. Having postulated this situation, he takes it for granted that with ten Americans to four Chinese the Chinese race will inevitably be "absorbed." One wonders just how the absorption would be brought about; but Sun Yat-sen was not concerned with such a speculative detail.

He conjures up a yet more terrible fear—extinction of China by a force that works subtly and unseen—"economic pressure." He represents China as a land which has already lost its independence and is actually lower in status than a very subsidiary colony. He tells the Chinese they are not like the people of Annam or Korea, slaves of one country, but slaves of ten "imperialistic Powers." He enlarges the indictment against the nations who are thus oppressing China, robbing her of actual silver dollars. By specious arguments and uncritical statistics he makes this sum go up and up, until he declares that by "six kinds of economic domination" China is annually fleeced of not less than one billion two hundred million dollars. Whereas "racial extinction" is a hundred years off, extinction by "economic pressure" is an imminent peril. He warns his people that China will hardly last more than ten years, if she does not throw off this terrible bondage to the imperalistic Powers.

Over and over in the lectures he returns to this appalling picture. He thinks up other ways of frightening the people. He speculates about what will be the state of oppression in ten years. At the present rate of increase he reasons that China will be paying foreigners three billion dollars a year; consequently, ten years hence, every able-bodied Chinese male will be paying foreigners a tax of forty-five dollars a year! What a figure with which to terrify every poor coolie!

It is very difficult, if not impossible, to reconcile Sun Yat-sen's attack upon "foreign economic pressure" with his own previous advocacy of foreign economic development of China on a scale well calculated to give the foreign investors the power of "economic pressure." No Emperor, and no other President had ever presumed to urge the borrowing of foreign capital on the scale that Sun Yat-sen did. And no one of them was ever blinder than he to the possibility of an unhappy sequel to "the influx of large-scale foreign capital on the largest possible scale." He seems never to have grasped the always possible sequence of foreign control upon foreign capital investment—an eventuality hardly to be avoided in a country unstable financially and disrupted politically. He would have tied China, regardless of the primitive stage of her economic development, in a network of financial indebtedness and risk so entangling and so vast that all that he was inveighing against in the *San Min Chu I* lectures would have been by comparison like the tying of a single loose knot. Startling as it may be, the fact is, that the same Sun Yat-sen who advocated the "International Development of China" at the staggering rate of sixty million dollars a day performed the feat of frightening China into nationalism with the bogey of "foreign economic pressure."

The *San Min Chu I* cannot produce the same effect upon a foreign and upon a Chinese mind. Its agglutination of Western-derived ideas, is so new to most Chinese that the impression on them is of wonderful and almost unlimited learning. Even Chinese "returned students" educated in the West, who should be able to expose the errors and the misuse of facts and figures, do not do so; some from sheer tolerance of inaccuracy, some because of well-grounded fear of incurring the displeasure of the government, others because they believe in the book's fundamental persuasion toward democracy and accept as essentially sound its protest against imperialism. To the Western mind, however, the large democratic principles are now commonplaces. Sun Yat-sen's exposition of them can seem neither learned nor original. The Western mind, moreover, has passed the crest of enthusiasm for them and has come out on an arid sort of plain, where the defects of democracy stand out in a hot sunlight. As for the indictment of imperialism—unfortunately, what is excellent propaganda for setting Chinese against foreigners does not work excellently as an argument to bring foreigners to a sympathetic attitude toward China's national ambitions. Hence the need of selective summaries of the *Three Principles of the People*. An intellectually creditable argument, and a very strong one, might have been made against the web of injustice in which China finds herself entangled. Instead, Sun Yat-sen, over-influenced doubtless by the Russians, used fallacy, misrepresentation, distortion and other forms of vitiated thinking to gain his end—the arousing of the people.

Sun Yat-sen's opinions are said to be China's opinions. If this is so, the violence of these judgments is not so much to be resented as to be observed. No nation in our time has so pitifully failed to understand itself as China. The Chinese people know themselves to be possessed of many abilities that are second to none, of large natural resources and of an unparalleled fund of human industry.

They believe that they are democratic at heart and peaceful in intention. Yet the reforms have gone wrong. What is the matter? Unable to analyze her own difficulties, China fell an easy prey to a rationalization of her failure that was considerate of racial pride. The Russians presented a brilliantly conceived, partially true and thoroughly palatable analysis of national frustration. Russia diagnosed China's plight as due to "foreign imperialism." Not so far gone that her mind was unclear, China knew that a certain amount of the trouble was due to rampant internal militarism. But the Russians affirmed that the Chinese militarists and foreign imperialists worked hand in hand; that when the militarists wanted money, they went to the foreign Powers; that when the foreign Powers wanted privileges they supported the militarists. Looked at through Russian eyes, the evil in China was the *bête noir* of communism, the "world evil" of "imperialistic exploitation," especially of an insidious, economic kind. China, wishing to throw off the disease, followed the doctor's advice. Sun Yat-sen aroused the people with the fear of racial extinction. He painted the "imperialistic powers" very black and sent China on a crusade for "national independence."

IV. SUN YAT-SEN'S POLITICAL PROGRAM FOR CHINA

Sun Yat-sen's passionate denunciations of imperialism brought him a greatly enlarged popular following. In the same year, 1924, he produced another writing which won him followers among the less volatile and less ardent classes. *The Outline of Reconstruction* is now ranked high among the party classics. It is to be distinguished from the *magnum opus* in many parts of which we have already given account, *The Principles of National Reconstruction,* begun in 1918 and not completed at the time of his death. The *Outline* is a concise statement, drawn up under twenty-five points.

It is not so long but that it can be posted on a capacious billboard. In two horizontal blue and white panels it decorates the faded red walls on both sides of the great south entrance of the Forbidden City in Peking. It is carved on the walls of the Memorial Hall in the Sun Yat-sen mausoleum at Nanking. Facsimiles of the original manuscript are frequently to be seen with the little note of attestation in the handwriting of Madame Sun (Ching-ling). It is signed by Sun Yat-sen and dated April 12, 1924. Its lucidity, compactness, and well-rounded theory appealed to the type of intellectual who does not rush into popular movements but sometimes finds them impossible to resist, and is glad to have an unimpassioned and reasoned statement of policy as his point of attachment. Some of these people had mistrusted Sun Yat-sen before. But, carried along by the general flow of sentiment, they seized upon *The Outline of Reconstruction;* in explanation of a changed attitude toward Sun Yat-sen they began to say: "He has made for our country a plan—a very good plan for China." In order to estimate this plan fairly, it is desirable to take a sweeping glance over the whole course of Sun Yat-sen's political thinking about his country.

In a previous chapter I have ventured to characterize Sun Yat-sen as a programatist. His most colossal plan, prodigious in extent, was a program for the material development of China through railways, roads and harbors, through the development of natural resources, and the creation of giant industries. In the political zone Sun Yat-sen was also a programatist, but his political plans never assumed so overgrown a size nor included such a multiplicity of details. Although a monumental treatise on the subject of "Political Reconstruction" was planned as the final part of Sun Yat-sen's comprehensive work on *National Reconstruction,* this was the part that was still unfinished at his death. Consequently, posterity must do without the fuller treatises that were projected on "The Five Power Constitution," "Local Government," "Central Government," "Foreign Policies" and "National Defense." If Borodin had not pushed Sun Yat-sen out on the lecture platform in 1924, posterity might never have had even the sections on "The Three Principles."

In lieu of detailed statements concerning the precise nature of the government which Sun Yat-sen desired for China, we must accept the broad outlines which he repeated over and over in addresses and in articles. As far back as the organization of the Revolutionary Brotherhood in 1905 the plan had been sketched: a republic; citizens with equal rights and privileges; a president elected by popular ballot of the citizens; a parliament of representatives elected by the citizens; a constitution to be drawn up and promulgated in written form. The stages in which the changes were to be brought about were also outlined in the "Manifesto of the Military Government of the Revolutionary Brotherhood" made public in 1911. There was to be a purely military government for a three-year period of reform; and next a six-year period of political tutelage, during which citizens were to learn local self-government in the administrative districts called *hsien;* in its eighteen provinces China had then over 1500 of these districts, each ruled by a district magistrate. While the people of the *hsien* were having their six-years training in local government, the central government was to continue to be a military one. The third period was to be the culmination of the nine-years process in a constitutional government with a popularly elected president and parliament, the adoption of a written constitution and the obliteration of the military government.

Certain main features remained constant in Sun Yat-sen's plans for his country: the three stages of development, the beginning of training in self-government in the 1500 administrative districts, and a central government entrusted during the period of preparation to a military group operating under a promulgated understanding with the provinces. As the failure of the republic became more and more manifest from 1913 on, Sun Yat-sen became increasingly insistent upon another early conception of his: what he called the "Five Power Constitution." This, he convinced himself would be the cure of China's constitutional maladjustments. The plan grew out of his reading of Montesquieu and his study of the classic example of the application of Montesquieu's theory—the Constitution of the United States of America, which defines three governmental "powers" or branches operating for the good of the whole but without subservience to one another. In Imperial China there had been no such differentiation of functions in government. The Chinese Republic, wishing to be entirely modern, modeled itself on the three power plan with executive, legislative and judicial branches. But, instead of checking one another in an integrated and flexible whole, the executive and parliamentary divisions quarreled disastrously; in fact the quarrel degenerated into a primitive struggle for existence that ended in the final extinction of the parliament. When that happened, Sun Yat-sen insisted that, with the addition of two more independent departments or powers, the difficulties would be overcome and the whole would function together with the proper equilibrium. To ensure the election of none but suitable officials and legislators he advocated the revival—in what form is not detailed—of the ancient Chinese system of examinations, then thoroughly destroyed by the reforms. Only those who passed the examinations were to hold either elective or appointive offices. Lest, in spite of this method of choosing government personnel, parliaments should become unruly and officials corrupt, there was to be another branch of the government with the power to observe, censure and punish—a Department of Control. This harked back to several practices of the Empire, especially to the custom of appointing censors who had a right to criticize officials, even the Emperor. Under the Empire these men exercised their function by moral force and knew better than to overuse it.

The appointment of a man as censor was a tribute to the ripened wisdom of age and to moral integrity—a political laureateship rather than a practical office. The picture of a five-powered central government was always completed in Sun Yat-sen's mind with the direct exercise by citizens of "four rights"—election, recall, initiative and referendum. He puts his case for the "five powers" and the "four rights" succinctly in one of his lectures:

These five powers belong to the government, and as the government is merely a machine, they are mechanical powers or powers to produce force and efficiency in performing a certain desired work. They are five in number because there are five different things for the government to do. . . . The people's political rights may be considered four safety-checks on the powerful governing machine. They are four in number because there are four ways of controlling the movements of the machine.[16]

The Outline of National Reconstruction, Sun Yat-sen's final formulation of his political plan for China, was signed just eleven months before his death. In an English translation it reads like a code of Twenty-five Political Commandments delivered to the people:

The national government shall reconstruct the republic upon the basis of . . . the Three Principles and the Five Power Constitution.
. . . .
The process of reconstruction shall be divided into three periods. . . .
. . . .
During the period of military operations the area of operations shall be subject to martial law.[17]

The document amounts to a briefly worded codification of Sun Yat-sen's previous planning for the Chinese Republic. Alterations are not many, and there are few new details. A change of emphasis is the immediately outstanding feature. "The Three Principles of the People" are reversed in order so that the emphasis of priority is thrown upon the socialistic principle, which had stood third.

The first principle of reconstruction is that of popular livelihood or the promotion of the general welfare. In order to meet the most urgent needs of the people for food, clothing, shelter, and communication with one another, the Government shall coöperate with the people in the improvement of agriculture so that all may have sufficient food, in the development of the textile industry so that all may have sufficient clothing, in the building of houses on a large scale so that all may have comfortable homes, and in the building and improvement of roads and waterways so that all may conveniently travel and transport their goods.[18]

Economic development is assigned—never before so explicitly—to the districts (*hsien*) as a part of their practice of local self-government. It is the districts that are to organize the land tax, gather in the unearned increments and develop public industries. The district governments are to receive the revenues from lands, forests, streams, water-power and mines for investment and expenditure. If additional capital is obtained from the central government for larger enterprises, it is to be on a coöperative basis with equal sharing of profits. From its revenues each district is to contribute to the support of the central government not less than ten per cent and not more than fifty per cent of its revenues.

There is in this final plan a noticeable omission of time-limits for the three stages of reconstruction, formerly set at three years of military rule and six years of political tutelage. Here allowance is made for variation in the speed of these processes in different provinces. As soon as order is restored in a province it may enter on the period of tutelage. When all the districts of a province become fully self-governing, the province is to begin constitutional self-government with popular election of a provincial assembly,

which in turn is to elect the provincial governor. The province, however, is to be simply a link between the central government and the
district governments, and is to be subject to the central government
in all national matters. When a majority of the provinces shall
have reached the period of self-government, a national congress is
to be elected—one deputy from each *hsien*—to adopt a constitution.
On the day of its promulgation the Period of Constitutional Government will be considered to have begun. A national election is then
to be held according to provisions of the constitution. The highest
power in the central government is to be vested in the People's
Congress, consisting of one deputy from each *hsien*. In relation
to the central government this Congress is to have the "four rights"
exercised by citizens in the affairs of local government, that is,
the People's Congress is to elect the central government officials
and to have the right to recall them; and in regard to legislation
it is to have the rights of initiative and referendum. The Congress is responsible for organizing a central government with five
departments, Legislative, Executive, Judicial, Examining and Controlling. Three months are allowed for this process; then the provisional government must retire in favor of the new one.

That Sun Yat-sen's planning for China involves a period of "enlightened despotism" was early pointed out by his critics, to whom
he replied that a despotism existing for the purpose of producing
a republic was very different from a despotism made benevolent to
prop up a monarchy. That Sun Yat-sen was compelled in his
thinking to admit the necessity of a central despotism *pro tempore*
is not surprising, considering the vast unpreparedness of China
for democracy. It is surprising that he seems to have failed to observe how opposed to each other were the tight centralization for
which the Kuomintang constitution provided and the local autonomy and local initiative which his *Outline* sets forth. Sun Yat-
sen's plan calls for the exercise by the people of all four of the

most advanced rights that citizens have acquired in democracies anywhere. That the people could be trained in such functioning without exercising the functions is impossible to suppose. But, as surely as they began to exercise them, it would mean the end of the Kuomintang form of government in the *hsien*. Perhaps Sun Yat-sen intended that it should be the end. The Kuomintang constitution, however, provided China with more than a party constitution; it initiated a political system by which power is handed down from a national government to a multitude of *hsien* and through them to smaller units. In it no provision was made for initiative or power to work upward from the *hsien* to the central government, unless it could get through by a national party congress whose whole method of election was in the keeping and control of the dictatorship. It would seem that emerging local initiative could scarcely fail to come into conflict somewhere with the party dictatorship. If these two forces could take the field for a fair trial of strength, the very struggling would educate the citizenship. But, here's the rub! The education of the people in self-government is, by bitter irony, entrusted to the central government, whose very hold on power consists of a high degree of centralization and the support, not of a universal citizenship but of a highly selected party membership. One can imagine such a central government concerned about the education of citizens and officials to function in the pattern of party government; but it seems very optimistic to believe that it will educate the people in a pattern of local government inconsistent with party power. The future must show how China is to resolve so fundamental a contradiction; and a critic must in all modesty remember that such difficulties do not always clear themselves by logical processes. It is enough for us as onlooking Westerners to remark that China has in her present make-up what seems to us to be contradictory elements. She has a large hold-over of regional administration, stubbornly defended by powerful militarists with armies of their own. Yet there is at the nation's heart a party dictatorship, which in its very structure is centralized to the last degree. Finally, China has abundant professions, on the part of militarists and of the central dictatorship alike, that Sun Yat-sen's plan of educating the people in "direct local self-government" is the only plan for the country. That Sun Yat-sen set the stamp of his approval on two conflicting patterns of government, the party dictatorship of the Kuomintang constitution and his own "direct democracy," is the irony of his end. Therein lies an inconsistency that will confuse his followers as long as they follow him.

On three great issues that confront China today, Sun Yat-sen's thinking has been confusing rather than clarifying. Let us summarize them.

What form of government should China have? Surely that is a cardinal question. We have seen that Sun Yat-sen spent his life advocating a constitutional and parliamentary republic—with the slight modification which made it what he called "five-powered." But, by the reorganization of the Kuomintang in 1924 he presented China with a government radically different—a party dictatorship.

What shall China do about communism? Already the confusion that was in Sun Yat-sen's mind on that point has become a bitter conflict spread out over China.

What is the way of life and freedom for China in her economic relations with foreigners? We have seen that Sun Yat-sen advocated—on a scale no one else ever dared to contemplate—the foreign economic development of China. But he also brought China to a resentment of foreign enterprises which will be a long time in passing. He taught his countrymen that, because of foreign economic "exploitation," they were already worse than slaves—an oppressed people that must fight for independence.

Sun Yat-sen's opinions, considered objectively as the changes of a mind in the course of its development and decline, would have biographical interest only. But, regarded as authoritative deliverances which set for China a program, his variable ideas have a tragic importance.

V. SUN YAT-SEN AND MILITARISM

If the Occident was slow to grasp Sun Yat-sen's "Russian orientation," it was not his fault. The policy was thoroughly understood in the reorganized Kuomintang, and Sun Yat-sen made enough public statements to leave no doubt of it. On Oct. 8, 1924, a Russian fleet made Canton a visit, bearing, as afterwards transpired, not a gift of money to the Kuomintang but a present of valuable furs which could be inconspicuously turned into money. Sun Yat-sen sent the Commander of the fleet an address of welcome in which he said:

The relationship between the Russian Soviet Socialist Republic and the Republic of China is of the most intimate kind. The Russian Soviet Socialist Republic recognizes its mission in the overthrow of brutal imperialism. I have always advocated the Three People's Principles, and am also fighting for the Chinese Revolution and for the world revolution. Now that you have come a long way with your fleet, the friendship between the two countries will thereby be rendered more intimate. In helping each other and in overcoming all obstacles the two countries will together serve world peace. This is a blessing not only for the two countries but also for the world.[19]

Misgivings as to the alliance, and particularly its involvement of Chinese Nationalism with the communist party, were felt by many of Canton's stabler citizens. They saw Sun Yat-sen developing his so-called "Red Army" in Kwangtung. The Russian advisers were doing this thoroughly on the principle of an active propaganda corps allied with the military units in order that the soldiers should be taught the principles for which they were preparing to fight.

Contemporaneously, there was developing in Canton, ostensibly with Sun Yat-sen's encouragement, an informal militia called the "Merchants' Volunteer Corps." The Merchants' had a difference with Sun Yat-sen over the importation of arms, a consignment of which was seized. Bitter feelings were aroused, and there was a bloody clash between the Merchants' Corps and the Red Army in October, 1924, in which many were killed and a large number of buildings destroyed by fire.

In all three of his Southern régimes Sun Yat-sen was in some degree entangled in the quarrels of Northern war lords. In this— the third—period he came near playing the rôle of a militarist himself. Sun Yat-sen was, however, essentially a civilian, not a soldier. A military rôle always sat awkwardly upon him.

A sensational issue with the North was created for Sun Yat-sen by the election of Tsao Kun to the presidency in 1923 by outrageous bribery of the Parliament. This scandal was resented by public opinion very generally in China. Wu Pei-fu was the militarist in control of Peking at the time; since he was of the same political faction as the President, there came upon him a reflected odium. Party enmities became tense, and in September, 1924, war broke out both in the Yangtze Valley and in the north. Sun Yat-sen at once began mobilizing forces to join the war, allying himself with Chang Tso-lin and the Anfu group. One of the most pleasing photographs I have seen of Sun Yat-sen and Chiang Kai-shek together shows them sitting in excellent light in adjoining windows of the railway train that was to take them to the front to direct the expedition; they look very unmilitary, it is true, but comfortably human.

Sun Yat-sen had announced the departure with his usual expert publicity. The "Manifesto on the Northern Expedition," issued Sept. 18, 1924, shows how completely he had adopted the Russian interpretation of a league between militarism and imperialism. "The direct cause," he says, "of our civil wars during the last thirteen years has been militarism, and the indirect cause has been imperialism." Concerning the war of the moment he affirms: "The Northern Expedition is being undertaken in order to coöperate with the rest of the country in destroying Tsao Kun, Wu Pei-fu and other traitors. . . . The war is not only directed against militarism, but against imperialism whose support has made the existence of militarism possible." The drastic foreign policy of the Kuomintang is reaffirmed:

We shall demand the revision of unequal treaties and the abolition of all special privileges in order to protect our national interests in foreign relations and to eradicate the imperialist influence in China. New treaties will be concluded in accordance with the principles of international equality and mutual respect of sovereignty. . . . After the abolition of unequal treaties, China's new laws will be applied throughout her territories, including the existing leased settlements.[20]

Like most of the *tuchun* wars this one ran a short course and, before Sun Yat-sen could get into action, the Christian General, Feng Yü-hsiang, brought the episode to an abrupt end by his *coup d'état* at Peking Oct. 23, 1924; he isolated his superior commander, Wu Pei-fu, and forced him to retreat before Chang Tso-lin. Then General Feng assumed an ultra-democratic rôle; he turned the "little Emperor" out of his palace home and took possession of it in the name of the people. For "Chief Executive" he recalled the old war horse, Tuan Chi-jui—a none too happy choice. Immediately there was talk of getting the North and South together in a conference for rehabilitating China. An invitation was sent to Sun Yat-sen to come to Peking. When a similar invitation had come from Li Yuan-hung in 1922 Sun Yat-sen had not responded. His refusal then had created adverse comment, for there was a rising sentiment in China that the North and South should get together. There was, however, a difference in the two situations. In 1922 Sun

Yat-sen was smarting from the failure of his own projected campaign against the North; moreover, the invitation had come from those whom he did not like. In 1924 his designated enemies, Wu Pei-fu and Tsao Kun, had been defeated by General Feng's *coup.* With good grace Sun Yat-sen could consent to confer with his victorious allies. Canton had ceased to be a comfortable environment; he could well get out of it. He was far from well. Borodin apparently favored the trip. That he was under any illusion that China was about to be reunited seems implausible. One wonders how clearly he was looking ahead at this time; did he know or suspect that Sun Yat-sen was a dying man? Did he foresee the effective drama that was to follow at the nation's capital? It was perhaps argument enough for Borodin that Russian influence was at a high mark in Peking. The Sino-Russian agreement had been concluded in May of that very year, 1924. Karakhan was occupying the former Russian Legation as the first representative of ambassadorial rank sent by any country to China. This unique ranking made him automatically doyen of the international diplomatic corps residing at Peking—a distinction that brought him scant honor from the other legations, but was used to the full in impressing susceptible young Chinese who showed an interest in communism. As an opportunity for publicity alone, the trip north must have seemed desirable to the propagandists of the Kuomintang. It promised an extension of the lecturing campaign upon which Borodin had so successfully launched Sun Yat-sen. The aging patriot had never done better as a speaker; he was not only sure to speak well of Russia, he was ready to speak dangerously and offensively of foreign imperialists. Before he left for the north a birthday dinner was given him in Canton, at which he indulged slightly in reminiscences. He was fifty-eight years old by occidental reckoning.

Accompanied by his young wife and a supporting staff, Sun Yat-sen left Canton by a government cruiser November 13th, took a

Japanese ship at Hongkong, arrived at Shanghai on the 17th, left for Kobe on the 21st, left Kobe for Tientsin on the 30th and arrived there December 4th. On his trip north he had many opportunities for public statements through the press and through popular addresses. At Shanghai he issued a vigorous statement against foreigners and their wrongs to China, and voiced the already current criticism of missionaries as running-dogs of imperialism. At Moji he is reported to have said: "China is ruined, and it is England that has done it." In a speech at Kobe he advocated a pan-Asiatic movement against European and American oppression. The Japanese, resentful of recent discrimination against them in American immigration laws, were all the more ready to lend an ear. As reported in the press, Sun Yat-sen said:

Russia symbolizes and practices a "live and let live" policy. Other powers aim at dominating the so-called weak nations. We Asiatics must emancipate Asia and the down-trodden states of Europe and America from European and American oppression. Japan and China must join hands and harmoniously lead the Asiatics to fight for a greater Asiaticism, thus expediting world-peace.[21]

On his journey Sun Yat-sen learned from press reports that the Chief Executive had not waited for conference with him, but had already issued his call for the Reorganization Conference. Neither had Sun Yat-sen waited for conference with the Chief Executive, but had sent broadcast at the very outset of his trip a characteristic manifesto, dated November 10th, stating what his ideas were as to the make-up of the projected national body. Extraordinary proposals they were! He wanted representatives from bodies whose progressiveness could be depended upon. He listed them: (1) Modern industrial organizations, (2) Chambers of commerce, (3) Educational associations, (4) Universities, (5) Provincial federations of student unions, (6) Labor organizations, (7) Peasant organizations,

(8) All anti-Tsao-Wu armies, (9) Political parties. It was at Tientsin that Sun Yat-sen was shown the basis of representation as worked out by the Peking Government and promulgated in the summons. He was very much disappointed that his suggestions had been ignored. It was also at Tientsin that Sun Yat-sen had a conference with his military ally, Chang Tso-lin; this overtaxed his strength so that he had to go to bed with a painful affliction of the liver.

On December 31st Sun Yat-sen arrived at Peking, a seriously sick man. He was taken to the *Hotel de Pekın;* doctors attended him, and the dread word, cancer, crept into the press reports. After consultation he was removed to the best equipped hospital in all China, the Peking Union Medical College Hospital, an institution whose roots were deep in missionary medical work. It had, however, been taken over in 1915 by the China Medical Board of the Rockefeller Foundation, and in the next few years was reorganized, liberally endowed and equipped with magnificent buildings and technical apparatus. In this new and expensive example of "modernization," built with funds that any Soviet Russian would have stigmatized as fruits of "economic exploitation," Sun Yat-sen had the expert care of foreign doctors drawn largely from the missionary class which he had recently criticized in Shanghai as "agents of imperialism." Here his radical Russian advisers called at his bedside, and his hospital room was frequented by political plotters. And all this extraordinary mixture of inconsistencies was no more than an index of Sun Yat-sen's conglomerate mental heritage and a clue to the hybridization of influences making modern China. In this Westernized hospital Sun Yat-sen was operated upon, January 26th, by Dr. Adrian S. Taylor, Head of the Department of Surgery, who had himself been a missionary until his appointment to Peking Union Medical College in 1916. It was found that the disease was cancer and that it had already involved the liver. The wound was closed, and Sun Yat-sen's friends were told that his condition was past curing; the hospital could do no more for him. The plotting about his bedside went on more actively. The hospital must have been relieved when his wife and friends took him away to a private house. Wellington Koo's Chinese home in the northern part of the Tartar City was taken for his use. There Sun Yat-sen spent the small remnant of his days. Western-trained though he was in medicine, he consented to the desperate plan urged by his friends—that old style Chinese doctors be called. He submitted to their treatment, but got no better. His young wife and his thirty-four-year-old son were in faithful attendance, and his daughter was summoned. The mother of his children was not there.

VI. THE LEGACY OF PROGRAMS

On his deathbed Sun Yat-sen was not forgotten by Borodin, who had come to Peking to be with him. He was also assiduously attended by a group of Chinese friends, among whom were certain notably radical leaders. Wang Ching-wei was there, and Mrs. Liao Chung-kai, wife of the organizer of a Russianized Chinese labor movement. The group about the deathbed deliberately planned for Sun Yat-sen an apotheosis after the pattern of Lenin's. They saw to it that Sun Yat-sen signed several important messages. On February 17th a message was made public addressed to the Chief Executive in regard to the Reorganization Conference; this criticized both its basis of representation and its agenda. Although this conference was held later, the Kuomintang would take no part in it, and nothing permanent resulted. The purpose for which Sun Yat-sen had come north, the reunification of China, thus failed of realization. But events that did ultimately help to reunite China were happening in the sick room.

The now famous Will was the most important product of the determined history-making. The story of the Will is already a tangle of hearsay and legend; one cannot be sure what to credit. A conservative Chinese authority represents it as having been subtly brought about. It was first suggested to Sun Yat-sen that he would necessarily have a period of long retirement for convalescence during which the party would be deprived of his leadership, and that consequently they wished a statement from him as to the policy he would like them to follow. Accordingly he made such a statement, which was taken down from his lips, and later signed. Another source—one of the little Chinese biographies—reports that on February 24th a small group waited by his bedside, listening for his every word—his wife, his son and Wang Ching-wei. Sun Yat-sen wearily opened his eyes and asked them what they wanted him to say. Wang Ching-wei offered to write down something and read it over to him. The sick man agreed; whereupon Wang Ching-wei produced a little statement and read it aloud. Sun Yat-sen said "Very good! Very good!" but the paper was put aside. The day before he died Sun Yat-sen called for it and signed it.

Although in Wang Ching-wei's handwriting, the document is thoroughly like Sun Yat-sen. It is so matter-of-fact and unsentimental that it might have been a statement in a committee meeting or in a public address. The large array of eight witnesses, however, suggests that, whatever Sun Yat-sen may have thought he was doing, the importance of the document was recognized by those around him. As translated by a Chinese, T. C. Woo, in *The Kuomintang and the Future of the Chinese Revolution,* the Will reads:

I have devoted forty years to the work of Nationalist Revolution, the aim of which is to secure the freedom and independence of China. After forty years of experience I am profoundly convinced that in order to reach this aim we must wake up the masses of the country and unite with those races of the world who treat us on an equality, and struggle together.

At present the revolution is not yet completed. All my comrades must continue to exert their efforts according to the General Principles of Reconstruction, the Outline of Reconstruction, the Three Principles of the People written by me, and the Declaration of the First National Congress of the Kuomintang, until this aim is realized. The calling of the People's Congress and the abolition of the unequal treaties that I have advocated recently must be realized within the shortest possible time. This is what I wished to call your attention to.[22]

Although written fully two weeks earlier, this document was not signed by Sun Yat-sen until March 11th. On the next day, March 12, 1925, at the age of fifty-eight he died. The newspapers of Peking on that very day published the substance of the Will as Sun Yat-sen's bequest to the party.

Before he passed away yet another document was signed for public use: A Message to Soviet Russia. Any one who has become familiar with Sun Yat-sen's cast of expression must suspect that this was drawn up for him by some one else; it is attributed to Eugene Chen. There is no reason to doubt that it was signed by Sun Yat-sen and that it expressed his feelings. When for Russia herself the alliance with the Kuomintang became a more vivid concern, this message became a potent sanction of "world revolution." It was addressed to the Central Executive Committee of the Union of Soviet Socialist Republics:

Dear Comrades:

While I lie here in a malady against which men are powerless, my thoughts are turned towards you and towards the fates of my Party and my country.

You are at the head of the union of free republics—that heritage left to the oppressed peoples of the world by the immortal Lenin. With the aid of that heritage the victims of imperialism will inevitably achieve emancipation from that international regime whose foundations have been rooted for ages in slavery, wars, and injustice.

I leave behind me a Party which, as I always hoped, will be bound up with you in the historic work of the final liberation of China and other exploited countries from the yoke of imperialism. By the will of fate I must leave my work unfinished, and hand it over to those who, remaining faithful to the principles and teachings of the Party, will thereby be my true followers.

Therefore I charge the Kuomintang to continue the work of the revolutionary nationalist movement, so that China, reduced by the Imperialists to the position of a semi-colonial country, shall become free.

With this object I have instructed the Party to be in constant contact with you. I firmly believe in the continuance of the support which you have hitherto accorded to my country.

Taking my leave of you, dear comrades, I want to express the hope that the day will soon come when the U.S.S.R. will welcome a friend and ally in a mighty, free China, and that in the great struggle for the liberation of the oppressed peoples of the world both those allies will go forward to victory hand in hand.

With fraternal greetings,

Sun Yat Sen.[23]

This message brought to the Kuomintang immediately after Sun Yat-sen's death a telegram from Stalin on behalf of the Russian Communist Party, and from Zinovieff, a cabled promise of the continued support of the Third Internationale.

A more intimate document, one that came directly from the heart of the dying man, was a short paper often spoken of as the "second will." It gave to his young wife, Ching-ling, the only property he died possessed of—his house in Shanghai and his books.

The scientific preparation of the body for indefinite preservation was the next imitation of the Russian technique of hero worship. For this work the body was taken back to Peking Union Medical College. In the face of considerable opposition, the family had the courage to arrange for a Christian funeral service to be held in the beautiful auditorium of the Medical College. This observance—so completely at variance with Soviet practice—doubtless met the wishes of the young widow; and there was poetic justice in it. For her sake Sun Yat-sen had lost the approbation of the Christian church. The Christian funeral pronounced oblivion upon the rift in which she was implicated. Evidently on his deathbed Sun Yat-sen's mind had reverted to the faith of his ardent youth. Grasping the hand of a Christian brother-in-law, he had said: "You are a Christian; I, too, am a Christian." Later he added, "I am a messenger of God to help men to obtain equality and freedom." When had he ever made so sharply limned a statement of his lifelong sense of mission? "Don't make trouble for the Christians!" was his deathbed injunction to one of his left-wing followers. When the family determined to have a Christian funeral, it was not hard to find in Peking a liberal-minded Chinese clergyman to conduct it. But the communists and many others of the Kuomintang were not pleased. There were rumors that the chapel would be blown up, or the funeral interfered with. Attendance was wisely limited to the invited, among whom, as it turned out, foreigners formed a large majority. Great Chinese crowds, however, gathered in the street between the chapel and the hospital on March 19th. A surpliced choir, carrying candles, followed the bearers of the coffin. In his youth Sun Yat-sen had worn a surplice and had sung in an Anglican choir. The service included the singing of hymns that were his favorites. Several addresses were made, in which incidents were related to show that Sun Yat-sen had not forgotten his Christianity, although he had long ceased to be a church-goer. "I do not belong to the Christianity of the churches," he had once said, "but to the Christianity of Jesus who was a revolutionary."

After the funeral the coffin was escorted to Central Park (formerly a section of the exclusive Imperial city) by crowds of students with banners, who almost fought for the honor of marching near the bier. Karakhan, Soviet ambassador, assumed the rôle of a chief mourner. In an Imperial pavilion inside Central Park the body lay in state, draped with the blue and white party flag of the Kuomintang. Thither the people came by thousands daily to gaze on the face of the dead patriot. Schools were given holidays that the boys and girls might come in groups. Students, both men and women, acted as ushers to control the movements of the crowds. In the open air of the park phonograph records of Sun Yat-sen's own voice reported his speeches to receptive listeners. For fully three weeks the wave of popular emotion was given this outlet.

Meantime the press all over China was printing eulogies of Sun Yat-sen. One of the most acute as well as most generous was from the first Premier of the Republic, Tang Shao-yi. Of Sun Yat-sen he said:

We were not only fellow-provincials, but natives of the same district, our homes being but eight miles apart in Heung-shan. For some forty years we have known of one another and since the founding of the Republic, we have often been associated in public service.

To Dr. Sun will have to go the credit of having made the revolution an effective force and of having crystallized public opinion behind a democratic movement, which has survived all the mistakes and the reactions of the past thirteen years. . . .

At the moment of mourning we shall forget everything about him but one outstanding fact and that is that he was the champion of democracy in China. Everything else will be forgotten. Every personal whim, every personal dissension, every difference of opinion will be forgotten, only the large fact of his life will remain, his struggle against despotism, his struggle against corruption, his struggle for the right of the governed to a say in the government. And throughout the country as this thought sweeps the minds of the people, as this thought becomes the cry of the suffering millions, as men speak it and write it and read it, a spirit will be abroad in the land which will make itself felt and which in the end will shake Peking to its very foundations.[24]

On April 2nd a semi-modernized Chinese funeral procession with certain military features escorted the heavy Chinese wooden casket to a beautiful temple in the Western Hills, Pi Yün Ssu, Azure Cloud Temple. There in a lofty chamber, accessible only by climbing many stairways, it rested for five years. During the disturbances of the Nationalist advance and during the dictatorship of Chang Tso-lin it awaited the arrival of the Kuomintang. Pilgrimages to the temporary resting place were for a while possible, but Chang Tso-lin quietly put a stop to them by ordering the chamber closed to the public. A much advertised metal coffin sent from Moscow arrived only tardily and proved to be as unsuitable as it was tasteless in design. It was shown to me and to other visitors lying discarded in a side corridor of the old temple, a temple splendidly oriental in its architecture and mellow with traditions that seemed rooted more deeply than the ancient white-barked pines of its courtyards. Sun Yat-sen could not have had a more beautiful final resting place, nor a more unfitting one. It was his wish that he should be buried at Nanking near the tomb of the first Ming Emperor. A project was shortly set afoot for the preparation of a suitably modernized mausoleum on Purple Mountain.

DOCUMENTATION OF QUOTED PASSAGES

[1] Holcombe: *The Chinese Revolution* (Cambridge, 1930), p. 359. [2] Translation by D. Willard Lyon, cf. *The World Mission of Christianity* [The Report of the Jerusalem Conference of 1928] (New York, 1928) Vol. I, p. 80. [3] From address on *The Five-Power Constitution*, 1921, cf. Hsü: *Sun Yat-sen*, p. 108. [4] Sun Yat-sen: *San Min Chu I*, trans. Price (Shanghai, 1927) p. xii. [5] Ibid., pp. 415, 416. [6] Ibid., p. 423. [7] Ibid., pp. 428, 429. [8] Ibid., pp. 434, 435. [9] Ibid., p. 439. [10] Ibid., p. 440. [11] Ibid., p. 444. [12] Ibid., p. 85. [13] Ibid., p. 84. [14] Ibid., pp. 17, 18. [15] Ibid., pp. 87, 88. [16] Sun Yat-sen: *San Min Chu I*; Hsü: *Sun Yat-sen*, p. 384. [17] Sun Yat-sen: *Outline of National Reconstruction*; Holcombe: *The Chinese Revolution*, Appendix B, p. 352.

[18] Ibid., p. 352. [19] Woo: *The Kuomintang and the Future of the Chinese Revolution* (London, 1928) p. 127. [20] Hsü: *Sun Yat-sen His Political and Social Ideals* (Los Angeles, 1933) p. 144. [21] A Tokyo despatch of Nov. 30, 1924, to *The New York Times*. [22] Woo: *The Kuomintang and the Future of the Chinese Revolution* (London, 1928) p. 253. [23] Tang Chin Che: "Sun Yat Sen's Life and Work," *Labour Monthly* (London, May, 1925) Vol. 7, p. 287. Published also in *The New York Times*, May 24, 1925. [24] *Far Eastern Review*, March, 1925, Vol. 21, p. 103.

SOURCES AND AUTHORITIES: See Appendix C, p. 403.

CHAPTER X

Demigod or Man?

THE sequel to Sun Yat-sen's death is history so recent that it needs no retelling. The unfortunate incident of May 30, 1925, in Shanghai, in which students lost their lives at the hands of the police in the International Settlement, and "the Shanghai mind" held out stubbornly against Chinese opinion, furnished just the heated atmosphere in which anti-imperialistic propaganda could thrive. The equally bad Shameen incident at Canton in June, and similar shootings elsewhere, were all fuel to the Nationalist flames. They also gave great stimulus to the development of the Communist Party in China; in two years after the Shanghai shootings communists increased four-fold—so it is affirmed by a Chinese authority.

At Moscow in September, 1925, the "Sun Yat-sen University" was founded to attract Chinese students to Russia, and Radek was put at its head. Its objects were clearly explained to an American journalist by one of the professors:

Our purpose is two-fold: first, to offset the pro-Western cultural propaganda of foreign mission schools in China by giving Chinese students a taste of Soviet culture; second, to teach the Chinese the lessons of our revolution, so that they can duplicate our successes and avoid our mistakes.[1]

To this university youths were sent from all over China by Kuomintang branches. There were as many as three hundred students in 1926; among them were the young son and daughter of the "Christian General," Feng Yu-hsiang, both in their early 'teens.

When in January, 1926, the Second National Congress of the Kuomintang was held in Canton, the Sun Yat-sen Cult began to take form. The Will was read and accepted as a sacred party legacy. The writings of Sun Yat-sen named in the Will thus became enshrined among the fundamental documents of the party, namely, *The Principles of Reconstruction, The Outline of Reconstruction* and *The Three Principles of the People.* Against these principles and plans no member is allowed to speak. Out of reverence for Sun Yat-sen the Second Congress refused to elect a successor as President of the party. Using a praesidium for practical purposes, the Kuomintang voted to look upon Sun Yat-sen as its "President and Director for all time to come."

The weekly memorial meetings to Sun Yat-sen became thenceforth a required feature in all Kuomintang branches. These are regularly held on Monday mornings, not only in government offices and party committee meetings, but in factories, barracks and schools. The triple bow before the portrait of Sun Yat-sen, the reading of the Will, and the three-minutes silence thereafter are the essential features of the ceremony. Sometimes a patriotic address follows, or the Nationalist song is sung. In homes also the portrait of Sun Yat-sen began to be displayed as the "father of his country," especially in the South: a practice deriving both from America and from the "Lenin corners" in Russia.

Following the example of its predecessor, the Second National Congress sent abroad a "Declaration." In this Sun Yat-sen's hand is missing but the philosophy of the Nationalist Revolution follows his lead though more obviously impregnated with Borodin's ideas. There is no gainsaying the brilliancy of Borodin's tactics in persuading the Kuomintang that the world was in bondage to imperialism, and in motivating the Chinese Revolution as a phase of a world-struggle against bondage. In this document "the tools and puppets of the aggressive powers" are pilloried in turn:—the militarists; the official classes who "cater to the militarists for personal promotion"; the compradores as the cat's-paw of foreign capitalism; and the country landlords as survivals of mediaeval feudalism. Sun Yat-sen's Will is specifically cited as enjoining sincere coöperation with Soviet Russia.

At the first anniversary of Sun Yat-sen's death, there were cere-monies for laying the corner-stone of the mausoleum at Nanking. The anniversary was celebrated with Soviet fervor in many places, although clashes between communists and "rights" occurred. There was no attempt to apologize for or to conceal Sun Yat-sen's "Soviet orientation." It is significant of an undercurrent of dissent that an anti-Russian society showed its head in Peking. A meeting was held in which China's relations with Russia were the subject of criticism; whereupon a communist precipitated a fight, in which chairs were smashed and bodies wounded. In spite of this episode March 12th and several days following were marked by notable memorial demonstrations in Peking. An illumination was staged at the magnificent south entrance of the Forbidden City. A lantern parade wound its way through the Tartar city; in it over thirty student-bodies took part. Enormous lanterns were inscribed with slogans, such as, "Abolish the unequal treaties," "Down with all anti-Sun forces." A portrait of Sun Yat-sen was placed over the Emperor's dais in the throne-hall of the ancient palace (by that time a public museum); by its sides scrolls were hung to eulogize Sun Yat-sen as the uncrowned king of New China. Thither in-numerable organizations and schools made pilgrimages of respect that continued for three days. On the street-corners students, dele-gated to the task of speaking, enlarged upon Sun Yat-sen's meaning for the instruction of the populace.

The Nationalist drive northward carried with it propaganda of Sun Yat-sen's ideas; his books were widely read; his utterances were expounded in public addresses and in outdoor harangues. Everywhere instruction in the "Three Principles" became a part of the "political tutelage of the people." Popular biographies were produced to make Sun Yat-sen a hero for the everyday man. His birthday and his deathday became public holidays and occasions of patriotic observances. Thus Sun Yat-sen has become a national symbol and the Cult something akin to a religion. If in its initiation the Sun Yat-sen Cult was a Russian suggestion, it was not and could not have been foisted on China by the Russians. No foreign nation, by any persuasion or diplomacy, could have induced China to worship a man against her will. Why then is Sun Yat-sen worshipped?

He is first of all the symbol of unity in the Kuomintang. The sentiment for him is almost the only sentiment that appeals to all alike—lefts, rights and center.

He is the symbol of disinterested love of country. It is really remarkable that in a land where men are so habitually suspected of self-interest and self-seeking, Sun Yat-sen remains unsmirched by such criticism. He literally lived for his country. He doubtless was wrong-headed at times, and sometimes hard to work with, but he loved China and lived for China's good as he saw it. He was a patriot of unique purity of purpose.

He is the symbol of his country's purpose to reconstruct herself along modern lines after the manner of the West. There he is an exact symbol; he himself was a Westernized Chinese, thinking in terms of the West more than in Eastern terms.

He is the symbol of an unfinished revolution, which China is determined to realize. That the task is enormous, far exceeding his apprehension or the apprehension of his countrymen, makes no difference. Sun Yat-sen's courage to attack it, and his lifelong courage to remain with it at all odds is the people's inspiration.

He is the symbol of the very idea of democracy which he unfail-

ingly preached. The appeal of this idea to the great unvocal masses
of China is beyond estimate; out of their poverty and illiteracy
they have listened to his evangel of a day when the country shall be
theirs to govern and to enjoy.

Whatever may be Sun Yat-sen's significance for future generations, he is also for this generation a flaming symbol of China's revolt against the wrongs of foreigners. At present the Chinese are
too wrought up about these wrongs to admit that their own forbears are responsible, along with our occidental forbears, for the
anomalous relationships that exist between Chinese and Westerners
in China. Although in neither case is the present generation to
blame for having created the bad situation, there is this difference:
the present generation of foreigners has few motives for change,
whereas the present generation of Chinese has an urgent desire for
change. When, filled with combustible grievances, Sun Yat-sen ex-
ploded in denunciation of foreign-controlled customs and of the
unequal treaties, his words detonated over China. They met a sensational response. With the Russian reorganization of the Kuomintang behind him, the whole force of his long-thwarted personality
was thrown into the assault upon vaguely defined "foreign imperialism." The *San Min Chu I* lectures opened what became a terrific attack. The blame for China's republican failure was heavily
placed on "foreign imperialism." The prescription for national success was revolt against the unequal treaties and all the other forces
declared to be strangling China. Henceforth, Sun Yat-sen was more
than "the father of the republic"; he was the sign and symbol of
the inflamed anti-imperialistic resentment. And that is still a large
part of his meaning in China. School children who bow to Sun Yat-
sen's portrait today are taught to hate "imperialism" as the arch-
enemy of China, the all-oppressing tyrant.

Why does the admiration of such a hero need a cult? Obviously
the Cult is at present a means to an end, and that strikes through it

a note of psychological practitioning, if not of insincerity. The *raison d'être* of the Cult is not hard to understand; it is the attempt to find some cohesive in the pitiable disintegration of China today. One sympathizes with the desire to create cohesion, especially if one thinks of the disintegration not as a cold evolutionary process, but as a humanly conditioned evil which must be humanly dealt with. If the Sun Yat-sen Cult could be divorced from its canonized documents, which are chiefly Sun Yat-sen's writings, it would be easy to be tolerant of it in the hope that it might contribute something toward the needed fusion. But by the acceptance of the Will as much more binding than Sun Yat-sen ever intended it to be, and by the mesmeric repetition of it in the weekly ceremonies of the Cult, an homage that should be spiritually liberating has been bound up with a dead man's thinking. The ideas and plans of Sun Yat-sen have been elevated as the not-to-be-questioned program for China's national development; and all the prejudices and resentments that are wrapped in their exposition have become sacrosanct. This intellectual halting of a nation is, to my mind, the most dangerous feature of the Sun Yat-sen Cult. It amounts to an attempt to create integration by a required conformity, instead of by the fusing power of intelligence and emotion. From conformity there will always be dissenters. While political thinking is controlled by authority and creativity is suppressed or regimented, the more vigorous dissenters of China will, in desperation, go over to communism; equally able but less headstrong young people will turn aside from public life, to which they would gladly give their talents, and go into scientific work or some other form of neutral service.

What the Cult may yet become no one can prophesy. If it is essentially a political instrument, it may die with a turn in politics. If it is a moral movement, it will have a longer and more significant life. Its future hangs now in the balance. That it may become a dead hand of authority inhibiting the creativity of China is a possibility to be fought against by the intelligentsia of the world. It may become in truth a religion; the rate at which it is accumulating myths suggests that it may elaborate its ritual and attach to itself dogmas and superstitions. It may become a dramatization of the bitter failure-psychosis of China; then Sun Yat-sen's resentments will fill the whole picture, his optimism will be forgotten, and his arraignment of foreign imperialism will become the central gospel. In short, the Sun Yat-sen Cult may become anything foreseen or unforeseen. Its possibilities for good are foremost in our minds at present, but it would be foolish to overlook the possibilities of bane and bale. Certainly it has not yet exhausted its potentialities; the direction of its future should not be left to the fanatic and the unscrupulous; it is a movement for the healthy-minded to keep a hand in.

II. THE UNREAL AND THE REAL SUN YAT-SEN

It is one of the difficulties of the biographer that already legend has spun a tangled web about Sun Yat-sen. Biographical material that has been published, both in Chinese and in English, forms a mass of uncriticized episode and estimate. It is difficult, even now, to recover the man from the distortions of idealization and romance, and the misrepresentations of propaganda.

As a result of assiduous heroizing in China the common man in the street today sees Sun Yat-sen only in an envelope of glamour: as a man who adventured abroad and came back with prodigious learning in Western matters, as a dauntless reformer who suffered many reverses but was never for one moment discouraged, as a leader whose judgment though many times frustrated was not once found to be in the wrong. His love of country is presumed to have been without a flaw or a stain, and his wisdom in things political is not to be doubted for a moment. In sacrificing the real man for such an incredible idol China is shutting her eyes to the vivid picture she might see in him of her own irregular progress toward an elusive ideal.

Nor is it in China alone that Sun Yat-sen has been uncritically treated. Many may not be aware of the large contribution the Occident has made toward the unreal romanticizing of this man. The lifting of him with Russian help to a pedestal like Lenin's has been the climax of a long process. Ever since Sun Yat-sen became for a few days in 1896 a news sensation in London, his name has been something for journalists to play with. Incidentally, journalism has done not a little toward tangling the threads for a biographer. Exaggerated estimates of Sun Yat-sen have gone abroad, ranging from reports of his marvelous command of English—mistakenly inferred, it must be said, from publications scrupulously edited by unselfish friends—to the cumulative legend of him as a supreme commander of a ramifying and highly articulated conspiracy that wrought deeds in the dark in the manner in which the "inscrutable Chinese" are held to be peculiar: a picture that has little resemblance to the listed revolutionary abortions of those hot-headed and often quarrelsome young modernists that formed the *Tung Meng Hui*. The first of the heroizing biographies was produced by an American. Judge Linebarger's *Sun Yat-sen and the Chinese Republic* antedates the Cult by several years, yet no Chinese biography has surpassed it in fulsomeness and in usefulness to the Cult.

After we have tried to sift the facts from the fiction and to weigh all our estimates, does Sun Yat-sen still remain for us a man mysteriously unreal? As he has been sometimes presented, with whole major motivations of his life blurred or left out, Sun Yat-sen is admittedly difficult to understand. But of all Orientals Sun Yat-sen was the least mysterious. He had none of the sophisticated craftiness that made the old mandarins difficult antagonists in diplomacy. He could be as abruptly outspoken as ourselves, and the furniture of his mind was of our own Western ideas. In so far as he patterned himself after us, surely, we should be able to understand him. Not all the mystery we feel is Sun Yat-sen; the great mystery is China herself, and not even the modern Chinese understand China. When the world begins to comprehend China, Sun Yat-sen will seem incidental and inevitable.

In youth his countenance was frank, self-confident and unsuspicious. Photographs of him in his prime, of which there are scores in existence, show the low-browed, squared-off face of a kindly and tolerant man, who only on occasion, appears a little vain or fanatic. His weakest features were his sensuous mouth and his small chin. The level, glowing, patient eyes, set wide apart, were anything but scrutinizing: they could never have made any one uncomfortable with the sense of being looked through and appraised. They have been described as "magnetic," but not as keen eyes. Indeed, a fault which Sun Yat-sen recognized in himself was that he was no keen judge of other men.

Neither was he an interested observer of his own inner nature. He showed no tendency toward undue self-analysis or accounting for his own reactions and impulses. He held himself, however, in considerable esteem and in certain periods of his life over-estimated the value of his thinking to the nation. Sun Yat-sen did not live perpetually in a concrete world outside himself. His objective world included the realm of books and of intellectual theories; it was only after filling his mind from these that he indulged in spinning rationalizations out of his own brain.

His reserve, I surmise, was due more to lack of imaginative and dramatic interest in his own inner life than to any intentional reticence. But this kind of inert reserve is perhaps more difficult to penetrate than any other. Judge Linebarger was granted special opportunities to draw out of Sun Yat-sen the materials of a biography, but he apparently found much difficulty in inducing anything but superficial revelation. *Sun Yat-sen and the Chinese Republic* contains happenings of childhood in plenty, but very little illumination of the triumphs and crises of mature life.

This kind of unintentional reserve can, however, coexist with quiet friendliness, and in Sun Yat-sen's case did so. He had, especially in his prime, the power of attracting people, both Chinese and foreign. Among his friends he appears to have lost only a few. There was something in him that called out loyalty to a remarkable degree. The attraction must have been both in his character, in which men placed reliance, and in some charm which drew men to him.

Sun Yat-sen's personality had its marked phases. To look over even the best of his photographs is to be set wondering how they could all be of the same man. The delightfully eager youth, one feels, might have developed into the idealistic first President of the Republic, although the younger face gives no hint of the stubborn strength of the revolutionary. But between the magnanimous patriot who relinquished the presidency and the aging egoist there yawns a great gulf. The disastrous "Second Revolution" was a parting of the ways in personality, if ever there was one; that period of hiding in Japan when Sun Yat-sen took a second wife, and privately traded with his country's economic resources for help against Yuan Shih-kai, gave China a changed Sun Yat-sen. Nevermore the magniloquent rhapsodist of the ceremony at the Ming tombs in 1912! Nevermore the simple faith that others also had the good of China at heart! Increasingly mistrustful, arbitrary, dogmatic and hard to work with, Sun Yat-sen became a programizing theorist. The man the Russians dealt with was Sun Yat-sen in his final phase, a singular mixture of rigidity and weakness, of egoism and compliance, of set-theory and mental confusion. Unyielding toward his fellow countrymen, he was pitifully ductile in the hands of his Russian instructors. Photographs of this period show a face curiously emptied of its flame and fervor. Gone is the stiff backbone of his prime; his chin is not held up so confidently; the eyes are not so warm or so direct; and sometimes around his lips lurks the suspicion of a sneer.

Throughout his life Sun Yat-sen's personality found its freest outlet in the propaganda of ideas, most of which he absorbed from foreign sources—first the idea of a republic to replace the Manchu Empire, and subsequently of other ideas related to democracy. With this propaganda he is now identified. When he was expressing himself in direct contact with people he showed unusual power of carrying others out of their own opinions and into his; but when men got away from his personality, his ideas seemed to relax their hold. Just as Sun Yat-sen's ideas benefited from his actual presence, they are bound to suffer from the permanent withdrawal of it. For the millions of Chinese who never saw Sun Yat-sen a glamour-substitute has been provided in the cult. Concerning the impression created by his personality one of the most convincing records is from the pen of Nathaniel Peffer:

I have never left him without feeling convinced—that is, before analyzing what he had said to me—that, in my judgment of him, I had done him wrong. There is perhaps no fallacy that he could not make plausible to me while I was with him. My feeling is not a merely personal reaction. I have never known anybody who has been face to face with Dr. Sun who has not been imprest by him. It is not in any respect his physical presence that engages attention; for it is not at all commanding. His eyes do not "pierce yours till they see the inmost recesses of your soul." He is short and now rather inclined to be plump. His face is as unrevealing as that of most Chinese. Nothing about him strikes you until he talks—in a low and uninflected tone, with a rapid flow of words. Then his poise, his dignity, his enthusiasm, and, above all, his utter sincerity record themselves on your memory forever.[2]

Again and again Sun Yat-sen has been described as dramatic. But there was nothing in his deportment that was histrionic. He was quiet and modest in demeanor, and in speech he was deliberate and only cumulatively impressive. On the public platform he was earnest and forcible but undramatic; he is described as an almost monotonously even public speaker, never raising his voice or indulging in impassioned phrasing, and making few gestures if any. Certainly none of his published lectures and few of his writings can be described as dramatic. His account of his own revolutionary career in the little *Autobiography* is almost unbelievably undramatic. No one but Sun Yat-sen would have been content to write it with so few dramatic details. His Will is, in its statement, as undramatic as any document could be. One feels like challenging any one to say what is there said less dramatically.

There is no question that Sun Yat-sen had a dramatic sense of publicity; it may have been his journalistic acumen—his sixth sense for effectiveness in press utterances—that is accountable for the oft-repeated description of him by journalists as dramatic. Early in his career he learned the power of newspaper publicity; he owed to it his release from his secret imprisonment in the Chinese Legation in London in 1896. Many times in his life he played for public attention through the press, particularly for world-attention. When he had a chance to speak through a great newspaper, he rarely failed to give good copy. And he knew how to time his public utterances, and how to make them bold enough to attract attention. He knew when to criticize the World War, and he knew when to announce that he was turning to Soviet Russia. But not always were his sensational publicities effective. At times they fell flat. His frantic telegram to England in 1913 about the Five Power Loan which Yuan Shih-kai was negotiating had about as much effect as a mosquito buzzing in the ear. His most stupendous play for world attention, the publication just after the World War of his mammoth project, *The International Development of China*, elicited only politely guarded comments. There he overshot his mark; the plan was too big and too bold to receive serious consideration in the war's aftermath.

But there is a sense in which Sun Yat-sen was dramatic—a sense so profound that others than myself may have felt after it for a long time without being able to define it. Sun Yat-sen was more than the sum of his qualities or the total of his gifts and powers; his career surpasses the tale of his narratable deeds. He attained significance because of Something which was added to all these. Because of that added Something, a man of little more than mediocre parts has been given the garment of greatness to wear— perhaps forever. How shall the truth about him be expressed?

Sun Yat-sen did that presumptuous thing, so rarely done that we think of it as daring: he assumed a rôle in history, and he played it to the end, in spots ineffectively, even incompetently, sometimes pompously, sometimes tragically; but he played it—that is the point. How he got in touch with the Director of the great drama we call History, and learned how the play was to be plotted, is the mystical core of his life—mystical but not mysterious to those who agree with its fundamental assumptions. If Christianity frequently gave its adherents such a sense of historic direction, we might say Sun Yat-sen's Christianity helped him to know. Perhaps it did. The Christianity he came in contact with was expressed by people who lived with a sense of mission; in their own degree they were obsessed with a historic purpose. Possibly it was from the missionaries that Sun Yat-sen got his strong feeling of responsibility to his age, and with it the root-belief that an individual may come to know his proper life-direction. But, except in the illuminating Western education they gave him, the missionaries had no part in Sun Yat-sen's choice of the life of a revolutionary in the service of China. Somehow this offshoot of the peasantry oriented himself in relation to his people and his times, envisaged his rôle and stuck to it tenaciously. When, as the result of many frustrations, he developed a defensive egoism, his sense of destiny assumed monumental proportions. It was a destiny not to be shared with others; it left all too little room for generosity toward the able men who supported his causes. It is this narrow individualism that makes it difficult to yield ground to apologists who would have us believe that the inflated ego of the aging Sun Yat-sen was simply his country writ large. If China had been the real Ego, surely there would have been honor and fame for more than one man. But as Sun Yat-sen grew older he thought more and more of himself as the center of the revolution and the sole creator of its only valid programs.

This egoism was nothing other than the matured bulk of his life-long sense of mission, grown out of all bounds from perpetual cultivation of it. It became so large and so integral to his personality that others were impressed into accepting it. He won Judge Linebarger to belief in it, and through the Judge's biography the obsession has been passed on to many. It became a vortex, gathering to Sun Yat-sen all that could be caught in its swirl—intellectual leadership, programatic infallibility, spiritual dictatorship. The group that watched about the deathbed was caught in its sucking eddy. In Sun Yat-sen's lifetime it was by reason of his sense of mission that his moderate gifts were brought to bear so effectively upon China. His identification with his narrow age and with the thrust of his race lifted him to a height of achievement to which his abilities would not otherwise have carried him. The Cult has been China's acceptance of his monumental sense of destiny and the projection of it beyond the years of his life.

So in the final analysis it was Sun Yat-sen's sense of mission that has made him memorable. Without it China would probably have neglected him, as she has neglected men abler than he. It was in this respect that Sun Yat-sen was dramatic. When the curtain lifted upon the Drama of Change in China, he was in the flies with his part already conned; he stepped upon the stage and played the rôle. No one else coveted the playing of the first act. A greater actor might have played the part better, but there was no other actor waiting. And so the mighty play went on, sweeping Sun Yat-sen up to a climax much greater than any he could have conceived or plotted. No one will deny that Sun Yat-sen's life was dramatic.

III. THE EPITOME OF HIS AGE

Sun Yat-sen's chief interest to a historian is that he seems an epitome of his age—a transition period with all the faults and interest of transitions. In it there has been much exuberance and much confusion. It has been a period characterized by over-confidence and under-thinking.

Sun Yat-sen is typical of the impact of Western ideas upon China. If we do not admire the result of our influence, we must at least recognize it as our handiwork. One of Sun Yat-sen's Chinese critics says that he "never permitted other men to influence his thought or to revise his plans." If Sun Yat-sen seemed so to Chinese, he does not seem so to Occidentals. Western teaching was formative in his educational period. His malleability under foreign influences persisted throughout his life; it reappeared in accentuated form in his last two Russianized years. Occidentals are bound to criticize him as being too impressionable to foreign influences and too icono-clastic toward Chinese tradition. In his openness toward foreign influences he is more characteristic of his period than many Chinese would like to admit.

Sun Yat-sen was typical also of the half assimilation of Western ideas which has been an inevitable but an unlovely phase of the transition. The cleverness of such assimilation can for a little while blind the Occidental's eyes to the superficiality of it, but it cannot permanently do so. It is when the Western-trained Chinese is talking in his own tongue to his fellow-countrymen who have no means of checking his accuracy that the fault of malassimilation appears at its worst. Because the *San Min* lectures were just such talks, Sun Yat-sen's assimilation appears there most faulty.

Sun Yat-sen is also typical of his period in his ardent ambition for the "modernization" of China—meaning the introduction of Western science, Western institutions of government and Western methods in industry. Because Japan has progressed along this path, it seems to the present generation to be the only one for China. Sun Yat-sen was always looking abroad for the cue to the lines of development China should take. What is the Western tendency in government? Democracy. Then China must have democracy. What is the Western tendency in production? Machine production. Then China must have mechanical industry and huge manufactories. At China's present problem, the small working-shop and handicraft industry, he does not even take a glance. Instead, he works out programs for the industrialization of China, possible only with fabulous foreign loans, and he elaborates a "practicable socialism" to forestall the evils of an industrial age of the future. The ambition to see China modernized is not Sun Yat-sen's alone; it is typical of the thinking of the transition. With the assumption of the desirability of modernization goes the pursuit of the most modern. Being over-sensitive about the backwardness of China, Sun Yat-sen and his age have been seeking shortcuts to the Utopia of Modernization. Consequently, they have been looking abroad not only for "world tendencies" but for the latest tendency. They realize that the world moves on, and that while China is catching up, the world may have advanced a step or two more. This is just where the appeal of Russia to the Chinese mind is particularly strong. It is accepted that Russia is in the van of human progress, so by catching up with Russia, it is believed, China can steal a long march on Britain and America.

Sun Yat-sen is also typical of his period in his faith in reforms by rationalization; of this faith the program is the solidified expression. As the mere theorizing of a man with little scope for activity Sun Yat-sen's programs would be simply an intellectual curiosity. But Wang Ching-wei capped the climax when he influenced Sun Yat-sen on his deathbed to bequeath this huge unwieldy bulk of programs to his people as a sacred legacy. Many men in smaller ways have made just such programs and have believed that a movement rationally programized was as good as realized. When the Chinese get a little farther away from this period, they will see how, for thirty years past, the leaders of the nation have thought in terms of programs. The "returned students" have been particularly prone to admire the program as a contribution of great value.

In his inconsistencies of thinking and in his blindness to those inconsistencies, in his shifts of opinion, and his seeming irresponsibility in shifting, Sun Yat-sen is typical of far too much in the mentality of China today. By virtue of his inconsistencies Sun Yat-sen is a leader whom any one may follow. Those who believe in communism can and do cite his utterances; those who hate and dread communism can and do quote him. Foreigners who seek economic concessions may point to a whole volume; Chinese who mistrust the insidious entry of foreign domination by way of economic development have the *San Min* lectures to support their resentment at its bitterest. China will not have to make up her mind on these policies as long as she follows Sun Yat-sen. She can shift as he shifted.

It is because modernist China shares Sun Yat-sen's faults that she does not see them. She instinctively worships the man who best epitomizes the national urge forward. Optimistic by temperament, caught by the glamour of newly discovered Western ideas, adventuring for changes, expectant of not-too-difficult success, defeated over and over, turning for help first to one quarter and then to another, proudly concerned for the place and honor of the nation, and finally developing the resentments of a world sadly out of joint, Sun Yat-sen is typical of both the brighter and the darker side of China's momentous struggles. Sun Yat-sen is the epitome and Republican China is the exposition in full. The acceptance of change as the line of destiny, laborious learning from the West, the recklessness of revolution, the disillusionment of the sequel, repeated efforts and repeated failures, the desperate desire to retain self-respect by developing more assertiveness, by rationalizing more explanations, or by discovering others on whom to lay the blame—all of these and the resulting sad confusion are phases of the life of the Republic as well as phases of the life of Sun Yat-sen.

IV. LEADER OR MISLEADER?

Was Sun Yat-sen a great leader? That question is not answered by affirming that he was the epitome of his age.

At the beginning of his so-called *Autobiography* Sun Yat-sen reveals what he himself considered to be the elements of greatness in a political leader. The great men of Chinese history, he says, have succeeded in accomplishing memorable things by working "in conformity with the laws of nature, with the sentiments of men, and with the trends of world progress, and because they met a real need of the time." Notice the elements of great leadership: understanding the sentiments of men, and the trends of world progress; meeting a real need of the time; working in conformity with the laws of nature; and as a result accomplishing some great work.

There is no question that Sun Yat-sen was an assiduous student of world trends. The direction of world progress was to his mind always the direction that China should take. But he assumed too readily that China's progress must be along the specific progress-paths of other lands—of Japan, of the United States of America, of Russia.

In understanding "the sentiments of men" Sun Yat-sen at times showed extraordinary acuteness, and at other times amazing dullness. He was almost uncannily right about the amount of anti-Manchu sentiment there was in China and about the crumbling state of the old régime. But he was in as high degree mistaken about the mental preparedness of China for democracy; and he was nothing short of fatuous in his assumption that the young modernist leaders of China would prove adept at democratic functioning. In common sagacity as to how men would act and react Sun Yat-sen often seemed less gifted than the average man of his own people. He lacked that finer insight that in a few men amounts to genius, the ability to penetrate human behavior and discover motives by which men may be deeply enough moved to sustain action and to endure the frictions of group effort. Sun Yat-sen was fairly successful in inciting people to action; the difficulty was that he stirred people who either had motives too superficial to sustain the undertaking, or who had motives of the wrong kind—sure to thwart or wreck his causes. He did not know how to bring to birth in men the qualities that make creative group relationships possible. The skill to do that is, of course, a rare power; precisely that, I take it, is what makes a man significant religiously, no matter what religion he professes or prefers not to profess.

That the establishment of the Republic in 1911 met "a real need of the time" would be a very difficult proposition for a historian to defend. It would be much easier to support the statement that it anticipated the needs of China by two or three generations. Surely it must be clear to every one now that the Republic was established at a time when China lacked the collective ability to operate a republic. Chinese historians may one day be describing it as a stupendous and tragic prematurity.

With this observation one is plunged into the next question: Is the fastening upon a people of a form of government in which they are not prepared to function "working in conformity with the laws of nature"? It would seem rather to be working contrary to natural laws, and thus putting nature under the great strain of repairing the resultant damage. Not only the shift to a republic but a good deal else of what Sun Yat-sen advocated seems now to have been badly out of conformity with the phase of nature that he was dealing with, namely, the social habits and aptitudes of the Chinese of his generation. The last thing that could be said of Sun Yat-sen is that he was "a realist in politics." Therein lies his inferiority to Lenin, with whom he has been inaptly compared in Russia and in China. The revolution for a republic, to which he expected to give his whole life, fell, untimely ripe, into his hands when he was forty-five years old. This premature success seems to have dislocated what judgment he previously had, especially of the fundamental processes of social change. Everything looked too easy to Sun Yat-sen after that. He grossly underestimated the time required for reforms. Consequently, his programs sound like plans made for gods, not for men. The social conditioning of his contemporaries and his planning were incompatible.

Can one then say that Sun Yat-sen accomplished a great work as a political leader? He will have to be seen down a longer vista of time before a final judgment can be pronounced on that point. Any attempt to cite accomplishments for Sun Yat-sen in practical affairs is doomed before it is made. In spite of his expanded programs for the modernization of China he has no piece of significant work to his credit. He planned a fabulously expensive railway system, but most of the railways that China yet has were built under the monarchy. Even the long-projected modernization of Canton, which made some headway in the early '20's, was due more to an energetic group of younger men than to Sun Yat-sen himself. The Republican Revolution, with which Sun Yat-sen's name is forever associated, was by no means purely of his doing. He worked for it as others did, but he was not even in China when it was carried through to its first success. Much of the change that has been coming over China cannot fairly be credited to the Republic, much less to Sun Yat-sen. Certain of the durable major reforms were made under the monarchy; so, also, one of the major disruptions of centralization was accomplished, as has already been pointed out, under the Empress Dowager.

In the blind urge of his country toward change Sun Yat-sen was a vital element. But he was only one element; he was not the creator of the urge, as he liked to think he was. China in her present worshipful attitude toward him is for the moment acquiescing in his self-estimate. But some day China will know that she is attributing to a patriotic citizen a propulsion that was really in her great collective self.

If Sun Yat-sen was distinguished above his age, it was in an educated sense of trends or in some mystical surrender to them, by virtue of which he broadly foresaw the paths along which his country must ultimately travel and projected all his personal force along those paths. But let us not dehumanize him by attributing to him a superhumanly clear and highly inspired prophetic vision. His was a pedestrian and stumbling progress. Slowly he made his way in spite of intellectual limitation, crude intrigue, bad judgment, faulty coördinations, and wild misreckonings of the human equation. Yet in all Sun Yat-sen's unrealized plans the core was an indisputably laudable ideal. That is what makes the popular acclaim of him as a hero so inescapable. Although China could not possibly have become a republic at the moment when Sun Yat-sen tried to make her into one, the dream of an ultimate democracy will intrigue her for centuries to come. "The Three Principles of the People," looked at in the large, are as sound and inevitable as growth. Who would do other than applaud the striving of a people toward national individuality, popular government and a decent livelihood? In the present stage of China's development these "Three Principles," especially when presented by a party as a promise of things to be brought about, have an electrical appeal for the emerging masses. In their convincing desirability they are in a large degree independent of the passionate prejudice, the doctrinaire planning and the boyish economics in which Sun Yat-sen swaddled them.

If we are compelled to admit, as I feel I must, that Sun Yat-sen in his lifetime fell short of being a great leader of his people, is it still possible to believe, as the Chinese do at present, that Sun Yat-sen remains the undying leader of the future into which he projected his plans? Sun Yat-sen dead and lifted to a position of not-to-be-questioned authority is a much more disturbing phenomenon than the mistake-making, now-in-and-now-out Sun Yat-sen of history. He is disturbing not because of his radicalism—the world absorbs radical leaders; he is disturbing not for his criticism of imperialism or his alliance with Soviet Russia; he is disturbing because of the limitations of his mind. Even a great mind is not great enough for an absolute throne and crown. It is pitiful to see a whole nation regimented into shut-eyed following of a leader whose abilities appear inadequate for such titanic leadership. I can view only with foreboding such intellectual paralysis at this time when China needs every unit of brain-power that can be stimulated to function.

Persistent as I have been in trying to learn from Sun Yat-sen, I am one with many Westerners who fail to find in him either a profound or very original thinker. I see in him an effective propagandist of the elemental ideas of democracy; I see him as a stubborn protagonist of his own articulated program; I recognize his service in propagating varied Western ideas that were novelties to the Chinese; and I have taken notice that in his later, as well as in his earlier years, he fanned smoldering prejudices into passionate resentments. But as a thinker, Sun Yat-sen's leadership of China has not been clarifying.

Probably the current exaltation of Sun Yat-sen's intellectual leading will be as difficult for future generations of Chinese to understand as at present it is difficult for most Westerners. But just now it is only the Occidental who becomes easily cynical about this laborious but far from brilliant mind, doggedly interpreting Western ideas to a populace lacking the means of judging the limitations of his knowledge. It seems almost as if he feared "loss of face" if he was not ready to discuss without hesitation carbohydrates and calories, Henry George and Karl Marx, electric lighting and cellular tissue, evolution, Russia, ventilation, liberty, *The Wealth of Nations,* ship building, trench warfare and yellow fever. This encyclopedic flow of information is the element in Sun Yat-sen's books that most quickly palls on a Western reader, who finds mushing through pages of glib expositions of occidental commonplaces a high price to pay for a few ideas that are really Sun Yat-sen's. All this educational bulk of his works is distinctly of the transitional period in which China finds herself today; it cannot hope for life or usefulness when the period has passed. China is in a phase of tutelage to Western ideas in which Sun Yat-sen's expositions serve a useful end. When she grows out of this tutelage, she will discard the teaching just as a schoolboy puts his primer on the shelf. Then, whatever residuum there may be of Sun Yat-sen's own thinking will be more objectively examined; and by that he will ultimately be rated as a thinker. The observation to be made just now is that his thinking has not clarified the great issues before the China of today. Sun Yat-sen has left his country a legacy of confusion.

Yet in spite of my profound revulsion at the idea of a China repressed into conformity with Sun Yat-sen's thinking, my hope would be that the Cult should not receive a violent set-back, but be allowed to settle slowly down into a liberal estimate of a man who had many admirable points and who was of decided historical interest. I should not like to see the current sentiment for him iconoclastically assaulted. So far as it is the spontaneous enthusiasm of a people for a man who expressed and interpreted their instinctive urge forward, sentiment should be free and unhampered to rise to any heights of genuine expression. This sentiment should be free also in regard to his books. The writings of Sun Yat-sen should be as open to intelligent inquiry and disputation as the books of any other man. The protective circle now drawn about them to hinder criticism is a threatening mistake in the present Nationalist policy; it is difficult to be patient with it even through one misguided decade. If the influence of Sun Yat-sen is to be the healthy and inspiring stimulus to unselfish patriotism that it should be, some way out of the present impasse must be found—a way through to intellectual integrity, not only for those who should be dealing with his books as products of thought, but for those whose task it becomes to lead China through her difficult political development on toward the distant ideal democracy with which Sun Yat-sen's name should be always honorably associated.

China must not stop at Sun Yat-sen's level of political intelligence. That the rising generation has not the ability to surpass his thinking would be difficult to believe. Yet nothing could be clearer than that the country has no need of another schematic thinker to dispute Sun Yat-sen's place of honor by putting forth a rival program. China needs no more thousand-year plans. She needs thinking that digs deep into the actual present. Nobody yet seems to be getting below the surface of the national policy of Change. I use the word, Change, as the simplest and most generic term. In whatever form Change is advocated—whether it be revolution, reform, or reconstruction, modernization, socialization, collectivism or communism —there is a unique and stubborn problem underlying it for China. Occupied with imitation of the West, the country has not made a fair beginning on this problem which has been waiting for a day when China should become original enough to understand herself and be done with naïve expectation of turning up some magic formula in the Occident.

DOCUMENTATION OF QUOTED PASSAGES

[1] Roots: "The Moscow End of China-Soviet Affairs," *Asia* (New York, June, 1927) p. 468. [2] Peffer, Nathaniel: "One of Asia's Three Great Moderns," *Asia,* Vol. 24, p. 658 (August, 1924).

SOURCES AND AUTHORITIES: See Appendix C, p. 405.

CHAPTER XI

The Future of Sun Yat-sen's Republic

I. THE PROBLEM OF A CHINA NOW CHANGED

IT would be difficult to imagine a boyhood and youth more completely interfused than was Sun Yat-sen's with the potent forces of change. Bred in the region most alive with foreign trade, caught in the flux and re-flux of overseas migration, educated from boyhood to manhood by foreigners, molded in impressionable years by the alien environments of Hawaii and Hongkong, converted by an American missionary, disciplined by Western scientific studies and socialized by the humanitarianism of medicine, Sun Yat-sen became what these forces made him.

It should not be forgotten, however, that in Sun Yat-sen's youth these influences were little reckoned with; some of them were working very obscurely. When Sun Yat-sen was a boy, China seemed the most unchangeable human unit in the world. In Western minds she was the very synonym of change-resistance. The world contemplated her immemorial traditions, her intensely race-centered egoism, her proud self-sufficiency, and her age-settled habits of thinking and acting, and wondered whether such a country could ever change. Perhaps it was our inner doubt as to whether change was possible to China that made us Occidentals so bold and so crass in urging changes upon her. It is easy to be reckless where one anticipates no result from one's daring. We realized neither the thing we were doing nor the scale on which we were doing it. Today the broad fact is written large upon the page of history and there it confronts us—that we Occidentals, whether consciously or unconsciously, intelligently or unintelligently, directly or indirectly, have been exerting great pressure upon China to change. Now that she is changing, it is easier to see what we have been doing than it is to justify what we did.

What a drama it has been—the history of China in relation to our occidental world!

On our side it began with the curiosity of the early travelers who, like Marco Polo, pushed a little farther along the highways of Central Asiatic trade and made the great discovery of China. Marco Polo returned to Europe with vivid details of China's colorful and elaborate civilization and of the subtleties and luxuries of her arts— only to be disbelieved and accounted half mad. And for their unbelief his fellow-Europeans knew little more of China for several centuries.

What instinct was it, pure commercial greed, or greed tempered by some thirst for expanding adventure, that made us Occidentals, first by fits and starts, and then pertinaciously thrust ourselves upon China? Something in us knew China for a great potential market, and something in us coveted the luxury of China's silks and porcelains. Seeking our advantage, we pressed upon the Chinese, profiting by the integrity of their business transactions, forcing them to open ports to our ships, and extracting from them pieces of land on which to build our trading-posts. When, on occasion, we got into difficulties or desired more advantages, we called on our governments to help us by sending embassies to the Emperor of China, bludgeoning him, if necessary, with the threats or actualities of war, in order to secure for ourselves further ports for our commerce and the concession of larger trading areas. It was in serving us in such ways that our governments came to see possible political advantages, and then the motive of national aggrandisement grew apace.

Meantime, in doing business with the Chinese, we discovered the delights and comforts of living among a people so dependable, so industrious, and so interesting in their artistic expressions and in the refinements of their cultural life. The commercial posts developed into foreign communities, until, along with our business activities, we had carried into China our social philosophies and social groupings, our methods of community government and our standards and styles of living.

While our traders were developing business with the Chinese, we initiated also another kind of penetration, not a whit less adventurous, and considerably more pervasive, in the missionary migration. It is easier to explain why we traded than why we missionized. If we could sit above ourselves like judges, aloof and indifferent, we might be able to analyze and understand our missionary impulse toward the Orient. At the present time we are too deeply and too emotionally bound up with it to treat it quite objectively. Perhaps there was something in the *zeitgeist* that started missions on the mutation so conspicuously manifested in the later decades of the nineteenth century. Perhaps it was some forgotten emphasis in Christian theology (possibly only in Protestant theology) that provided the significant urge. Whatever the causes may have been, the history of China must be written differently today because of that amazing centrifugal propulsion which after the middle of the nineteenth century whirled faster and faster at the heart of Protestant Christianity. These missions form one of the most vivid and romantic aspects of the relation between West and East. Not every age in the world's history sees one of its major religions develop a significant movement of expansion and propaganda. What made our missions the more consequential to China was the fact that just when, under the insistence of the traders, China was opening slowly and reluctantly to the outside world, our missions became most expansive and most enterprising. The missionary movement had one of its propulsive centers in the United States of America. Britain throbbed with it, and Germany, Scandinavia, France and Italy in their degree. With greater and greater force the migration spread, until the mission stations in China were numbered by hundreds, whereas the trading centers were counted by tens. Missionaries lived in the interior where traders were excluded from residence. They learned the language of the people; most of the traders did not. Except incidentally the traders were not much concerned to change China, but the missionaries were apostles of change. They were sent with the purpose of changing fundamental modes of thinking and standards of conduct. Moreover, they were not only zealots for a religion, but carriers of that religion's environmental civilization. Above all they were educational in the Western sense of education. They created centers of Western learning, building from primary schools patiently up to colleges and professional schools. For many years the only Western education in China was in mission schools. The missionaries fostered scientific knowledge and translated scientific books. It was they who developed the humanitarian knowledge of healing and sanitation, and relief in plague and famine. They introduced clubs and societies on foreign patterns, and associations for the diffusion of popular knowledge. They translated and distributed secular as well as religious books. One may safely say that there was nothing that might be done to stimulate intellectual progress or social betterment that some missionary somewhere did not undertake—from the better tanning of leather to the creation of a university. History may care little how many converts Christian missions have made in China, but it will never cease to reckon with the diffusion of Western ideas, which seems now to have been only a by-product of the missionary penetration. Sun Yat-sen had much of his education in mission schools and hospitals, and his experience is typical of that of hundreds of the modern leaders of China.

In all these ways, both directly and indirectly, through our traders, our governments and our missionaries, we have been urging the most ancient, homogeneous and stable nation of the Orient to change.

Now the change has begun! And before it we stand dazed and perplexed. The drama is taking on the tone and tenseness of a tragedy. We see a protean urge for variation taking possession of a stable people, who over centuries and millenniums had worked out their own original ideas of human relationships and their own schemes of social and political grouping, and had worked them out so well that China achieved social integration over a vaster population, and survived over a longer period than any other national grouping anywhere in the world at any time in history. Before this marvelous demonstration of stability in social living we of the rest of the world may well stand admiring and awed. In our tardy admiration we are beginning to inquire into the causes of such long-lived and widely diffused vitality. But just as we are about to sit at China's feet and learn, the whole marvelous structure seems about to crumble before our eyes. We are no more than awake to the nobility of this ancient, coherent and vital people than they take to imitating us!

Their motive for imitation is mixed. By no means is it all admiration. Back of the imitation is a protective instinct. The Chinese are trying to adapt themselves to an outside world which once could be haughtily ignored, but cannot now, by any force of their own, be so much as held off. In order not to be at a disadvantage with the world that is pressing upon them, the Chinese feel they must learn the ways of the West. They learn by imitation, and one imitation leads to another in a seemingly endless chain. And in the confusion resulting from so much imitation China's individual genius is thwarted of its own expression.

The process of adaptation, as we have seen, is much more than the adaptation of individuals by education. A whole generation of Western-educated men has not been enough to stabilize China. There are immeasurably greater social problems involved. No sooner is a strong individual educated in the thinking and institutions of the West—Sun Yat-sen for instance—than he wants to change the social structure of China, at one point or at many points, by persuasion or by force. He idealizes these changes under some large alluring word—"modernization" or "revolutionary reconstruction"—and he aspires to lead his yet unenlightened fellow-countrymen in a mass movement in order that the changes may be brought about rapidly and brilliantly. Wisely or unwisely he effects the destruction of something old, but has difficulty in creating a social entity to replace it. There is "revolution" without "reconstruction"; instead of "modernization" there is chaos. That, in brief, is the life-story of Sun Yat-sen.

It is at this unhappy juncture that we long-interfering Occidentals sit up to contemplate the appalling spectacle of a China now changed. What has become, we ask, of the skill that caused China to make for herself a racial grouping on the grandest scale and with the utmost permanence the world has ever witnessed? Have the Chinese people of today lost the wisdom of their ancients? The growing illness of China's body-politic would make us think so.

But where is our own boasted occidental intelligence that we should have been party to the muddling of social changes in this horrible fashion? The sad fact of the matter is that we of the West seem to have no intelligence of a social kind great enough to lend to China in her dire need. We make sad failures in attempting very much smaller problems of our own. But to confess this is not going to save ourselves, much less another people. Where are there resources of intelligence able to make headway against the disaster that has come upon China? We rush to her aid in famines and in floods—disasters petty compared with the afflictions that change has brought upon her. Are we at the end of our resources now? If so, we must simply say to China: You must be as much greater than ourselves as your problem of adaptation is greater than any that we know.

II. THE RÉGIME THAT WAS WRECKED

China is not easy to understand. We of the West know it, and we have been shirking the arduousness of the understanding; we have been throwing it back on the Chinese. But we Occidentals who would rather see China's difficulties diagnosed by Chinese are in the end denied this easier way out. Instigators of the whole modernizing movement in China, we are now being called upon to take our share of the responsibility for understanding why things have gone wrong. We have been impelling China toward changes so drastic that we have got her into a maze of confusion in which she seems incapable of understanding herself. I speak as an individual when I say that I have been as baffled as the Chinese to understand why things have gone so persistently wrong for them. Other people in other lands undertake to function in new patterns calling for democratic coöperation; some of them manage to do it; China undertakes it and fails, not once, not twice, but many times over. Surely this recurrence means something. What it means should be discussed and, if possible, understood. I should today have no courage to undertake a discussion of it, were it not that all my life I have been feeling China as a part of myself. China belongs to me by right of my birth there; when I discuss her failures, it is as if I were confessing my own. I have, moreover, the right of one who has been toiling with the problem. I have been working through and around the life of Sun Yat-sen in an endeavor to understand him and the whole republican development of which he is the nationally worshipped exemplar. The confusions of the study have been blinding beyond belief. Perhaps because I have worked long enough in the darkness, I think I begin to see.

Not less confusing than the influence of the Western world has been the influence of Japan, the country which has been the exponent and the exemplification of the values of "moderniza-tion." It was Japan's brilliant example that started China on the heedless pursuit of modernization. It was to Japan that thousands of Chinese youth went in the first flush of eagerness for Western education. It was in Japan that many of the students turned into ardent revolutionaries. It was Japan that gave asylum to banished reformers and defeated revolutionists. It was from Japan that a new Chinese public opinion was molded by Chinese writers—no-tably, Liang Chi-chao. Japan's triumph in the war with Russia was as stimulating to China as it was to Japan herself; that an oriental nation had fairly met a European power and had defeated her gave the Orient a new confidence in itself and unbounded optimism re-garding the future. It was just when the world was ringing with acclaim for Japan that Sun Yat-sen and several other plotters against the Manchus called a meeting of Chinese students in Tokyo in the fall of 1905. They responded in large numbers and, with such enthusiasm as had never been known among them, organized the Revolutionary Brotherhood, which carried the Chinese Revolu-tion to its consummation in 1911. Japan might have gone on in-definitely in the rôle of patron of modernization for China, if she had not allowed self-interest to lead her into policies antagonistic to China's well-being. Japan took a bad turning, which became apparent in the Twenty-one Demands of 1915; and since then she has not ceased to entangle her China-relations in tortuous un-fairness and black wrongs. Japan began by being a helper in China's quest for modernization, only to turn into the most insidious enemy that China has, the one that now presumes to arraign China before the bar of the world for the chaos which Japan has, time and again, not scrupled to foster.

While we are lamenting China's chaos, we must not fail to lay a large share of the blame for it upon the world's plain lack of intelligence where changes in a highly wrought social fabric are concerned. In revolution China has been a disciple of the Occident. But where are those among us who know the A B C's of social change? In China's case our human ignorance has affected the largest homogeneous bloc of people in the world. Mankind has never seen an illustration on so great a scale as in China of the effects of revolutionary change upon an old and highly correlated civilization. China's condition stands today a condemnation of the insufferable superficiality of Western thinking in dealing with that sensitive tissue, community life. An earthworm can be cut in two anywhere and its parts survive; cutting into the complex flesh of a bird is a different matter. China's civilization was no earthworm civilization. Its wounded tissues are now a pitiful sight.

If we are to attempt to say how much of the blame for China's chaos must be laid upon China herself, we must first try to see sharply and clearly how much it was that Sun Yat-sen and his fellow-revolutionists expected of their country. Such a cold consideration as this seems not to have occurred to the daring spirits who were ready to venture everything for a gloriously modernized China. Being radicals, they thought of the old régime as so much obstruction to be cleared away. It seems scarcely to have entered their minds to ask what demands the revolution was making upon the adaptability of the Chinese.

In 1911 Sun Yat-sen spoke of China as "the country in the world most fitted to be a republic." The over-confidence of the revolutionists in setting up a republic was due in some measure to their wrong estimate of the amount of democratic experience China had had. Much that was misleading was said then and has since been said about the essential democracy of China. The facts call for scrutiny.

In old China, as in all human society, there were large areas in which the people managed their own affairs. They cultivated their farms, held their markets, made things to sell, kept their shops, raised their families, conducted schools, built temples—all without the government either helping or hindering. It would have been an extraordinary and ultra-modern situation if the government had managed such affairs for the people.

In China the farmers had the habit of living in communities, rather than on separated farmsteads; so they naturally developed community organization in these farming villages. In other communities craftsmen organized in occupational guilds, traders in business guilds. Old China was full of organizations with many purposes. Families had their own organizations of varying sizes, running up to clans of a hundred to two thousand people. Inevitably these organized groups overlapped or became linked together. A trade might become a family business; villages were usually clannish; guilds might be clans or groups of clans. All these organizations were social and lay beneath the purview of the government, although they furnished channels through which the government might conveniently convey orders. Even the villages were far too numerous and too trivial for the government to bother itself about. The district magistrate (the lowest governmental official) was only too glad to let the villages—of which there might be hundreds in a single district—manage their own affairs.

Among these social organizations some grew vigorously in old China and acquired weight and importance in their communities. In the Chinese cities, which had no geographical wards, the guilds and clans were the natural units of subdivision, and had to be reckoned with. The tranquillity of the countryside depended upon the inconspicuous functioning of the primitive village councils. It is all the more true in the disturbed conditions of today that the order and stability of China depend in large degree on the functioning of the organizations that are non-political. Governments may come and go, armies may march and harass, but these social organizations have so far been able to persist. Not everything in China has disintegrated.

It is to these interesting social organizations that attention is called by those who say that China is essentially self-governing and democratic. But, it is just here that one of the bad jumps is made in thinking about China's problem. A separately managed group is not necessarily democratic; if that were true every independent nation in the world would be a democracy. Because a superior power is not interfering from the outside of a country, or of a county, does not make it certain that that country or county is democratically administered. The fact that its form of government has not been externally foisted upon a community proves nothing about the community's organic character. It is essential to clear that point before going on. No matter how important these social groupings may have been in the general life of old China, they must be looked at before they are pronounced democratic.

The social organization that seems most fundamental in Chinese society is the family; it is relatively more important than the family is in Western civilization. Certainly in China the family is not democratically organized. It is doubtful whether, in the nature of things, a family can be democratic anywhere. In a family some are old and some are young, some are productive and some are non-productive, some are experienced and some are inexperienced. These inescapable differences make it inevitable that some individuals will be subordinated and others will control—and that without "the consent of the governed." Whether in the dim ages past the father seized the government of the Chinese family and has simply held it ever since, or whether it has come about some other way, the fact is that in China the family is more than ordinarily autocratic. For one thing it is more than ordinarily large; it usually comprises all the married sons and their families, as well as an accretion of other relatives. The large Chinese family is held together in an autocratic pattern in which the father is the undisputed head. The relation of wife to husband, of children to parents, of younger brothers to the eldest brother, of daughters to the family into which they were born, and of daughters-in-law to the family into which they are married—all these relations have been worked out thoroughly in China and are regulated, not only by custom but by an ancient and authoritative ethical code. Of the "five human relationships," with which Chinese ethics concerned itself, three were relationships within the family.

Furthermore, the Chinese family organization was and still is a restraint upon individualism that can be at times very severe and despotic. When the Chinese excuse themselves to us for failure by saying "We are too individualistic," they presume somewhat upon our foreign ignorance of Chinese family discipline. In the Chinese family there developed also a group spirit—an *esprit de corps*— which our Western family never approximates. Families had their group ambitions, promoted the advancement of their members and asserted their group rights in the larger society.

The clan was a bigger family group, never, however, enlarging to the size that Westerners sometimes fancy when they try to visualize the ramifications of an ancient family tree. The clans were usually small groups ranging from about a hundred to perhaps two thousand members. Among the men of one surname there were many clans.

The working shop was a family big enough to take in apprentices. The guild was often a ramifying family connection specializing in one line of business. A village might be made up of a single clan or of several coöperating clans. In this development the group pattern and group spirit derived from the family were carried into other organizations, and along with them a great deal of the autocracy of family management. In so far as the derived organizations stuck to the family pattern in their organic functioning they cannot be called democratic. The survival of the autocratic head-of-the-family idea in the social organizations calls for a good deal more study, before it should be presumed that the experience gained in these organizations is training for democracy. The idea of one head man with autocratic powers is so thoroughly ingrained in the Chinese mind and so abundantly supported by Chinese ambition, that every movement toward democracy should soberly reckon with it. Yuan Shih-kai could not get away from it. Neither, in actual practice, did Sun Yat-sen. He, too, was autocratic, and demanded obedience to his personal authority. Whether he was called generalissimo, or president, or chairman, he instinctively functioned on the autocratic principle, not on the equality principle. When he was leveled to a committee membership in his first Canton period, he resigned and went off to Shanghai. He ended his life with the most complete imaginable autocracy guaranteed to him by the constitution of the Kuomintang.

While emphasizing the very large survival of the authoritarian family concept in Chinese society, we should recognize also that the social organizations did develop interesting practices that may be considered foreshadowings of democracy. The clans held stated conclaves, at which the clan-head was chosen by an elective procedure and clan business was discussed. Some of the business guilds had federated branches located in different cities, sometimes in different provinces, and fell into the habit of holding a gathering of branch representatives. Various forms of committee administration grew up in the guilds. These and other incipient democratic practices need to be studied more thoroughly to discover what elements of autocracy remained actively functioning within the organization at the same time. The general statement may be made, that, at most, the clans, guilds and other social organizations were qualifications of the fundamental family autocracy by practices that tended toward democracy. It often seems to an outsider that the relationship the Chinese best understand is the authoritarian one —an autocratic head set over subordinates—the "number one man" designated and accepted. They have yet to bring to maturity the practice of coöperation among equals; and that is at the very heart of successful democratic functioning.

Because of the importance and stability of China's social organizations, there has been a recent tendency to belittle the place of the actual government in the life of China, treating it as if it were something like a cap that the country might casually wear or change or dispense with. Even Sun Yat-sen went out of his way to assert in one of his lectures on Democracy, in 1924, that the old government had really nothing to do with the people except to collect taxes. In making such a remark Sun Yat-sen was trying to score a point for the solicitude of the Kuomintang on behalf of the people, and history went glimmering. Doubtless taxes bulked large in the popular Chinese mind (though one notes that they were not as productive, as in Europe and America, of demands for a share in the government). The part of the government that sat at the capital might have been a matter of indifference to the Chinese people, but there was no unconsciousness of, or indifference toward, the ramification of government that ultimately touched every village and hamlet. The pervasiveness of the government was a striking characteristic of the old régime. This ramifying system did much more than collect taxes. It maintained order by means of a wide-flung militia. It administered justice through its officials according to a fairly well developed code of penal offenses; for, even after the clans and guilds had done their best in judicial administration, there were plenty of quarrels and crimes left that crossed clan and guild lines, and only a magistrate could attend to these. On its various levels the government also took considerable responsibility for public works—canals, highways, railways, bridges, dykes and municipal improvements. Under good rulers the welfare of the people was actually promoted, as it is—let us hope—today. It was the government that developed and administered the extraordinary system of examinations, which set standards for education and passed upon the fitness of men for offices in the governmental hierarchy. The government of the old régime had its faults and its abuses, but it was no mere toy of the reigning family; it was a huge administration, well organized according to its own principles.

Old China was governed by a vast outreaching network of officials organized upon the strict principle of graded subordination. From the Emperor at the top, power and responsibility were handed down to viceroys of regions, provincial governors, intendants of divisions, heads of prefectures and sub-prefectures, and magistrates of districts. Of the district magistrates alone there were over fifteen hundred; in each upward-climbing grade there were diminishing numbers. None of these officials ruled in collaboration with equals; each was a highly individualized trustee of power stationed at a particular post. All officials had at their bidding recognized underlings—executives, secretaries, guards, police—to whom they gave commands, but with whom they never conferred on an equal footing. When the Emperor met his Council of State, it was as a superior announcing orders and policies. If a regional viceroy called in a governor of a province, or the head of the military garrison, it was for a courteously extended consultation with men whose position relative to his own was thoroughly understood. Nowhere was there any blurring of precise subordinations with pretenses of equality. Except in military organization, the citizens of the Occident know no such consistent subordination and definition of responsibility as was characteristic of China under the old régime.

The logic of this old hierarchy seemed to be the diffusion of functions as widely as possible. Responsibility was placed as low down as it could be. The people did everything they could for themselves through their social units, such as the clans and guilds; what they and the villages could not take care of was the business of the district magistrate, the hardest worked official of the old régime. What he could not correlate was the business of the official who presided over a group of districts; and so on up. The province was an extremely important large unit about which grew up a rather sensitive regional consciousness, and not a little regional jealousy. Roughly speaking, the government was as local or regional as it could be made. But except on the ignored level of clans, villages and guilds, it cannot be described as local *self*-government or regional *self*-government. It was local and regional administration from above through officials appointed by the central government to carry it on. Checks were actually devised against the possibility of its becoming self-government; for example, the governor of a province could never be a native of the province; he must be always from some other province.

This very clear organization with its defined subordinations made for an effective and cohesive administration over the huge area that old China was. But in all this admirable scheme nothing remotely analogous to a national parliament or a provincial legislature was known. Group responsibility and group administration was unheard of so far as the government was concerned. The old régime was a hierarchically organized system of government through highly empowered individuals. Since the functioning together of groups of equals had no place in the scheme, the old government inevitably fostered individualism in its officials and put the premium of promotion upon strong administration.

Back of this political practice—its immemorial base and its age-long justification—were the Confucian education and the Confucian philosophy. The derivation of the government from the family was philosophically acknowledged and ethically enlarged upon. The Emperor was the father of the nation or the head of the national clan. Paternal solicitude for the people was the ideal held up before every official, no matter what unit he was set over. Emphasis was placed upon the character and ability of the official who was to sustain the relationship of father to the people. To discover talented individuals was conceived of as the first function of education; then to develop them to the highest individual potential of ability and character; after that to select those best qualified for public service in official positions. Because it was believed that the betterment of society must come from the development of gifted individuals, the emphasis of Confucian philosophy was upon the "princely man," that is, the man distinguished above his fellows both in character and in ability. Thus the old education, fortified by the ethical philosophy of Confucius, was concentrated—in theory, certainly, and in a considerable degree successfully—upon producing the highly potential individual. No wonder that there came to be associated with the very idea of leadership a high valuation of individualism. The conception that society might be better served by grouping individuals on the principle of equality and requiring them to function as democratic groups had no place in the Confucian philosophy and the Confucian education.

III. THE EXPECTATION AND THE CHAOS

Toward the end of his life Sun Yat-sen was fluent with protests against slavish copying of the West, especially in political practice. He assured his countrymen that they were capable of creating something new and better in government. Yet when one looks at Sun Yat-sen's planning for his country, one finds a web of imitation. He is typical of his age in being so intent upon mastering what the West had to offer that his mind did not function creatively. He seems never to have had a truly creative inspiration as to a kind of government suited to the genius of the Chinese people. That he came to a theoretical recognition of the paramount place of the family system in Chinese social life is clear from certain expositions in his later lectures—notably those on the "Three Principles." His very phrase for Nationalism is the People's Clan. He definitely attributed the long-lasting stability of Chinese civilization to its foundation upon the family. But, when Sun Yat-sen undertook to plan a government for China, the fundamental structure of Chinese society counted for nothing; the family-derived pattern of coöperation was cast to the seven winds of heaven, and utterly alien forms of functioning were put in its place. What Sun Yat-sen substituted was so new to the Chinese that to them it has seemed original. But the West, from which he borrowed the ideas, knows that his planning was imitative, not creative. The creative man would have understood—both instinctively and intellectually—the inherent structure of Chinese civilization and the habits of the Chinese people, and he would not have disregarded them in planning a government.

By the Revolution of 1911 the huge nation that is China was required to transform itself by the mere writing of a constitution from a close-knit hierarchy of individual officials to a federation of popularly elected provincial legislatures, each with its attendant executive and judiciary *à la* Montesquieu's theory of government and the practice of the United States. To head this federation—called a republic—a supreme parliament was summoned at Peking. The first difficulty these legislatures experienced was of discovering anything like a group mind; political parties were not sufficiently developed to create a majority. The National Assembly rapidly became a disorderly conglomeration of factions. Inchoate as it was, the Assembly had to coöperate with a president, a premier and a cabinet. Even the President was not a highly individualized trustee of power; he found himself tied up with the Premier, and they had no end of trouble hitting it off as a pair. Cabinets were formed but they could not agree; they broke, were re-formed only to break again. A struggle developed, as we have seen, between the executive branch of the government, dominated by the President, whose training had all been in the old strong-man type of administration, and the unwieldy legislative body; this deepened into a quarrel, and then into a fight for the survival of the fittest. It was the President who survived, and the National Assembly that was scattered and ended.

What Sun Yat-sen and his co-revolutionaries had taken for granted was that the leaders of China could be thrown into equality-groups as large as a parliament, as small as a cabinet—and that they would be able from innate intelligence to function in these groups. Although there were many other mis-reckonings of China's preparedness for democracy, that, it seems to me, was the fundamental mistake of the Chinese Revolution. A people habituated by ages of tradition to individualized administration in governmental affairs was not able to take up quickly a form of government whose proper functioning depends upon the smooth coöperation of groups of men brought together on a basis of equality.

The most radical change that has taken place in the government of China since 1911 was that made at Nanking in 1928 after the success of the Nationalist Revolution. This also goes back to Sun Yat-sen, whose reorganization of the Kuomintang with Russian help in 1924 determined the constitution of the party under whose committees the government functions. Like the government of the Empire the Kuomintang system is also a hierarchy. In it power is handed from the top down on a strict principle of graded subordination. It is not, however, a hierarchy of responsible individual officers, but a hierarchy of committees ramifying through five grades of subordination from the National Executive Committee at the top to the Executive Committees of the sub-precincts at the bottom. It is a thorough-going plan of government by groups. At the points where government functions, the Kuomintang installs a committee instead of an individual.

This new system, introduced even on a small scale, would have seemed a marked departure for China. What shall be said when the change is simultaneously attempted at every governing center of every grade in the vast expanse of the country? Fortunately the committees are more compact and manageable in size than the groups which attempted to function together under the early republican form of government patterned after the United States and France. But compared with the old Imperial system it is heavily weighted and cumbersome. For the single-mindedness of the individual official there is substituted the unpredictable mind of a group; and for the decisiveness and despatch of a strong man there are substituted the deliberations of a committee. Manifestly, the success of such a government depends upon the ability of the groups to stick together and work together. And that brings upon this experiment also the fundamental criticism passed upon the earlier experiment—that it proceeded upon the unwarranted assumption that a people accustomed to an unusual degree of administrative individualism will from innate intelligence function smoothly and effectively when thrown into groups. The history of the first years of the National Government demonstrates again that to take this for granted is a notable error of judgment.

What has happened under the Kuomintang is the old trouble under a new form. There have been repeated break-downs of the functioning groups; simultaneously there have also been compromises and conflicts with strong men of the individualistic tradition, who, impatient of the impracticalities of group functioning, have retrieved for themselves something of the power with which the old officials were authorized to rule. In spite of the theoretical firmness of the Kuomintang hierarchy, the central Government has not been able to keep strong men in their theoretical place of subordination. In other words, it has proven impossible to set up again the graded subordination which the old régime accepted with little questioning. China has lost both ways: she has destroyed the centralizing hierarchy—apparently beyond repair—and has not yet learned to function satisfactorily in equality-groups. She is no longer an empire and she is not yet a democracy.

When Republican China becomes less imitative in the political sphere—if she has not by that time wrecked all that was good— she may begin to call in question such rash attempts at new modes of behavior. She may even begin to think that some of her old ways were better ways. The Chinese family pattern is surely one of the world's great patterns in group relationships and in group functioning. Great, too, in its way was the Chinese governmental system which was derived from it. Whereas the family organization enlarged no further than rather small clans, the government took the family principle—the highly empowered administrator— and gave it an effective spread over an enormous area by a logical pattern of graded subordination. The empowered individuals were kept in control by central appointment on the basis of competitive examinations.

The incomparable examination system was first ruthlessly wrecked by the monarchy, because a discrimination was not made between its need of educational reform and its usefulness as an organ of control and cohesion in the government. Next the governmental hierarchy was wrecked by the Republic because the topmost pinnacle was a resented Manchu family. The smashing is not over. The stabilizing social organizations are now being attacked, not only by "tutelage of the people" in unnatural ways, but by communistic iconoclasm. Why smash ahead? If China's indigenous patterns of coöperation are at cross-purposes with theoretical democracy, why not modify democracy instead of the habits of a whole people? Novel forms of democracy are being invented elsewhere; why should not China have her own original variation?

One of the most admired characteristics of Chinese craftsmanship is the imagination which seems never to fail to see the artistic possibilities latent in its material. Whether working in stone or wood or ivory or seeds of fruit, the Chinese artist first observes the contour, the texture, the color, and the unique decorative incidents inherent in his material; it is about them that his fancy builds creatively. Chinese social structure should not be less respectfully carved at than a gnarled root or a peach stone or a block of quartz. The artist in social reform will begin with what he has, and glory in its unique tones and shapes, even in its oddities. Inspired by them, and working within their limitation, he may create something tremendous, beautiful, original.

But, alas! it is suggestions such as these that are branded by modernist China as "reactionary"—a word made so odious by Sun Yat-sen that it is now almost synonymous with traitorous. The current mood of intolerance of the past gives one no choice but to take it for granted that nothing will deter China from attempting democracy according to Sun Yat-sen's plans—no matter how prolonged and difficult may be the process of learning alien forms of coöperation. So, we Westerners can only suppress our judgments and take it for granted that the way out for China is not revival of an old decent order (one of the ancient values, now to be thought of as lost forever) but forward through the weltering chaos to actual and effective coöperation in the democratic group patterns so prematurely thrust upon her.

IV. DISINTEGRATIVE BEHAVIOR

Republican China's end and aim is democracy: that must be considered settled. China's most fundamental problem is then not her foreign relations, important as they are; it is not militarism: that is symptomatic rather than basal; it is not the economic relief of the masses, appealing as that is to every humane person; it is not the ardent rush of her youth into communism as the only promising activity in a society gone wrong; it is something deeper, about which neither nationalist nor communist has had constructive words to say: it is the disintegrative behavior which appears in Chinese attempts at democratic functioning.

As I read the history of the Republican régime in China, I cannot fail to see the reiteration of a deadly sequence: an existing governmental pattern is destroyed; a new pattern—always borrowed from some other country or built of borrowed parts—is substituted; there is a getting-together on a larger or smaller scale of a group committed to coöperative functioning in that pattern; but the functioning breaks down, or breaks off bit by bit; it in turn is destroyed and a new pattern is put in its place. This is an old story now—twenty-two years old—the story of a new pattern attempted in coöperative government with disintegration as the outcome.

Sun Yat-sen apprehended this only darkly. He was in the habit of alluding to a foreign criticism of the Chinese as unable to hold together, and he quoted many times the phrase first given currency, I am told, by Liang Chi-chao—that the Chinese are like "a stretch of scattering sand" (*i p'ien san shah*). In one of his lectures Sun Yat-sen attributed this to the possession by the Chinese of too much of that which the West values so highly—Liberty. But when he suffered from outbreaks of disintegration, he was ready enough to put the blame on the older officials, who played a reactionary game of politics, and other dissenters from his plans. Sun Yat-sen seems never to have looked at himself to observe how he functioned when he got into a democratic group, else he would have discovered that there was much to be desired even there. He was not easy to work with. There are many men living in China today who can remember his inflexibility and his arbitrariness, his unwillingness to take as well as give, his lone-hand methods, and his lack of skill in developing men to carry responsibility with him. He made men his henchmen rather than his partners, and worked with inferiors in age or ability better than with his equals. His three attempts at republican government in Canton all ended quickly in dissension and in his own withdrawal, either voluntary or compelled. Yet Sun Yat-sen apparently never noticed in himself any lack of skill in democratic group functioning. His blindness has been characteristic of the modernist leaders in China generally; they see the disintegration—that is obvious—but they think themselves free of responsibility for it, and fail to see their own disintegrative behavior. The reasons which they put forward to convince themselves that they are blameless should not be allowed to blur the point. The reiteration of the behavior-pattern is the significant fact that should not be obscured by a variety of condoning circumstances. Disintegrative behavior has been recurring far too regularly under the Chinese Republic for it to be without meaning. It has appeared so often that there is but one sure prophecy in the parlous uncertainties of China today, that is, that disintegration will go on occurring until it is intelligently dealt with as a baleful disease in the Chinese body politic.

Processes of disintegration that frustrate group functioning may be observed breaking out from time to time in all modern equality-groupings in China, whether student societies, college faculties, religious organizations, charity boards or political bodies. Such an outbreak always results in waste of what has been gained and a consequent set-back, and it frequently entails a tragic wreck of human ability and personality, which should be the very agencies by which progress is made. Lest I should be thought of as arraigning the Chinese in a spirit of boastful occidental superiority, let me grant that in all governments and in all our imperfect human society there are disruptive elements constantly or periodically at work: nothing is truer, to our shame be it said! But it is also true that there is a quantum of coöperation that must persist in order to neutralize the disruptive forces and make democracy a functioning possibility. It is only a plain observation to say that the Chinese have not yet achieved this coöperative minimum.

Why have the Chinese failed to function coherently in the new democratic groupings? That is something they themselves must probe into and understand. A Westerner can only make suggestions.

Sun Yat-sen did not realize what he was asking of his people, else "reconstruction" would not have looked so easy to him. One of the inescapable criticisms of his leadership is that his intelligence was not keen enough to know a thing for difficult when it was difficult. Perhaps it is not putting it too strongly to say that Sun Yat-sen's plans and policies demanded of his fellow-countrymen a degree and kind of adaptability that neither they nor human beings anywhere should be expected to attain. Chinese in all walks of life understand what it is to be trusted with authority, and what it is to be subordinated to authority. But to be thrown into equality-groups with no one in authority and no one subordinated calls for a radical change of their whole sense of human relationships. To have made a success of the Revolution of 1911 would have required of the Chinese an intuitive perception of the authority of the group will, and an unheard-of genius for quick and effective coöperation in patterns created on an entirely new principle. Now, after twenty-two years of trying to do what should not have been expected, the plucky attempters of the impossible may be ready to analyze the unfortunate results.

Because a misconception that touches on this point may be getting abroad, it should be emphasized that the republican failure is not due to fundamental inability on the part of the Chinese to coöperate. Chinese history covering thousands of years has its over-whelming testimony on that point. Chinese are capable of coöpera-tion in patterns to which they are habituated. Surely we have made that clear in commenting on social organizations, such as the fam-ily, the clan, the guild. The republican overturn demanded a revo-lutionary alteration of modes of coöperation long established among an ancient and habit-formed people. Westerners who have grown up to the principles that underlie cabinets and committees and parliaments, and have been educated in the technique of equality-coöperation, have no idea how difficult that kind of group function-ing can be for people with age-old traditions of definitely designated personal authority and clearly understood subordinations.

Is it possible to be more concrete? The Chinese are perhaps too clever as organizers on paper. The sangfroid with which they will set up a modern organization would deceive any one except very experienced observers. The modernized Chinese does not do much hesitating; he adventures. When he adventures into foreign func-tioning, it is only with such understanding as his foreign tutors have given him; and that is not enough. Chinese habits have to be understood, too. When an equality organization is attempted in China, this is what often happens: the one who is chosen dean, president, chairman or head-by-some-other-name, instinctively sup-poses himself to be the traditional "number-one man," vested with authority; he naturally treats his confrères as if they were his subordinates. If they happen to be enlightened to a sufficient degree in the theory of democratic functioning, they resent being subordi-nates, and raise an outcry or start a ruction.

There is not a little behavior in the modern groupings that is unconsciously disintegrating; it has no malice aforethought. It is part ignorance, part inexperience and part human frailty. But none the less it contributes toward China's national disintegration. It should be remembered that in the modern groupings people are handling new potencies; they have powers in committees, cabinets, bureaus, boards and assemblies that are new to them. An inept individual may become a member of some equality-grouping; he may be an able man; he is almost sure to be an ambitious one; in his group relationships he may offend sensibilities by aping the brusqueness of the bluntest foreigner (never the kind of foreigner the Chinese like), or he may affect the garrulous forthrightness of some deceptively frank American, thereby sowing disagreements and spreading alienation; he may have some other simple fault or misapprehension; soon friability appears in the group in which he is working—it does not cohere; presently his committee, or faculty, or board, or department goes to pot—a short and simple annal of disintegration. When the breakdown comes, feelings are already so irritated that it is impossible for the Chinese group to locate and cure the cause of the trouble. It takes a disinterested and more than ordinarily intelligent man to analyze the group's functioning and detect the node of disintegration. But it is just this that Chinese wits must be sharpened to do.

Disintegration may result from attempting to do something that calls for a skill not yet acquired. Disintegration may also be caused by outside attacks upon the insecurely functioning group. Acquiring skill in a new form of coöperation is difficult enough; acquiring it in the midst of a society which actively practices a politics of disintegration is a super-added difficulty about which the Chinese should clear their minds. Therein lies what I believe to be the most distinctive and the most disruptive element in the Chinese political practice of today. Under the Republic there has been going on not only the struggle to coöperate in unaccustomed democratic patterns, but the disabling practice of a politics of disintegration. By this phrase I mean designing attempts to gain political advantage over an opponent by inducing disorganization and chaos within his zone of influence. There should be no need of a foreign critic to point out that an appalling amount of disintegration is craftily produced in China by calculated policies of attack. To create chaos for political ends is an enemy practice—anti-national and anti-patriotic; no palliating argument from the past or present can make it anything else. This threatening game may be an unconscious hold-over from practices of the Empire. It should be pointed out, however, that it does not in the least resemble those old bad habits which Sun Yat-sen inveighed against, namely, the corrupt practices and reactionary conservatism of the old mandarins. This is something that manifests itself in so many ways that I am compelled to believe that it taints the minds of all Chinese leaders, even the minds of the Western-educated and the youngest of the student class. Chinese leaders—including the potential leaders among students—seem instinctively to employ the tactics of disintegration. Possibly none of them realize that this political practice is the very antithesis of the democracy they so ardently advocate. A democracy that perpetuates the politics of disintegration will either die of the violence, or revert to the tyranny which alone can survive that kind of politics.

In China the politics of disintegration has been played with many variations; some of its forms are crude, some are subtle; some are so easily observable that the whole world knows that they are being practiced; some have passed unobserved and are doing their deadly work unchallenged.

One of its crudest forms is the resort to ruction. Both Confucius and Mencius conceded the right of the people to revolt against bad rulers. In spite of the large place that clans, guilds and other social organizations had in the community life, they had no share or privileges in the old government. To secure attention the people had to resort to some form of eruptive tactics—a clamorous protest or disturbance of the peace. I remember seeing a classical Chinese play in which the process was vividly portrayed while the audience cheered the action: the responsible magistrate had been guilty of unjust government; the people in protest mobbed him, beat him, left him badly scuffed and half dead. This method of bringing a government to book, although very ancient, is not obsolete in China; it has been practiced by modernized students in modernized Nanking. If better organized and equipped with firearms, a similar rising becomes a civil war—a method of disintegration so notorious that all the world now associates it with China.

An oft-repeated and peculiarly modern method of bringing about disintegration (the more baleful because of its possibilities in destroying all kinds of group enterprises) can be reduced to a typical formula running something like this. A group is nucleating about some project which shows promise of success. Those who wish the project ill or those who covet it for themselves attack it with criticism, severely, often violently, insisting that the organization of the nucleus is wrong, or arguing for drastic modification of its purposes and objectives, or for the removal of this or that person from the group. They may even convince individuals within the group that such changes are imperative, and of course they convince themselves that their own motives in attacking are of the best. The promising nucleus is—in the China of these days— learning its A B C's in group functioning, and it readily disintegrates before such an attack. The result is that a fresh nucleus must be formed, and it is subjected to a similar attack, and in turn disintegrates. The process repeats itself in many places and with many kinds of projects besides the governmental ones; and China wonders why there is chaos. In operation this formula is the more deadly, because, as I have tried to point out, the nuclei are frail young organisms struggling into being, whereas the disintegrative forces that attack them have an expertness and cruelty bred of long development under the Empire. The precariousness of the national life of China in this situation is a serious matter; it is doubtful whether its democratic nucleations can any of them survive, unless some measures are taken to put an end to the politics of disintegration.

V. SCATTERING SAND

The only hope of China ever becoming a democracy is by an educational process: Sun Yat-sen was right about that. But, by what educational process? It is possible to pursue education and miss the essential kind of education. Sun Yat-sen was very well educated, but that did not make him democratic in his functioning. From "political tutelage," as Sun Yat-sen conceived it, the whole nation might emerge, and fail of democracy. Before democracy can function in China, a body of people must be brought along to the point where they can function together in equality-groupings without recurrent breakdown.

To bring a large body of illiterate adults to sufficient literacy to read newspapers and simple books is a stupendous educational undertaking, as the brave mass-educationists know. To educate the children and youth of four hundred million people in the Western knowledge that alone can form the background for "modernization" and for Westernized democratic institutions calls for a well-financed and coördinated educational effort on a gigantic scale. But both these educations are in more or less explored regions, and are simple in comparison with China's unique problem of reëducating an old and habit-formed people in new habits of group functioning. But without this habit-education the other two educations, useful as they are in themselves, will fail of realizing a democracy in China: that is the conclusion to which one is driven. This task of habit-education will call for creative genius of a very high order, as well as for system and method applied with infinite patience. Optimists must be warned that it will not be accomplished without engaging the most spiritual forces in education, and only by using methods of the utmost enlightenment. It cannot be done by repressive force of any kind; repression will only entrench more strongly the old habit of playing with disintegration.

The functioning of individuals in groups and of groups in relation to society calls for many judgments of conduct which carry over into the region of ethics. Responsibility becomes moral; what destroys social effectiveness becomes a sin. Many such sins will turn out upon investigation to be the old depravities—corruptibility, jealousy, treachery. But that is not all. These are nice points in group behavior which must be discerned. It may surprise the Chinese or even the occidental reader to have me affirm that the democratic people of the Occident are in possession of a considerable body of accepted judgments as to what is fair play and defensible procedure in democratic functioning. As a matter of fact we are almost unconscious of the possession of such a body of common judgment. The infringement of these judgments is the experience which makes us aware that they exist.

That a nation so superbly ethical as the Chinese should be found lacking in the ethics of democracy may to some appear puzzling. Really it should cause no wonder. Group functioning on the principle of equality has not been attempted in Chinese politics until recently; the ethics of such group functioning could not have been discovered by the Chinese earlier. Among the five human relationships once regarded as fundamental, there was no such relationship envisaged as the democratic group. So it is little wonder that when the Chinese are required to function in new equality-groupings, they are found to be ethically at sea. They cannot apply to the new functioning the ethics of any other relationship they know; indeed, to carry over into democratic groupings their well-understood ethics of the family or of the relation of sovereign and subject is nothing short of disastrous. The Confucian philosophy which furnished the education for the old government was intensely ethical. Through all the abuses of the old régime it kept alive not only the ideal of rule by good men, but likewise the ideal of a loyal people, also ethically minded. The new democracy requires a new ethics based upon a sound philosophy of the value of group intelligence, group will and group action, and the perfecting of all these.

Lest I should be accused of criticizing China and letting the Occident off with a pat on the back, I want to say as forcibly as it can be briefly said, that, in my judgment, there is nothing the whole world needs so much to be getting about as certain aspects of this same problem of group functioning. Great forces are pressing us toward more and more socialization of our functioning over wider and wider areas of economic and political life; so it behooves us to apply the utmost intelligence we can summon to the discovery of the underlying principles of group determination and group effort. Unless we can make some clear discriminations between the fallacious and the sound, the blundering and the skilful, the progressive and the retrogressive, we also may suffer disintegration through undertaking to function in patterns alien to our habits, and unsuited to the degree and kind of our social development. The ethics of groups is the ethics with a future.

The creation of an ethic of democracy for China and the correlation of it with the already formulated ethics of other human relationships is an opportunity for thinkers. It would seem that the keenest philosophical minds, as well as teachers and writers of the finest ethical insight, could do nothing more serviceable than to bring order out of the chaos in this region. The ethics of democratic functioning might well become a subject of discussion by students and teachers everywhere, and by every club, society or party organized on modern lines. Many of the already nucleated modern groups may become centers of vitalizing experiment for the perfection of group functioning. When the smaller democratic groups become alive to ideals of coöperation and make themselves proficient in the practice of group enterprises, the beneficial effects on governmental groupings will begin to be felt. Indeed, it would seem that the only way to eradicate disintegrative habits from governmental groups is to build up cohesive and flexible coöperative habits in the small democratic groupings in schools, colleges and everyday life. If I have any suggestion for the educators of China, it is to set consciously about the developing of equality-group functioning in every kind of school by every kind of means—play, athletics, dramatics, exploration, group study and discussion, group management and any other commendable activity that can cause people to function together as equals. Disintegration should become the cardinal sin and some penalty be devised for it. Reversion to "scattering sand" should be the occasion for "a day of humiliation."

All this will admittedly be a slow educational process. If the present—which always seems to be an emergency in Republican China—calls for emergency education, that should be taken in hand by its potential leaders of the near future: if not studying abroad, they are students in China's middle schools, colleges and universities. Wherever they are, they may be called upon to discipline themselves in group functioning. Skill, of course, cannot be conjured up in a generation or two generations, no matter how earnest their effort, but great improvement is a possibility. In current attempts to make Sun Yat-sen's program of "tutelage of the people" effective, political tutelage is too generally thought of as education of the ignorant masses. It is too readily taken for granted that the educated classes are already prepared for democracy and qualified to tutor the masses. So students are sent out to harangue the farmers and the artisans on the technique of democracy. If I understand the history of Sun Yat-sen's period, it is the educated leaders of the people who have so far been tested in democratic functioning; it is by them that all the experiments have been made; it is not the masses but the educated leaders who have over and over failed, chiefly, if I read the history aright, because they do not naturally function well in the new groupings but develop a pernicious behavior of disintegration. There is an insidious fallacy in the turn of thinking toward the undereducation of the masses as the chief cause of China's failure in modern forms of government. Granted that a republic cannot mature with a largely illiterate or undereducated citizenship, and that any policy looking toward a republic should make provision for an educated electorate, it is, however, dodging an important point to fail to see that China could by now have progressed much farther on the long road toward democracy, if its already educated leaders had shown the qualities of coöperative functioning that the world optimistically expected of them. No amount of mass education is going to cure this serious fault of the leadership. In the present stage of leader-development the tutelage of the common people in new patterns of local self-government is a very doubtful policy. If the traditional patterns of local government are replaced with the new patterns in which not even the tutors themselves have skill in functioning, the last stabilizing governmental habit of the Chinese people will have been destroyed. What is to be expected then but a stretch of sand even more scattering?

Can a nation when it is old remake its habits of group functioning? All cynics and many "practical men" will say "No." Educationists—especially the great ones—may say soberly, "It is conceivable." National reconstruction is a popular phrase in China to-day; it is on the lips of every student, every militarist, every politician and every awakening citizen. I wish that I could associate an idea with this phrase so that it could never come to the lips or even arise in thought without there coming with it the realization that one thing is needful before reconstruction of any kind can be brought about, that is, effectiveness in the new group functioning.

Unless the Chinese can learn to work together coherently in the new democratic groups, it is preposterous national self-deception to talk about the country's reconstruction. Without proper group functioning the result realized will not be nationalism or democracy or the betterment of the livelihood of the people, but only disintegration, sadder and sadder disintegration. It is the crowning irony of China's recent history that Sun Yat-sen's socialistic policies have become a battle-ground of factions—ironical, because until the Chinese leaders have learned the art of working together in the simpler democratic groupings without recurrent breakdown, the application of any of Sun Yat-sen's socialistic policies is as impossible and as visionary as a parliamentary republic was in 1911. If group functioning is the very heart of democratic government, it is the whole body of a socialistic democracy. Much as one longs for the relief of the deplorable condition of the Chinese masses, one must set it down plainly in glaring black and white that the masses will suffer more and yet more until leaders are educated to coöperate without the perpetual appearance of the vicious behavior pattern of today, disintegration. China will have to choose between being a "stretch of scattering sand" existing for nobody's good, or going into the slow educational process of learning to function coherently in democratic groupings. Over-sloganized as China is she needs a new "mouth-cry"—"Check the scattering sand!"

To integrate China's prodigious crumbling mass will call for an unparalleled effort of the human will; it numbs one's imagination to conceive the human energy that will be required to do it. But there is no doubt that in her huge collective mass there is sufficient energy, if it can be rightly directed. In all social advances the people's will must be directed by right discriminations and clear insights. For the making of intelligent choices and for shaping the course of the nation China needs a new generation that shall far outstrip Sun Yat-sen and his generation. And when that generation has made its utmost possible advance, it must be outstripped by a more intelligent and more determined succeeding generation. Only thus will China ever win through.

Yet what will happen in the end may be this: greater intellects and more dynamic spirits may arise, labor, and perchance be forgotten, while Sun Yat-sen is remembered and exalted as a symbol of China's first struggle to become a democracy. But the future of China is the important matter, not the reputations of men. It may be true that, among the men of China's transition there has not appeared a greater than Sun Yat-sen. But the time is not far off when he that is but little in China's democracy must be greater than Sun Yat-sen:—greater in the insight to see what is worthy to endure in China's own social fabric; ready to humble himself to the drudgery of ingloriously restricted tasks; determined to resist the temptation to short cuts suggested by pride; patient to endure the reproach of failure while slowly retrieving past mistakes; willing to discipline himself severely in the art of functioning in groups; eager not only to build but to let others build.

Epilogue

Too much have I seen for one not born a prophet;
  I am too weak and bound to set men free;
Let me discharge my pen from the inky battle,
  And watch some braver seer outstrip me.

Now let me close my eyes and rest from seeing!
  Let those whose sight is strong lead on before!
I shudder at precipices and crashings headlong;
  O, give me a while in a room with a shut door!

APPENDIX A

The Christian-Father Myth

I. THE PROBLEM STATED IN A LETTER FROM THE AUTHOR TO THE HOME SECRETARY OF THE LONDON MISSIONARY SOCIETY

New York City,
Nov. 11, 1929.

Reverend Nelson Bitton,
London Missionary Society,
Livingstone House, Westminster, S.W.
London, England.

Dear Mr. Bitton:

May I trouble you to answer what may at first sight seem a deceptively easy question?

In your book *Our Heritage in China* you make this statement on page 58:

"No account of our South China Mission should close without an emphatic reference to the magnificent *human* results of their past and present labours. The great succession of Chinese pastors, beginning with Liang Ah-fa, has brought honour to the cause of Christ throughout the whole land of China. Dr. Sun Yat-sen's father was among that number."

Can you tell me whether your statement that Sun Yat-sen's father was a Christian pastor was based upon London Missionary Society records—either printed or unprinted—or whether it was based upon the article published in the *Strand Magazine* in March, 1912, entitled *My Reminiscences* by Sun Yat-sen? Lest you may not have that statement at hand, I quote it:

"Up to the year 1885, when I was eighteen years of age, I had led the life of any Chinese youth of my class, except that from my father's conversion to Christianity and his employment by the London Missionary Society I had greater opportunities of coming into contact with English and American missionaries in Canton."

Perhaps you will recall that Dr. Cantlie made a similar statement in his book *Sun Yat Sen and the Awakening of China,* which appeared about the same time in 1912 (p. 27):

"Sun Yat Sen was born in 1867. . . . His father was a convert to Christianity, and was employed as a missionary agent by the London Missionary Society. An English lady connected with the mission interested herself in the young lad, and by her help Sun was well grounded in English."

You will understand why I am coming to you about this, when I tell you that for over a year I have been working on a book-sized biography of Sun Yat-sen.

One of the points that I have not been able to clear to my satisfaction is the Christian connection of Sun Yat-sen's early youth. Accounts about his father's relation to Christianity are confusing. On the one hand there is the tradition that his father was a Christian employed by the London Mission. Elsewhere his father is described as an idol-worshipper and a very conservative and unenlightened Chinese: Linebarger's biography so represents him, and it is known that Sun Yat-sen himself coöperated in the preparation of that biography. I want very much to know what the truth is.

While in China I wrote to —— —— of the L.M.S. mission in Fukien, whom I had met personally, and presented my questions. I knew that —— was a scholarly person and interested in Sun Yat-sen. The reply gave me nothing definite but said that my letter had been sent to a member of the London Mission in Hongkong (unnamed) who would certainly be able to find the information. Although that was eight months ago, I have received no communication.

When, a few weeks ago, I came to New York, I was hopeful that the publications of the London Mission contained in the Missionary Research Library here would be found to throw light on the point. So far I have found nothing except the above quotation from the *Strand* printed with a comment of gratification. (*Chronicle of the London Missionary Society,* April, 1912, p. 99.)

In another quarter I learn (*The Missionary Herald* A.B.C.F.M. April, 1912, p. 171) that Sun Yat-sen was baptized in late 1883 or early 1884 by Dr. Charles R. Hager, an American Congregational missionary in Hongkong. He published an interesting article in that number entitled *Dr. Sun Yat Sen, Some Personal Reminiscences*. The accuracy of this article I am able to check at so many points that I have great confidence in it. While not definitely disposing of the Christian-father tradition, this article does not contain any detail which could be used to give it the color of probability.

I am beginning to wonder whether the statements about Sun Yat-sen's father being a Christian and an employee of the London Mission can be substantiated from any records other than the statement in the *Strand* which purports to have come from Sun Yat-sen. You are probably aware how widely this has been repeated. You can tell me whether in making the statement in your own book you did it on the authority of mission records, or whether you trusted—as would be eminently natural for you to do—the reliability of the statement by Sun Yat-sen in the *Strand*. If you can furnish me any London Mission records that support the Christian-father tradition, I should be glad to pay a competent research worker any sum up to five pounds sterling for examining old London Mission records and reporting to me on the findings.

If I must finally, on the basis of evidence or lack of evidence, abandon the tradition as unfounded, I think an appendix in my book which dealt with it would be worth while.

You have perhaps noticed that a life of Sun Yat-sen is running in a new Hawaiian monthly called *The Honolulu Mercury* beginning June, 1929. The life is by Bishop Restarick, who has gathered material from Hawaiian Chinese who knew Sun Yat-sen. He definitely takes issue with the whole line of statements I have been putting before you, and bluntly says that the *Strand* statement is "absolutely false," adding:

"If Dr. Sun did authorize the article, it must have been in order to deceive the English people as to his youth, and to enlist the sympathy of English Christians. He must have wished the public of Great Britain to believe that his early life was influenced by their missionaries and so gain support for his revolutionary projects." See the June issue; also the July issue in which Dr. Cantlie is named in connection with the story.

I wish Dr. Cantlie and his wife were alive to throw light on this question. Dr. Hager is also deceased. Perhaps you have already cleared the problem, or could suggest some one who could untangle it. If the London Missionary Society cannot, I think I should despair. . . .

NOTE: *Knowing to whom to turn, the Home Secretary drew forth a lucid statement from one qualified to speak, and very kindly sent me a copy of it. It is convincing beyond anything I had dared to hope for.* —THE AUTHOR

II. REPLY FROM A MISSIONARY LONG RESIDENT IN HONGKONG

Foreign Missions Club,
151, Highbury New Park, N. 5
7th. December, 1929.

Rev. Nelson Bitton,
Home Secretary, L.M.S.

Dear Mr. Bitton:

I have the pleasure to acknowledge with thanks the receipt of your letter putting to me the question whether the father of Sun Yat Sen was at any time a Christian preacher, serving in the Gospel under the auspices of the L.M.S.

The reply has to be in the negative. Sun's contacts with this Mission did not begin through his parentage; nor had we knowledge of the man until, at the age of 21, on his return from sojourning with his elder brother in Honolulu, he became a student of the Hongkong College of Medicine for Chinese, then newly formed and now merged in the Hongkong University. . . .

To the best of my knowledge, recollection and belief Sun's father was a typical villager, a peasant farmer, cultivating his own little ancestral holding at Ts'oi Hang, in the district of Heung Shan, distant from Canton about 25 miles. The only work that the L.M.S. has had, and still has, in this district is and has been from the beginning in the Portuguese Colony of Macao. This work was initiated by Pastor Wong and myself more than 30 years ago and has been from the outset supported by the Chinese, without financial assistance from the Society. Sun's district is one in which other Societies have worked with good results. It has not, however, outside Macao itself been an L.M.S. area.

It remains to be added that I have not met in the course of my service any person who claimed acquaintance with Sun Yat Sen's father. Had I lighted upon an informed person acquainted with Ts'oi Hang village, my first impulse would have been to full detailed inquiry. Had Sun been of Christian parentage I was in a good position to learn the fact, as were also Chinese friends with whom I companied at the time when Sun himself was a much discussed, and I may add a much criticised, personality. . . .

With kind regards,
Believe me,
Yours very truly,
(Signed) THOMAS W. PEARCE

APPENDIX B

Doctor Sun Yat Sen

SOME PERSONAL REMINISCENCES
BY CHARLES R. HAGER, M.D., OF HONGKONG

From *The Missionary Herald*.
Boston, April, 1912, p. 171 f.

Dr. Hager went to South China as a missionary of the American Board in 1883, and for twenty-seven years he has resided in the city of Hongkong, conducting missionary work in that city and in country towns, chiefly in the province of Kwangtung. Two years since he was compelled by ill health to return to America, and is now residing in Claremont, Cal. Dr. Hager has been in close contact with the Chinese, especially those who have passed through Hongkong going to or from America. He has counseled and befriended thousands of them, both as a physician and a preacher of the gospel.—THE EDITOR

So much has been written of this noted Chinese that has not always been in accordance with truth, that it has seemed best to me to record a few facts of my relation with him. It was in the autumn or possibly the winter months of 1883 that I first met him and judged him to be sixteen to eighteen years of age. He had returned to China from Honolulu, where he had spent a number of years in study, while his older brother was there engaged in business.

Of course, I could not help asking him whether he was a Christian, to which he replied that he believed the doctrine of Christ. "Then why do you not become baptized?" "I am ready to be baptized at any time," he replied; and so after some months of waiting he received the ordinance in a Chinese schoolroom where a few Chinese were wont to meet with me every Sunday, about a stone's throw from the present American Board mission church in Hongkong.

It was a humble building in which the future provisional president of China's first republic received the sacred ordinance. During the week a Chinese boys' school was taught there, while our young friend lived in the second story with some other Chinese, and an American Bible Society's colporter and I lived in the third story. In this way I saw a great deal of Sun, and always liked him.

For a time he attended the diocesan school of the Church of England, but soon changed to go to Queen's College.

It was some time in 1884 that an Englishman and I accompanied Sun Yat Sen to his home in Heung Shan. We decided to sell a number of Gospels on the way, and in passing through the Portuguese colony of Macao we disposed of a great many Scriptures. Sun Yat Sen took us to a Chinese inn, where a bed and two meals cost us about thirty or forty cents a day. Of course we ate with Chinese chopsticks and slept on Chinese bed boards, just as did our friend. After a day or two we went to his home and for several days enjoyed his hospitality; and if I remember rightly we also saw his wife. I concluded that Sun Yat Sen belonged to one of the more well-to-do families. The house in which we lodged was of a superior type. This was probably due to the elder brother's prosperity in business in Honolulu.

After Sun Yat Sen became a Christian he immediately began to witness for Christ, and such was his earnestness that in a short time two of his friends accepted Christianity. This was at a time when few converts were made and when many feared to identify themselves with Christians. But so great was the influence of Sun that he won these men to the truth. It was the same power that he has always had of making men accept his opinions. That is the reason nearly all of the 7,500,000 Chinese who are now abroad in other countries came to hold his views that the Manchus must go. True, many of the Christians could not ally themselves with him, but at heart they were one with him. It was the same power by which he has given to China a republic, instead of continuing the old monarchy.

Sun Yat Sen has learned many lessons in the hard school of adversity. No sooner had his brother at Honolulu heard that the young man had become a Christian than he sent word home that unless he gave up his Christianity he himself would no longer send any money home; and an elder brother in China, in case of the father's death, has almost un-limited authority and power. This dire threat had no effect upon our young, enthusiastic Christian, who did not cease promulgating his views on the Christian religion and the falsity of idols. Finding his threats unavailing, the elder brother sent for Sun Yat Sen to come once more to Honolulu, as he wanted to effect a certain sale to which the younger man's signature was necessary. This was, however, a mere subterfuge to get him away from China. After his arrival in Honolulu, his brother not only threatened him, but absolutely refused to give him any money; at length the Chinese Christians contributed the funds to send him back to China to study for the ministry; for at this time he had a strong conviction that he must become a preacher of the gospel.

The above incident was told me by Sun Yat Sen himself after his return to China.

Perhaps if there had been a satisfactory theological seminary at that time in Hongkong or in Canton, and some one to support him, Sun Yat Sen might have become the most famous preacher of his time, by the magnetic power of personal contact with men in winning them to Christ. After several months of inactivity he decided to take up the study of medicine, which has always been held in high esteem and next to the ministry by the Chinese. At his personal request I gave him a letter to the venerable Dr. J. G. Kerr, asking him if he would not remit a part of the medical fees, which were at that time about twenty dollars a year. For one or two years Sun studied Western medi-cine in the Chinese language, but came to Hongkong once more, after the opening of the Hongkong Medical College, and matriculated for four years in an English medical school, taught by the various physicians and doctors of Hongkong.

It was probably about this time that Sun Yat Sen began to express his ideas on the reforms needed in China and secretly to lay plans for the great changes that have now occurred. It was then, too, that he impressed himself and his views so favorably upon his associates, Chinese pastors, and others who have secretly rallied to his standard for nearly twenty years.

After his graduation in medicine and while I was in America taking my own degree in medicine, he devised a scheme of medical work for the Chinese in Macao upon a large scale, and for a time, at least, the wealthy Chinese contributed large sums of money for a free hospital in that colony; after several years the scheme was given up on account of financial difficulties.

Not long after my return to China, in 1894, Sun Yat Sen called upon me with a former pastor of the London Mission. He seemed the same kind and respectful young man that he always was; what surprised me was the remark of the native pastor, who had just returned from a three years' sojourn in Germany as a teacher of Chinese in Berlin. "How were you able," he asked, "to persuade such a man to become a Christian?" Today it seems clearer to me than ever before that even at that time Sun Yat Sen had already impressed himself upon the most progressive element of Chinese society, so that they were following him as their leader.

A few months later an attempt was made to take possession of Canton; the scheme leaked out and the reformers barely escaped with their lives; even Sun Yat Sen was almost seized and some Christians were beheaded.

After this Dr. Sun, as we shall now call him, became a wandering refugee, never sure that he might not fall into the clutches of the Chinese government, which had set a large price upon his head. At length being in London, pursuing still further his medical studies, he was decoyed into the Chinese Embassy and made a prisoner, with the view of taking him back to China to secure the large reward offered; but Dr. Sun found a way to communicate with Dr. Cantlie, who was once his teacher in Hongkong, and through his teacher's efforts and Lord Salisbury's action he was released. It was while here that I wrote him several letters, receiving a reply to each one. From this time on he never came openly to Hongkong, and even Japan as well as the Hongkong Government was obliged to refuse him residence within its territory.

Another lapse of years followed, and I saw him no more until 1904, when I conversed with him for a little time at San Francisco. He told me that nothing less than a change of dynasty was needed in China.

I tried to show him that the reforms which he formerly advocated were being adopted, to which he replied merely by saying that the Manchus must be ousted. During the same year (1904) I met him once more in a Chinese mission service in New York. He had lost much of the vivacity of his youth, and seemed careworn and oppressed with anxiety, but he was still loyal to the Christian faith. As I was anxious to raise some money among the Chinese for our Hongkong mission church, he told me of a relative of Tang Shao Yi, the new premier, and from the same district of Heung Shan, who might be able to assist me.

Dr. Sun undoubtedly has been collecting funds for many years for this revolution, and the Chinese of America have given large sums to aid him. His first attempted revolution was financed from the Hawaiian Islands and Hongkong. It need not be thought strange that Dr. Sun should attempt to change China's government. He had learned the lesson from the lips of missionaries and others in Hawaii, where they deposed a queen, who was perhaps not quite so bad as the former empress dowager of China. In resigning the presidency of the Chinese Republic in favor of another Chinese, Dr. Sun has shown himself the same simple-hearted and really earnest Christian patriot that he is. Personally I am sorry that he found it necessary to do so; but he has not buried himself, rather has he cemented China as a whole; if he lives, he may yet become a shining light in the history of the republic of China. Whether in or out of service, he will always be a moving power in the affairs of the nation. For eighteen years he has been banished from his own country and in constant danger of losing his life. When he returned at last he was immediately made president of the republic that he largely created, and even won over the premier of China.

The name he bears is significant of his life. The word Sun or Suen is the clan name and means "descendant." He has borne three given names within the last twenty years. The first is Yat Sen, "Day New" or "Daily Renewal" or "Daily Reform." Another name is Man,[1] which is the character for "Literary," and by which he was chiefly called after

---

[1] Clearly a misprint for Wen.

his banishment. Now he bears another name of Yat Sen, which means "Day's Genii," or the "Sun's Immortal One." In all these names there is a semblance of his character, and if the republic of China lives it will be due to his untiring zeal and self-abnegation for the good of his own countrymen.

Once I coveted him for the gospel ministry; but if he is true to his God and his country in the present crisis, I shall be satisfied that he found his path of service.

APPENDIX C

Sources and Authorities

I. THE TERRAIN AND ITS PITFALLS

If restrictions upon freedom of speech present difficulties to a biographer of Sun Yat-sen, the written sources, too, have their limitations. First of all one must reckon with the character of the biographies already published.

The earliest appeared in London immediately after the success of the republican Revolution—*Sun Yat Sen and the Awakening of China* by James Cantlie and C. Sheridan Jones. Dr. Cantlie had known Sun Yat-sen personally, and that which seems to be his contribution to the book is useful, but it is a slender part supplemented by many optimistic pages on China and the Chinese, lacking biographical value. Unfortunately for my purposes, the book was published in 1912, when neither the career of Sun Yat-sen nor the awakening of China had more than got under way.

The second of the biographies in English was also written too soon— *Sun Yat Sen and the Chinese Republic* by Paul Linebarger. Sun Yat-sen authorized Judge Linebarger to produce a biography and coöperated with him. A reviewer characterized the result as the life of Sun Yat-sen as he himself wished to have it written. Certainly, it is eulogistic to a degree. While giving an altogether disproportionate space to childhood and youth, it omits vitally important ranges of mature life. The relation of events comes to an inconclusive end about 1920; the climax of Sun Yat-sen's life came after that.

Whereas Judge Linebarger placed his reliance upon Sun Yat-sen personally for material, a more recent biographer, Bishop Restarick, has drawn upon Chinese who knew Sun Yat-sen. He made this venture, be it stated, in Honolulu, at a safe distance from the disciplinary arm of the

Kuomintang. By this method he has released some vivid materials, but he has involved himself in confusions; he was evidently without the orientation which might have come from personal knowledge of China and from access to certain sources in the Chinese language. *Sun Yat Sen* by Henry Bond Restarick appeared serially in the *Honolulu Mercury* from June, 1929, through January, 1930. With some revisions it was issued as a volume by the Yale University Press, October, 1931. I had some correspondence with Bishop Restarick concerning certain points on which I take issue with him. A letter setting forth a few of these has been published in the *Journal of the North China Branch of the Royal Asiatic Society*, Volume LXIII, 1932.

My biography profits by these biographies having preceded it. All of them I have searched for materials. It is not unnatural that I have found the usefulness of each to lie chiefly within a zone of special knowledge. Cantlie is a first-rate source for Sun Yat-sen's medical days, both of study and of practice; also for the vivid happenings of his earliest visit to London. Linebarger's book is particularly valuable for episodes of childhood and youth; in this region Sun Yat-sen seems to have opened up to him with reminiscences. Restarick's volume contains the fullest account there is of Sun Yat-sen's sojourn in Hawaii and the residence there of members of his family. I have tried to mention these books in the chapter-lists of Sources and Authorities as often as they have proven useful.

Many shorter sketches of Sun Yat-sen's life exist as chapters in English books. Most of these are uncritical of current traditions. An exceptionally vivid, but extremely vulnerable life forms the first chapter of Upton Close's *Eminent Asians*. It gives further currency to demonstrable errors, and some of its racy characterizations are more vivid than true. The latter parts, which grew immediately out of the author's period of newspaper work in China, furnish an interesting mirror of the impression made by Sun Yat-sen upon a contemporary foreign journalist.

Of the shorter lives one of the most competent—though not without some errors—is by a Jesuit father who teaches in a suburb of Shanghai. It stands as a thirty-page introduction to the author's translation of the *San Min Chu I*, originally done into French, but now accessible in English under the title, *The Triple Demism of Sun Yat-sen* by Paschal M. D'Elia, S.J., Franciscan Press, Wuchang, 1931.

Sketches of Sun Yat-sen's life are now frequently produced in English by the publicity department of the Nanking government. My friends in China often send me these, clipped from the English press. It goes without saying that they do not approach Sun Yat-sen with freedom or objectivity.

As I was nearing the completion of this book, another source appeared to be reckoned with—*The Gospel of Chung Shan according to Paul Linebarger*, Paris (France), 1932. It contains the much-to-be-regretted announcement of the complete loss of biographical materials which Linebarger had collected and worked upon with further books in mind. These had been deposited with the Commercial Press in Shanghai, and were all lost in the destruction of the Press's properties by Japanese bombs in January 1932. The present volume, it is stated, "offers what little records the author has remaining as source-material to the historian of the future." Reconstructed under difficulties from notes and diaries, the book is far more illuminating in regard to the career of Sun Yat-sen's biographer than in respect to the life of Sun Yat-sen himself. When the history of these times in China has been clearly narrated, certain historians may perhaps interest themselves in the amazing phenomenon of Sun Yat-sen worship, and they will find this book illuminating: it will show them how rapidly history can become obscured by reading-in sentiments and judgments that are *ex post facto*. This book is nothing if not a cult book: its *raison d'être* is manifestly to heighten the worship of Sun Yat-sen in China and to stiffen the popular resentments useful to the Kuomintang. From many internal evidences it appears that it has been primarily written to be translated into Chinese, and that its English publication in France is only the tee from which to drive the ball.

In the Chinese language there are many short biographies, about whose comparative value there is no consensus of opinion. They are popular primers in democracy, propagandist and heroizing in purpose. Much more useful to a historian are the chronologies of Sun Yat-sen's life, quite a number of which have been produced. It is in these that the Chinese historical spirit is seen at work on the events. One of the earliest and most interesting was done by Wu Chih-hui, a man who is now "one of the old guard" of the Kuomintang. Those that I have made use of are named in lists of Sources and Authorities.

The published material on the life of Sun Yat-sen forms a difficult and confusing mass to work upon. There are amazing contradictions as to fact; there are deflections of representation due to partisan feeling and to left or right leanings; there is a repulsive overload of fulsome flattery. I have not undertaken to discuss the multitudinous discrepancies in footnotes; that would cumber the book with the mechanism of scholarship. It must not therefore be inferred that I have failed to scrutinize them; I have had painful struggles to separate the man from the misrepresentations. That with all my pains I have myself avoided errors would be presumptuous to suppose. I shall be grateful to those who will write and tell me where I have erred.

Because the biographical material is more than ordinarily confused, I went eagerly to Sun Yat-sen's own writings. Here, thought I, one might hope to find the real Sun Yat-sen. Here, indeed, one does find his opinions and his habits of thinking, but these are wrapped and re-wrapped in borrowings from Western learning and endless expositions of occidental commonplaces for untutored Chinese audiences. Although by tearing off this sheathing one can reach Sun Yat-sen's views, one can discover very little of the processes by which he arrived at them. As for personal revelations, they are of rare occurrence. A man who could not disclose his inner self to his most favored biographer could not be expected to wear his heart on his sleeve in public addresses, magazine articles, and controversial manifestoes; and these make up the main body of Sun Yat-sen's published books. Little revealing correspondence seems to exist. How serious this lack is may be realized by a moment's thought concerning the place of personal letters in Western biography.

Sun Yat-sen did leave a few autobiographical narratives. The most vivid were published in English and were translated later into Chinese. In these he had the collaboration of occidental journalists and other writers. They are not without pitfalls for a biographer. One such narrative, printed over Sun Yat-sen's own signature, is responsible for the most persistently circulated untruth I have had to wrestle with, namely, the statement that his father was a Christian and an employee of the London Missionary Society. If that had been true, Sun Yat-sen's childhood environment and opportunities would have been quite different from what I have to report. It is no wonder that the misleading statement has traveled far, and that both the secular and religious presses have repeated it: it was first made in an article entitled "My Reminiscences" which was said to have been "taken down from Sun Yat-sen's own lips and signed by him." (*The Strand Magazine*, London, March 1912.) For a discussion of the Christian-father myth the reader is referred to Appendix A. The writing of a biography of Sun Yat-sen is no undertaking for the naïvely credulous.

Even when Sun Yat-sen thought he was making revelations, he failed to do so in any Western sense. There exists a pamphlet-sized production known as his *Autobiography*. Produced soon after the success of the republican Revolution, it is an ultra-condensed and very bare recital of eleven successive revolutionary uprisings in which Sun Yat-sen himself had some share. I have followed the Chinese chroniclers in accepting this *Tzu Chuan* as in the main a dependable source for the revolutionary history through 1911. Some errors have already been detected in it, and more may be discovered. Yet, because it deals with a series of events which no one could have known so completely or so intimately as Sun Yat-sen, a heavy burden of proof will always rest upon any oral or written testimony that may appear to challenge or to contravene its statements. My own disappointment with the *Tzu Chuan* is not that in some details it may be in error (that would seem to be only humanly probable), but that it lacks details where the Western mind wishes more circumstantiality and vividness. As an account of a hazardous revolutionary career it is, judged by occidental standards, singularly cold, laconic and uninspired.

If any one supposes that I have exaggerated the amount of misrepresentation which has appeared in print in regard to Sun Yat-sen, he should gain access to a first-class newspaper "morgue" and look over the Sun Yat-sen clippings. I have thought at times of devoting an Appendix to categorical denials of currently circulated untruths. But that might appear too funny to be taken seriously. Worse than that, it might give an altogether erroneous impression of worthlessness in newspaper sources.

When dealing with events that are current, newspapers furnish indispensable sources, especially for Sun Yat-sen's political life. It is chiefly in feature articles sketching events which have slipped off into the past that newspapers have shown themselves all too fallible. They have given wide currency to many an irresponsible story. An illustration of the rapid growth of legend may be found in the widening area of romantic misrepresentation which has developed in regard to Sun Yat-sen's relations with his secretary, Soong Ching-ling, who became his second wife. It has been an extraordinarily delicate matter to separate the facts from the accretions in this much-exploited region. I believe my account is nearer the truth than any that has yet appeared.

For the relief of the biographer the tracking down of truth has its amusing episodes. Again and again I have been driven back to the most primitive of historical criteria. The simple principle that a person cannot be in two places at the same time has cleared away a lot of doubtful tradition. If Sun Yat-sen was in Hongkong all of 1884 and the evidence is complete, he certainly did not spend 1884 in Honolulu. If he was overseas during the whole of 1904, there is something shaky in a story that he was hatching a conspiracy in China in that particular year If a certain young lady was a resident student in Macon, Georgia, during 1911 and 1912, a journalist's sensational report that she was acting as Sun Yat-sen's secretary during his Presidency at Nanking and following him adoringly about China during the remaining months of 1912 takes on the hue and color of outrageous fiction. How grateful I have come to be for school records! Where they have not been destroyed by fire, or incinerated by the route of the waste-basket, they are the staunchest of chronologers.

Another test of truth that has proven very useful is the one employed by everybody, historian or no historian—the way purported facts fit together. As long as reports of events are at sixes and sevens, the discouraged biographer knows something is wrong somewhere. When testimony from different sources fits together like bits of a jig-saw puzzle, one feels a growing presumption of reliability. In fitting things together I have had exasperating struggles with mere dates, but in the end the effort has been worth while. After all, that prosaic thing called chronology

is the bony structure of biography; while it is out of joint, the figure of
the hero looks awry; but when the sequences are rightly understood, there
come sudden and thrilling revelations of the man himself.

Another principle on which I have relied is no more than a common-
sense rule of caution: when in some doubt about reports to be frank
about it; when in grave doubt to avoid the matter as untouchable. At
times this calls for severe restraint of one's dramatic impulses. From
many a tempting bit I have turned aside, telling myself that when the
truth had worked out its own consistencies, a larger drama would result than could ever come from seizing upon details because they were
dramatic.

A final canon concedes the possible contiguity of truth and untruth
within the same source. The most difficult problem in biographizing
Sun Yat-sen is that of erring sources. All the sources seem to contain
errors—chronologies, biographies, autobiographies, and journalistic write-
ups. The nearest to a hole-proof account of any phase of Sun Yat-sen's
life that has passed under my scrutiny is Dr. Hager's article which I have
reprinted as Appendix B. So far I have discovered only two or three unimportant errors in it, and I have had verification of many a curious
detail. It goes without saying that it is not easy to build on sources in
any one of which an undetected error may make the building insecure.
Yet sources cannot be discarded because errors are found in them; if
that were our procedure, we should have no sources left for a life of
Sun Yat-sen. Fortunately, sources are numerous enough to be checked
one against another. Both specialty and bias can be reckoned with, and
sometimes oral testimony can be had for confirmation or discrediting.

The discrimination between probable errancy and probable truthful-
ness is most difficult of all in Sun Yat-sen's own writings. The natural
presumption is that no source can be more ultimate than a man's own
account of himself. Unluckily, conspiracy and secret plotting do not confirm a man in habits of candor and consistency. Sun Yat-sen has been
convicted, not only of withholding the truth, but of actual misrepresentation. Must we then distrust and discard everything he says about himself?
Surely not. We cannot accord him less generous treatment than we accord to lesser sources. It becomes, however, a delicate and complicated

matter to judge how likely Sun Yat-sen would be to tell the truth about himself at any given time. Critical judgment is bound to play a part in concluding when he had motives for concealment, when he had motives for candor, and when he might have been simply off his guard.

Unless my reader happens to be interested in the vagaries of that none too correct lady whom we call Tradition, he is not likely to envy me the experience of biographizing Sun Yat-sen. Certainly I could not find it in my heart to wish upon another person the tedious pains and tantalizing labors that have been mine.

It is next to impossible to be entirely consistent in the anglicizing of Chinese names in a book such as this. Some names have become so standardized in English that no one would attempt to conform them to set rules now, *e. g.,* Canton, Peking, Manchu. Sometimes it seems very desirable to follow the dialect of the district in anglicizing a place name or a personal name, as in the name of Sun Yat-sen's birthplace, Choyhung, and his own name also; but this is impossible as a general practice.

Because it is better that a reader should mispronounce a Chinese name than be conquered by it, I have avoided adding difficulty to difficulty by complicating any name in my text with the odd-looking breathings whose significance is occult to all except initiates in the Chinese language. But, in quoting a Chinese phrase, they seem indispensable; and I have used them regularly in the book lists.

It should be stated that the lists of Sources and Authorities, which follow next, are not general reading lists, but specific acknowledgments of source-material found useful in making the chapter under whose number they stand. The order of the titles represents, in general, the sequence of their usefulness.

II. SOURCES AND AUTHORITIES CHAPTER BY CHAPTER

CHAPTER I

LINEBARGER, PAUL: *Sun Yat Sen and the Chinese Republic,* New York, 1925. No other biography contains so many episodes of childhood and youth.

LINEBARGER, PAUL: *The Gospel of Chung Shan according to Paul Linebarger,* Paris, 1932, pp. 197, 223.

"Madame Sun Yat-sen's Statement on the Political Situation," July, 1927, Woo: *The Kuomintang and the Future of the Chinese Revolution,* p. 270.

CHINESE CHRONOLOGIES of Sun Yat-sen's life, though often at variance, have been invaluable, particularly:

WU CHIH-HUI: *Sun Chung-shan Hsien-sheng Nien Piao;*

Chung-shan Hsien-sheng Nien P'u, an appendix to the Chinese translation of Linebarger's biography;

Chung-shan Hsien-sheng Nien Piao, published in the Memorial number of *The Young Companion,* Shanghai; November, 1926;

HSU MIN: *Chung-shan Hsien-sheng Ta Shih Nien Chih.*

SUN YAT-SEN: *Tzu Chuan (Autobiography).* An English translation by Leonard S. Hsü was published in *China Tomorrow,* June to December, 1929; also accessible in Hsü: *Sun Yat-sen: His Political and Social Ideals.* University of Southern California Press, 1933, p. 44.

SUN YAT-SEN: "My Reminiscences," *Strand Magazine,* March, 1912.

COOLIDGE, MARY ROBERTS: *Chinese Immigration,* New York, 1909.

COMAN, KATHERINE: *The History of Contract Labor in the Hawaiian Islands.* Publications of the American Economic Association, Third Series, Vol. IV, No. 3, August, 1903.

CHEN TA: *Chinese Migrations, with Special Reference to Labor Conditions.* Bulletin of the United States Bureau of Labor Statistics, No. 340, July, 1923.

RESTARICK, HENRY B.: *Hawaii from the Viewpoint of a Bishop,* Honolulu, 1924.

RESTARICK, HENRY B.: *Sun Yat Sen, Liberator of China,* Yale University Press, 1931. Useful for its contributions to the Hawaiian episodes; also contains information about Lu Hao-tung.

HAGER, CHARLES R.: "Doctor Sun Yat Sen, Some Personal Reminiscences." *The Missionary Herald,* Boston, April, 1912. See Appendix B.

Sun Chung-shan Ch'uan Chuan, a popular Chinese biography, contains material about Lu Hao-tung.

CANTLIE, JAMES, and C. SHERIDAN JONES: *Sun Yat Sen and the Awakening of China*, London, 1912. The American edition (New York, 1912) contains different illustrations, also some additions to the text.

HSÜ, LEONARD S.: *Sun Yat-sen His Political and Social Ideals*, University of Southern California Press, 1933.

The Regulations of the *Hsing Chung Hui* may be found in Sun Yat-sen's Collected Works.

CHAPTER II

"Former Chinese Student at Trinity Won High Renown," *Duke University Alumni Register*, September, 1931, p. 285.

SUN YAT-SEN: *Tzu Chuan (Autobiography)*; Translation by Leonard S. Hsü, *China Tomorrow*, Peking, June to December, 1929; also accessible in Hsü: *Sun Yat-sen*, 1933, p. 44.

SUN YAT-SEN: "My Reminiscences," *Strand Magazine*, March, 1912.

RESTARICK, HENRY B.: *Sun Yat Sen, Liberator of China*, Yale University Press, 1931.

SUN YAT-SEN: *Kidnapped in London*,[1] Bristol, 1897.

CANTLIE, JAMES: *Sun Yat Sen and the Awakening of China*, London, 1912.

WU CHIH-HUI: *Sun Chung-shan Hsien-sheng Nien Piao*.

T'ANG LEANG-LI: *The Foundations of Modern China*, London, 1928. Short Sketches of the lives of K'ang Yu-wei and Liang Ch'i-ch'ao.

[1] No other episode in Sun Yat-sen's life has been so fully reported from all possible angles as the sensational event which made his name famous in the Western world. It became news for the London press at once. A complete narrative of the incident from Sun Yat-sen's own standpoint was published, with the help of British friends in Bristol, in 1897 under the title *Kidnapped in London*. A concise account, accurate in details, was issued in Chinese in 1899 at the time when Sun Yat-sen again appeared in the Orient as a plotter; this is the Legation's side of the story. Dr. Cantlie wrote from his knowledge for *Sun Yat Sen and the Awakening of China*, 1912. The story is more briefly told on behalf of the English Counsellor to the Chinese Legation in Boulger's *Life of Sir Haliday Macartney*, London, 1908. Much ado about this one episode has tended to emphasize romantic adventure as the keynote of Sun Yat-sen's career, especially for the minds of Occidentals. A serious biographer cannot but wish that the plethora of material here could somehow retrieve the scantiness of material in some other areas.

LIANG CH'I-CH'AO: *History of Chinese Political Thought,* London, 1930.

CHANG CHIH-TUNG: *China's Only Hope,* Translated by Samuel G. Woodbridge, New York, 1900. This was previously issued in Shanghai as a paper-covered book under the title *Learn.*

LINEBARGER, PAUL: *Sun Yat Sen and the Chinese Republic,* New York, 1925.

LYNCH, GEORGE: "Two Westernized Orientals," *The Outlook,* Vol. 67, No. 12, March 25, 1901, p. 671.

CHAPTER III

WU CHIH-HUI: *Sun Chung-shan Hsien-sheng Nien Piao.*

LYON, D. WILLARD: *Chinese Students in Japan,* Shanghai, 1906.

SUN YAT-SEN: *My Reminiscences;*
    Tzu Chuan (Autobiography);
    Chung Kuo chih Ke Ming (China's Revolution);
    The True Solution of the Chinese Question, 1904.

HU SHIH: "What I Believe," *The Forum,* February, 1931.

WANG, TSI C.: *The Youth Movement in China,* New York, 1927.

HSU MIN: *Chung-shan Hsien-sheng Ta Shih Nien Chih.*

ANON: *Chung-shan Hsien-sheng Nien P'u.*

ANON: *Chung-shan Hsien-sheng Nien Piao.*

FINCH, PERCIVAL: "A Chinese Sage Speaks to the World," *New York Times* Magazine, June 21, 1925.

T'ANG LEANG-LI: *The Foundations of Modern China,* London, 1928;

T'ANG LEANG-LI: *The Inner History of the Chinese Revolution,* New York, 1930.

RESTARICK, HENRY B.: *Sun Yat Sen, Liberator of China,* Yale University Press, 1931, especially Chapter IX.

San Francisco Examiner, April 7, 1904, p. 5; April 29, p. 7; May 7, p. 1.

CULIN, STEWART: *The I Hing or "Patriotic Rising,"* The Numismatic and Antiquarian Society of Philadelphia, 1887.

JORDAN, DAVID STARR: *The Days of a Man,* New York, 1922, Vol. II, p. 32–34.

Anon: "Gen. Homer Lea's Career That of a Hero of Romance," New York *Sun,* February 18, 1912, Sunday features, p. 3.

Correspondence from David Starr Jordan, *New York Evening Post,* December 19, 1913.

Hager, Charles R.: *Doctor Sun Yat Sen, Some Personal Reminiscences.* See Appendix B.

Huie Kin: *Reminiscences by Huie Kin, Pastor Emeritus, First Chinese Church, New York City,* San Yu Press, Peiping, 1932.

Public Ledger, Philadelphia, June 23, 1905.

Soong Ong Siang: *One Hundred Years' History of the Chinese in Singapore,* London, 1923.

CHAPTER IV

Sun Yat-sen: *Tzu Chuan (Autobiography);*
Chung Kuo chih Ke Ming;
San Min Chu I: Nationalism, Lecture III;
My Reminiscences.

T'ang Leang-li: *The Inner History of the Chinese Revolution,* New York, 1930.

Linebarger, Paul: *The Gospel of Chung Shan according to Paul Linebarger,* Paris, 1932.

Restarick, Henry B.: *Sun Yat Sen, Liberator of China,* Yale University Press, 1931.

Ball, Dyer: *Things Chinese,* Hongkong, 1888, article on Secret Societies.

Wu Chih-hui: *Sun Chung-shan Hsien-sheng Nien Piao.*

Woo, T. C.: *The Kuomintang and the Future of the Chinese Revolution,* London, 1928.

Wang T'ien-hen: *Sun Chung-shan Chih Shih* contains the T'ung Meng Hui Manifesto, which may also be found in Sun Yat-sen's Collected Works.

Barker, J. Ellis: "Dr. Sun Yat Sen and the Chinese Revolution," *Fortnightly Review,* November, 1911, Vol. 96, p. 778.

Soong Ong Siang: *One Hundred Years' History of the Chinese in Singapore*, London, 1923.

CHAPTER V

Sun Yat-sen: *Chung Kuo chih Ke Ming.*

Chinese Recorder, 1911, 1912, contains valuable currently published annals of the Revolution.

The China Year Book, Ed. Bell and Woodhead, Shanghai, of which 1912 was the first issue, furnishes summaries of current events and many important government documents.

The Missionary Herald, Boston, 1912, 1913, contains a larger body of valuable information than any other missionary journal I have discovered.

Barker, J. Ellis: "Dr. Sun Yat Sen and the Chinese Revolution," *Fortnightly Review*, November 1911, Vol. 96, p. 778.

Nelson, Charles A.: "Dr. Sun Yat Sen in Canton," *Missionary Herald*, August, 1912, p. 355.

Martin, Henry S.: "Peking Churches' Reception to Dr. Sun," *Missionary Herald*, 1912, p. 512.

Sun Yat-sen: "To the Friends of China in the United States of America," New York *Sun*, Sept. 24, 1912. Printed also at the end of the American edition of Cantlie: *Sun Yat Sen and the Awakening of China.*

The China Year Book, 1929–1930, article "Railways," p. 344.

The North China Herald, 1913, Vols. 106–109, contains news despatches concerning Sun Yat-sen's visit to Japan and the "Second Revolution."

Linebarger, Paul: *The Gospel of Chung Shan according to Paul Linebarger*, Paris, 1932.

Woodhead, H. G. W.: *The Truth about the Chinese Republic*, London, 1925.

T'ang Leang-li: *The Inner History of the Chinese Revolution*, New York, 1930.

CHAPTER VI

HARDY, G. L.: "China's Arabian Nights President," *New York Tribune,* Sunday Magazine, June 7, 1914, p. 5.

RESTARICK, HENRY B.: *Sun Yat Sen, Liberator of China,* Yale University Press, 1931. A useful source on Sun Yat-sen's family.

LINEBARGER, PAUL: *Sun Yat Sen and the Chinese Republic,* New York, 1925. Chapter XXXVIII.

SOONG, CHUNG-LING: "The Greatest Event of the Twentieth Century," an article reprinted in *The Wesleyan Alumnae,* April, 1927, Macon, Georgia.

Kuo Fu, A Supplementary Issue of *The Young Companion* in Commemoration of Dr. Sun Yat-sen, Father of the Chinese Republic, Shanghai, November, 1926.

DOOLITTLE, JUSTUS: *Social Life of the Chinese,* New York, 1865.

The North China Herald, Vols. 110–114, contains some current material on the obscure years in Japan. The "Letter alleged to have been written by Dr. Sun Yat-sen to a high personage in Japan" may be found in Vol. 111, p. 898.

T'ANG LEANG-LI: *The Inner History of the Chinese Revolution,* New York, 1930.

The Chinese Chronologies, *Chung-shan Hsien-sheng Nien P'u,* and *Chung-shan Hsien-sheng Nien Piao* contain only a very little on the years 1913–1917.

WEALE, B. L. PUTNAM: *The Fight for the Republic in China,* London, 1918. Contains the "Alleged Secret Agreement" between Sun Yat-sen and the Japanese, and the "Secret Memorandum of the Black Dragon Society." The Agreement, though not so fully translated, may also be found in *The North China Herald,* Shanghai, Vol. 115, p. 254.

WHEELER, W. REGINALD: *China and the World War,* New York, 1919.

CHAPTER VII

SUN YAT-SEN: *Chung Kuo chih Ke Ming.*
Chung-shan Hsien-sheng Nien P'u.

Chung-shan Hsien-sheng Nien Piao.

Kuo Fu, A Supplementary Issue of *The Young Companion,* November, 1926.

The China Year Book, 1916, 1919, 1921 and following. During the European War the annual appearance of this useful summary suffered interruptions.

The Far Eastern Review, 1917 and ff.

The North China Herald, Vols. 119, 120.

Who's Who in China, China Weekly Review, Shanghai.

DEWEY, JOHN: *Letters from Japan and China,* New York, 1920.

HU SHIH: *The Chinese Renaissance* (Bulletins on Chinese Education. Vol. II, Bulletin 6), Shanghai, 1923.

DE VARGAS, PHILIP: *Some Elements in the Chinese Renaissance,* Shanghai, 1922.

YEN, Y. C. JAMES: *The Mass Education Movement in China,* Shanghai, 1925.

WHEELER, W. REGINALD: *China and the World War,* New York, 1919.

RESTARICK, HENRY B.: *Sun Yat Sen, Liberator of China,* Yale University Press, 1931.

CLOSE, UPTON: *Eminent Asians,* New York, 1929.

Some Aspects of Chinese Civilization, Shanghai, 1922.

CHAPTER VIII

SUN YAT-SEN: *Sun Wen Hsueh Shuo (Sun Wen's Philosophy).* The Preface is dated December 30, 1918. This was later to become the section, "Psychological Reconstruction," in the large work called *Chien Kuo Fang Lüeh (General Principles of National Reconstruction).* An English translation, through the Russian, forms the major part of *Memoirs of a Chinese Revolutionary,* London and Philadelphia (no date).

SUN YAT-SEN: *The International Development of China,* Shanghai, 1920. This is the English form given to material which had been published in Chinese as articles and essays, afterward included in *Chien Kuo Fang Lüeh* under the sub-heading, "Material Reconstruction."

SUN YAT-SEN: Address on *San Min Chu I* delivered March 6, 1921. A translation forms Appendix I of *Memoirs of a Chinese Revolutionary.*

Chung-shan Hsien-sheng Nien P'u.

Chung-shan Hsien-sheng Nien Piao.

Chung-shan Hsien-sheng Ta Shih Nien Chih.

The People's Tribune, Peking. Special Memorial Edition, March 12, 1926, on the first anniversary of the death of Sun Yat-sen, especially an article by Eugene Chen, "Sun Yat-sen: Some Memories."

Woo, T. C.: *The Kuomintang and the Future of the Chinese Revolution,* London, 1928.

T'ANG LEANG-LI: *The Foundations of Modern China,* London, 1928.

BAU, MINCHEN JOSHUA: *China and World Peace,* New York, 1928.

Far Eastern Review, October, 1922, an article: "Will China Come Under the Influence of Germany and Russia, or Drift into an Alliance with Japan?" by G. B. R.

ABEND, HALLETT: *Canton Now,* Peking Leader Press, 1926.

BROCKMAN, FLETCHER S.: "Foreign Control at Peking Means War, Says Sun Yat-sen," *New York Times,* July 22, 1923.

Declaration of the First National Congress of the Kuomintang, January, 1924. A translation may be found in Appendix C of Woo: *The Kuomintang and the Future of the Chinese Revolution.*

The Constitution of the Kuomintang. A translation may be found in Appendix C of Holcombe: *The Chinese Revolution.*

MONROE, PAUL: *China, A Nation in Evolution,* New York, 1928.

HOLCOMBE, ARTHUR N.: *The Chinese Revolution,* Harvard University Press, 1930.

CHAPTER IX

The Constitution of the Kuomintang, Holcombe: *The Chinese Revolution,* Appendix C.

CHEN, EUGENE: "Sun Yat-sen: Some Memories," Special Memorial Edition of *The People's Tribune,* Peking, March 12, 1926.

SUN YAT-SEN: *San Min Chu I.* This has been more than once translated: *The Three Principles by Sun Yat-sen. Known to the Chinese as San*

Min Chu-i. Translated from the Original Chinese by a Well-known Sinologue, with Notes by an Independent Commentator. Shanghai, 1927 (North China Daily News). This is not a complete translation. The "Notes" unfortunately have an unpleasant and obvious animus.

San Min Chu I, The Three Principles of the People by Dr. Sun Yat-sen Translated into English by Frank W. Price. Edited by L. T. Chen. Under the Auspices of the China Committee, Institute of Pacific Relations, Shanghai, 1927. This is a complete translation made with a desire to be scrupulously fair.

The Triple Demism of Sun Yat-sen, Translated from the Chinese, annotated and appraised by Paschal M. D'Elia, S. J. with Introduction and Index. English Edition by The Franciscan Press, Wuchang, 1931. Done from the French edition published in 1929.

Yet another translation—made by a Chinese—is the major text of *Sun Yat-sen. His Political and Social Ideals,* A Source Book Compiled, Translated and Annotated by Leonard Shihlien Hsü. University of Southern California Press, Los Angeles, 1933. Any one who wishes to get the feel of Sun Yat-sen's elementary education of his people, and is willing to take the full blow of his anti-imperialism should read Dr. Hsü's translation.

WILLIAM, MAURICE: *Sun Yat-sen versus Communism,* Baltimore, 1932.

WOU SAOFONG: *Sun Yat-sen: Sa Vie et Sa Doctrine,* Paris, 1929.

Sources for Sun Yat-sen's Political Planning for China:

Manifesto of the Military Government of the Revolutionary Brotherhood (in Chinese), 1905 (circa) and 1911.

Problems of the Revolutionary Reorganization of China, January, 1919. *Memoirs of a Chinese Revolutionary,* p. 119–146.

Address on the San Min Chu I, March 6, 1921. *Memoirs of a Chinese Revolutionary,* Appendix I.

Address on the Five-Power Constitution, July, 1921. *Memoirs of a Chinese Revolutionary,* Appendix II.

Chung Kuo chih Ke Ming (China's Revolution), January, 1923.

San Min Chu I, especially the lectures on *Democracy,* 1924. Translated by Frank W. Price. See above.

Outline of National Reconstruction, April 13, 1924. Woo: *The Kuo-*

mintang and the Future of the Chinese Revolution, Appendix B; also Holcombe: *The Chinese Revolution*, Appendix B.

Manifesto on the Northern Expedition, September 18, 1924.

Manifesto on Going to Peking, November 10, 1924.

Letter to the Chief Executive, February 17, 1925.

These three are now accessible in English in Hsü: *Sun Yat-sen His Political and Social Ideals*, pp. 142–157.

The Will, accessible in English in many books, among which are those by Woo and Holcombe already referred to.

Letter to Soviet Russia, contained in Tang Chin Che: "Sun Yat-sen's Life and Work," *Labour Monthly*, May, 1925.

WANG T'IEN-HEN: *Sun Chung-shan Ch'uan Chuan*, Shanghai, 1927.

Woo, T. C.: *The Kuomintang and the Future of the Chinese Revolution*, London, 1928.

Kuo Fu, A Supplementary Issue of *The Young Companion*, Shanghai, November, 1926.

Contemporary newspapers and periodicals and private letters.

Despatch from Riga, March 16, published in the *New York Times*, March 17, 1925, reports the Russian response to Sun Yat-sen's deathbed message to Moscow.

CHAPTER X

Woo, T. C.: *The Kuomintang and the Future of the Chinese Revolution*, London, 1928.

ROOTS, JOHN McCOOK: "The Moscow End of China-Soviet Affairs," *Asia*, June, 1927, p. 468.

Declaration of the Second National Congress of the Kuomintang. Eugene Chen published an English translation in *The People's Tribune*, Peking, in March, 1926.

INDEX